Washington, DC

"Washington, America's capital, is a world capital—a city
of remarkable strengths. Its proud face reflects many
of our nation's greatest memories, achievements
and aspirations."

President William J. Clinton, *Extending the Legacy*, 1997

D1039228

Travel Publications

Michelin North America
One Parkway South, Greenville SC 29615, U.S.A.
☎ 1-800-423-0485
www.ViaMichelin.com
TheGreenGuide-us@us.michelin.com

Manufacture française des pneumatiques Michelin
Société en commandite par actions au capital de 304 000 000 EUR
Place des Carmes-Déchaux – 63 Clermont-Ferrand (France)
R.C.S. Clermont-Fd B 855 200 507

© Michelin et Cie, Propriétaires-éditeurs, 2001
Dépôt légal décembre 2001 – ISBN 2-06-100078-9 – ISSN 0763-1383
Printed in France 11-01/5.1

Typesetting: Nord Compo, Villeneuve-d'Ascq
Printing and binding: CLERC, Saint-Amand-Montrond

Cover design: Carré Noir, Paris 17e arr.

THE GREEN GUIDE:
The Spirit of Discovery

Leisure time spent with The Green Guide is also a time for refreshing your spirit, enjoying yourself, and taking advantage of our selection of restaurants, hotels and other places for relaxing. Immerse yourself in the local culture, discover new horizons, experience the local lifestyle— The Green Guide opens the door for you.

Each year our writers go touring: visiting the sights, devising the driving tours, identifying the highlights, selecting the hotels and restaurants, checking the routes for our maps and plans.

Each title is compiled with great care, giving you the benefit of regular revisions and Michelin's first-hand knowledge. The Green Guide responds to changing circumstances and takes account of its readers' suggestions; all comments are welcome.

Come share our enthusiasm for travel, which has led us to discover over 60 destinations around the world. Let yourself be guided by the best motive for travel-the spirit of discovery.

Contents

Introduction   19

Address Book   41

Sights   69

Department of the Treasury, detail

Adams Morgan Restaurants

© Mike Mitchell/FOLIO, Inc.

Chess Players, Dupont Circle

Statue of George Washington, George Washington University

5

Maps and plans

COMPANION PUBLICATIONS

Map 491 Northeastern USA/ Eastern Canada

Large-format map providing detailed road systems and including driving distances, interstate rest stops, border crossings and interchanges.

– Comprehensive city and town index

– Scale 1:2,400,000 (1 inch = approx. 38 miles)

Map 930 USA Road Map

Covers the principal US road network and presents shaded relief detail of the overall physiography of the land.

– Features state flags with statistical data and state tourism office telephone numbers

– Scale 1:3,450,000

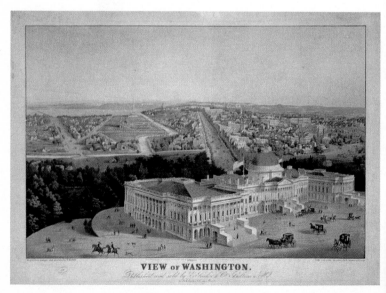

View of Washington (1852) by E. Sachse

LIST OF MAPS

MUSEUM PLANS

Using this guide

The Sights section of this guide is divided into twelve areas: Washington, DC's Capitol Hill, The Mall, White House Area, Downtown, Foggy Bottom, Georgetown, Arlington Across the River, Dupont Circle, Embassy Row, Anacostia and the Eastern Riverfront and Excursions from the city. Within these sections, each **Entry Heading** is followed by public transportation information.

In the text, useful information such as sight location or street address, opening hours, admission charge, telephone number and Web address appears in *italics*. In addition, symbols indicate the nearest Metro or bus stop Ⓜ; wheelchair access ♿; on-site eating facilities ✗; camping facilities △; on-site parking ◘; sights of interest to children [Kids]; and long lines ⅢⅡ. The presence of a hotel swimming pool is indicated by the symbol ♨.

Many entries feature **digressions**—entertaining breaks from sightseeing that are marked by a purple bar and indicated on maps by a black dot ❶ with the corresponding map reference number.

The **Address Book** section, edged with a marbleized band, at the front of the guide features detailed information about hotels, restaurants, entertainment, shopping, sightseeing, sports and recreational opportunities.

At the back of the guide, the section of blue pages offers **Practical Information** on planning your trip, getting there and getting around, basic facts and tips for international visitors.

Addresses, phone numbers, opening hours and prices published in this guide are accurate at press time. We welcome corrections and suggestions that may assist us in preparing the next edition. Please send your comments to:

Michelin Travel Publications
Editorial Department
P. O. Box 19001
Greenville, SC 29602-9001
Email: TheGreenGuide-us@us.michelin.com
Web site: www.ViaMichelin.com

Legend

★★★ **Highly recommended**
★★ **Recommended**
★ **Interesting**

Sight symbols

➡ ▬▬▬ Walking tour with departure point and direction

♦ ⚱	Church, chapel	☀ ♈	Panorama – View
✡	Synagogue	▬	Building described
AZ B	Map co-ordinates locating sights	▭	Other building
▪ ▲	Other points of interest	▪	Small building
▪	Statue, monument	♠	Lighthouse
⊚	Fountain		Cemetery described – Other

All maps are oriented north, unless otherwise indicated by a directional arrow.

Other symbols

🛡 Interstate Highway   🛡 US Highway   ⬭ Other Route

▬●▬	Highway, interchange	🅸	Visitor information
▬▬	Toll road, bridge	⊞	Hospital
⊐ - - -	Tunnel with ramp	🎁	Gift shop
→▶	One way street	🚻 ✕	Restrooms – Restaurant
▬▬ ▭▭▭	Pedestrian street – Steps	↕ ⤴	Elevator – Escalator
✈ ●	Airport – Subway station	🅿 ✉	Parking – Post Office
🚆 🚌	Train station – Bus station	▬▬●▬▬	Railroad passenger station
⛴	Ferry: cars and passengers	▬▪▬	Gate
⛵	Ferry: passengers only	▶ (⁼⁼⁼)	Golf course – Stadium
▬▬	Harbor cruise	❶	Digressions
⊡	Sight of special interest for children	‖‖‖	Long lines

Abbreviations and special symbols

⚑ ⚐ Embassy: described – mentioned   🌸🌸 Japanese cherry trees

9

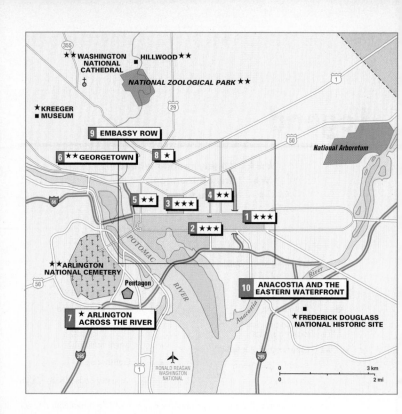

Principal Sights

CENTRAL WASHINGTON DC

1 ★★★ CAPITOL HILL Area number and name

★★★ Highly recommended

★★ Recommended

★ Interesting

● *Smithsonian* Metro entrance/station name

0   500 m
0   1500 ft

Florida   Ave.

Q   St.

P   St.

N   St.

York   Ave.

3rd   St.

Massachusetts   St.

New   Jersey   Ave.

1st   St.

M   St.

L   St.

I (Eye)   St.

H   St.

Capitol   St.

North   Capitol   St.

K   St.

4th   St.

G   St.

F   St.

2nd   St.

Capital Children's Museum

P

★ **NATIONAL POSTAL MUSEUM**

Union Station

★ **UNION STATION**

National Building Museum

Pension Bldg.

● *Judiciary Square*

E   St.

D   St.

C   St.

National Japanese American Memorial

Department of Labor

Louisiana   Ave.

Delaware   Ave.

Senate Office Buildings

★★★ **NATIONAL GALLERY OF ART**

East Bldg.

1 ★★★ CAPITOL HILL

Sewall-Belmont House

Constitution   Avenue

★★★ **THE CAPITOL**

NW   NE

SW   SE

★★ **SUPREME COURT**

East   Capitol   St.

★ **FOLGER SHAKESPEARE LIBRARY**

★★ **LIBRARY OF CONGRESS**

US Botanic Garden

Independence   Avenue

1st   St.

Seward Square

House Office Buildings

Washington   Ave.

South   Capitol   St.

Federal Center SW

Capitol South   St.

Folger Square

2nd   St.

3rd   St.

North Carolina   Ave.

C   St.

D   St.

E   St.

F   St.

South Carolina   Ave.

Virginia   Ave.

New   Jersey   Ave.

Garfield Park

G   St.

I (Eye)   St.

4th   St.

5th   St.

395

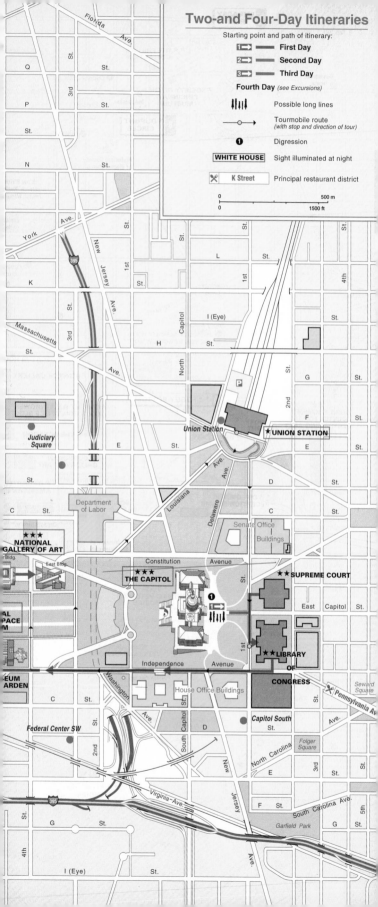

Two- and Four-Day Itineraries

Planning Tips

The fast-paced itineraries mentioned below and shown on the fold-out map to the left are designed for visitors pressed for time and are best suited to the period from April to September, when daylight is more plentiful. To avoid long lines, it is best to reserve White House, Capitol and FBI tours in advance *(see Reservations for Sights)*. Purchasing advance tickets for the Holocaust Museum is also strongly advised.

Shuttle buses – Travel by **Tourmobile** shuttle bus is incorporated into the second day. **Old Town Trolley** also serves some of the sights below.

Eating – On-site eating facilities are indicated in the individual sight descriptions in this guide by the symbol ※. In warm seasons snacks are available from kiosks on the Mall or from street vendors along Independence Avenue. Picnicking is permitted on the Mall. Union Station, the Old Post Office *(Pennsylvania Ave. & 12th St. NW)* and the Shops at National Place *(Pennsylvania Ave. & 13th St. NW)* house a multitude of eateries for all tastes and budgets. Upscale establishments on K Street and Connecticut Avenue offer formal dining, while the large waterfront restaurants on Maine Avenue SW specialize in seafood. Many Asian eateries are located in **Chinatown** and the Arlington-Clarendon area *(p 193)*, while the vibrant **Adams Morgan** neighborhood in the vicinity of Columbia Road and 18th Street NW, known mainly for its Hispanic and Ethiopian cuisine, hosts a wide variety of ethnic restaurants. Historic **Georgetown** and **Alexandria**, each with a large concentration of restaurants, offer a full range of dining experiences. *See Address Book.*

Two-Day Itinerary

First Day	Itinerary in red ➡
Morning	The Capitol★★★, Supreme Court★★, Library of Congress★★
Lunch	Supreme Court★★ or National Air and Space Museum★★★
Afternoon	National Air and Space Museum★★★, National Gallery of Art★★★
Evening	Kennedy Center★★

Second Day	Itinerary in purple (with Tourmobile) 2➡
Morning	White House★★★, National Museum of American History★★
Lunch	National Museum of American History
Afternoon	US Holocaust Memorial Museum★★, Jefferson Memorial★★★, Lincoln Memorial★★★, Vietnam Veterans Memorial★★★, Arlington National Cemetery★★ *(open until 7pm Apr–Sept)*
Evening	City lights. Begin at the observation room of the Washington Monument★★★ *(open until 11:45pm Late-May–Labor Day)*, then tour by car the other illuminated sights shown on the map

Four-Day Itinerary
(For the first two days, follow the itinerary described above.)

Third Day	Itinerary in green 3➡
Morning	National Museum of Natural History★★, Arthur M. Sackler Gallery★★ or Freer Gallery of Art★★, National Museum of African Art★★ or Hirshhorn Museum and Sculpture Garden★★
Lunch	On the Mall *(See Eating above)*
Afternoon	National Archives★★, FBI★, Ford's Theatre and Petersen House★, National Portrait Gallery★★ *(return to Pennsylvania Ave. and take any no. 30s bus to Georgetown)*
Late-Afternoon/ Evening	Georgetown Walking Tour and dinner in Georgetown

Fourth Day	Map p 228
Morning	Mount Vernon★★★, Woodlawn Plantation★
Lunch	Mount Vernon
Afternoon/Evening	Gunston Hall★, Alexandria Walking Tour: Old Town★★ and dinner in Alexandria

Lincoln Memorial, Washington Monument and US Capitol

Introduction
to Washington, DC

The District of Columbia

Location and Climate – Washington, DC lies approximately in the middle of the eastern seaboard of the US, about 90 miles inland from the Atlantic Ocean. Situated on the northern banks of the Potomac River, the city rises from low bottomland along the riverfront to a series of hills in the north. At its highest elevation in the Northwest quadrant of the city, it is 390ft above sea level. Rock Creek, a tributary of the Potomac, follows a shallow, wooded valley extending through the heart of the city from north to south. Located at 39° north latitude and 77° west longitude, the city has a temperately continental climate. Winds are generally from the west, and humidity is often high because of proximity to the ocean and the Chesapeake Bay, 25 miles east of the city. In the vicinity of Washington, the Potomac River has an average channel depth of about 14ft, making it unnavigable for large cargo-carrying vessels.

Size and Population – Shaped like a truncated diamond, each side measuring 10 miles, the city is carved out of Maryland and separated from Virginia by the Potomac *(map p 32)*. It covers 67 square miles and is divided into four quadrants: **Northwest** (NW), **Northeast** (NE), **Southeast** (SE) and **Southwest** (SW). The longest distance from its southern to its northern tip is 12 miles. The population decreased by about 35,000 in the past decade, to 572,059, making Washington the 21st largest city in the US. The decline can be attributed to an exodus of blacks from the district, which is now 60 percent black and 32 percent white. In the Northeast, Southeast and Southwest quadrants, blacks predominate; the Northwest quadrant is largely white. The neighborhood known as Adams Morgan, concentrated mainly in the area of Columbia Road and 18th Street NW, is the hub of Washington's growing Hispanic community, which constitutes about eight percent of the population. Since 1990 a quarter of a million immigrants, primarily Asians, have settled in the Washington metropolitan area, mainly in the suburbs. The region's Indian immigrant community has doubled in the last decade, to 80,000, among them many engineers attracted by Northern Virginia's booming high-tech economy.

The District Government – After a century of congressional rule, Washington was given the federally mandated authority to govern itself under the Home Rule Act of 1973. Headed by an elected mayor and a 13-member legislative council, the city government, by merit of the District's unique status, undertakes all local, county, and state government responsibilities—the schools, the police, the courts, the department of motor vehicles, etc. Though the city functions somewhat independently of the federal legislature, Congress retains veto power over bills passed by the District council. In addition, many agencies and commissions exercise oversight jurisdiction in District matters. The National Capital Planning Commission, a 12-member body appointed by the president and the mayor, reviews city development plans, while the Commission of Fine Arts oversees the design of buildings, parks and monuments. Congress itself sets height restrictions on all District buildings, and the President's Office of Management and Budget establishes limits for the city budget. In 1995, in an attempt to stem the city's growing indebtedness, Congress passed legislation, signed by the President, that created a 5-member financial control board, with power of approval over the city's budget, and in fact all legislation passed by the council. The city has recently produced balanced budgets and met the fiscal goals mandated by Congress, triggering the dissolution of the financial control board in September 2001.

Historically, suffrage has been a matter of concern to the citizens of Washington. In 1964 they were allowed to vote in the presidential election for the first time. As part of the 1973 Home Rule Act, they were also allowed to elect one delegate to the House of Representatives. The delegate serves a two-year term and, though not granted a vote on the floor of Congress, the delegate is allowed to vote on issues within the congressional committees on which he or she serves. Unbowed by the failure of a proposed constitutional amendment in 1978, the defeat in the House of DC statehood legislation in 1993, and the denial of a voting-rights lawsuit by the Supreme Court in 2000, DC residents continue to push for a voice in Congress. Recently the city government showed its support, offering license plates with the slogan "Taxation Without Representation."

The Metropolitan Area – The Washington, DC metropolitan area comprises 18 counties in Maryland, Virginia and West Virginia, and the District of Columbia itself. The total metropolitan area encompasses 6,510 square miles. With a population of 4,923,153, it ranks ninth among the nation's 280 metropolitan areas. Between 1990 and 2000 the area's population increased by nearly 17 percent.

Continued growth has drawn many of the outlying towns and villages into a steadily expanding ring of suburban settlements. The municipalities bordering the Capital Beltway (Interstate 495), which encircles the District at a distance of approximately 12 miles from the center, tend to be suburban "bedroom" communities closely attached to Washington culturally and economically. As the suburban reach of Washington extends farther west and south into the hinterland, more distant and traditionally more rural counties in Virginia and West Virginia—as well as independent cities of Virginia, such as Fairfax, Manassas, and even more remote Fredericksburg—serve as commuter communities as well.

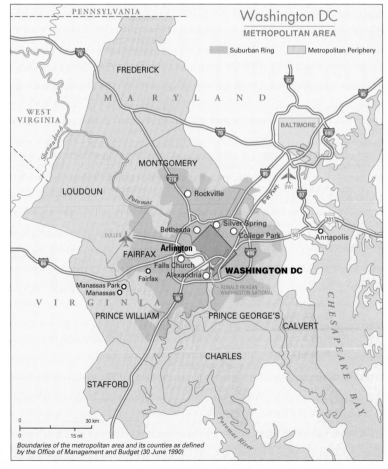

Boundaries of the metropolitan area and its counties as defined by the Office of Management and Budget (30 June 1990)

The Federal Government

Under the system of checks and balances established by the US Constitution, the federal government is composed of three branches: the Legislative (both houses of Congress), the Executive (the president and the executive office) and the Judicial (the Supreme Court and all other federal courts). The White House, seat of the executive branch, is situated within a mile of Capitol Hill, where the Capitol, home of Congress, and the Supreme Court building are located. Each of these branches fulfills specific functions and duties of its own, as well as overseeing and keeping in check the powers exercised by the other two branches.

The Legislative Branch – Conceived by the Founding Fathers as a bicameral system of government, the Congress comprises two bodies: the Senate and the House of Representatives. Jointly they are responsible for drafting and passing laws; for handling matters of national finance, such as setting and collecting taxes and coining money; for ensuring, in conjunction with the president, the defense of the nation; for regulating commerce; and for admitting new states to the Union. Within these broadly defined powers, each body has separate duties, as described below.

A specific Congress serves for two years (the 107th Congress convenes from 2001 to 2002), beginning new sessions each year in late January and generally recessing in August and again in the fall.

The **Senate** is composed of 100 senators, two from each of the 50 states in the Union. Senators are elected to six-year terms by popular vote, in accordance with the 17th Amendment, which was added to the Constitution in 1913 (originally, the Constitution specified that senators be elected by state legislatures).

Senate terms are staggered so that no more than one-third of the Senate seats are renewed each year. The vice president is the official presiding officer of the Senate, but in his absence, senators elect a president pro tempore from among their ranks. The Senate's specific duties include approving presidential appointments; ratifying foreign treaties by a two-thirds majority (a power now little used); and trying federal officials impeached by the House. (Only two US presidents have stood trial before the Senate: Andrew Johnson, Abraham Lincoln's successor, in 1868, and Bill Clinton in 1999. Both presidents were acquitted.)

The **House** is composed of 435 representatives (often referred to as congressmen and congresswomen), with the number of representatives per state based on population. California has the greatest number of representatives (53). The District of Columbia and the US territories of Guam, the Virgin Islands and American Samoa are represented by nonvoting delegates to the House, and the commonwealth of Puerto Rico sends a nonvoting resident commissioner.

Members of the House serve two-year terms, and their presiding officer is the Speaker of the House, elected anew with each Congress. Under the Constitution the House is responsible for originating all bills relating to taxes; impeaching (that is, charging federal officials with criminal actions); and determining the outcome of a presidential election if there is no clear electoral majority.

Historically Congress has been dominated by two opposing political parties, whose names and policies have changed over time. Today the major parties are Democratic and Republican, though nothing prevents "independents" or members of smaller parties from running for office.

In both houses, the dominant party elects a **majority leader** and a deputy, the **majority whip**. The minority party, likewise, elects its own leader and whip. If the majority party in one or both houses of Congress is different from the party of the president, legislation may bog down, as Congress votes against supported initiatives or the president vetoes congressional acts.

In both chambers, much of the work of formulating and drafting new laws is done within **standing committees**. There are 19 such committees in the House and 16 in the Senate. Normally a representative serves on two committees, a senator on three or four.

How a Bill Becomes Law – Any interested person or group, whether within or outside the political system, may draft a bill and seek the support of a US senator or representative to introduce it for congressional consideration. Of the many bills proposed annually, only a handful are enacted into laws. Throughout the legislative process described below, a corps of lobbyists is generally operating behind the scenes to persuade legislators to protect the interests of their clients.

Each bill begins its journey when it is introduced on the floor of either the House or the Senate chamber; in many cases a similar proposal is introduced simultaneously in both houses. The chamber's parliamentarian then assigns it to an appropriate **standing committee** for consideration, and if deemed worthwhile, the proposal is normally referred

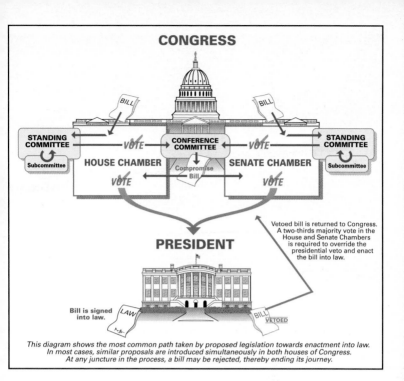

CONGRESS

STANDING COMMITTEE
Subcommittee

CONFERENCE COMMITTEE

STANDING COMMITTEE
Subcommittee

HOUSE CHAMBER

SENATE CHAMBER

VOTE

VOTE

Compromise Bill

VOTE

VOTE

BILL

BILL

PRESIDENT

Vetoed bill is returned to Congress. A two-thirds majority vote in the House and Senate Chambers is required to override the presidential veto and enact the bill into law.

Bill is signed into law. LAW

BILL VETOED

This diagram shows the most common path taken by proposed legislation towards enactment into law. In most cases, similar proposals are introduced simultaneously in both houses of Congress. At any juncture in the process, a bill may be rejected, thereby ending its journey.

to a **subcommittee** for further study. The subcommittee holds hearings in which it elicits the opinions of experts and interested parties. Such hearings, especially in the House, are generally open to the public. The subcommittee must then "mark up" the bill, or rework the language and intent of various sections in light of the conclusions drawn from hearings. The marked-up bill then passes back to the full standing committee, which after further study either rejects the bill or "reports" it—that is, recommends its passage to the chamber. In the House, reported bills are then submitted to the Rules Committee before returning to the chamber. In the Senate, the leadership determines the course of action on each piece of legislation.

Having received committee approval, the bill is placed on the chamber's calendar, and at the scheduled time, it is debated, amended and put to a vote. At this point, a bill that has been introduced in only one chamber is sent to the other chamber, where the legislative process begins anew. If the bill has been introduced simultaneously in the Senate and the House and passed by both, the two versions are then referred to a **conference committee**, composed of members from both chambers who meet to resolve differences in wording and intent. Their compromise version is then sent back to both the House and Senate, which separately vote on the identical version of the bill. After passage in both houses, the approved legislation next proceeds to the president, who may sign it into law or exercise his **veto** power by returning the bill to Congress unsigned, with a statement of his objections. Congress may override a presidential veto with a two-thirds majority vote in both chambers. The president has a third option: If he wishes to register his disapproval without actually vetoing, he may simply retain the unsigned bill, and after 10 days, it automatically becomes law, provided Congress is in session. If Congress is adjourned at that time, the president's failure to sign constitutes a "pocket veto," and the bill dies.

The Executive Branch – The president and vice president are the only elected officials of the branch's 4 million employees (including armed forces personnel). Presidential elections are held every four years, and a president may serve a maximum of two four-year terms in office, as stipulated by the 22nd Amendment (1951) to the Constitution.

The Constitution also requires that a presidential candidate be at least 35 years old; be born in the US and live in the US for 14 years prior to running for office. Presidential candidates choose their running mates at the commencement of campaigns. In the event of the president's resignation, impeachment, incapacitation, or death, the vice president assumes the presidency.

The president serves as commander-in-chief of the Armed Forces, with ultimate control over the defense of the nation. However, as required by the Constitution and the War Powers Act of 1973, a protracted military action must be approved by Congress, which solely holds the power to declare war. In addition the president serves as the nation's chief executive. In this capacity he appoints all ambassadors, ministers, consuls and persons serving in cabinet-level positions and approves the appointments of

Historical Documents, National Archives

many policy-making personnel within the Executive branch. Whenever a vacancy occurs on the Supreme Court or among other judges on the federal bench, the president makes a new appointment (which is subject to Senate approval). Through such appointments the president exerts an influence that may last far beyond his own tenure in office. The president is also empowered to grant pardons and reprieves to those convicted of committing crimes against the US government. Finally, the president, through his veto power, is instrumental in the lawmaking process *(See How a Bill becomes Law p 22)*.

The Executive branch comprises the **Executive Office of the President**—independent federal agencies, and all 14 **cabinet departments** (Departments of State, Treasury, Defense, Justice, Interior, Agriculture, Commerce, Labor, Health and Human Services, Education, Transportation, Housing and Urban Development, Energy, and Veteran Affairs). The "secretary," or head, of each cabinet department advises the president on setting national policy.

The Executive Office of the President includes the White House staff and a number of departments that assist and advise the president on policy, such as the Council of Economic Advisers and the Office of National Drug Control Policy (run by the nation's "Drug Czar"). A powerful component of the Executive Office is the **Office of Management and Budget**, which prepares the president's annual federal budget, works with Congress on legislative objectives and acts as an organizational overseer for the entire Executive branch.

Many crucial government responsibilities are executed by the dozens of federal agencies chartered by Congress and overseen by the president, such as the Central Intelligence Agency, the Post Office, the National Security Agency and the National

President Bill Clinton Addressing Congress, January 19, 1999

Aeronautics and Space Administration and such important regulatory bodies as the Environmental Protection Agency, the Federal Trade Commission and the Securities and Exchange Commission.

The Judicial Branch – The smallest of the three branches, the Judiciary interprets the law of the land. It is composed of three levels: **US District Courts** (numbering 94), **US Courts of Appeals** (13) and the **US Supreme Court**. Judges at all three levels are appointed for life to the federal bench by the president and must be confirmed by the Senate.

Federal cases may be civil or criminal in nature. Criminal cases must concern a violation of federal law. For a civil case to be heard in federal court, it must involve one of the following criteria: a federal statute, a constitutional issue, or litigants from different states in a case involving a sum in excess of $75,000.

Normally, federal cases are first filed and tried at the district level, though they may begin in special federal courts, such as the US Claims Court or the Tax Court. Once a decision has been handed down in district court, a dissatisfied party who feels that the district wrongly applied the law may file an appeal with the US Court of Appeals serving his or her district.

The final court of review, the Supreme Court, is made up of eight associate justices and a chief justice. This body hears only about two percent of the petitions it receives annually, focusing attention on cases that call into question the constitutionality of existing laws or that challenge lower court interpretations of federal laws. Decisions handed down by the Supreme Court set the legal precedents for all other courts of the land.

How Washington Works

Washington's principal industry is government. The federal presence in the metropolis dominates the economy, directly through the civil service bureaucracy and indirectly through government-related businesses. Politics and government also influence the social climate of the capital city. With less than two percent of its work force involved in manufacturing, Washington functions like a white-collar town.

Federal Government – Some 322,000 people living in the metropolitan area are on the federal payroll, from the president to park rangers, custodians to museum curators. Most permanent government positions are within the purview of the Office of Personnel and Management, an independent agency of the Executive branch. However, higher-level jobs are generally held by presidential appointment, and new appointees are customarily brought in with each change of administration.

Daily, hordes of employees commute from the surrounding suburbs to work in the government offices scattered throughout the city. Some 23 percent of the city's land is federally owned. After hours, whole corridors of the city where government buildings are concentrated (particularly in Foggy Bottom) are virtually deserted.

Social life in the capital city tends to be conducted at private gatherings, where the nation's leaders, foreign diplomats and prominent figures in the business world informally share political and economic ideas that ultimately influence the direction of government. The national and international elite may meet in private homes, at embassy receptions, in reception rooms on Capitol Hill and in such private clubs as the Cosmos Club, Sulgrave Club and Metropolitan Club.

Government-Related Sector – In order to be near the federal nerve center, hundreds of national and international organizations have offices in Washington. The Pentagon, wellspring of the military industrial complex, supports innumerable defense contracting companies throughout the metropolitan area.

Since the 1970s a number of research and development complexes have been built around the Capital Beltway. Their fortunes are very much dependent on the political climate and the congressional appropriation of federal resources.

As many as 90,000 people engage in lobbying work in the capital. Washington-based **Lobbyists** representing some 23,000 special interest groups, political action organizations (PACs), professional and trade associations, and foreign countries and businesses, work to persuade legislators to support laws helpful to their clients' interests. Many organizations employ their own staff lobbyists, but often such work is undertaken by well-connected attorneys at DC firms. The term "lobbyist" derives from the 19C, when such influence peddlers would haunt the lobbies of public buildings where politicians congregated. Today lobbyists conduct their business at fine restaurants and well-orchestrated social gatherings.

Private Sector – Exerting a powerful influence on the city's sociopolitical fabric is the **fourth estate**. Washington's formidable press corps is comprised of correspondents from national and regional newspapers, many of whom maintain Washington offices in the National Press Building *(14th and F Sts. NW)*. *The New Republic, National Geographic, US News and World Report,* and *USA Today* (with its parent company, newspaper and media giant Gannett), are among the publications with their headquarters in or near the capital. Dominated by the *Washington Post,* one of the country's most influential newspapers, the press has become a major player in shaping public opinion. The *Post's* involvement in uncovering the Nixon-Watergate debacle in the mid-1970s broke new ground in investigative reporting.

The District also serves as headquarters for large corporations, such as MCI and Marriott; and for more than a thousand associations and interest groups, such as the AFL-CIO and AARP. Internet giant AOL makes its home in Northern Virginia's high-tech corridor.

Tourism – Attracted by the capital's renowned monuments and museums and by the numerous conventions held in the area, nearly 21 million visitors come to Washington each year. Tourism, the city's second largest industry, brings in more than $4 billion a year to hotels, restaurants and other service-related businesses that cater to visitors. Traditionally a place of pilgrimage for Americans, in recent years the capital has begun to draw more foreign tourists.

The International Element – Once a rather provincial town with only a small contingent of foreigners, Washington has become, in recent decades, a cosmopolitan city. Over 150 foreign missions maintain embassies and consulates here, and such international organizations as the World Bank, International Monetary Fund and Organization of American States are based in the city.

The influx of Asian, Middle Eastern and African immigrants that began in the late 1970s has given the city a distinctly international flavor. Washington's shops, restaurants and festivals reflect this urban mix of cultures.

Washington DC Time Line

The Colonial Period

1608	Capt. John Smith sails up the Potomac.
1662	The first land patent on the future site of the District is granted.
1749	**Alexandria** is laid out.
1751	**Georgetown** is established.
1763	The **French and Indian War** ends, affirming British supremacy in eastern North America.
1775-83	The **American Revolution** takes place.
1776	Members of the Continental Congress meeting in Philadelphia sign the **Declaration of Independence**.
1783	Britain recognizes the independence of the 13 colonies.
1788	Maryland cedes territory on the north shore of the Potomac for the establishment of a new federal city.
1789	The **US Constitution** is ratified. New York is designated capital. **George Washington** is elected first US president.
1790	The nation's capital is moved to Philadelphia. Congress passes the **Residence Act**, giving George Washington the power to choose the site for the new capital and 10 years in which to create a federal city.

George Washington
1789-1797

Building a Capital

1791	President Washington selects a site along the Potomac for the federal district and authorizes **Pierre Charles L'Enfant** to draft city plans. Congress appoints three commissioners, who name the 10sq mi diamond-shaped area the Territory of Columbia (subsequently known as the District of Columbia) and the capital the City of Washington.
1792	L'Enfant is dismissed by President Washington. The cornerstone is laid for the White House.
1793	The cornerstone is laid for the Capitol.
1800	President John Adams is the first occupant of the White House. Congress convenes for the first time in Washington in the unfinished Capitol building.
1801	Thomas Jefferson is the first president to be inaugurated in Washington.
1802	Under congressional jurisdiction, the City of Washington is chartered. The first district government buildings are erected. City population: 3,000.
1808	Construction begins on the Washington Canal along present-day Constitution Avenue.
1812	**War of 1812** begins. The US declares war on Britain.
1814	The British invade Washington and burn the Capitol, the White House and other public buildings. Washington banks offer $500,000 in loans to help rebuild the city and to quell a movement to abandon the capital.
1815	President James Madison signs the Treaty of Ghent, ending the War of 1812.

© White House Historical Assn.; photos by National Geographic Society

Thomas Jefferson
1801-1809

Library of Congress

Abraham Lincoln
1861-1865

A Century of Growth

1824	Citywide celebrations take place on the occasion of the second visit of the **Marquis de Lafayette**, America's Revolutionary ally.
1832	A severe cholera epidemic sweeps the city.
1835	The Baltimore and Ohio Railroad reaches the District, initiating the eventual decline of canal traffic through Georgetown and Washington.

1836	Construction of the Treasury and Patent Office buildings gets under way.
1846	Congress establishes the **Smithsonian Institution**.
	District territory south of the Potomac is retroceded to Virginia, reducing the District by one-third of its original size.
1850	Chesapeake and Ohio Canal is completed.
1855	The Castle, the Smithsonian's first building, opens on the Mall.
1861	Beginning of the **Civil War**. Many public buildings in the District become hospitals and barracks for Union soldiers. A network of forts is erected around the city's southern edge.
1862	Congress grants compensatory emancipation of all slaves in the District.
1863	President Abraham Lincoln issues the **Emancipation Proclamation**.
1864	Confederate Gen. Jubal Early is repulsed at nearby Fort Stevens, saving the capital from capture by the South.
1865	End of the Civil War. Gen. Robert E. Lee surrenders to Gen. Ulysses S. Grant at Appomattox. President Lincoln is assassinated five days later while attending a performance at Ford's Theatre.
1867	DC citizens are granted suffrage. Howard University, the capital's first black university, is chartered by Congress.
1871	DC population (over 130,000) has doubled since the beginning of the decade due largely to the influx of former slaves.
	Georgetown is incorporated with Washington.
1871-74	An act of Congress establishes a brief period of territorial government for the District.
	Alexander "Boss" Shepherd begins a major citywide public works project that results in a much beautified but near-bankrupt city.
1874	The city's first art museum, the Corcoran Gallery of Art, opens on Pennsylvania Ave.
1880s	Establishment of streetcar lines leads to the growth of outlying areas.
1884	The Washington Monument, begun in 1848, is completed.
1897	The first Library of Congress building opens.

"The City Beautiful"

1900	Washington celebrates its centennial.
1901	The **McMillan Commission** is established to beautify the capital.
1908	Union Station is completed.
1914	The Lincoln Memorial is begun in the reclaimed **West Potomac Park**.
1917	US enters **World War I**. Washington experiences a wartime boom. Rows of temporary war buildings, or "tempos," are erected around the Mall.
1918	Armistice ends World War I. DC population has risen to nearly 440,000.
1926	National Capital Park and Planning Commission is established. The Public Buildings Act leads to the construction of many federal edifices.
1931-32	Hunger marchers demonstrate in Washington.
1941	US enters **World War II**. DC experiences another wartime boom.
	The National Gallery of Art opens on the Mall.
1945	World War II ends in victory for the US and Allied forces.
1950-53	Korean War takes place.
	DC population peaks at 800,000.
1961	**John F. Kennedy** is inaugurated 35th US president and appoints a committee to study the rejuvenation of Pennsylvania Ave.
	Congress ratifies the 23rd Amendment to the Constitution, giving District residents the right to vote in presidential elections.
1963	**Martin Luther King Jr.** leads 200,000 in the March on Washington for Jobs and Freedom. King delivers his "I Have a Dream" speech from the Lincoln Memorial.
	President Kennedy is assassinated in Dallas and buried in Arlington National Cemetery.
Late 60s	Racial riots erupt in the capital. Areas of the city are looted and burned.
Early 70s	Anti-Vietnam War demonstrations are staged on the Mall.
	District residents are allowed to elect one nonvoting delegate to the House of Representatives.

Toward the 21C

1971	John F. Kennedy Center for the Performing Arts opens.
1973	Congress passes the **Home Rule Act**, establishing self-government for DC.
	US troops are withdrawn from Vietnam.

1974	President Richard Nixon resigns in the wake of the Watergate scandal.
1976	US bicentennial celebrations. **Metrorail**, the city's first subway system, begins operations. The Cooperative Use Act is passed, allowing commercial activities in federal buildings and encouraging restoration of historic government structures.
1979	Farmers' Tractorcade invades Washington; protesters camp on the Mall. Pope John Paul II delivers a mass on the Mall.
1982	The Washington Convention Center opens, spurring downtown development.
1983	The renovated Old Post Office opens, heralding the rebirth of Pennsylvania Ave.
1987	The Smithsonian Quadrangle opens.
1990	The Washington National Cathedral, begun in 1907, is completed.
1991	Bicentennial of L'Enfant's plan of Washington.
1993	The US Holocaust Memorial Museum and the Smithsonian Institution's National Postal Museum open. The Vietnam Women's Memorial is dedicated. Bill proposing DC statehood is defeated in Congress.
1995	Million Man March terminates at the Lincoln Memorial. Korean War Veterans Memorial is dedicated.
1996	Last Washington Redskins football game is played in RFK Stadium. New stadium to be built outside DC by 1997.
1997	Memorial to President Franklin D. Roosevelt opens to the public. Construction of the Ronald Reagan Building completes the Federal Triangle complex.
1998	National Airport officially named in honor of President Ronald Reagan. President Bill Clinton is impeached by the House of Representatives. He is later acquitted by the Senate.
2000	After six weeks of recounts and lawsuits in Florida, the battle to determine the winner of the presidential election moves to the capital, where a Supreme Court decision gives the final victory to George W. Bush.
2001	In the worst terrorist attack in US history, the Pentagon suffers damage resulting in over 180 fatalities. The Twin Towers and surrounding buildings of the World Trade Center in New York City are destroyed, resulting in the loss of approximately 5,000 lives.

200 Years of Growth

Selecting a Site – After the Revolutionary War the delegates of the newly formed government expressed interest in designating a federal district to be the seat of power for the new country. A number of existing cities, including New York and Philadelphia, vied to be selected, offering money and land as incentives. Rivalry between the northern and southern states concerning the site of the new capital was resolved through a political compromise: In exchange for agreeing to locate the city in the "southern" precinct, the northern states would be relieved of the heavy debts they had incurred during the Revolution.

In July 1790 Congress passed the Residence Act empowering President George Washington to select a site for the new federal district. Ultimately Washington designated a tract on the Potomac River in the vicinity of Georgetown, though he left its exact boundaries and size undefined. Washington was well acquainted with this area, as his own plantation, Mount Vernon, was 16 miles down the Potomac, and he believed that the site had great commercial potential as a port if it were linked by canal to the productive lands of the Western frontier. In order to facilitate its development, Washington convinced major landholders in the area to give portions of their land to the new capital.

L'Enfant's "City of Magnificent Distances" – In 1789, even before Congress voted to create a federal district, the French Maj. **Pierre Charles L'Enfant** (1754-1825) expressed to President Washington his eagerness to draw up the plans for the new capital. Trained at the Royal Academy of Painting and Sculpture in Paris, L'Enfant arrived in the US in 1777 at the age of 22 and fought under General Washington in the American Revolution. After the war, L'Enfant established himself in American social circles and enjoyed a fine reputation as a designer and architect, particularly for his work in remodeling Federal Hall in New York City. Impressed with L'Enfant's ideas, and realizing that there were few trained engineers from which to choose, Washington eventually appointed him to design the city and its public buildings.

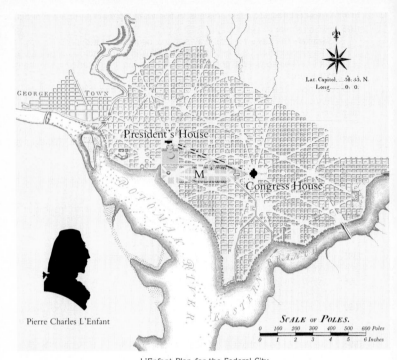

L'Enfant Plan for the Federal City
Adapted from Thackara & Vallance plan, 1792. Silhouette redrawn from a work in the collection
of the Diplomatic Reception Rooms, Department of State

Following his appointment by Washington, L'Enfant traveled to Georgetown, arriving in March 1791. He had in hand a city layout sketched by Thomas Jefferson, who, along with Washington, was instrumental in fostering the early development of the federal city. L'Enfant immediately began reconnoitering the area, which at that time had been settled by several landowners and contained three settlements: the well-established Georgetown and the fledgling towns of Carrollsburg (adjacent to present-day Fort Lesley J. McNair) and Hamburg (now the site of the State Department Building in Foggy Bottom).

One of L'Enfant's first decisions was to situate the future "Congress house" on Jenkins Hill, which had a commanding view of the Potomac River. Along this east-west axis, L'Enfant planned a 400ft-wide "Grand Avenue" (now the Mall) to be lined by foreign ministries and cultural institutions. The avenue would culminate in an equestrian statue of George Washington, connected on a north-south axis with the "president's house." This mansion in turn would be linked back to the Capitol via a mile-long commercial corridor (present-day Pennsylvania Avenue). Tiber Creek, a tributary of the Potomac situated south of this projected corridor, would be transformed into a city canal that would run along the northern side of the Grand Avenue, turning south at the foot of Jenkins Hill before emptying into the Eastern branch. The watercourse was to be decorative as well as functional, punctuated by reflecting pools and fountains.

L'Enfant laid out the remainder of the city in a grid pattern of streets intersected by broad diagonal avenues at "round-points," each intended to serve as the focus of a neighborhood area. In emphasizing monumental buildings, grand perspectives, gracious circles, wide avenues and expansive views, the Frenchman was influenced by the Baroque notions of urban planning then prevalent in Europe. L'Enfant's widely dispersed, multi-centered city, which later earned the sobriquet "the City of Magnificent Distances," anticipated a population of approximately 800,000 people and extended north to the present Florida Avenue escarpment, encompassing an estimated 6,000 acres.

Dreams and Realities – Once Washington had approved the expanded city plan, L'Enfant directed his energies toward implementing his grand scheme. Refusing to divert his attention to practicalities, L'Enfant was seen as uncooperative and peremptory by the city surveyor, **Andrew Ellicott**, by Jefferson and by the three city commissioners appointed by Washington to oversee the capital's development.

In September 1791 the commissioners named the new diamond-shaped federal district the "Territory of Columbia" (the current designation, "District of Columbia," came into use in the 19C). Ten miles long on each side, the territory encompassed the County of Alexandria on the Virginia shore of the Potomac and portions of Maryland on the northern shore. The commissioners named the capital itself the City of Washington and stipulated that its street grid be designated by numbers and letters.

To generate revenue for public works and buildings, the commissioners held an auction of lots in October 1791, but only 35 parcels in the as-yet-undeveloped city were sold. Before long, a series of conflicts arose between L'Enfant and the commissioners. Finally, in February 1792, unable to defend the designer's recalcitrance any longer, Washington dismissed him. Gathering up most of his plans and drawings, L'Enfant left the town he had conceptualized. Thirty-three years later the talented Frenchman died penniless and forgotten in nearby Maryland, having never received just compensation and recognition during his lifetime. (In 1909 L'Enfant's remains were transferred to Arlington National Cemetery. The L'Enfant Plan of 1791, restored in 1991, is now in the custody of the Library of Congress.)

Andrew Ellicott took over where L'Enfant left off, reconstructing the Frenchman's original plan from preparatory sketches. Ellicott recruited the gifted, self-taught mathematician Benjamin Banneker, a free black, to assist with the surveying, and proceeded to lay out streets and avenues. On instructions from Jefferson and Washington, Ellicott named the latter after states of the Union.

During the same period, competitions were held to design the president's house and a home for Congress, but even after architects were chosen, work proceeded slowly because the lot sales needed to finance construction continued to lag. A syndicate of private financiers was formed in the late 1790s to act as a real-estate development company for Washington, but the syndicate's bankruptcy in 1797 curtailed further growth. In addition to the lack of an economic base, the city suffered from a critical shortage of stonemasons and other skilled laborers.

"City of Magnificent Intentions" – When Congress and President John Adams relocated from Philadelphia to Washington in November 1800, they found the skeleton of the nascent city etched into the wilderness. Both the Capitol and White House were incomplete; Pennsylvania Avenue was a rutted, marshy thoroughfare; and the town was bereft of finesse or comfort. In August 1814 the fledgling capital suffered a major setback when the British invaded the town and set fire to the Capitol, the White House and other public buildings.

After the war a contingent of federal officials, despairing that the town would ever become a capital, lobbied to desert Washington and move the federal government to a more established city. A group of local entrepreneurs put up their own funds as loans for rebuilding, thereby successfully persuading the lawmakers to remain in Washington. Congress appropriated additional monies to repair the damaged Capitol and Executive Mansion, and development continued as before, slowly but a little more surely.

In 1815 the Washington Canal opened along Pennsylvania Avenue. Unfortunately, the canal provided neither the decorative element intended by L'Enfant nor the commercial boon that had been hoped for by George Washington and others. In 1835 the Baltimore and Ohio Railroad reached Washington, at once signaling the age of rail transport and the doom of the canal trade so necessary to the prosperity of Alexandria and Georgetown. Alexandrians, feeling they had suffered economically and politically by their integration into the federal district, petitioned for retrocession to Virginia. Their petition was granted in 1846.

In spite of numerous setbacks, by the mid-19C Washington was on its way to becoming a city, and its prevailing Neoclassical flavor had been established, thanks to such monumental structures as the Old City Hall, the Treasury Building and the Old Patent Office Building. Impressive Federal-style residences were also scattered throughout the burgeoning city. Washington had newspapers, theaters and, if not a rich, at least a respectable cultural life.

Pennsylvania Avenue and 15th Street (c.1900)

Kiplinger Washington Collection

31

In 1850 President Millard Fillmore commissioned **Andrew Jackson Downing** to devise a major landscape plan for Washington's central quarters, particularly Lafayette Square and the present-day Mall. Although Downing's plans were never funded, they represented an early and instrumental effort to unify the green spaces of the "monumental city." In 1855 the newly created Smithsonian Institution opened its brick Castle on the Mall.

> *"It is sometimes called the City of Magnificent Distances but it might with greater propriety be termed the City of Magnificent Intentions... spacious avenues that begin in nothing and lead nowhere; streets mile long that only want houses, roads and inhabitants; public meetings that need but a public to be complete; and ornaments of great thoroughfares, which only lack great thoroughfares to ornament...."*
>
> Charles Dickens, while visiting DC in the 1840s

During the Civil War, development in Washington came to a halt as the city turned its attention to national and local defense. A ring of forts was built along the Potomac, and several of the city's grand public structures became hospitals for the Union wounded.

The brief period of territorial government that began in 1871 was dominated by **Alexander "Boss" Shepherd**, the driving force behind a citywide public works program that resulted in the development of such outlying areas as Dupont Circle; the alteration of street levels to improve drainage; the paving over of the old, unsanitary canal; and the planting of thousands of trees. Shepherd's grand plan also bankrupted the city, which, as always, relied on federal coffers for support. A disgruntled Congress revoked territorial government and returned the city to district status in 1874. In 1871 Washington was significantly enlarged by the incorporation of Georgetown. As the century drew to a close, railroad, streetcar and trolley lines led to the growth in nearby Virginia and Maryland of suburban communities that were linked economically and culturally to the city.

"The City Beautiful" – In 1901 the US Senate appointed the four-member **McMillan Commission** to recommend an overall building and landscape plan for the Mall area, which was then an unsightly hodgepodge. The commission's report, inspired by L'Enfant's original plan, established an 800ft greensward for the Mall and extended it west and south along the reclaimed Potomac flats, where the grand monuments to Lincoln and Jefferson were subsequently positioned.

To oversee all future planning for and building in the capital, the Commission of Fine Arts was created in 1910. In the same year, the Height of Buildings Act stipulated that no structures exceed 15 stories, thus ensuring that Washington would remain a horizontal and spacious city. Another law, the Public Buildings Act of 1926, resulted in the construction of a number of the city's monumental Classical Revival buildings, including those on the Federal Triangle and the structures housing the National Archives and the Supreme Court.

During the first half of the 20C, Washington's population increased from 278,000 to 800,000. The two world wars and the 1930s Works Progress Administration attracted an influx of workers to the city and its suburbs. To meet the administrative needs of the war efforts, a number of temporary buildings were constructed in the Mall area.

The District:
TAKING SHAPE IN THE 19C

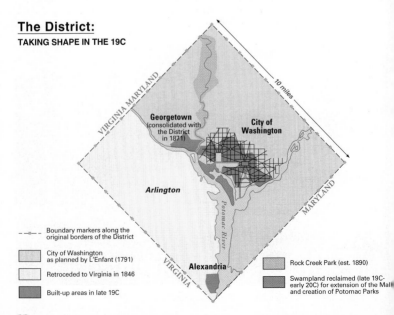

10 miles

VIRGINIA MARYLAND

Georgetown
(consolidated with
the District
in 1871)

City of
Washington

Arlington

Potomac River

MARYLAND

VIRGINIA

Alexandria

----- Boundary markers along the
original borders of the District

City of Washington
as planned by L'Enfant (1791)

Retroceded to Virginia in 1846

Built-up areas in late 19C

Rock Creek Park (est. 1890)

Swampland reclaimed (late 19C–
early 20C) for extension of the Mall
and creation of Potomac Parks

© Patricia Fisher/FOLIO, Inc.

Metro Station

In the postwar decades, Washington became a decentralized city with a decaying central core and an ever-increasing dependence on the automobile. While a system of expressways was built around the periphery of the District, traffic remained a critical problem. To alleviate congestion, a subway system, the **Metrorail**, began operations in 1976 and has since continually expanded its intercity and suburban service. The system's efficiency and elegant, albeit stark, design by the architect Harry Weese has won national acclaim.

■ National Capital Planning Commission

The National Capital Region covers the District of Columbia, the city of Alexandria and Maryland's Prince George's and Montgomery counties as well as Virginia's Arlington, Fairfax, Prince William and Loudoun counties. The National Capital Planning Commission is the central planning agency of the federal government in the Capital Region.

First established in 1924 by a congressional act as the National Capital Park Commission, the agency was authorized to acquire land for a park and recreation system for the nation's capital. Renamed by congressional act in 1952, the National Capital Planning Commission today consists of five planning experts, three of whom are appointed by the president and two by the mayor of DC, and seven ex officio members, including the mayor and the Secretary of the Interior.

Responsibilities include approving new federal building plans in the District, reviewing plans for federal structures in the Region and preparing a yearly analysis of all federal agency capital project proposals for the Region. Major federal laws underpinning the commission's decisions include the Height of Buildings Act of 1910, the Commission of Fine Arts Act of 1910 and the Commemorative Works Act of 1986.

The Commission, in 1997, released its *Extending the Legacy* plan—measures for preserving and enhancing Washington, DC's Monumental Core, from the Mall to the Potomac and Anacostia Rivers, as well as 22 miles of waterfront from Georgetown to the National Arboretum. However, a battle over the World War II Memorial, to be built directly between the Washington and Lincoln memorials, underscored the vulnerability of urban planning principles in a city where politics reigns supreme. Amid growing fears that demand for such projects threatens to overwhelm the Mall's historic character, a task force of interested commissions released a plan in spring 2001 to preserve the site's present character by halting approval for new construction along the central axis and identifying sites across DC for new memorials.

Soon after issuing the Memorials and Museums plan, an emboldened Commission further voted to reconsider the scale of the already-approved World War II Memorial and its impact on the Mall's vistas. But Congress, to the satisfaction of veterans' groups, quickly passed legislation overruling the Commission and approving the project; fittingly, the president signed the bill into law in a Memorial Day ceremony.

The Contemporary City – In the 1960s and 70s, tax laws favored the demolition of the city's old structures, and many charming architectural features were removed forever from the cityscape. At the same time, however, an awareness of historic preservation was burgeoning. The Kennedy administration (1961-63) began efforts to rejuvenate and restore historic Pennsylvania Avenue. In 1978 the city passed the Historic Landmark and Historic District Protection Act, which set guidelines for the designation and protection of historic structures and districts. By the 1980s the growing awareness of Washington's architectural heritage was reflected in commercial, as well as public, endeavors. Old buildings were renovated rather than demolished, new buildings were designed to interface with traditional architecture and the resuscitation of Washington's historic Downtown was well under way.

In addition to this architectural awareness, increasing focus was placed on developing and maintaining the parks and green spaces for which the city is famous. During her tenure as First Lady, **Ladybird Johnson** was instrumental in a city beautification process that led to the landscaping of park areas and public squares. Throughout the late 1960s and 70s, the National Capital Planning Commission instituted long-range plans that strove to achieve an integrated look for the city and its natural areas. The District's public parkland, some 7,000 acres that include the elm-lined lawns of the Mall and the hilly, forested terrain of Rock Creek Park, is administered and maintained by the National Park Service.

Development in the city is now closely monitored by a number of local and federal commissions and agencies, which combine their efforts to ensure that the capital retains its reputation as "the City Beautiful."

Architecture

From its inception Washington has attracted the talents of nationally prominent architects whose skills and vision are reflected in the city's many historic buildings. Because of the dominance of the Neoclassical style within the city and the strict building codes that set a 15-story height limit, modern Washington never developed as a center of innovative, high-rise architecture. Designed as a showcase for the new democracy, it remains in appearance a city of government, featuring massive, columned buildings adorned with allegorical motifs that recall the democratic and aesthetic ideals of ancient Greece and Rome. The District inventory of historic sites currently lists some 396 buildings, parks and historic districts, including lesser-known treasures such as the Classical Revival-style Embassy Gulf Service Station, a less prominent but enduring symbol of the capital.

18C – Washington preserves few vestiges from the 18C, since the city's foundation dates back to the 1790s. During the colonial period, the **Georgian** style, so named because it was popular in England under kings George I-IV (1714-1830), predominated in the design of brick and stone plantations and manor houses in nearby Virginia and Maryland. Existing examples of this style, which is typified by porticoes, cornices, quoins (prominent corner masonry) and hipped roofs, include Carlyle House, and Gunston Hall in Virginia.

In Georgetown the simple Old Stone House is one of the few extant buildings that reflect colonial vernacular architecture prior to the Revolution. Following Independence, the influence of the successful English architects the **Adam brothers** was seen in the work of colonial designers who adapted the Adam style to an American idiom that became known as **Federal** architecture. This style relies on symmetry and decorative elegance, often integrating such adornments as delicate columns, rosettes, urns and swags. The circular and oval-shaped rooms that characterize this style were used to great effect in The Octagon and Tudor Place, both private residences designed by **Dr. William Thornton** (1759-1828), the first architect of the Capitol. Many of the late-18C and early-19C row houses in Georgetown and Old Town Alexandria also exemplify the Federal style.

R. Corbel/MICHELIN

The Octagon

19C – In America as in Europe, the 19C gave rise to an eclectic mix of revival styles. In Washington, however, the prevailing taste for Neoclassical style frequently led to criticism of buildings that broke with this tradition. Some fine 19C structures that did not adhere to classical principles, such as the Old Post Office, the Old Executive Office Building and the Pension Building, were little appreciated, neglected and even threatened with demolition.

The **Greek Revival** style, modeled on the Doric temple, gained prominence in the 1800s under the talented hands of **Benjamin H. Latrobe** (1764-1820), who modified the original White House design and was responsible for many small architectural gems, such as Decatur House and St. John's Church. Another proponent of this style, **Robert Mills** (1781-1855) created the Treasury Building, the Old Patent Office Building and the original design of the Washington Monument. By mid-century a few architects began experimenting with the **Romanesque Revival** style, as exemplified in the turrets and battlemented cornices of the Smithsonian Castle, designed by **James Renwick** (1818-95). In the 1870s and 80s, Henry Hobson Richardson (1838-86) modified this approach into the popular **Richardsonian Romanesque**. Distinctive for its massive stone constructions that feature arched windows, doorways and turrets, this style can be found in the Old Post Office and in private residences in the Northwest quadrant, such as the Heurich Mansion. The **Italianate**, a simpler residential style, can be seen in several of the 19C brick row houses in Georgetown, the Dupont Circle area and Foggy Bottom.

Old Post Office

One of many versions of what is popularly called Victorian architecture, the Italianate employs overhanging cornices, decorative brackets, bow windows and porches.

Library of Congress

The **Second Empire** style, a mid-19C French innovation, first made its appearance in America in the early 1860s, with the building that now houses the Renwick Gallery. Named after its architect, James Renwick, this building features the characteristic Second Empire mansard roof—a dual-pitched roof pierced with dormer windows on the steep lower slope. During the Grant administration (1869-77), the style became so prevalent that it was known as the General Grant style. The massive Old Executive Office Building is one of the nation's finest examples of the style.

At the turn of the century, the exuberant **Beaux-Arts** style dominated the new buildings of Washington. Developed in France's famous École des Beaux-Arts, where many prominent American architects studied, this style was typified by a monumentality that reflected the optimistic spirit of the nation in the late 19C and early 20C. Its eclecticism combines classical elements with elaborate detailing, as seen in such public buildings as Union Station by **Daniel H. Burnham** (1846-1912), one of the leading advocates of Beaux-Arts, and the Library of Congress. In residential architecture, Waddy B. Wood and Jules Henri de Sibour designed a number of the palatial homes along Embassy Row in the Beaux-Arts manner.

20C – In the 1920s Beaux-Arts enthusiasm gradually became restrained, evolving into the more formal **Classical Revival** architecture that again dominated Washington from the 1920s through World War II. The Federal Triangle complex, built in the 1930s, includes seven buildings designed in the Classical Revival style by seven different architects, one of whom was **John Russell Pope** (1874-1937). The most prolific proponent of this style, Pope is responsible for such grand public buildings as the National Gallery of Art, the National Archives, the Scottish Rite House of the Temple *(1733 16th St. at S St. NW)* and the Jefferson Memorial. Sweeping staircases, pedimented porticoes, domes, and unadorned surfaces are all hallmarks of Pope's edifices.

Post-World War II Modernism has had little impact on Washington architecture. Rather than producing innovative architectural design, the 1950s, 60s and 70s saw the loss of many fine 19C structures, as undistinguished boxlike office buildings proliferated throughout the city. It was during this uninspired period that the Kennedy Center and the National Geographic Society building, both by **Edward Durell Stone**, were erected.

Washington does, however, possess a few exceptional examples of modern architecture: Dulles International Airport (1962, Eero Saarinen), the Martin Luther King Memorial Library (1972, Mies van der Rohe) and the East Building of the National Gallery of Art (1978, I.M. Pei).

National Archives

In recent years the currents of **post-Modernism** have resurrected the use of columns, arches and other embellishments that had been banished during the austere Modernist period. Washington Harbour, designed by Arthur Cotton Moore, embodies the extravagances of the 1980s, while a more restrained and academic approach can be seen in the newer structures along the historic Pennsylvania Avenue corridor, where classical elements are used in an attempt to integrate new architecture with the existing building stock. The Market Square complex *(between 6th and 7th Sts.)* by Hartman-Cox, exemplifies this trend. A decidedly post-Modern influence is apparent in the architecture of the US Holocaust Memorial Museum (James Freed), which opened in 1993. The new Italian chancery, clad with pink marble imported from Asiago and juxtaposing elements of a Tuscan villa and a Florentine palazzo, provides Embassy Row with an eye-catching, if nonindigenous, example of historical eclecticism (2000, Piero Sartogo).

Cultural Scene

Traditionally considered a cultural backwater, Washington has emerged in recent decades as a vital center for the performing arts, thereby taking its place among the nation's leading cultural hubs.

Museums – Founded in 1846 through a bequest to the US from an English scientist named James Smithson, the **Smithsonian Institution** now constitutes the largest complex of museums in the world. Of its 16 museums and galleries in Washington, DC, nine are located on the Mall. (Although loosely affiliated with the Smithsonian, the National Gallery of Art is an independent institution.) The Smithsonian's National Zoological Park and five of its six other museums are also located in Washington.

The collections of the Smithsonian contain some 140 million objects, including cultural and scientific artifacts and artworks ranging from the prehistoric to the contemporary. Among them are revered relics that define the country's heritage: the Star Spangled Banner, the Wright Brothers' *1903 Flyer*, Dorothy's ruby slippers, Woody Guthrie's "This Land is Your Land" and the entire Folkways Records collection. The institution also maintains six special facilities supporting work in the arts and sciences and sponsors public lectures, concerts, classes, festivals and tours.

In addition to the Smithsonian attractions, the capital boasts several fine privately owned museums created through the generosity of prominent Washington collectors. Foremost among these institutions are the Corcoran Gallery of Art, the Phillips Collection, Hillwood and Dumbarton Oaks. The area has preserved many historic house museums *(p 38)* that offer visitors glimpses into the capital's illustrious past. The federal city also abounds in exemplary public buildings, many of which are open to the public. A visit to such sights as the Capitol, Supreme Court, FBI or the Bureau of Engraving and Printing can provide a unique learning experience in the workings of the US government. Throughout the year the area's cultural and educational institutions—both public and private—sponsor an impressive schedule of (usually free) exhibits, lectures and concerts catering to a wide range of tastes and interests.

Performing Arts – *For addresses, telephone numbers and other practical information, consult the blue marbled pages of the Address Book.* With the opening of the John F. Kennedy Center for the Performing Arts in 1971, Wash-

---

■ SMITHSONIAN INSTITUTION

Mall museums

Arthur M. Sackler Gallery
Arts and Industries Building
Freer Gallery of Art
Hirshhorn Museum and Sculpture Garden
National Air and Space Museum
National Museum of African Art
National Museum of American History
National Museum of Natural History
National Museum of the American Indian
(projected opening date: 2004)
Smithsonian Institution Building:
Smithsonian Information Center
(The Castle)

Off the Mall

Anacostia Museum
National Portrait Gallery
(closed for renovation; scheduled reopening fall 2004)
National Postal Museum
National Zoological Park
Renwick Gallery
Smithsonian American Art Museum
(closed for renovation; scheduled reopening fall 2004)

New York City

Cooper-Hewitt National Design Museum
(THE GREEN GUIDE New York City)

ington finally began to attract an increasing number of world-class performers. Housing four theaters and the resident National Symphony Orchestra, the center offers drama, concerts and dance performances, and a regular schedule of film festivals and events through its affiliation with the American Film Institute. The well-respected Arena Stage complex, entering its 51st season, anchors the city's diverse and thriving theater community. Woolly Mammoth Theatre Company produces new and experimental works, while Shakespeare is the house playwright at the Folger Theatre. Touring Broadway musicals stop at the historic National Theatre, established on Pennsylvania Avenue in 1835 (and now a Kennedy Center affiliate). The National Park Service maintains two theaters: historic Ford's

© Everett C. Johnson/FOLIO, Inc.

Performance at the National Gallery of Art, West Garden Court

Theatre located downtown and the highly acclaimed Wolf Trap Farm for the Performing Arts, an outdoor summer theater in the nearby Virginia suburbs, which features world-renowned dance troupes and musicians.

In addition, the city benefits from an exceptional number of free summer concerts given by US military bands at various locations in the city *(see Military Band Concerts)*.

Further Reading

Above Washington by Robert Cameron
(Cameron and Co., San Francisco, 1989)

AIA Guide to Washington DC
(Johns Hopkins University Press, Baltimore MD, 1994)

Buildings of the District of Columbia by Pamela Scott and Antoinette J. Lee
(Oxford University Press, New York, 1993)

Kidding Around Washington, D.C.: A Young Person's Guide to the City by Debbie Levy
(John Muir Publications, Santa Fe, 1997)

The United States Capitol
(Stewart, Tabori & Chang, New York, 1996)

The White House: The History of an American Idea by William Seale
(AIA Press, Washington DC, 1992)

Washington, D.C.: A Book of the Nation's Capital
(Smithsonian Press, Washington DC, 1992)

Washington: Then and Now by Charles S. Kelley
(Dover Publications, New York, 1996)

Art and History of Washington, DC by Bruce Smith
(Bonechi, Florence, 2001)

Where to Find It

Locations of Washington's distinctive collections, houses and gardens:

American Decorative Arts	Carlyle House
	Daughters of the American Revolution
	Diplomatic Reception Rooms
	Dumbarton House
	Gunston Hall
	White House
Pre-Columbian Art	Dumbarton Oaks
	The Textile Museum
Byzantine Art	Dumbarton Oaks
Russian Decorative Arts	Hillwood
20C Art	Art Museum of the Americas
	Corcoran Gallery of Art
	Hirshhorn Museum and Sculpture Garden
	Kreeger Museum
	National Gallery of Art (East Building)
	Smithsonian American Art Museum
	Phillips Collection
House Museums	Arlington House
	Carlyle House
	Decatur House
	Dumbarton House
	Frederick Douglass National Historic Site
	Gunston Hall
	Hillwood
	Historical Society of Washington DC
	Lee-Fendall House
	Mount Vernon
	The Octagon
	Society of the Cincinnati Museum
	Tudor Place
	Woodlawn Plantation
Gardens	Dumbarton Oaks
	Gunston Hall
	Hillwood
	Kenilworth Aquatic Gardens
	National Arboretum
	Woodlawn Plantation
	Bishop's Garden (Washington National Cathedral)

Where to Find It

Locations of Washington's popular artifacts and treasures:

Archie Bunker's chair .... National Museum of American History

Athenaeum portrait of George
Washington by Gilbert Stuart .... National Portrait Gallery

Charters of Freedom .... National Archives

Derringer used to assassinate
Abraham Lincoln .... Lincoln Museum at Ford's Theatre

Fabergé Imperial Easter eggs .... Hillwood

First Ladies' gowns .... National Museum of American History

Giant pandas .... National Zoological Park

Ginevra de' Benci by
Leonardo da Vinci .... National Gallery of Art

Gutenberg Bible .... Library of Congress

Hope Diamond .... National Museum of Natural History

Japanese cherry trees .... Tidal Basin

Kennedy graves .... Arlington National Cemetery

Kitty Hawk 1903 Flyer .... National Air and Space Museum

Luncheon of the Boating Party
by Pierre-Auguste Renoir .... Phillips Collection

Michael Jordan's jersey .... National Museum of American History

Niagara by Frederic Edwin Church .... Corcoran Gallery of Art

Spirit of St. Louis .... National Air and Space Museum

Star-Spangled Banner .... National Museum of American History

George Washington's tomb .... Mount Vernon

Watergate tapes .... National Archives (College Park MD)

Food Stand along the Mall

Address Book

Where to Eat

Dine side by side with famous politicians or conduct your own "external investigation" at establishments owned by political pundits. Search out the best chili-cheeseburger in town or "make a deal" in the hush-hush wood-paneled interiors of not-so-politically-correct steak houses. Visitors to the nation's capital can sample the same delicacies enjoyed by some of the world's most visible leaders—from old-fashioned barbecue to red Thai curry prawns and lamb vindaloo. A city for the people, Washington, DC boasts restaurants that typify the variety of tastes and pleasures of the nation it represents.

The venues listed below were selected for their ambience, location and/or value for money. Rates indicate the average cost of an appetizer, an entrée and dessert for one person (not including tax, gratuity or beverages). Most restaurants are open daily—except where noted—and accept major credit cards. Call for information regarding reservations and opening hours.

Additional restaurants are listed throughout this guide in the form of Digressions. See Index for a complete listing of eateries described in the text.

$$$$	over $50	$$	$15-$30
$$$	$30-$50	$	less than $15

What you should know about Washington, DC restaurants:

Smoking is generally not allowed in Washington, DC restaurants, although some may permit it in the bar area. Although **jackets** may not be required, gentlemen might feel more comfortable wearing one in the more expensive restaurants. **Reservations** are highly recommended. Gratuities are generally not included on the bill; a **tip** of 15 to 20 percent is considered standard.

Luxury

Bistro Bis – *15 E St., NW.* ☎ *202-661-2700. www.bistrobis.com.* **$$$$ French.** Located in the hip, stylish Hotel George, this decisively French bistro swarms with political figures. Washington celebrities hover around the zinc bar and nestle into cozy leather booths, while three dining levels compliment the contemporary bistro offerings. Worth trying: chef Jeffrey Buben's mussels marseillaise and seared sea scallops provençale.

Butterfield 9 – *600 14th St., NW.* ☎ *202-289-8810.* **$$$$ American.** Evoking the subtle glamour of black-and-white Hollywood, Butterfield 9's creative American menu skillfully combines retro and modern flavors. Start with gnocchi laced with flavorful truffles or a delicate napoleon of red and golden beets layered with piquant cheeses. From there, move on to a traditional steak or an inventive crab-stuffed flounder, before feasting on baked Alaska for dessert.

The Caucus Room – *401 9th St., NW.* ☎ *202-393-1300. www.thecaucusroom.com.* **$$$$ American.** The consummate Washington steakhouse, where power players disappear into the rich, dark wooded interior and enjoy a tender steak and a glass of merlot. Truly a bipartisan venture, The Caucus Room is partially owned by notable Republican Haley Barbour and Democrat Tom Boggs and boasts a colorful William Woodward mural of a jovial donkey and elephant amicably enjoying a lavish feast. Generous portions and impeccable service justify the high prices.

DC Coast – *1401 K St., NW. www.dccoast.com* ☎ *202-216-5988.* **$$$$ New American.** A towering bronze mermaid sculpture greets hungry locals at this hot downtown restaurant. Housed in an Art Deco-era bank, the contemporary dining room features lantern-style chandeliers, oversized oval mirrors and spiral-shaped booths. Chef Jeff Tunks' tri-coastal specialties (Mid-Atlantic, Gulf and West) include tuna tartare chunks with lime and coconut milk, and beef tenderloin medallions with creamed leeks and port glaze.

Oceanaire – *1201 F St., NW.* ☎ *202-347-2277.* **$$$$ Seafood.** Washington's new seafood restaurant offers over two dozen fresh catch options each day in a rambling downtown setting. Chef Jason Tepper features two menus each day, to accommodate fresh arrivals. Start with the regional favorite Maryland blue crab soup or zesty oysters Rockefeller before moving on to the peppery cioppino. Nostalgia triumphs for dessert: Fresh-baked Toll House cookies and frosty glasses of milk have been eagerly received by discerning Washington diners.

Restaurant Nora – *2132 Florida Ave., NW.* ☎ *202-462-5143. www. noras.com.* **$$$$ New American.** America's first certified organic restaurant, Nora is housed in a 19C grocery store in Dupont Circle. Nora Pouillon's politically

TenPenh

correct, new American menu featuring delights such as roasted heirloom-tomato soup and pan-roasted Maine lobster with saffron risotto and pesto sits well with Washington diners, who have praised her innovative organic creations for 22 years. Nora's sister restaurant, Asia Nora, *(2213 M St., NW ☎ 202-797-4860)* boasts an intriguing Asian influence.

701 – *701 Pennsylvania Ave., NW. ☎ 202-393-0701. $$$$ **New American.*** Tucked behind the Navy Memorial, 701 recalls the elegance of a sumptuous supper club, with its enticing piano music and vast selection of vodkas and caviar. The fresh fish selections are dramatic preludes to performances at the nearby Shakespeare Theatre. For elegance at an affordable price, try the pre-theater menus, or stop by for dessert after the performance.

1789 – *1226 36th St., NW. ☎ 202-965-1789. $$$$ **American.*** This Washington fine-dining legend is named for the year in which nearby Georgetown University was founded. Executive Chef Ris Lacoste has made 1789 a culinary landmark, whose roaring fires and country-inn setting compliment a seasonal American menu. Pumpkin ravioli and glazed roast pork chops entice in autumn, while fresh seafood delights year-round.

TenPenh – *1001 Pennsylvania Ave., NW. ☎ 202-393-4500. www. ten penh.com. $$$$ **Asian.*** The sumptuous décor and notable flavors of one of Washington, DC's most popular Asian restaurants resulted from a six-week shopping and tasting journey to South Asia. Begin with the Thai-style coconut and chicken soup with portabella mushrooms before moving on to the macadamia and panko-crusted halibut or the red Thai curry prawns. Wash it down with the sake or ginger limeade.

Vidalia – *1990 M St., NW. ☎ 202-659-1990. $$$$ **Southern.*** With upscale versions of shrimp and grits and chicken and dumplings, Vidalia is an oasis of Southern comfort food in Washington's bustling business district. Vidalia's sunny yellow walls match the warm cornbread and refreshing lemonade that accent a summer lunch. Try the signature roasted Vidalia onion in season, and close your meal with sticky pecan pie paired with bourbon-laced ice cream.

Mid-Range

Café Atlantico – *405 8th St., NW. ☎ 202-393-0812. $$$ **Latin American.*** Café Atlantico is widely considered conservative Washington's most daring restaurant. Lively and unconventional, chef Christy Veile tastefully modifies Nuevo Latino flavors to suit Washington's conservative and liberal taste buds. Updated versions of traditional favorites, such as the Puerto Rican *asopao* (shrimp and crab stew), ceviche and empanadas are suitably paired with refreshing rum-based mojitos or cachaça-inspired caipirinhas.

District ChopHouse – *509 7th St., NW. ☎ 202-347-3434. www.districtchophouse.com. $$$ **American.*** Carved out of an old bank building, District Chophouse's thick steaks and smooth beers have earned it local honors. Order the signature crispy onion rings and jumbo hamburgers before heading to the MCI Center for a sporting event, or stop in for Sunday brunch, when cake-like German apple pancakes and steak and eggs are accompanied by live jazz music.

Jeffrey's – *2650 Virginia Ave., NW. ☎ 202-298-4455. $$$ **Southwestern.*** Opened in April 2001, Jeffrey's accompanied President George W. Bush and Laura Bush to Washington, DC from Austin, Texas. David Garrido's contemporary Texas

43

Seared Salmon

menu was a Bush favorite, and the couple has been known to sneak out for a quick bite at the new DC location in the notorious Watergate complex. Start with the crispy gulf oysters on yucca root chips, then move on to a tender bison steak.

The Mark – *401 Seventh St., NW.* ☎ *202-783-3133. www.themarkrestaurant.com.* **$$$ American.** This casual Penn Quarter bistro creatively jumps from country to country for an enticing menu. Bypass the theater-going crowds and sample The Mark's contemporary menu on Monday nights, when all bottled wines are half price. Don't skip dessert; the chef's signature white-chocolate cheesecake is a sinful treat.

The Occidental Grill – *1475 Pennsylvania Ave., NW.* ☎ *202-783-1475. www.occidentaldc.com.* **$$$ American.** One of Washington's most historic restaurants, the Occidental cozies up against the stately Willard Hotel, near the White House. The contemporary American menu features a simple, tasty selection of grilled meats and fish with cameo appearances by a trendier Chilean sea bass and marinated veal cheeks.

West 24 – *1250 24th St., NW.* ♿ ☎ *202-331-1100. www.west twenty-four.com.* **$$$ American.** Notable Washington political figures and incongruous couple James Carville and Mary Matalin crossed party lines to open this relaxed bistro, between M and N Streets, NW. Rich jewel tones and deep woodwork compliment the selection of bold Southern tastes and innovative variations on American favorites. A retro-style bar offers an inviting, neutral meeting ground for Capitol Hill staffers and well-known political figures. Tangy fried green tomatoes usher in a delightful lunch menu, while a cornmeal-crusted cod fillet with jicama slaw proves a satisfying dinner choice.

Bangkok Bistro – *3251 Prospect St., NW.* ☎ *202-337-2424.* **$$ Thai.** The smooth lines and soothing violet and green colors of Bangkok Bistro garnered an award from *Architectural Digest*. With its outdoor café and garden seating, the Georgetown restaurant invites a lively summer dining crowd, while the fiery Thai flavors sizzle all year long. Bangkok Bistro eschews potent chiles for subtler flavors in its best dishes.

Café Deluxe – *3228 Wisconsin Ave., NW.* ♿ ☎ *202-686-2233. www.cafe deluxe.com.* **$$ American.** With the feel of a trendy brasserie, Café Deluxe eases patrons into a menu of traditional comfort foods. Soothing, dark booths provide a relaxing backdrop for the grilled meatloaf with Creole sauce and applewood-smoked pork chops, while the contrasting Art Deco décor prompts the spontaneous ordering of new renditions on old cocktails such as sour-apple martinis. Café Deluxe placates vegetarian patrons with generous salads, pastas and pizzas smothered with vegetables and cheese. Gooey chocolate-chip-cookie pie guarantees a satisfying ending.

Capitol City Brewing Company – *2 Massachusetts Ave., NW.* ☎ *202-842-2337; also 1100 New York Ave., NW.* ☎ *202-628-2222. www.capcitybrew. com.* **$$ Pub.** Casual and comfortable, the District's oldest microbreweries serve up simple bar tastes in two restored historic buildings. Beer fans can try a Sampler, consisting of all four in-house brewery blends. Servers promptly bring soft, warm pretzels to munch on while perusing the menu. Giant sandwiches and ample salads rejuvenate after a lengthy day of sightseeing. For dessert, share the massive Monumental Brownie.

Clyde's of Georgetown – *3236 M St., NW.* ☎ *202-333-9180. www.clydes. com.* **$$ American.** With several locations in the Washington metropolitan area, cheery, saloon-like Clyde's has burgeoned into a Washington legend. Casual diners can opt for traditional burgers, sandwiches and chili, while patrons with greater expectations can select from a lengthy list of fashionable martinis and fresh seafood catches.

Mama Ayesha's – *1967 Calvert St., NW.* ☎ *202-232-5431.* **$$ Lebanese.** This cozy Middle Eastern eatery emanates a welcoming air of family camaraderie. Start with one of the varieties of hummus or stuffed grape leaves before feasting on couscous smothered by seasoned vegetables or kabobs. Bigger appetites will be whetted by the daunting baked lamb shank. Dinners conclude with a cup of sweet Arabian coffee and decadent baklava.

Lauriol Plaza – *1835 18th St., NW.* ☎ *202-387-0035.* **$$ Mexican.** One of Adams Morgan's most popular eateries, Lauriol Plaza keeps pitchers of margaritas flowing freely during happy hour. Fabulous fajitas and other Tex-Mex mainstays are joined by Puerto Rican and Latin American selections on the extensive menu. With ample outdoor dining, Lauriol Plaza sizzles on summer evenings.

Lebanese Taverna – *2641 Connecticut Ave., NW.* ☎ *202-265-8681.* **$$ Lebanese.** One of the most popular restaurants in Woodley Park, Lebanese Taverna teems with young professionals and outdoor café enthusiasts. Large groups can begin with a savory array of mezze, a spread of hors-d'œuvres, paired with the warm, soft pita bread that emerges from the wood-burning ovens. The juicy rotisserie chicken and lemony chicken shish taouk are tasty and satisfying.

Old Europe – *2434 Wisconsin Ave., NW.* ☎ *202-333-7600. www.old-europe.com.* **$$ German.** One of Washington's only German restaurants, Old Europe draws a healthy contingency of beer and schnitzel lovers who find solace in few other locales. The walls are covered, as anticipated, with steins and wooden crests that create a perpetual air of Oktoberfest. Satisfying, hearty dishes are served up in a quick, friendly and unpretentious manner.

Red Sea – *2463 18th St., NW.* ☎ *202-483-5000.* **$$ Ethiopian.** An eye-catching red awning stands out amidst the colorful storefronts of Adams Morgan, broadcasting one of the neighborhood's best representatives of Ethiopian cuisine. The Red Sea presents a zesty spread of chicken, beef and lamb dishes, as well as an extensive, inviting array of vegetarian selections. Designed for family-style eating, the chewy enjira bread soaks up the blend of seasoning in the gingery split peas and other saucy selections.

Tortilla Coast – *400 First St., SE.* ♿ ☎ *202-546-6768. www.tortillacoast.com.* **$$ TexMex.** Wayward Texans have found their way to Tortilla Coast for potent margaritas and spicy tastes of home since 1988. Cleanse your palate with the Stars and Stripes margarita, a blend of traditional and strawberry margaritas laced with Blue Curacao. Spinach and mushroom enchiladas and soft tacos satisfy vegetarians, while southwestern flavors shine through in the hickory barbecue chicken fajitas.

Clyde's of Georgetown

White Tiger – *301 Massachusetts Ave., NE.* ☎ *202-546-5900.* **$$ Indian.** Just footsteps from Union Station, the tropical décor and Raji mystique of White Tiger seems a far cry from the nearby steakhouses. The menu weighs heavily on lighter, northern Indian fare, with impeccable chicken and lamb vindaloo and savory naan bread. Outdoor seating makes it a favorite for Capitol Hill employees.

Budget

Ben's Chili Bowl – *1213 U St., NW.* ☎ *202-667-0909.* **$ Chili.** Ben's is common meeting ground for DC's traditional African-American community and young urban dwellers; sloppy chili dogs, thick milkshakes and fries loaded with cheese and bacon have proven to be universal pleasers in this Washington dining landmark. The interior retains the nostalgic charm of a 1950s diner, while modern business lunchers swivel around on the barstools during their power lunches.

Firehook Bakery & Coffeehouse – *3411 Connecticut Ave., NW.* ☎ *202-362-2253. www.firehook.com.* **$ Bakery.** For a quick, tasty sandwich or a sugary snack, Firehook Bakery captures carbohydrate fiends with its tempting window displays. Mini-loaves of fresh, crusty bread compliment fresh mozzarella and pesto on a simple caprese sandwich, while cream-filled tarts beg to be taken home from behind old-fashioned glass cases. Other locations on Q, 17th, and M streets.

Old Glory – *3139 M St., NW.* ☎ *202-337-3406. www.oldglorybbq.com.* **$ Barbecue.** Don't miss this fun, lively barbecue joint perched on the busy Georgetown corner of M Street and Wisconsin Avenue. Settle into a booth, and a server will promptly arrive to powerfully "brand" your table with a purposeful slap of an iron stamp. Each table comes equipped with six regionally-inspired sauces to suit patrons' preferences. Mosey up to the lavish hickory bar, which boasts the largest selection of bourbons in DC. Children favor the draft root beer.

Oodles Noodles – *1010 20th St., NW.* ☎ *202-293-3138.* **$ Asian.** Oodles Noodles lives up to its name by playfully fusing Malaysian, Japanese, Indonesian, Thai and Chinese variations of noodles. Select from udon, ramen, egg, chow fun, then select a preparation style—the frenzied cooks do the rest. The savory satays and chicken-coconut soup are worthy introductions to a quick, simple menu.

Pizzeria Paradiso – *2029 P St., NW.* ☎ *202-223-1245.* **$ Pizza.** Tucked inside a tiny row house near Dupont Circle, Pizzeria Paradiso's delicate crust and fresh ingredients join forces to create one of the best pizzas in the nation's Capital. The exceptional crust soaks in a rich, smoky flavor from the wood-burning oven, as the fresh mozzarella melts over a bed of thinly sliced roma tomatoes.

Pizzeria Paradiso

Rockland's – *2418 Wisconsin Ave., NW.* ☎ *202-333-2556. www.rocklands. com.* **$ Barbecue.** For a quick, inexpensive meal in Georgetown, follow the sweet smell of hickory smoke up Wisconsin Avenue to Rocklands. Traditional barbecue staples, from ribs and pulled pork to jalapeño cornbread, are deftly handled here. If you're shopping for something a little different, try the smoky grilled swordfish or salmon sandwich.

Saigonnais – *2307 18th St., NW.* ☎ *202-232-5300.* **$ Vietnamese.** Located in the heart of Adams Morgan, Saigonnais tantalizes with aromatic Indochine creations. Stylish and simple, the spring rolls are crisp and flavorful, while the assembly-required, pork-filled crepe rolls offer a challenging prelude to the suave lemongrass chicken and other generous dishes. The walls of the tiny restaurant are covered with photos of celebrity patrons.

Where to Stay

Party lines aside, the city's range of accommodations is sure to please both discerning diplomats and budget-minded backpackers. Swank boutique hotels, charming guest houses, and the city's grande-dame luxury establishments provide sanctuary to the thousands of families, journalists, politicians, and international visitors who come to the capital each year. Most hotels are located in the downtown and Georgetown areas while less-expensive rooms can be found in the Dupont Circle and Adams Morgan neighborhoods.

For general information about hotel chains in Washington, DC see the Accommodations section in the back of this guide.

The properties listed below were selected for their ambience, location and/or value for money. Prices reflect average cost for a standard double room (two people) in high season (not including any applicable city or state taxes). Room prices may be considerably lower in off-season, and many hotels offer discounted weekend rates. The presence of a swimming pool is indicated by the ☒ symbol.

$$$$$	over $300	$$	$75-$125
$$$$	$200-$300	$	less than $75
$$$	$125-$200		

What you should know about Washington, DC hotels:

■ Quoted rates do not include the city's substantial **hotel tax** of 14.50 percent. For example, with a quoted room rate of $139, you will actually pay $159 for that night's stay.

■ Rate categories below should be taken as a general guideline only. **Rates** can be higher or lower depending on season, day of the week and volume of advance reservations.

■ Guest **parking** will cost from $15 to $30 per day.

■ For **price-shopping**, and to find available rooms during the high season, consider using a rooms broker like Hotel Reservations Network *(www.hoteldiscount. com)*, Travelscape *(www.travelscape.com)*, Capitol Reservations *(www.hotelsdc. com)* or Quikbook *(www.quikbook.com)*. **Pet owners** should contact hotels directly or peruse *www.petswelcome.com* for a list of establishments that are dog- and cat-friendly.

■ In-room **telephone charges** can range from 50¢ to as much as $2 for local calls. Be especially prudent when making calls using the hotel's long-distance provider. Some establishments will charge as much as four to five times the usual rate. Even using a long-distance calling card can sometimes incur connection fees. When checking in, be sure to ask the price for local calls and connection fees for toll-free numbers. When in doubt, use the pay phones in the lobby.

Luxury

Four Seasons – *2800 Pennsylvania Ave., NW.* ✗ ♿ 🅿 ☒ ☏ *202-342-0444. www.fourseasons.com. 259 rooms.* **$$$$$** With an unassuming brick exterior, this upscale hotel earns its distinguished marks with luxurious furnishings and impeccable service. Original art adorns the walls of the roomy suites, complimenting the flavor of surrounding Georgetown. Guests can also take advantage of the state-of-the-art fitness center and spa.

Ritz Carlton – *1150 22nd St.* ✗ ♿ 🅿 ☏ *202-835-0500. www.ritzcarlton. com. 300 rooms.* **$$$$$** This new addition to the Washington luxury hotel landscape brings sought-after amenities to the West End. The luxurious rooms are bathed in mossy tones, with sumptuous bedding and high-tech business perks. A magnificent fitness center that overlooks the street draws envious looks from those hurrying past.

Hay-Adams – *16th & H Sts., NW.* ✗ ♿ 🅿 ☏ *202-638-6600 or 800-424-5054. www.hayadams. com. 143 rooms.* **$$$$** With a picturesque view of the Executive Mansion from its location across Lafayette Square, the Hay-Adams is closer to the White House than any of Washington's grande-dame hotels. Steeped in Washington lore, this elaborate, Renaissance-inspired beauty repeatedly houses world leaders and discerning travelers.

Hotel George – *15 E St., NW.* ✗ ♿ 🅿 ☏ *202-347-4200 or 800-576-8331. www.hotelgeorge.com. 139 rooms.* **$$$$** Washington's hippest hotel stormed onto the hotel scene in 1998 to the chagrin of hotel traditionalists and to the delight

of style-hungry liberals. With vibrant colors and contemporary artistic tributes to the first President of the United States, the Hotel George's very vogue minimalist interior and its proximity to Union Station have made it a staple of business and leisure travelers and celebrity guests.

Hotel Washington – *515 15th St., NW.* ⅹ ঐ ⬜ ☏ *202-638-5900 or 800-424-9540. www.hotelwashington. com. 340 rooms.* $$$$ Sporting one of the best views of Washington atop its rooftop terrace, the Hotel Washington sits a mere block and a half from the White House. Luxuriously appointed bedrooms feature marble bathrooms, elegant décor and spectacular views of historic Pennsylvania Avenue.

View of Lafayette Park and the White House
from the Hay-Adams Hotel

Courtesy DC Convention & Visitors Bureau

Jefferson Hotel – *1200 16th St., NW.* ⅹ ঐ ⬜ ☏ *202-347-2200 or 800-368-5966. www.thejeffersonhotel.com. 100 rooms.* $$$$ Built as a grand private residence in 1923, the Jefferson dazzles with its established reputation and classic exterior. A cheery courtyard leads into a Federal-style lobby with simple, tasteful furnishings. The guest rooms are quietly washed with neutral tones and exquisitely furnished with inviting four-poster beds.

The Latham Hotel – *3000 M St., NW.* ⅹ ঐ ⬜ ☏ *202-726-5000 or 800-368-5922. www.thelatham.com. 143 rooms.* $$$$ With a primo Georgetown location that houses **Citronelle**, one of Washington's most revered restaurants, the Latham's comfy guest rooms and rambling suites readily impress. The hotel boasts nine unique, two-story carriage suites and elegantly appointed guest rooms with generous amenities.

The Madison – *15th & M Sts., NW.* ⅹ ঐ ⬜ ☏ *202-862-1600 or 800-424-8577. www.themadisonhotel.net. 341 rooms.* $$$$ Perhaps better known for its graceful collection of antiques, The Madison proudly markets itself as "Washington's Correct Address." Located just a few blocks from the White House, the Madison's guest rooms are exquisitely furnished with custom-made French Provincial furnishings reflecting the Williamsburg and English Regency styles.

Monarch Hotel – *2401 M St., NW.* ⅹ ঐ ⬜ ⤢ ☏ *202-429-2400 or toll free 877-222-2266. www.washingtonmonarch.com. 415 rooms.* $$$$ The great outdoors reigns in the Monarch, as sunlight pours through the glassy atriums where trees flourish. Ample guest rooms contain clothed in elegant furnishings and sunny hues; posh executive suites are tailored to suit business travelers and to accommodate small meetings. Ideally located on the fringes of Georgetown, the Monarch provides easy access to shops and restaurants.

Morrison-Clark Inn – *1015 L St., NW.* ⅹ ঐ ⬜ *www.morrisonclark.com* ☏ *202-898-1200 or 800-332-7898. 54 rooms.* $$$$ This turn-of-the-century mansion seems misplaced in the middle of downtown's business district. Past the antiques-filled parlor, with lace curtains and burgundy wall coverings, you'll find three styles of accommodations. Choose from neutral-toned Neoclassical, opulent Victorian, and country-style distressed woods and wicker. The restaurant's Southern-style specialties have made it a national favorite.

Phoenix Park Hotel – *520 N. Capitol St., NW.* ⅹ ঐ ⬜ ☏ *202-638-6900 or 800-824-5419. www.phoenixparkhotel.com. 150 rooms.* $$$$ Situated between Union Station and the US Capitol, Phoenix Park pairs a convenient location with generous amenities and live Irish entertainment. The welcoming exterior harkens back to an 18C Irish manor, while the lively downstairs pub draws a steady crowd of Capitol Hill staffers.

Renaissance Mayflower Hotel – *1127 Connecticut Ave., NW.* ⅹ ঐ ⬜ ☏ *202-347-3000 or 800-468-3571. www.renaissancehotels.com/wassh. 660 rooms.* $$$$ A perennial favorite of frequent visitors, the Mayflower flaunts the splendor of Washington's golden age along busy Connecticut Avenue. The lobby of Washington's largest luxury hotel is graced with Federalist furniture and gilded accents, while the guest rooms recollect the genteel elegance of a distant era with their marble bathrooms and antique furniture.

St. Regis Washington, DC – *923 16th St., NW.* ⚹ ♿ 🄿 ☎ *202-638-2626 or 800-325-3535. www.stregis.com. 193 rooms.* **$$$$** The St. Regis looms over Washington's thriving business district with an air of distinction and aloofness. Inside, it's a glorious window into Washington's history of politics and intrigue. Since Calvin Coolidge cut the ribbon for the hotel's grand opening, every president has stopped by this hotel, which frequently hosts royal guests.

Swissotel Washington-The Watergate – *2650 Virginia Ave., NW.* ⚹ ♿ 🄿 ≋ ☎ *202-965-2300 or 800-424-2736. www.swissotel.com. 250 rooms.* **$$$$** Few Washington hotels are as cloaked in scandal as the Watergate, but Swissotel management has restored dignity and grace to the riverside property. The swirling complex offers stunning river views and easy access to the Kennedy Center and Georgetown. Rooms are simple, yet tasteful, and the rooftop bar serves an enticing summer martini.

Willard Inter-Continental – *1401 Pennsylvania Ave., NW.* ⚹ ♿ 🄿 ☎ *202-628-9100 or 800-327-0200. www.washington.interconti.com. 341 rooms.* **$$$$** A bastion of Washington tradition and opulence, the Willard towers over historic Pennsylvania Avenue. Inside, the dreamy Beaux-Arts lobby recalls an earlier age of opulence and political mystique with its grand columns and glittering chandeliers. The Round Robin Bar has served many a president mint juleps and potent brandies. Rooms reflect a tasteful, antique-drenched opulence, with views of the Washington skyline.

Mid-Range

Embassy Square – *2000 N St., NW.* ⚹ ♿ 🄿 ≋ ☎ *202-659-9000 or 800-424-2999. www.staydc.com. 278 rooms.* **$$$** Surrounded by colorful Dupont Circle's unpredictable sites and sounds, the Embassy Square is a simple, comfortable retreat ideally located near attractions, shops, restaurants and nightlife. The spacious suites are adorned with dark woods and deep green tones. Guests are greeted with a complimentary continental breakfast each morning.

Georgetown Inn – *1310 Wisconsin Ave., NW.* ⚹ ♿ 🄿 ☎ *202-333-8900 or 800-368-5922. www.georgetowninn.com. 96 rooms.* **$$$** Combining European elegance and colonial charm, the Georgetown Inn sits along bustling Wisconsin Avenue, in the heart of toney Georgetown's shops and restaurants. Luxurious marble bathrooms and heavenly four-poster beds lend an air of regal warmth to a hotel that has housed the Duke and Duchess of Windsor during past visits to Washington, DC.

Georgetown Suites – *1111 30th St., NW.* ♿ 🄿 ☎ *202-298-7800 or 800-348-7203. www.georgetownsuites.com. 214 rooms.* **$$$** Perfect for families and long-term visitors, this all-suite hotel is just minutes from historic Georgetown's shops and restaurants. The spacious suites come equipped with kitchenettes and generous amenities. Newly remodeled, each suite is tastefully decorated with modern furnishings.

Henley Park Hotel – *926 Massachusetts Ave., NW.* ⚹ ♿ 🄿 ☎ *202-638-5200 or 800-222-8474. www.henleypark.com. 96 rooms.* **$$$** The Henley Park Hotel's Tudor-style exterior and meticulously restored rooms reflect the classic elegance of Washington's earlier days. Conveniently located near the Washington Convention Center, the Henley Park offers complimentary limo service to downtown or Capitol Hill. Gargoyles and lead windows guard the entrance to the charming hotel.

Hotel Lombardy – *2019 Pennsylvania Ave., NW.* ⚹ ♿ 🄿 ☎ *202-828-2600 or 800-424-5486. www.hotellombardy.com. 125 rooms.* **$$$** Restored to reflect its original 1929 character, the Hotel Lombardy is located just four blocks from the White House in the center of Washington's business district. Sumptuous bedding compliments the densely woven oriental rugs and sleek chrome bath fixtures. Technological amenities coexist with the quaint ambience of this bastion of traditional DC hospitality.

Hotel Monticello of Georgetown – *1075 Thomas Jefferson St., NW.* ⚹ ♿ ☎ *202-337-0900 or 800-388-2410. 47 rooms.* **$$$** The Hotel Monticello's cozy, sunny suites brim with European charm and Georgetown sophistication. Just footsteps from the starting point of the historic C & O Canal and lively Wisconsin Avenue, the Monticello's bright, ample rooms provide an excellent base for exploring Georgetown.

Jurys Washington – *1500 New Hampshire Ave., NW.* ⚹ ♿ 🄿 ☎ *202-483-6000 or 800-423-6953. www.jurysdoyle.com. 314 rooms.* **$$$** Flanking Washington's beloved Dupont Circle, the Jurys Washington's spacious guest rooms boast technological amenities and business comforts such as voice mail and a trouser press. Along the circle, Claddagh's Restaurant and Biddy Mulligan's bar reflect the hotel's Irish ownership, complimenting the cosmopolitan neighborhood spirit.

The Melrose Hotel – *2430 Pennsylvania Ave, NW.* ✗ ♿ 🅿 ☎ *202-955-6400 or 800-635-7673. www.melrosehotel.com. 239 rooms.* **$$$** Sporting a catchy new name and fresh look, the Melrose reopened its doors in Foggy Bottom after an extensive remodeling project. The rooms bespeak flawless elegance, while nightly rates have not raced to catch up. Located within walking distance of the Kennedy Center and Georgetown, the Melrose's sunny, cheery rooms are a Washington bargain.

Washington Court Hotel – *525 New Jersey Ave., NW.* ✗ ♿ 🅿 ☎ *202-628-2100 or 800-321-3010. www.washingtoncourthotel.com. 264 rooms.* **$$$** Luxurious suites offer an unparalleled view of the Capitol dome in this charming Capitol Hill hotel. Independently operated, the Washington Court Hotel provides easy access to Washington's monuments, attractions and hot new eateries.

Budget

Channel Inn Hotel – *650 Water St., NW.* ✗ ♿ 🅿 ⚓ ☎ *202-554-2400 or 800-368-5668. www.channelinn.com. 100 rooms.* **$$** Billed as Washington, DC's only waterfront hotel, the Channel Inn offers comfortable, affordable rooms with breathtaking views of the Washington Marina. Several neighboring seafood restaurants and DC's nearby fresh-fish market accentuate the riverside hotel with fresh catches and homemade flavors. Airy rooms offer full amenities and inviting balconies on which to watch graceful sailboats and river cruise ships glide past.

Doolittle Guest House – *506 E. Capitol St.* ☎ *202-546-6622. www.doolittlehouse.com 3 rooms.* **$$** Though situated on a quiet, tree-lined street, this 1866 Victorian stands only four blocks from the US Capitol. From here, guests can walk to almost all DC attractions, including the Smithsonian museum and the Union Station train terminal. Three antique-appointed guest rooms and a library stocked with magazines and newspapers make for a comfortable night's stay. Breakfasts prepared with local organic produce and a gourmet's flair provide fuel for more sightseeing.

Hotel Tabard Inn – *1739 N St., NW.* ☎ *202-785-1277. www.tabardinn.com 40 rooms.* **$$** A Dupont Circle institution for 80 years, this hotel oozes charm with its scarlet walls, twisting staircases, stained-glass lamps and heavy antique furnishings. Rooms vary in size and décor; some share bathrooms. The plush couches and overstuffed chairs in the rustic lounge on the main floor are great places to kick back and unwind over cocktails. For lunch or dinner, the restaurant's acclaimed New American fare can be savored in the simple dining room or on an enclosed patio. A continental breakfast is included in the room tab.

Kalorama Guest House – *1854 Mintwood Pl., NW.* ♿ ☎ *202-667-6369. 19 rooms.* **$** Nestled in culturally diverse Adams Morgan, this charming assortment of Victorian townhouses pampers visitors with homey comforts, such as afternoon sherry and tasty continental breakfast selections. Rooms are sparse and simple, tinged with Victorian flair that mirrors the well-loved neighborhood.

Out on the Town

PERFORMING ARTS

Washington provides visitors with a great diversity of performing-arts offerings year-round. Highly respected dance, symphony and opera performances are held primarily at the Kennedy Center. Located in Vienna, Virginia, just 30 minutes from Washington, **Wolf Trap Farm Park** is the country's only national park dedicated to the performing arts. Visitors can enjoy a relaxing dinner under the stars on the grounds or bring a picnic for concerts, dance, jazz, opera and other performances from late May to early September. In the DC area, several downtown live-performance **theaters** mount a variety of stage productions performed by traveling Broadway companies and acclaimed regional and local groups. DC's main theater district centers on E Street between 7th and 15th Streets NW (the National, Warner, Ford's and Shakespeare theaters), while the Arena Stage along the southwest waterfront presents classic and contemporary drama in its three theaters. Catering largely to DC's African-American community is the newly renovated Lincoln Theatre on U Street. Popular rock and alternative **music** is performed at intimate and large-scale nightclubs as well as at stadiums and other large venues throughout DC, northern Virginia and neighboring Maryland. Area bookstores, coffeehouses and other locations host **public readings** or talks by both established and up-and-coming authors through-

Starring DC

Mr. Smith Goes to Washington (1939)
The Day the Earth Stood Still (1951)
Advise and Consent (1962)
The Exorcist (1973)
Three Days of the Condor (1975)
All the President's Men (1976)
First Monday in October (1981)
Protocol (1984)
The Distinguished Gentleman (1992)
Dave (1993)
In the Line of Fire (1993)
The Pelican Brief (1993)
Clear and Present Danger (1994)
The American President (1995)
Independence Day (1996)
My Fellow Americans (1996)
Contact (1997)
Wag the Dog (1997)
The West Wing (TV series; 1999–)
The Contender (2000)

out the year. *For a detailed listing of events, consult the* Washington City Paper *(distributed Thursday),* Washingtonian *magazine, the "Weekend" supplements in the Friday edition of the* Washington Post *and in the Thursday edition of the* Washington Times, *or the free publications listed on p 58 and p 60.*

Below is a selection of the area's venues and performing arts organizations:

Music and Dance

Classical Music	Venue	Season	☎	www
Folger Consort	Folger Shakespeare Library	Oct–May	202-544-7077	folger.edu
Juilliard Quartet	Library of Congress	Oct–Nov	202-707-5502	loc.gov
National Gallery Orchestra	National Gallery of Art	Oct–Jun	202-842-6941	nga.gov
National Symphony Orchestra	Kennedy Center	Sept–Jun	202-467-4600	national symphony.org
	Wolf Trap Farm Park	Jun–Sept	703-255-1900	
Washington Opera	Kennedy Center	Nov–Mar	202-295-2400	dc-opera.org
Washington Symphony	Various locations	Year-round	202-986-6030	wsodc.org
Wolf Trap Opera Company	Wolf Trap Farm Park	May–Sept	703-255-1868	wolf-trap.org

Dance				
Carla & Company (and other troupes)	Dance Place	Oct–May	202-269-1600	danceplace.org
Washington Ballet	Kennedy Center	Sept–May	202-362-3606	washington ballet.org

Rock/Pop	Address		☎	www
9:30 Club	815 V St. NW		202-265-0930	930.com
Nation Nightclub	Half & K Sts. SE		202-554-1500	
DAR Constitution Hall	18th & D Sts. NW		202-628-4780	dar.org
Lisner Auditorium (GWU)	21st & H Sts. NW		202-994-6800	gwu.edu
Robert F. Kennedy Stadium	E. Capitol & 22nd Sts. SE		202-547-9077	rfkstadium.com
USAir Arena *(map p 259)*	1 Harry S. Truman Dr. Landover, MD		301-350-3400	
Wolf Trap Filene Center	1551 Trap Rd. Vienna, VA		703-255-1900	wolf-trap.org

	☎	www
US Air Force Band	202-767-5658	af.mil/band
US Army Band	703-696-3718	army.mil/armyband
US Marine Band	202-433-4011	marineband.usmc.mil
US Navy Band	202-433-2525	navyband.navy.mil

Theaters and Companies

Curtain Up, a free quarterly publication available at area theaters and from TICKETplace (p 53), provides descriptions and schedules of plays currently being performed.

Theaters	Address	☎	www
African Continuum Theatre Company	3523 12th St. NE	202-529-5763	
American Century Theater	2700 S. Lang St., Arlington, VA	703-553-8782	americancentury.org
Arena Stage	6th St. & Maine Ave. SW	202-488-3300	arena-stage.org
Church Street Theater	1742 Church St. NW	202-265-3748	
Eisenhower Theater	Kennedy Center	202-467-4600	kennedy-center.org
Elizabethan Theatre	Folger Shakespeare Library	202-544-7077	folger.edu

Theaters	Address	☎	www
Ford's Theatre	511 10th St. NW	202-347-4833	fordstheatre.org
GALA Hispanic Theatre	1625 Park Rd. NW	202-234-7174	
Horizons Theatre	4350 N. Fairfax Dr., Arlington, VA	703-243-8550	horizonstheatre.org
Le Neon Theatre	1611 N. Kent St., Arlington, VA	703-243-6366	leneon.org
Lincoln Theatre	1215 U St. NW	202-328-6000	thelincolntheatre.org
National Theatre	1321 Pennsylvania Ave. NW	202-628-6161	nationaltheatre.org
Shakespeare Theatre	450 7th St. NW	202-547-1122	shakespearedc.org
Signature Theatre	3806 S. Four Mile Run, Arlington, VA	703-820-9771	sig-online.org
Source Theatre	1835 14th St. NW	202-462-1073	sourcetheatre.org
Studio Theatre	1333 P St. NW	202-332-3300	studiotheatre.org
Sylvan Theatre	Washington Monument grounds	202-619-7222	
Teatro de la Luna	3700 S. Four Mile Run, Arlington, VA	202-882-6227	teatrodelaluna.org
Warner Theatre	13th & E Sts. NW	202-783-4000	warnertheatre.com
Washington Shakespeare Company	601 S Clark St., Arlington	703-418-4808	crystalcity.com/shakespeare
Washington Stage Guild	At Source Theatre (above)	240-582-0050	
West End Dinner Theatre	4615 Duke St., Alexandria	703-370-2500	wedt.com
Woolly Mammoth Theatre Company	Various locations	202-393-3939	woollymammoth.net

Long-Running Performances			
Shear Madness	Kennedy Center	202-467-4600	shearmadness.com
Capitol Steps	Ronald Reagan Building	703-683-8330	capitolsteps.com

Tickets

As some of the more popular events sell out months in advance, it is advisable to buy tickets early. Full-price tickets can be purchased directly from the venue's box office or from one of the brokers listed below; a service charge of 10% or more may be added to the ticket price. Ticket brokers sometimes have tickets available when the box office is sold out, but expect to pay a substantial service fee. Hotel concierges may also be able to help secure tickets.

Tickets.com (☏ 703-218-6500; www.tickets.com) takes phone and online reservations for selected events and sights in DC and environs. Major credit cards are accepted. The service charge added to the price of each ticket varies, depending upon the event. Tickets may be purchased in person at various Olsson's Books & Records locations throughout the DC area. These locations only accept cash for ticket purchases.

Ticketmaster (☏ 202-432-7328 or 800-551-7328; www.ticketmaster.com) outlets are conveniently located throughout the area; call or check online for locations. Major credit cards are accepted. A convenience charge is added to the ticket price.

TICKETplace offers tickets for selected events on the day of the show at half price, plus a service charge of 10% of the full face-value of the ticket. Purchases must be made in person (cash or traveler's checks only) from the box office in the Old Post Office Pavilion, 1100 Pennsylvania Ave., NW (open year-round Tue–Fri noon–6pm, Sat 11am–5pm; ☏ 202-842-5387).

NIGHTLIFE

Tysons Corner

eCiti Café and Bar – 8500 Tyco Rd. www.eciticafe.com ☏ 703-760-9000. Housed in a former warehouse, eCiti quickly became the toast of the Northern Virginia tech quarter. Designed to satisfy the thousands of young professionals who work in quickly growing Tysons Corner, eCiti has also become popular with Washington, DC residents and workers. Though better known for its nightlife scene, eCiti took home the highly coveted Best New Restaurant honors in the 2001 Restaurants Association of Metro Washington Awards dinner.

Adams Morgan

Cities – 2424 18th St., NW. www.citiesrestaurant.com ☏ 202-328-2100. Brimming with smartly dressed professionals, Cities is quite a departure from the casual bars that line the streets of Adams Morgan. If you're looking to sample the cuisine, the nightlife or the culture of far-off places in Washington, DC, Cities is worth the visit—the club is themed after an international city and changes every few months.

Habana Village – 1834 Columbia Rd., NW. ☏ 202-462-6310. Forget the embargo on Cuba; Habana Village does its best to re-create the ostracized island in Washington, DC. Sultry and sexy echoes through all three stories of the club, where women never pay cover charges and even shrinking violets kick up their heels. Cigar smoke lingers in the air, as the bartenders pour mojitos by the hundreds on busy weekends.

Madam's Organ – 2461 18th St., NW. www.madamsorgan.com ☏ 202-667-5370. "Sorry, we're open" reads the mural outside, just below a busty redhead's boldly painted portrait. The bright colors and brazen sarcasm of Madam's Organ have made it one of the most familiar sites in DC. Inside, it's just as quirky. Take the stairs up to Big Daddy's Love Lounge & Pick-Up Joint, but beware...it's aptly named.

Chief Ike's Mambo Room – 1725 Columbia Rd., NW. ☏ 202-332-2211. Not much Mambo about it—George Stephanopoulos made frequent visits to this Adams Morgan haunt, setting off an invasion of preppie Capitol Hill staffers. Chief Ike's packs a big crowd on weekend nights, but the kitschy bar spills out onto a roomy terrace for fresh air and less harried conversation.

Dupont Circle

18th Street Lounge – *1212 18th St., NW.* ☎ *202-466-3922.* Celebrity residents and visitors are often spotted in the 18th Street Lounge, one of Dupont Circle's most coveted places for nightlife. Bouncers stand guard over the beautiful property—a historic mansion that was once home to Teddy Roosevelt—and maintain a strict admissions policy. Leave the jeans and sneakers at home, though; if you want to experience the ESL (as it's known to locals), you've got to project a level of "cool."

MCCXXIII – *1223 Connecticut Ave., NW. www.1223.com* ☎ *202-822-1800.* Billing itself as Washington's "Premier Champagne and Caviar Club," this is a place for those who like rubbing elbows with the rich and famous. Located in the heart of Dupont, MCCXXIII adds a touch of elegance to the Circle's entertainment options.

Dragonfly – *1215 Connecticut Ave., NW.* ☎ *202-331-1775.* Dragonfly filled a void in Washington, providing a cosmopolitan, trendy, yet unique nightlife option with its extensive sushi menu and liquor to match. The décor within is surreal, yet minimalist—Bruce Lee footage races across the whitewashed walls while music trickles out from the dance floor.

Gazuza – *1629 Connecticut Ave., NW.* ☎ *202-667-5500.* Sleek furnishings and outside seating overlooking busy Connecticut Avenue have placed newcomer Gazuza on the Washington nightlife map. The chic ambience and enviable property doesn't engender a sense of exclusivity, though; Gazuza's Dupont Circle location attracts a healthy mix of revelers seeking house music and trendy martinis.

Downtown

Ozio – *1813 M St., NW.* ☎ *202-822-6000.* Marketing itself as a "cigar and martini lounge," Ozio paints a tempting picture of urban chic to Washington's international crowd. It's got the martini menu and lingering cigar smells to match, though the splashy murals and muted walls detract from its loungy qualities.

Coco Loco – *810 Seventh St., NW. www.cocolocodc.com* ☎ *202-289-2626.* One of the staples of Washington's Latin Dancing for Dummies crowd, Coco Loco thrived even before downtown Washington became safe and cool again. It's a good place to practice your salsa moves or to take lessons on Thursday nights. If your hips start to ache from too much Latin dancing, a second floor belts out international and house music.

Polly Esther's – *605 12th St., NW. www.pollyesthers.com/dc* ☎ *202-737-1970.* If you're looking for a no-frills, no-pressure place to dance, you can't beat Polly Esther's. Three floors, dedicated to the 70s, 80s and 90s, pulse with familiar music and display memorabilia from earlier days. People of all ages crowd into the club on weekends, finding solace in the music of their past. Drinks also bear the names of pop culture icons from each decade, and era-appropriate movie and television clips play on big-screen televisions.

Georgetown

Blues Alley – *1073 Wisconsin Ave., NW. www.bluesalley.com* ☎ *202-337-4141.* Few Washington nightlife places have enjoyed the success and notoriety of Georgetown's Blues Alley, which has been praised by New York Times critics and Dizzy Gillespie alike. Since it opened in 1965, Blues Alley has touted itself as "DC's Best Jazz Supper Club" and is worthy of the distinction; some of the biggest names in jazz have played and recorded albums here.

Sequoia – *Washington Harbour, 3000 K St., NW. www.arkrestaurants.com* ☎ *202-944-4200.* Yachts and sporty racing boats sidle up to the Georgetown waterfront on warm summer evenings to enjoy the dockside nightlife scene. A constant stream of music wafts from the docked boats into the bar, where DC's bold and beautiful down beer and margaritas in the two-level glass-front restaurant.

Paper Moon – *1073 31st St., NW.* ☎ *202-965-6666.* A sleek international crowd flocks to this Tuscan villa-inspired Italian restaurant that morphs into a lively dance party on weekend nights. Playing largely house and international music, Paper Moon bursts with nearby Georgetown and George Washington University students and internationals who make their home in DC.

Third Edition – *1218 Wisconsin Ave., NW.* ☎ *202-333-3700.* This Georgetown mainstay served as the backdrop for the 1985 movie *St. Elmo's Fire* and has hosted many a beleaguered college student since it opened in 1969. On Wednesday through Saturday nights, a dance party erupts on the upper level, leaving the mellow downstairs beer-sippers and game-watchers in the wake of pop and rock classics. In the summertime, a lively Tiki Bar opens to offer one of Georgetown's few opportunities for outdoor nightlife away from the riverfront.

U Street Mural

U Street

Bohemian Caverns – *2001 11th St., NW.* ☎ *202-299-0800.* One of DC's best jazz spots in the days of Duke Ellington, Bohemian Caverns recently reopened with a fresh new look and a pleasing lineup of performers. An upscale restaurant occupies the upper level, while the live music trickles up from the caverns below.

The Black Cat – *1811 14th St., NW. www.blackcatdc.com* ☎ *202-667-7960.* Live-music lovers flock to The Black Cat for a sneak preview of some of rock's rising stars. With an ample space that can hold 550 fans, The Black Cat is readily packed with pierced and tattooed punk– and alternative-music fiends. The familiar U Street haunt is co-owned by former Nirvana drummer and current Foo Fighter Dave Grohl.

Shopping

Visitors to Washington can find everything from specialty shops and boutiques in **Georgetown** to established department stores situated in and around **Downtown**. Scattered throughout the city are several enclosed malls featuring multilevel arcades and offering a wide selection of shops, restaurants and movie theaters. Some of the more exclusive malls (Willard Collection, Mazza Gallerie) house boutiques of internationally renowned designers.

Galleries, antique shops and bookstores can be found in the neighborhoods of **Adams Morgan**, **Dupont Circle** and around **Eastern Market** on Capitol Hill. Fashionable **Connecticut Avenue** from K Street to Dupont Circle presents fine shops and specialty stores. In **Old Town Alexandria**, visitors can find an array of gift and antique shops and galleries.

Downtown and Vicinity

Department Stores	Address	☎	www
Hecht's Metro Center	12th & G Sts. NW	202-628-6661	hechts.com
Filene's Basement	1133 Connecticut Ave. NW	202-872-8430	filenesbasement.com

Shopping Malls			
La Promenade, L'Enfant Plaza	480 L'Enfant Plaza One level below Loews Hotel Lobby	202-485-3300	
Pavilion at the Old Post Office	12th & Pennsylvania Ave. NW	202-289-4224	oldpostofficedc.com
Shops at National Place	1331 Pennsylvania Ave. NW	202-662-1250	
Union Station	Massachusetts Ave. & 1st St. NE	202-371-9441	unionstationdc.com

Specialty shops and Trademark Stores

Banana Republic	601 13th St. NW	202-638-2724	bananarepublic.com
Discovery Channel Store	601 F St. NW	202-639-0908	discovery.com
ESPN Zone	555 12th St. NW	202-783-3776	espnzone.com
Hard Rock Café	999 E St.	202-737-7625	hardrockcafe.com
Political Americana	1331 Pennsylvania Ave. NW	202-547-1685	politicalamericana.com
Planet Hollywood	1101 Pennsylvania Ave. NW	202-783-7827	planethollywood.com

Connecticut Avenue/Dupont Circle

Specialty shops and designer boutiques

Betsy Fisher	1224 Connecticut Ave. NW	202-785-1975	betsyfisher.com
Burberry	1155 Connecticut Ave. NW	202-463-3000	burberry.com
Montblanc	1006 Connecticut Ave. NW	202-466-5001	montblanc.com
Rizik's	1100 Connecticut Ave. NW	202-223-4050	riziks.com
Shake Your Booty	2324 18th St. NW	202-518-8205	

Bookstores

Kramerbooks & Afterwords Café	1517 Connecticut Ave. NW	202-387-1462	kramers.com
Politics & Prose	5015 Connecticut Ave. NW	202-364-1919	politics-prose.com

Georgetown

Shopping Malls	Address	☎	www
Georgetown Park	3222 M St. NW	202-298-5577	gtpark.com

Specialty shops and designer boutiques

Bee Market	3300 M St.	202-337-6602	
The Coach Store	1214 Wisconsin Ave. NW	202-342-1772	coach.com
Soco	1250 Wisconsin Ave. NW	202-337-6790	
BCBG Max Azria	3210 M St. NW	202-333-2224	bcbg.com
Banana Republic	3200 M St. NW	202-333-2554	bananarepublic.com
Betsey Johnson	1319 Wisconsin Ave. NW	202-338-4090	betseyjohnson.com
Benetton	1200 Wisconsin Ave. NW	202-625-0443	
French Connection	1229 Wisconsin Ave. NW	202-965-4690	frenchconnection.com
Kenneth Cole	1259 Wisconsin Ave. NW	202-298-0007	kennethcole.com
MAC Cosmetics	3067 M St. NW	202-944-9771	maccosmetics.com
Pirjo	1044 Wisconsin Ave. NW	202-337-1390	
Restoration Hardware	1222 Wisconsin	202-625-2771	restoration hardware.com
Steve Madden Shoes	3109 M St. NW	202-342-6195	stevemadden.com
Patagonia	1048 Wisconsin Ave. NW	202-333-1776	patagonia.com

Maryland

Shopping Malls	Address		
Chevy Chase Pavilion	5335 Wisconsin Ave. NW	202-686-5335	
Landover Mall	Landover & Brightseat Rds.	301-341-3200	
Mazza Gallerie	5300 Wisconsin Ave. NW	202-966-6114	
Montgomery Mall	7101 Democracy Blvd., Bethesda	301-469-6000	montgomerymall. Shoppingtown.com
White Flint Mall	11301 Rockville Pike	301-468-5777	

Specialty shops and designer boutiques

Cartier	5454 Wisconsin Ave.	301-654-5858	cartier.com
MicMac Bis	5301 Wisconsin Ave. NW	202-362-6834	
Saks Fifth Avenue	5555 Wisconsin Ave. Women's Store	301-657-9000	saksfifthavenue.com
Saks-Jandel	5510 Wisconsin Ave.	301-652-2250	
Tiffany & Co.	5500 Wisconsin Ave.	301-657-8777	tiffany.com
Lord & Taylor	5255 Western Ave.	202-362-9600	
Gianni Versace	5454 Wisconsin Ave.	301-907-9400	versace.com

Virginia   Address

Shopping Malls

Ballston Commons	4238 Wilson Blvd., Arlington	703-243-8088	
Fashion Centre at Pentagon City	I-395 at S. Hayes St., Arlington	703-415-2400	
The Galleria	2001 International Dr. & Rte. 123, McLean	703-827-7700	mallibu.com
Landmark Shopping Center	I-95 South, Alexandria	703-941-2582	
Springfield Mall	I-95 South, Springfield	703-971-3000	springfieldmall.com
Tysons Corner Center	1961 Chain Bridge Rd., McLean	703-893-9400	shoptysons.com

Museum Shops

	☎	www
Arthur M. Sackler Gallery	202-357-4880	asia.si.edu
Arts & Industries Building	202-357-1369	si.edu/ai
Corcoran Gallery of Art	202-639-1700	corcoran.edu
Decatur House	202-842-0920	decaturhouse.org
Folger Shakespeare Library	202-544-7077	folger.edu
Freer Gallery of Art	202-357-4880	asia.si.edu
Hillwood Museum	202-656-8500	hillwoodmuseum.org
Hirshhorn Museum	202-357-1429	hirshhorn.si.edu
Library of Congress	202-707-8000	loc.gov
National Air & Space Museum	202-357-1387	nasm.si.edu
National Building Museum	202-272-7706	nbm.org
National Gallery of Art	202-842-6476	nga.gov
National Museum of African Art	202-786-2147	nmafa.si.edu
Smithsonian American Art Museum	202-357-2700	americanart.si.edu
National Museum of Natural History	202-357-1535	mnh.si.edu
National Portrait Gallery	202-357-2700	npg.si.edu
National Postal Museum	202-633-8180	si.edu/postal
Renwick Gallery	202-357-1445	americanart.si.edu
Lyceum (Alexandria)	703-548-1812	lexandriahistory.org

Spas

	Address	☎	www
Celadon	1180 F St. NW	202-347-3333	
Elizabeth Arden Red Door Salon & Spa	5225 Wisconsin Ave. NW Chevy Chase, MD	202-362-9890	reddoorsalon.com
Jolie Day Spa	7200 Wisconsin Ave. Bethesda, MD	301-986-9293	joliespa.com
Georgetown Aveda	1325 Wisconsin Ave. NW	202-965-1325	aveda.com
Bluemercury	3059 M St. NW Georgetown	202-965-1300	bluemercury.com
	1745 Connecticut Ave. NW	202-462-1300	
Jacques Dessange	5410 Wisconsin Ave. Chevy Chase, MD	301-913-9373	dessange.com

Sightseeing

Visitor Information

Free publications such as *Where Washington, Washington D.C. Quick Guide* and the *Washington Flyer* magazine (the latter available at local airports) offering information on events, attractions, shopping and dining can be found at hotels and visitor information kiosks. Contact the **Washington, DC Convention and Visitors Association**, 1212 New York Ave. NW, Suite 600, Washington DC 20005 (☎ *202-789-7000; www.washington.org*) to obtain these publications or visit the **Visitors Information Center** (☎ *202-328-4748 www.visitdc.com*) in the Ronald Reagan Building. The **Smithsonian Information Center** is located at 1000 Jefferson Dr. SW in the Castle *(open year-round daily 9am–5:30pm; ☎ 202-357-2700; www.si.edu)*. This state-of-the-art visitor center (interactive touch screens, video disks, electronic wall maps) is the place to plan your visit to Smithsonian attractions. The **White House Visitor Center** on Pennsylvania Ave. between 14th and 15th Sts. provides information about White House tours *(open year-round daily 7:30am–4pm; ☎ 202-208-1631; www.whitehouse.gov)*.

Tours

For visitors with little time at their disposal, we recommend following the two– or four-day itineraries on p 17. Addresses, opening hours, admission charges and other useful information designed to help you organize your visit are included with each of the sight descriptions in this guide.

A variety of guided tours (sightseeing buses, walking tours, cruises and special tours) are available to the visitor. Here is a selection of the principal tours:

Tourmobile Sightseeing – ☎ *202-554-7950; www.tourmobile.com. One bus route is indicated on the itinerary map pp 14-16.* Operating a concession authorized by the National Park Service, this company is the only sightseeing service allowed to take visitors up to the monuments and through Arlington National Cemetery. Tourmobile offers shuttle-bus service to the principal Mall and Capitol Hill sights, as well as to the White House, Kennedy Center, Arlington National Cemetery, Frederick Douglass National Historic Site and Mount Vernon. Daily tours *(except Jan 1 & Dec 25)* are offered mid-Jun–Labor Day 9am–6:30pm; the rest of the year 9:30am–4:30pm. Tickets *($18)* can be purchased from Tourmobile ticket booths located near many of the sights or from the driver of any of the blue and white buses; tickets are valid all day and entitle you to unlimited reboarding at any of the stops indicated with a blue and white Tourmobile sign. Tickets may also be purchased from Ticketmaster (☎ *202-432-7328; 800-551-7328 or www.ticketmaster.com)*. On-board commentary is provided by trained guides. Twilight Tours *($18)* are offered mid-Jun–Labor Day daily 7:30pm and Sept–Dec daily 6:30pm. Combination tours are available to Mount Vernon/ Washington/ Arlington *(Apr–mid-Nov daily; $45)* and Frederick Douglass National Historic Site/Washington/Arlington *(mid-Jun–Labor Day & Feb daily; $34)*.

Old Town Trolley – ☎ *202-832-9800; www.trolleytours.com.* Tours of Washington operate Memorial Day-Labor Day daily 9am–5:30pm; rest of the year daily 9:30am–4:30pm, except Thanksgiving Day and Dec 25. Visitors can board the orange and green trolleys every 30min at any of 17 locations. The complete itinerary lasts about 2hrs and the same ticket *($24)* allows free reboarding the entire day. After-hours tours *(2hrs 30min)* depart from Union Station *(Mar–Oct 7:30pm, rest of the year 6:30pm; $25)*.

Sightseeing Tour Bus

Gold Line-Gray Line – ☎ *202-289-1995 or 800-862-1400; www.gold-linegrayline.com.* This company offers a wide variety of tours year-round in and around Washington. Fares range from $28 for a 4hr tour of Arlington, Embassy Row and Capitol Hill to $78 for a 2-day "grand tour" of the principal sights. Excursions to Alexandria, Mount Vernon, Williamsburg, VA, Civil War battle sites, Charlottesville, VA and Atlantic City, NJ are also available.

Special Tours – The following **annual tours** allow you to visit sights that are usually closed to the public: Georgetown House and Garden Tours and the Embassy Tour *(p 206).* Advance reservations are strongly recommended for these popular tours.

Cruises on the Potomac River – Tours along the Potomac River offer views of the capital city by day and by night, when many sights are illuminated. Some companies offer dinner/dance cruises in addition to lunch and party tours. All cruises are round-trip. Below are the principal boat cruises operating on the river.

Departing from DC – **DC Ducks** takes occupants in amphibious open-air "boats" on a land tour of major sights, followed by a half-hour cruise on the Potomac *(departs from Union Station Mar–Nov daily 10am–4pm on the hour; 1hr 30min; $24;* ☎ *202-832-9800; www.historictours.com).* **Spirit Cruises** offers lunch, dinner and party cruises: dinner cruises aboard the *Spirit of Washington* head south beyond Alexandria before returning to DC *(depart from Pier 4, 6th & Water Sts. SW; Mar–Dec Tue–Sun 6:30pm; 3hrs; $57-$75).* The *Potomac Spirit* cruises to Mount Vernon *(departs from Pier 4 late Mar–Oct, Tue–Sun 9am; $26.50).* Reservations recommended for both cruise boats (♿ ▯ ☎ *202-554-8000; www.spiritcruises.com).* **Odyssey** offers year-round dinner cruises to Georgetown aboard the glass-atrium yacht *Odyssey III (depart from Gangplank Marina, 7th & Water Sts. SW; year-round Mon–Thu 7pm, Sun 6:30pm, $75 & Fri–Sat 8pm, $86; 3hrs; coat & tie recommended; board 1hr before departure time).* Lunch and brunch cruises are also available. Reservations required for all cruises (♿ ▯ ☎ *202-488-6000; www.odysseycruises.com).*

Departing from Alexandria *(map p 228)* – **Potomac Party Cruises, Inc.** offers dining cruises to DC aboard the *Dandy (departs from Prince St. year-round daily 11:30am; 2hrs 30min; $31-$38; dinner cruises 7:30pm; 3hrs; $62-$75; board 1hr before departure time).* A midnight dance cruise departs from Old Town or Washington Harbour in Georgetown. Reservations required for all cruises (♿ ▯ ☎ *703-683-6076; www.dandydinnerboat.com).* The **Potomac Riverboard Co.** features a narrated sightseeing cruise along Old Town's waterfront aboard the *Admiral Tilp (departs from Cameron St. Apr–Oct Tue–Sun; 40min; $8; phone for departure times* ☎ *703-548-9000; www.potomacriverboatco.com).*

Walking Tours

DC Sightseeing – Interesting, informative and fun summarizes these five area tours led by author and former editor for the Associated Press, Anthony Pitch. Visitors walk the streets of Georgetown, Adams Morgan or Capitol Hill, visit historically significant or insignificant sights, learn fun facts and explore the secrets of our nation's capital. *(Tours year-round Sun 11am—weather permitting, or by reservation; $10; phone for schedule and departure locations;* ☎ *301-294-9514; www.dcsightseeing.com.)*

Washington Walks – Licensed guides walk you through the DC area while sharing anecdotes and ghost stories: what skeletons are in whose DC closet and what past DC residents still linger in the present. Regularly scheduled tours are available throughout the week; other tours are available by reservation *(call for tour times and departure locations; $10-$20;* ☎ *202-484-1565; www.washingtonwalks.com).*

Other Tours

Bike The Sites, Inc. – Why walk when you can bike? Guided tours offered through downtown, Georgetown, Mount Vernon and other area DC points of interest. Bicycles, helmets, water and a snack are included in the cost of the guided tour *(call for tour availability; $40;* ☎ *202-966-8662; www.bikethesites.com).*

Spydrive – Uncover the important role that spies have played in the past and will play in the future of the United States. This tour takes you on a ride through DC with retired CIA, FBI and even KGB officials. You will learn about spies throughout history, their hangouts, their accomplishments and their weaknesses *($55;* ☎ *202-432-7328; www.spydrive.com).*

TechTours – Hop on the bus, hook up your headset and go! Bill Appell personally leads you through the Memorials, The White House and Arlington National Cemetery. Each person is hooked up with headphones so you can actually hear what the tour guide is saying. After your tour, you will have an online photo souvenir of your DC experience *(tours scheduled year-round Tue–Sat, 6am Apr–Aug, 7:30am Sep–Mar; reservations required; $39;* ☎ *301-261-2486; www.techtours.org).*

Crowds near White House Area

© Brigitta L. House/MICHELIN

Tips for Special Visitors

Children – Throughout this guide, sights of particular interest to children are indicated with a [Kids] symbol. Many museums and other attractions offer special children's programs and resource centers. Most attractions in Washington offer discounted admission to visitors under 18 years of age. In addition, many hotels offer family discount packages, and some restaurants provide a children's menu.

Travelers with Disabilities – Throughout this guide, wheelchair access is indicated on floor plans and in the admission information that accompanies sight descriptions by means of the ♿ symbol. Handicapped parking is available at most of the National Park Service sights in the city. The Smithsonian offers numerous services for visitors with disabilities. To obtain a copy of *Smithsonian Access* (large-type edition available), call or write Smithsonian Information, Smithsonian Institution, SI Building, Room 153, Smithsonian Institution, Washington DC 20560 ☎ 202-357-2700, TTY ☎ 202-357-1729 *(open year-round Mon–Fri 9am–5pm, weekends 10am–4pm; closed Dec 25)*.

The **Washington Metropolitan Area Transit Authority** has facilities and reduced fares for disabled riders on the **Metro** and public buses. For information and free publications, call ☎ 202-637-7000, TDD ☎ 202-638-3780; www.wmata.com.

Wheelchair Mobile Transport provides transportation for disabled individuals in the DC area. For more information or reservations, contact Wheelchair Mobile Transport, 1119 Taft St., Rockville, MD 20850; ☎ 301-294-0600.

Disabled travelers using Amtrak and Greyhound should contact these companies prior to their trip to make special arrangements and to receive useful brochures. For information about travel for individuals or groups, contact the Society for Accessible Travel & Hospitality, 347 5th Ave., Suite 610, New York NY 10016 ☎ 212-447-7284; www. sath.org.

DC Online

www.downtowndc.org – What to do and how to get there for Downtown DC, provided by the Business Improvement District.

www.whitehouse.gov – Information on White House events, history, past and present residents.

www.washingtonpost.com – Keep up with DC current events from what's in the news to where to see your favorite band.

www.thecapitol.net – Resource for business professionals visiting the DC area.

www.culturaldc.org – Information on the DC area's art exhibits, cultural events and activities. Festivals and little known treasures can be found on this online *"Insider's Arts Guide"*.

www.dcchamber.org – Chamber of Commerce informational site.

www.dc.gov – The government of DC site.

www.washington.org – Official visitors guide for Washington, DC.

www.dcvisit.com – DC Visitor Information Center web site.

www.firstgov.gov – All you need to know about our nation's government.

www.fly2dc.com – *Washington Flyer* magazine online.

www.where-events.com – *Where* magazine online.

DC For Kids

Where to eat ☜

ESPN Zone 202-783-3776
Hamburgers and games in one place; what more could a kid want?
555 12th St. NW

Air and Space Museum Gift Shop 202-357-2700
Astronaut Food
On the Mall

Hard Rock Café 202-737-7625
Rockin' hamburgers and ribs.
999 E St.

Palm Court Ice Cream Parlor 202-357-2700
Get a real taste of American history by indulging in an old-fashioned ice-cream soda.
National Museum of American History (on the Mall)

Planet Hollywood 202-783-7827
1101 Pennsylvania Ave. NW

Supreme Court Cafeteria 202-479-3211
Eat soup and sandwiches where history is made.
1st & E. Capitol Sts. NE

What to see

Bureau of Engraving and Printing *(p 128)* – Money!

Capital Children's Museum *(p 86)* – Dance in the streets of Mexico, hang out in a Japanese living room, drive a bus, be in your favorite cartoon and even conduct real experiments.

Mount Vernon *(p 240)* – Explore the 500-acre estate while following an Adventure Map, dress up in colonial clothing, and hang out in a Revolutionary soldier's tent.

National Air and Space Museum *(p 92)* – Gaze at the stars in the Einstein Planetarium.

National Archives' Charters of Freedom *(p 110)* – See the original copies of the Declaration of Independence, Constitution and the Bill of Rights.

National Aquarium *(p 170)* – Get up-close and personal with a sea urchin and his friends at the Touch Tank.

National Museum of American History *(p 115)* – Explore toys, clothes and tools of the past in the Hands on History Room.

National Museum of Natural History *(p 112)* – Have you ever seen a tarantula eat?

© Brigitta L. House/MICHELIN

Kids and Cats at the Zoo

National Postal Museum *(p 84)* – Make a postcard and send yourself some junk mail.

National Zoological Park *(p 221)* – Visit the pandas, learn about a rainforest in Amazonia and check out an orangutan using a computer!

Navy Museum *(p 215)* – Look at the world through a real submarine periscope.

The Castle *(p 90)* – Explore the Haupt Garden—and on a hot day the Persian-style *chadar* (water chute) is a great way to cool off.

Planning your trip

Children's Concierge – Consultants help you organize your trip from where to stay and where to go to how to ensure your children fully enjoy their trip. They even provide a Kidspack with age-appropriate supplies to enhance your children's visit. *($120/ hr; www.childrens concierge.com; ☎ 877-888-5468)*

What to do

"Goodnight Mr. Lincoln" – Put on your PJs and go to the Lincoln Memorial. Parents and children experience the life of Abraham Lincoln through stories, games and music *($10; www. washingtonwalks. com; ☎ 202-484-1565)*.

Carousel Ride – Ride an old-fashioned carousel on the Mall.

Online Info
www.whitehousekids.gov
www.our-kids.com

Sports and Recreation

Spectator Sports

Tickets for sporting events can usually be purchased at the venue or through **Ticketmaster** *(☎ 202-432-7328 for DC, ☎ 410-481-7328 for Baltimore, ☎ 703-573-7328 for Virginia; www.ticketmaster.com)*. When games are sold out, you can sometimes get tickets through a ticket agency *(see the Yellow Pages of the phone directory)*.

Bill Wood

Washington Redskins, #28 Cornerback Darrell Green

Professional Sports

Sport/Team	Season	Venue	☎ Information/Tickets
⚾ Baseball (AL) Baltimore Orioles	Apr–Sept	Oriole Park at Camden Yards 333 W. Camden St. Baltimore MD	Info: 410-685-9800 Tickets: 410-481-7328 www.baltimoreorioles.com
🏈 Football (NFL) Washington Redskins	Sept–Dec	FedEx Field Landover MD	Info: 703-478-8900 Tickets: 301-276-6050 www.redskins.com
🏒 Hockey (NHL) Washington Capitals	Oct–Apr	MCI Center 7th & F Sts. NW	Info: 202-628-3200 Tickets: 202-432-7328 www.washingtoncaps.com
🏀 Basketball (NBA) Washington Wizards	Nov–Apr	MCI Center 7th & F Sts. NW	Info: 202-628-3200 Tickets: 202-432-7328 www.washingtonwizards.com
🏀 Basketball (WNBA) Washington Mystics	May–Aug	MCI Center 7th & F Sts. NW	202-661-5050 Tickets: 202-432-7328 www.washingtonmystics.com
⚽ Soccer (MLS) DC United	Apr–Oct	RFK Stadium E. Capitol & 22nd Sts. SE	Info: 703-478-6600 Tickets: 202-432-7328 www.dcunited.com
⚽ Soccer (WUSA) Washington Freedom	Apr–Aug	RFK Stadium E. Capitol & 22nd Sts. SE	Info: 202-547-8351 Tickets: 202-432-7328 www.washingtonfreedom.com

Horse Racing

Racetrack	Season	Event	☎ Information
Laurel Park	Oct–Mar Jun–Aug	Thoroughbred racing	301-725-0400 www.marylandracing.com
Pimlico	Mar–Oct 3rd Sat/May	Thoroughbred racing Preakness Stakes	410-542-9400 www.marylandracing.com
Rosecroft Raceway	Year-round	Harness races	301-567-4000 www.rosecroft.com
Charles Town Races	Year-round	Thoroughbred racing	304-725-7001

Polo

Venue	Season	Event	☎ Information
Lincoln Memorial Polo Field	Jun–Oct Wednesdays 5pm Saturdays 1pm	local tournaments	301-972-7288 www.gopolo.com

Recreation

The District's two main recreational areas are the Mall and Rock Creek Park, both situated in the northwest quadrant and administered by the National Park Service. The **Mall**, with its sprawling lawns, planted gardens and waterfront parks, is well suited to outdoor activities such as jogging, biking, picnicking, paddleboating and a variety of sports (tennis, baseball, football, soccer and polo).

© Ed Castle/FOLIO, Inc.

Rock Creek Park

Covering some 2,100 acres astride scenic Rock Creek in the heart of the north-west quadrant, the rugged terrain of **Rock Creek Park** is crossed by an extensive network of paved roads, trails, and bicycle and bridle paths. Facilities include picnic groves, playgrounds, tennis courts, a golf course and stables.

Biking – There are many bike routes in and around Washington. Parts of **Potomac Park** are designated for cyclists. The picturesque **Chesapeake and Ohio Canal towpath**, which meanders 184mi from Georgetown to Cumberland, Maryland, is very popular with cyclists and hikers. Extending 17mi from the Arlington Bridge to George Washington's estate in Virginia, the **Mount Vernon Trail** borders the western shore of the Potomac River alongside the George Washington Memorial Parkway.

For information concerning cycling events and bike routes, contact:

National Park Service (bike-route maps) ....☎ 202-619-7222
www.nps.gov

Potomac Pedalers Touring Club ....☎ 202-363-8687
www.bikepptc.org

Washington Area Bicyclist Assn. ....☎ 202-628-2500
www.waba.org

Maryland National Capital Parks & Planning Commission ....☎ 301-699-2407
www.mncppc.org

Alexandria Department of Recreation & Parks ....☎ 703-838-4343
www.ci.alexandria.va.us

Arlington County Department of Parks & Recreation ....☎ 703-228-3681
www.co.arlington.va.us

Bike shops and boating centers offering bike rentals and trail information include:

Big Wheel Bikes ....☎ 202-337-0254
1034 33rd St. NW
10-speeds, hybrid, mountain   www.bigwheelbikes.com

Blazing Saddles Bicycle Rental ....☎ 202-544-0055
445 11th St. NW   www.blazingsaddles.com
hybrid, mountain

City Bikes ....☎ 202-265-1564
2501 Champlain St. NW   www.citybikes.com
hybrid, mountain

Fletcher's Boat House ....☎ 202-244-0461
4940 Canal Rd. NW   www.fletchersboathouse.com
landcruisers

Thompson's Boat Center..☎ 202-333-9543
Rock Creek Parkway & Virginia Ave.   www.guestservices.com/tbc
hybrid, mountain, landcruisers

Washington Sailing Marina ....☎ 703-548-9027
One Marina Dr., Alexandria, VA   www.guestservices.com/wsm
landcruisers, mountain

Boating – *For sightseeing and dining cruises on the Potomac, see p 59.* Because of its location on the **Potomac River** and its proximity to the Chesapeake Bay, Washington offers a range of activities for boating enthusiasts. Renting a paddleboat on the **Tidal Basin** is a classic DC activity and a favorite with children. Boats can be rented by the hour from the Tidal Basin Boat House *(15th St. & Maine Ave. SW; photo ID required; ☎ 202-484-0206)*. Boating on the **Chesapeake and Ohio Canal** between Georgetown and Violettes Lock can be a delightful excursion. Mule-drawn barge trips depart from the towpath in Georgetown Jun–Oct *(☎ 202-653-5190; www.nps.gov/choh)*. Canoes and rowboats can be rented from **Fletcher's Boat House** or **Thompson's Boat Center** or from **Swain's Lock House** *(☎ 301-299-9006)*. Sailboats can be rented from **Washington Sailing Marina** *(Alexandria, VA ☎ 703-548-9027)*.

Marinas (docking facilities only – no rentals)

Buzzard Point Boat Marina ....☎ 202-488-8400
Half & V Sts. SW

Capital Yacht Club ....☎ 202-488-8110
1000 Water St. SW   www.capitalyachtclub.net

Washington Marina ....☎ 202-554-0222
1300 Maine Ave. SW   www.washingtonmarina.com

For information on sailing and boating events on Chesapeake Bay, contact the **Chesapeake Bay Yacht Racing Assn.**, 612 Third St., Ste. 401, Annapolis MD 21403; ☎ 410-269-1194; www.cbyra.org.

Hiking – **Rock Creek Park** offers year-round hikes and nature walks guided by US park rangers. Favorite walks within the District include a 5mi loop around Hains Point and the **Tidal Basin**, especially when the famous Japanese cherry trees are in bloom. **Theodore Roosevelt Island**, located off the banks of Foggy Bottom, has 2.5mi of footpaths through woods, swamp and marshland with a variety of native plants and animals. The only access to the island is provided by a footbridge on the Virginia side. Free parking is available. For information: ☎ 703-289-2500; www.nps.gov.

For a hike outside the city limits, take the **Chesapeake and Ohio Canal towpath** to Old Anglers Inn (12.5mi), Great Falls Park (14mi), or Violettes Lock (22mi). Hikers to Glen Echo Park (7mi) have the option of returning to Washington by Metrobus. The trail system provides scenic but sometimes rugged hiking terrain. Maps and books about the canal are sold at some visitor centers along the trail. For further information, call the C&O Canal National Historical Park *(☎ 301-739-4200)*. The Mount Vernon Trail is also designed for bikers *(see Biking p 64)*.

For further information on hiking in the metropolitan area:

National Park Service ....☎ 202-619-7222
                                                                                www.nps.gov

Sierra Club ....☎ 202-547-2326
                                                                               www.mwrop.org

Maryland National Capital Parks & Planning Commission ....☎ 301-699-2407
                                                                               www.mncppc.org

Horseback Riding – There are numerous stables in and near the metropolitan area that provide mounts and riding instruction. Rock Creek Park has miles of designated bridle paths. **Rock Creek Park Horse Center**, managed by the National Park Service, offers trail riding, lessons and boarding year-round *(☎ 202-362-0117; www.rockcreekhorsecenter.com)*. Full riding and horse-care facilities are offered by **Meadowbrook Stables**, 8200 Meadowbrook Lane, Chevy Chase MD; *(☎ 301-589-9026)*. The city's main equestrian event is the **International Horse Show** held annually at the end of October at the USAir Arena *(map p 259; ☎ 301-840-0281; www.wihs.org)*.

Golf – The following public golf courses are maintained by the National Park Service (www.nps.gov); all rent clubs and other equipment.

East Potomac Park (par 65)
Hains Point SW ....☎ 202-554-7660

Langston Park (par 72)
25th St. & Benning Rd. NE ....☎ 202-397-8638

Rock Creek Park (par 65)
16th & Rittenhouse Sts. NW ....☎ 202-882-7332

Pros N Hackers – Provides information on over 100 public golf courses in DC, Virginia and Maryland. Available information on each course includes course details, cost, location, contact information, local pro and course reviews by other golfers *(☎ 703-495-9227, www.prosnhackers.com)*.

In addition, there are numerous country-club courses in the District where only members or guests of members can play, including the well-known **Congressional Country Club** in Bethesda, MD.

Ice Skating at National Sculpture Garden & Ice Rink

Ice-Skating – There are two major outdoor skating rinks in Washington (skates are available to rent):

National Sculpture Garden & Ice Rink ....☎ 202-289-3361
On the Mall at Madison Dr. & 9th St. NW.

Pershing Park Ice Rink ....☎ 202-737-6938
Pennsylvania Ave. & 14th St. NW

Swimming – In general, hotel pools are reserved for guests only. Some private clubs with pools offer short-term memberships. The DC Department of Recreation operates several outdoor pools in the summer *(open mid-Jun–Labor Day)*. For locations and opening hours, call the DC Department of Recreation's Aquatics Division *(☎ 202-576-6436; www.dcparksandrecreation.org)*.

Tennis – About 150 public courts are available on a first-come, first-served basis at no charge. For more information and a list of court locations and schedules, contact the DC Department of Recreation *(open year-round Mon–Fri 8:30am–6:30pm ☎ 202-673-7672; www.dcparksandrecreation.org)*.

The National Park Service maintains the following courts:

East Potomac courts ....☎ 202-554-5962
Hains Point SW.
(indoor and outdoor courts)

Rock Creek Park courts ....☎ 202-722-5949
16th & Kennedy Sts. NW. ....www.guestservices.com/rcp
(outdoor)

Montrose Park court
R St. between 30th & 31st Sts. NW, Georgetown
(outdoor)

Working Out – The **National Capitol YMCA** is open only to YMCA members and guests of members *(1711 Rhode Island Ave. NW, ☎ 202-862-9622; www.nationalcapitalymca.org)*. The clubs listed below allow nonmembers to use their facilities (weight rooms, aerobics classes and pool, if available) for a nominal daily fee *($10-$25)*.

Members of IHRSA should ask if they are entitled to a lower daily fee.

City Fitness ☎ 202-537-0539
3525 Connecticut Ave. NW

Sport House ☎ 202-887-0760
19th St. and Pennsylvania Ave. NW
McPherson Square ....☎ 202-638-3539

Tenley Sport and Health ....☎ 202-362-8000
4000 Wisconsin Ave. NW   www.sportandhealth.com

Washington Sports Club   www.washingtonsportsclub.com
214 D St. SE ....☎ 202-547-2255
1835 Connecticut Ave. NW ....☎ 202-332-0100
2251 Wisconsin Ave. NW ....☎ 202-333-2323
1990 M St. NW ....☎ 202-785-4900

Must-See Sights
of Washington, DC

Monuments and Memorials

Washington★★★ (Mall)

Jefferson★★★ (Mall)

Lincoln★★★ (Mall)

Franklin Delano Roosevelt★★★ (Mall)

Korean War Veterans★★★ (Mall)

Vietnam Veterans★★★ (Mall)

Vietnam Women's (Mall)

Marine Corps War (Iwo Jima)★ (Arlington)

Women in Military Service for America (Arlington National Cemetery)

Museums and Collections

National Air and Space★★★ (Mall)

National Gallery of Art★★★ (Mall)

National Archives' Charters of Freedom★★★ (Mall)
Declaration of Independence, Constitution, Bill of Rights

Natural History Museum's Gems and Minerals★★★ (Mall)

Freer Gallery of Art★★ (Mall)

US Holocaust Memorial Museum★★ (Mall)

National Portrait Gallery★★ (Downtown)

Phillips Collection★★ (Dupont Circle)

House Museums and Gardens

The White House★★★

Dumbarton Oaks★★ (Georgetown)

Dumbarton House (Georgetown)

Arlington House/Robert E. Lee Memorial★ (Arlington National Cemetery)

Frederick Douglass National Historic Site★ (Anacostia)

Mount Vernon★★★ (Alexandria, VA)

Addresses, telephone numbers, opening hours and prices published
in this guide are accurate at press time. Because of security concerns,
certain buildings may close unexpectedly. To verify opening times,
consult web sites or call using the information listed
under the times and charges for each site.

Air Transportation Hall, Gallery 102, National Air and Space Museum

Sights

Capitol Hill

The city's high eastern ground, bearing the popular designation Capitol Hill, is crowned by massive stone buildings serving the legislative and judicial branches of the federal government. Beyond them stretch the Hill's residential streets, neighborhoods of 19C row houses that reflect a true cross section of Washington's population.

Seat of Government – In 1791 when L'Enfant chose this hilltop (then known as Jenkins Hill) as the site of the future home of Congress, he expected the city's residential core to develop on its east flank. In order to stimulate growth in that area, George Washington himself constructed two town houses on North Capitol Street, while several wealthy individuals began their own mansions in the vicinity. In his design for the Capitol, William Thornton positioned the main facade on the building's east side, presumably in anticipation of the area's development. The establishment of the Navy Yard and the **Marine Barracks** *(8th and Eye Sts. SE)* in the early years of the 19C provided employment in the vicinity of the Hill and encouraged the growth of neighborhoods extending from the Capitol southeast to the river.

In 1814 the British invaded the area and burned the Capitol, but the Hill quickly recovered. In the decades following the War of 1812, it grew steadily as a residential area, though never to the degree L'Enfant had expected. Opened in 1870 on the 200 block of 7th Street SE, **Eastern Market** extended the reaches of Capitol Hill eastward. As the 19C drew to a close, the Hill became a middle-class enclave of pleasant brick row houses and neighborhood churches.

Federal Building Boom – At the turn of the century, the grandiose Beaux-Arts edifice housing the Library of Congress, now known as the Thomas Jefferson Building, was erected across from the Capitol. Several years later two other colossal Beaux-Arts structures—Union Station and the City Post Office, both designed by Daniel H. Burnham—were built at the northern foot of Capitol Hill. In the 1930s a flurry of construction resulted in the Folger Shakespeare Library, the John Adams Annex of the Library of Congress and the Supreme Court building, all in the immediate vicinity of the Capitol. Meanwhile, Congress was steadily adding new buildings to the Hill. The Senate erected three office buildings to the northeast of the Capitol: the **Russell Building** (1909, designed by Carrère and Hastings), the **Dirksen Building** (1958) and the **Hart Building** (1982). Similarly, the House erected three buildings on the south side: the **Cannon Building** (1908, Carrère and Hastings), the **Longworth Building** (1933) and the **Rayburn Building** (1965). In 1980 the Library of Congress added a third building, the James Madison Memorial Building, to its complex.

Revitalized Neighborhood – The social composition of Capitol Hill's residential streets has fluctuated throughout the 20C. In mid-century its middle-class population gradually moved to suburban Maryland and Virginia. Meanwhile, low-income families began to occupy the old, often run-down row houses. At the same time, the streets between the Capitol and Lincoln Park underwent renovation and restoration as well-paid professionals bought up the 19C homes here. Since the 1970s the Hill's residents have gained notoriety as civic activists capable of effectively preventing development that would alter the residential character of this area. Today Eastern Market, reputedly the city's only surviving market, has become the nucleus for a pleasant commercial area of small shops and restaurants. Independence Avenue, another commercial corridor, serves the Capitol's legislators and their staffs, while renovated Union Station, still the city's major rail terminal, also houses shops, restaurants and a cinema complex. The latest landmark to grace the neighborhood is the **Japanese American Memorial** located in the triangular park at Louisiana and New Jersey avenues and D Street, NW.

THE CAPITOL★★★

1st St. NW between Independence and Constitution Aves.
Ⓜ Capitol South or Union Station.
Plan pp 74-75

Extending along the eastern end of the Mall, the labyrinthine Capitol building, with its cast-iron dome topped by the statue of Freedom, is the city's most prominent landmark. This massive symbol of democracy in progress has housed the US Congress since 1800.

Historical Notes

Early Construction – When L'Enfant chose Jenkins Hill as the site for the Capitol in 1791, the Frenchman characterized it as "a pedestal waiting for a monument." L'Enfant himself was called upon to design the Capitol and other public buildings, but he was dismissed in 1792 before realizing a single project. President Washington and Secretary of State Jefferson elicited architectural plans for the Capitol by holding a public competition, but the entries proved so uninspiring that **Dr. William Thornton**, a respected amateur architect, was allowed to submit a drawing five months late. His entry called for a stone structure of classical proportions with a low-domed central section modeled after the Pantheon in Rome. The design met with immediate approval, winning Thornton $500 and a city lot.

Thornton's Design for the Capitol

Library of Congress

On September 18, 1793, Washington presided over the laying of the cornerstone in a ceremonial Masonic service that would be repeated in the building of future additions to the Capitol. A lack of skilled workers, tools and supplies in the then virtually nonexistent city hampered construction, as did a lack of funds. The revenue from the sale of city lots in the new capital was expected to finance building costs, but few people were attracted by the high prices and rudimentary conditions. By 1800, however, Congress was able to leave the temporary capital of Philadelphia and move to the nascent federal city. On November 22, 1800 President John Adams addressed the first joint session of Congress in the completed north wing (the original Senate wing) of the new Capitol. Professional rivalry among the various architects working on the Capitol (including James Hoban, designer of the White House) led to Thornton's resignation. In 1803 British architect **Benjamin Henry Latrobe** was appointed surveyor of public buildings, and by 1807 he had succeeded in completing the south wing (the original House wing). The two wings were linked by a wooden walkway crossing the present site of the rotunda. Latrobe's first House chamber featured a half-domed coffered ceiling. With the south wing completed, Latrobe began renovating and improving the north wing and submitted revised plans for the Capitol exterior that included a colonnaded central section.

Conflagration and Restoration – The War of 1812 saw the only enemy attack on the Capitol. In August 1814 the British set fire to it, gutting the interior. A providential downpour prevented total ruin, but when Congress returned in the fall, many members advocated abandoning the building and the city and finding a new home for the federal government. To discourage such a desertion, a group of private citizens had a temporary brick structure erected for Congress on the site where the Supreme Court now stands.

From 1815 to 1817 Latrobe worked at restoring the Capitol's interior, and in the process he added low domes over the building's two original wings and redesigned the House chamber (now Statuary Hall) into the semicircular shape it has retained to this day. Among the decorative elements that attest to Latrobe's inventiveness are the tobacco fronds and ears of corn that top the columns lining the House chamber. Though the building's grace was much admired, the echoes produced in the cavernous space led one representative to quip that it was "handsome and fit for anything but the use intended." Red draperies were hung behind the gallery to help muffle sounds. (The chamber is depicted in Samuel Morse's *Old House of Representatives*, on view in the Corcoran Gallery.)

When Latrobe resigned because of a clash with the commissioner of public buildings, Boston architect **Charles Bulfinch** took over and Congress was able to again meet in the Capitol in December 1819. Bulfinch served as the official architect of the Capitol until 1829. During his tenure he completed the building more or less according to Thornton's original plans, substituting a lofty copper-sheathed wooden dome for the hemispherical stone vault designed by Thornton.

Civil War Years – During the early 19C the legislature, keeping pace with the nation it represented, grew rapidly. By 1850 it comprised 62 senators and 232 representatives. Spurred on by Sen. Jefferson Davis, who later became president of the Confederacy, Congress appropriated $100,000 for two new wings to house the cramped Senate and House. Once again a contest was held, but no clear winner emerged. Rather, a composite design based on several entries was favored, and contestant **Thomas U. Walter** from Philadelphia was asked to draw up plans. Thomas Crawford was commissioned to design the statue topping the new dome. Crawford's 19 1/2ft bronze **Freedom** was outfitted with flowing robes and the liberty cap of a freed Roman slave. When Southerner Jefferson Davis objected to the implications of the statue's headdress, Crawford changed it to the present feathered, eagle's-head helmet. With civil strife in the air, construction began. When war finally did come, Congress was not in session, and the War Department quartered troops in the Capitol for several months. Soldiers called it the "Big Tent," and Army bakers built enormous ovens in the basement committee rooms, producing enough bread to feed troops bivouacked around the city. A year later the Capitol served briefly as a hospital for the wounded. Throughout the war construction on the Capitol proceeded, as "a sign," President Lincoln declared, "that we intend the Union shall go on." Walter's enlarged dome, designed to replace the now disproportionately small dome built by Bulfinch, was made of cast iron and weighed almost nine million pounds. By 1863 the dome, considered a marvel of 19C engineering, was ready to receive Crawford's crowning statue. The two new wings were finally completed in 1867.

Expansion – The nation's foremost landscape architect, **Frederick Law Olmsted**, was appointed in 1874 to lay out the grounds. Olmsted's landscaping reflects his propensity for natural sweeps of lawn and trees. His addition of the broad plaza on the east and the marble stairway and terraces on the west facilitated the creation of much-needed office space on the lower levels of the building.

For the next 75 years, interior changes such as electrification (1897), fireproofing and improved plumbing continued. Under Elliott Wood's term as architect of the Capitol (1902-23), a fourth floor was added, and the Latrobe domes in the two original wings were rebuilt in fireproof cast iron.

By the late 1950s Congress had again outgrown the Capitol. To provide more space the central section of the east facade was extended 32 1/2ft *(see drawing)*. The new marble front was designed as an exact copy of the original sandstone facade so as not to alter the essential appearance of this national landmark (the columns of the original facade are conserved at the National Arboretum).

CONSTRUCTION OF THE CAPITOL

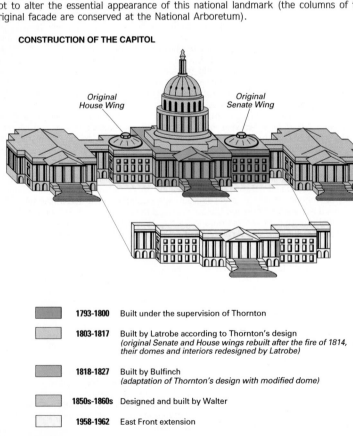

	1793-1800	Built under the supervision of Thornton
	1803-1817	Built by Latrobe according to Thornton's design *(original Senate and House wings rebuilt after the fire of 1814, their domes and interiors redesigned by Latrobe)*
	1818-1827	Built by Bulfinch *(adaptation of Thornton's design with modified dome)*
	1850s-1860s	Designed and built by Walter
	1958-1962	East Front extension

VISIT

Open Mar–Aug daily 8am–8pm. Rest of the year daily 9am–4:30pm. Closed Jan 1, Thanksgiving Day, Dec 25. Guided tours (30min) available. Congressional visits available. ✗ ⛓ ⅢⅢ ☎ *202-225-6827. http://webster.senate.gov. To reach main entrance from Mall walk around the building to east side. The general public is allowed free access to all areas described below. Only the rotunda, Statuary Hall and the crypt are included on guided tours of the Capitol.*

Main Floor

The Rotunda – On the east side of the rotunda, the eight-paneled, 10-ton bronze **Columbus doors** depict in high relief scenes from Christopher Columbus' life. Of the eight large paintings around the room, the four on the east side show early events in American history, such as the *Embarkation of the Pilgrims at Delft Haven, Holland* by Robert Weir, dated 1843 **(1)**. The ornate Capitol **dome**★★—180ft high and 98ft across—soars above rich artwork relating to the history of the country. The allegorical fresco in the eye of the dome, entitled the *Apotheosis of Washington*, was painted by Italian-born **Constantino Brumidi**, who had done restoration work in the Vatican. Brumidi worked on the Capitol from 1855 to 1880 and executed so many of its frescoes that he is often referred to as its "Michelangelo." The grisaille frieze circling the base of the dome (total length of frieze: 300ft) records over 400 years of American history, from the landing of Columbus to the birth of aviation. Brumidi began the fresco series when he was 72 but completed only six panels before an accidental fall on the scaffolding eventually led to his death. Filippo Costaggini carried on the work, but when he left in 1889 a 31ft gap remained in the frieze. Not until 1953 was the work completed by the American artist Allyn Cox.

The four paintings on the west side, all by John Trumbull, portray important moments of the Revolution, including the *Surrender of Cornwallis at Yorktown* (early 19C) **(2)**. Statues of American leaders from Washington **(3)** and Jefferson **(4)** to Martin Luther King Jr. **(5)**, encircle the room. During the Capitol's long history, such popular national figures as Abraham Lincoln and John F. Kennedy have lain in state here.

Statuary Hall – This elegant, semicircular, half-domed space was restored for the 1976 Bicentennial to its architectural appearance (unfurnished) of 1857, when it functioned as the House Chamber. A congressional act of 1864 allowed each state to place statues of two of its distinguished citizens in the Capitol. Until the 1930s these statues were all displayed in Statuary Hall. However, it was feared that their combined weight might cause the hall's floor to collapse, so some now stand in other Capitol corridors. Notable among the 38 still in the room are the statues of Robert E. Lee of Virginia **(6)**, 19C social reformer Frances Willard of Illinois **(7)**, 18C missionary pioneer Padre Junípero Serra of California **(8)** and King Kamehameha of Hawaii **(9)**. The room's unusual acoustics considerably amplify words spoken within.

Old Senate Chamber – Also restored for the Bicentennial, this room maintains the general appearance and several of the furnishings it had during the period the Senate occupied it (1810-14, 1819-59). Note the gilt shield and eagle over the vice president's desk and the porthole portrait of George Washington (1823, Rembrandt Peale). From 1860 to 1935, the chamber housed the Supreme Court.

Visiting the Offices of Your Senators or Representative – Offices are located in six buildings accessible from the Capitol via the basement-level subway: Russell, Dirksen and Hart Bldgs. (Senate); Cannon, Longworth and Rayburn Bldgs. (House). For assistance in locating offices, call ☎ 202-224-3121 or inquire at the Senate and House Appointment Desks *(ground floor)*. For an appointment with your senator or representative, write in advance *(p 255)*.

Viewing a Session of Congress *(3rd floor galleries)* – Passes to view a House or Senate session must be obtained at the office of your senator or representative (above). Certain committee sessions are also open to the public. Consult the *Washington Post* or ☎ 202-224-3121 for the recess schedule and the day's agenda. International visitors: Apply to the Senate and House Appointment Desks *(ground floor)*.

Ground Floor

Crypt – Forty Doric columns ring the low-ceilinged crypt directly below the rotunda. Original plans called for the body of George Washington to be enshrined in a vault below the crypt, but his descendants insisted that his remains be preserved at Mount Vernon. The crypt features displays on the history of the Capitol. The compelling sculpture of Lincoln's head **(10)** was done by Gutzon Borglum, who carved Mount Rushmore. Borglum intended the statue to show in Lincoln's face

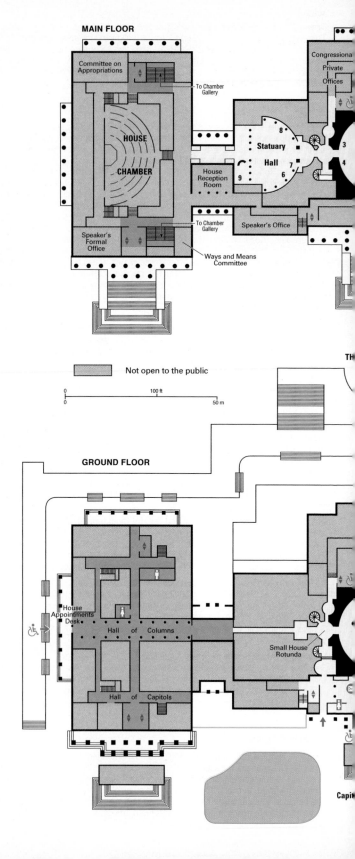

MAIN FLOOR

Committee on Appropriations

To Chamber Gallery

Congressiona[l]

Private Offices

HOUSE

CHAMBER

Statuary Hall

8

3

7

9

House Reception Room

6

4

Speaker's Formal Office

To Chamber Gallery

Speaker's Office

Ways and Means Committee

Not open to the public

0   100 ft
0   50 m

TH[

GROUND FLOOR

House Appointments Desk

Hall   of   Columns

Small House Rotunda

Hall   of   Capitols

Capi[

THE CAPITOL

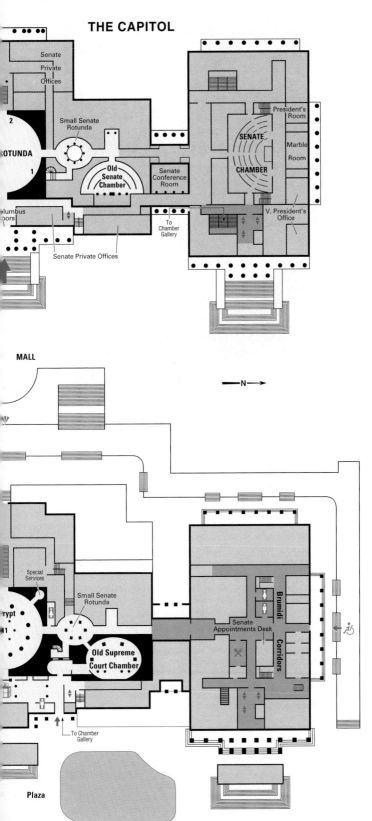

Senate Private Offices

Small Senate Rotunda

2

ROTUNDA

1

Old Senate Chamber

Senate Conference Room

President's Room

SENATE CHAMBER

Marble Room

V. President's Office

Columbus Doors

Senate Private Offices

To Chamber Gallery

MALL

—N→

Special Services

Small Senate Rotunda

Crypt

1

Old Supreme Court Chamber

Senate Appointments Desk

Brumidi Corridors

To Chamber Gallery

Plaza

The Capitol

"all the complexity of his great nature." He left off the statue's left ear as a symbol of Lincoln's unfinished life. A compass stone embedded in the floor **(11)** marks the zero point from which the city's four quadrants emanate.

Continue to the Senate wing.

Old Supreme Court Chamber – An intimate and gracious chamber with red carpeting and green-topped desks, this room housed the Supreme Court from 1810 to 1860, except during the period of reconstruction after the War of 1812. Note the many original 19C furnishings and the room's vaulting, designed by Latrobe. Here, the Marshall Court *(p 77)* heard many of the cases that would profoundly influence the development of the young nation.

Brumidi Corridors – The arched ceilings and walls of these two intersecting corridors are embellished with Brumidi's classically inspired murals depicting nature, famous Americans and historical scenes. Interspersed among the murals are works of later painters, such as Allyn Cox's mural of the 1969 moon landing. Minton floor tiles further enhance the decorative scheme of the corridors.

Return to the crypt and continue to the House wing.

A number of the state statues originally destined for Statuary Hall now stand among the tobacco-leafed pillars of the **Hall of Columns**. Paralleling this hall is the **Hall of Capitols**, which is decorated with murals by Allyn Cox depicting historic events as well as realistic scenes of everyday life.

Third Floor (Gallery Level)

House and Senate Chambers – *See Viewing a Session of Congress above.* The east stairway in the House wing *(not open to the pubic when the House is in session)* leads to the third-floor visitors' gallery for the House Chamber. The *Scene of the Signing of the Constitution of the United States* (1940) by Howard Chandler Christy hangs on the second-floor landing. The **House Chamber**, a richly appointed room, is dominated by a broad podium faced by the seats of the 435 members of the House (Democrats are placed to the right of the presiding Speaker of the House, Republicans to the left). Beside the podium hangs a full-length portrait of *George Washington* (1834) by John Vanderlyn, and to the right, a portrait of Washington's Revolutionary compatriot *General Lafayette* (1824) by Ary Scheffer. Medallions of historic figures hang on the gallery walls.

A third-floor hallway extends along the east face of the Capitol to the Senate wing. Round windows and the stone of the building's original facade (prior to the late-1950s extension) are visible along the interior wall of this hall.

The **Senate Chamber** is more soberly appointed than the House Chamber. The only works of art on display are the busts of early vice presidents that occupy the niches on the gallery level. When the Senate is in session, the vice president (in his absence, the president pro tempore), flanked by the secretary of the Senate, the sergeant at arms and various clerks, presides from behind the veined marble podium. The 100 senators are seated at dark mahogany desks (Democrats on the right, Republicans on the left). Note on

Band concerts
See Calendar of Events.
During the summer months, the Army, Navy, Air Force and Marine Bands offer a perpetual round of free concerts at 8pm on the east steps of the Capitol or at The Sylvan Theatre. The concerts last about an hour and a half, and range from classical to jazz to pop music. The Marine Corps Sunset Parade is Tuesdays at 7pm at the Iwo Jima Memorial.

the second-floor landing of the east stairway in the Senate wing W.H. Powell's monumental painting *Battle of Lake Erie* (1873).

Upon leaving the Capitol, stroll around the broad **west terrace**, where you can admire a sweeping **view**★★ across the Mall to the Washington Monument.

"If Washington should ever grow to be a great city,
the outlook from the Capitol will be unsurpassed in the world.
Now at sunset I seem to look westward far into the heart of the
Continent from this commanding position."

Ralph Waldo Emerson, 1843

SUPREME COURT★★

1st and E. Capitol Sts. NE.
Ⓜ Capitol South or Union Station.

Positioned directly across the street from the Capitol, this white marble monument to the supremacy of law houses the highest court in the land. Within its walls the third branch of government exercises its mandate to protect and interpret the spirit of the US Constitution.

Historical Notes

A Constitutional Basis – Article III of the US Constitution, ratified in 1788, called for a "supreme Court" of the land to act as a final arbiter of law and as a counterbalance to the other two branches of government (executive and legislative). The first US Supreme Court convened in 1790 at the Royal Exchange Building in the temporary capital of New York City. During the first three years, the Court, as a body, had little work. However, the individual justices were kept busy riding circuits, as they were required to do until 1891, hearing cases in their districts. Because of the difficulty of travel at the end of the 18C, many justices served only a few years.

One of the earliest judicial precedents was set in 1793 when President Washington asked the Court to advise him on questions of international law. Under its first chief justice, John Jay, it declined, explaining that in view of the Constitution's requirement of separation of powers, the Judicial branch had no place advising the Executive branch.

To jurists, the fourth chief justice, **John Marshall** (1755-1835), is the "Great Chief Justice." Appointed by President Adams in 1801, Marshall served until his death in 1835. During his long tenure he firmly established the fledgling Court as the supreme authority over the law of the land. Among the many important cases the Marshall Court ruled on, *Marbury v. Madison* (1803) set a critical precedent. In this case the Supreme Court affirmed its power to declare an act of Congress unconstitutional. Other important decisions reached under Marshall, in such cases as *McCulloch v. Maryland*, *Cohens v. Virginia* and *Gibbons v. Ogden*, reaffirmed the power of the Union and its authority over state laws.

A Body of Controversy – "We are very quiet here, but it is the quiet of a storm center," explained Justice Oliver Wendell Holmes Jr., who served from 1902 to 1932. Throughout its history the Court has been involved in controversy, sometimes settling it, at other times kindling it. In 1857 the Court handed down perhaps its most infamous decision, when, under Chief Justice Taney, it heard the case of a slave named Dred Scott. The Court's ruling—that Congress had no authority to limit the expansion of slavery—helped bring on the Civil War and badly damaged public respect for the Court.

■ The Supreme Court Justices

The nominating president and the year in which the judicial oath was taken are shown in parentheses:

Chief Justice

William H. Rehnquist *(Associate Justice: Nixon, 1972; Chief Justice: Reagan, 1986)*

Associate Justices

John Paul Stevens *(Ford, 1975)*
Sandra Day O'Connor *(Reagan, 1981)*
Antonin Scalia *(Reagan, 1986)*
Anthony M. Kennedy *(Reagan, 1988)*
David H. Souter *(Bush, 1990)*
Clarence Thomas *(Bush, 1991)*
Ruth Bader Ginsburg *(Clinton, 1993)*
Stephen G. Breyer *(Clinton, 1994)*

A Home of Its Own – In its early years the Court had no regular meeting place, convening in various public buildings in New York City, then Philadelphia. In 1800 it moved to the new federal city and occupied different rooms in the Capitol, including the room now known as the Old Supreme Court Chamber. After the British burned the Capitol in 1814, the Court was forced to meet in a number of temporary locations, including a private home and a tavern. When the Capitol was sufficiently repaired, the Court returned to the Old Supreme Court Chamber, which it occupied from 1819 to 1860. It then moved upstairs to the Old Senate Chamber, which remained its home for the following 75 years.

William Howard Taft (1857-1930), the tenth chief justice (1921-30) and the only US president to serve on the Court, convinced Congress in 1928 to allocate funds for a building to house the Court. In October 1935 the present edifice was completed at a cost of $9,650,000 but to mixed reviews from the justices. Justice Harland Fiske Stone called the new structure "almost bombastically pretentious...wholly inappropriate for a quiet group of old boys such as the Supreme Court."

A few of the precedent-setting cases heard in the courtroom of the current building include *Brown v. Board of Education*, which established school integration nationwide; *Engel v. Vitale*, outlawing school prayer; cases involving the constitutionality of abortion; and most recently the consitutionality of electoral procedures in the 2000 presidential election.

The Court at Work – Woodrow Wilson called the Supreme Court "a kind of Constitutional Convention in continuous session." As the highest court in the country, it is the court of last appeal. The chief justice and associate justices are appointed by the president, with Senate approval, as vacancies occur. Only death, voluntary retirement or resignation, or congressional impeachment can remove a sitting justice. Through his appointees to the Supreme Court, a US president might exercise influence long after his term has ended.

Congress, not the Constitution, sets the number of justices on the Court. In the Court's first century, that number changed six times. Now, based on the Judiciary Act of 1869, it is set at nine justices.

The Court's term begins on the first Monday in October. From October through April the Court hears oral arguments on cases it has consented to review. Of the over 7,000 requests for review it receives annually, the Court hears from 75 to 100 cases. It typically sits two weeks a month, Monday to Wednesday *(10am–3pm)* with a lunch recess *(noon–1pm)*. Most case arguments are limited to one hour, with 30 minutes allotted to each side. For the remainder of the week the justices review arguments and consider requests for future reviews. From mid-May through June the Court convenes on Monday *(10am)* to deliver its opinions on the cases argued in that term.

VISIT

Open year-round Mon–Fri 9am–4:30pm. Closed major holidays. ✗ ♿ ☎ 202-479-3211. www.supremecourtus.gov. Sessions are open to the public on a first-come, first-served basis. Consult the Washington Post *for the daily schedule of Court hearings. When the Court is not in session, lectures on the Supreme Court are held in the courtroom on the half hour 9:30am–3:30pm. For further information ☎ 202-479-3211.*

An oval plaza fronts the cross-shaped building of gleaming white marble, designed by Cass Gilbert. Flanking a broad staircase that leads up to a colonnade of 32 Corinthian columns are two massive allegorical figures. Sculpted by James Fraser, they represent the Contemplation of Justice (left) and the Authority of Law (right). Carved under the bas-relief in the pediment are the words "Equal Justice Under Law." A wide columned hall, adorned with a coffered 44ft-high ceiling and busts of chief justices, leads from the entrance to the **courtroom**. Here the justices sit on a raised bench positioned in front of 4 of the 24 massive veined columns that ring the 82ft-by-91ft chamber. The justices' places are ordered by their seniority, with the chief justice taking the center position.

© Brigitta L. House/MICHELIN

Supreme Court

Visitors may descend to the ground floor, which features changing exhibits on the history and function of the Court. Dominating the main hall on this level is a massive **statue of John Marshall**, depicting him in a relaxed seated pose that suggests his renowned affability and lack of pretense. *A film (24min) on the history and work of the Court is shown continuously in the theater at the end of the hall to the right of the Marshall statue.*

LIBRARY OF CONGRESS★★

1st St. and Independence Ave. SE.
Ⓜ Capitol South or Union Station.

A renowned Beaux-Arts landmark, the original Library of Congress is reputedly Washington's most richly ornamented building. The largest library in existence, it retains in its varied and ever-growing collections more than 18 million books, as well as myriad historical and artistic treasures.

Historical Notes

Congress' Library – In 1800, while still convening in Philadelphia, Congress appropriated $5,000 for the establishment of a library for its own use. Originally the library was housed in the Capitol for the convenience of the legislators. When the library's 3,000 volumes were destroyed in the Capitol fire of 1814, Thomas Jefferson offered his extensive personal library to Congress, which purchased the 6,487 volumes for $23,950. The collection was shipped in 10 horse-drawn wagons from Monticello, Jefferson's Virginia estate, to the Capitol. Unfortunately, another fire in 1851 destroyed two-thirds of the existing library collection. Congress immediately appropriated funds to replenish the holdings and to build a new, multitiered library along the west side of the Capitol. In honor of the Library's Bicentennial in 2000, an effort was begun to reconstitute the lost volumes as a gift to the nation.

A Library for the People – Though intended to serve only members of Congress and Supreme Court justices, the library was gradually opened to other governmental and diplomatic officials. In 1864 **Ainsworth Rand Spofford** was appointed librarian of Congress and began a process that changed the library into a public institution. In order to amass a more extensive collection, Spofford lobbied Congress to amend existing legislation so that the copyright for books, musical scores, maps and charts would be granted by the Library of Congress rather than

■ Lincoln's Pockets

The Library of Congress possesses the contents of Abraham Lincoln's pockets when he was shot. Presented to the library by the president's granddaughter, they include a watch fob, two pairs of spectacles and a pocket knife. A $5 Confederate note and nine newspaper clippings (supporting Lincoln for various actions he took while in office) were found in his billfold.

the Department of Interior. This procedure ensured that newly published materials would find their way into the library's holdings, a practice that continues to this day. The collection increased rapidly under Spofford, and all available space in the Capitol was quickly filled.

In 1873 Congress approved a separate building for the library. In 1886 ground was broken, but the work progressed slowly, causing Congress to dismiss the building's principal architects, **John Smithmeyer** and **Paul Pelz**. They were replaced by Thomas Casey, the chief of Army engineers, and Bernard Green, a civilian engineer. Along with Casey's son Edward, Green planned the interior artwork and commissioned a small army of American artists to execute the ambitious decorative scheme, which blended mosaics, murals, marblework and sculptures. The library opened in 1897, under budget (total cost: $6.5 million) and ahead of schedule; it has functioned as the "national library of the United States" ever since.

A Growing Concern – In 1939 the library expanded to a second structure, the **John Adams Building** *(2nd St. SE, behind the main building)*, noteworthy for its Art Deco ornamentation. At that time the original building was designated the Thomas Jefferson Building. A third facility, the austere marble **James Madison Memorial Building** *(Independence Ave., between 1st and 2nd Sts. SE)*, was opened in 1980 and contains more than twice the floor space of either of the two older library structures. Its Memorial Hall *(left side of the lobby)* is dominated by a seated statue of James Madison, the fourth US president.

Holdings – The Library of Congress retains more than 120 million items, which fill the equivalent of some 500 miles of shelves. These possessions include more than 27 million manuscripts, 4 million maps and atlases, and 8 million musical items, such as scores, instruments and correspondence among musicians, 12 million photographs and 18 million books. The library acquires new holdings at the rate of 10 items per minute. Foremost among the valuable works of art owned by the Library of Congress are two mid-15C masterpieces: the manuscript Giant Bible of Mainz and a Gutenberg Bible. American artifacts include Jefferson's rough draft of the Declaration of Independence and President Lincoln's handwritten drafts of the Emancipation Proclamation and the Gettysburg Address. The library's renowned music division contains a noted collection of Stradivarius violins and original scores by Brahms, Liszt, Beethoven and other composers.

Visiting the Library – The Library of Congress functions as a reference library and may be used by any individual 18 years or older pursuing research. The general public is welcome to visit the complex. All three buildings are open year-round. An orientation video *(12min)* is shown every 20min on the ground floor of the Jefferson Building in the new visitor center. **Guided tours** of the Jefferson Building are available Mon–Sat 10:30am, 11:30am & 1:30pm, 2:30pm, 3:30pm *(Mon–Fri only)*. Tour tickets (free) may be required; inquire at the visitor center. The Jefferson Building contains exhibits of items from the special collections. "Treasures of the Library of Congress" is an exhibit of continuously rotating rare library materials, such as George Washington's first inaugural address and Frank Lloyd Wright's architectural drawings. A copy of the

Great Hall, Jefferson Building, Library of Congress

Handbook of the New Library of Congress, which describes the library's history and architecture, may be purchased from the shop in the Jefferson Building or the Madison Building. A cafeteria is located in the Madison Building on the 6th floor *(open to the public for lunch beginning at 12:30pm)*; a snack bar is located on the ground floor.

For current visitor information or assistance in using the research facilities, consult the touch-screen terminals located in the visitor center. Visitor information ☏ 202-707-5000; research information ☏ 202-707-6500; tour information ☏ 202-707-9779; general information ☏ 202-707-8000. The library offers a regular series of concerts by its resident string quartet, the **Juilliard Quartet**. It also features public lectures and poetry readings, as well as showings of old films in its Pickford Theater, located in the Madison Building. For schedules, consult the touch screens at the visitor center in the Jefferson Building. For concert information, call ☏ 202-707-5502.

THE THOMAS JEFFERSON BUILDING

Open year-round Mon–Sat 8:30am–5pm. Closed major holidays. Guided tours (1hr) available. ♿ ☏ *202-707-8000. www.loc.gov.*

■ Q & A

Quoted from the Library of Congress brochure 25 Questions Most Frequently Asked by Visitors:

Question 4:

Does the Library have a copy of every book published in the US?

No, but it does have more than 27 million cataloged books and other printed materials.

Question 6:

Who is in charge of the Library of Congress?

The Library is directed by the Librarian of Congress, who is appointed by the president of the US and confirmed by a vote of the Senate.

Question 7:

How does Congress use the Library?

More than 500,000 requests are received annually by the Congressional Research Service (CRS), the part of the Library that serves Congress. Staffed by specialists on such topics as economics, foreign affairs and the environment, CRS supplies Congress with unbiased information on a wide variety of subjects.

Question 20:

Where is the Copyright Office?

On the 4th floor of the Madison Building. It has handled more than 20 million copyright registrations and transfers since 1790 and currently deals with more than 500,000 new registrations each year.

Exterior – This Beaux-Arts showplace occupies a full block across from the Capitol on 1st Street SE. At street level the exuberant **Neptune Fountain** by Roland Hinton Perry depicts the sea god and his cavorting entourage.

The building's central section is vaulted by a massive green copper dome surmounted by a lantern that supports the symbolic "torch of learning" *(step back from the facade across 1st St. to view)*. The intricate entrance stairway, replete with side flights, ornamented stone balustrades and candelabras, provides a ceremonial access to the edifice. The granite facade, which resembles the 19C Paris Opera House, features a second-story portico of paired Corinthian columns and massive quoins, or cornerstones. Busts depicting famous men of letters are framed in the oculi, or round openings, that punctuate the portico *(illustration p 35)*.

★★Interior – Murals, sculptures, detailed mosaics, marble columns and floors, and vaulted corridors make the two-story **Great Hall** one of the most impressive spaces in the city. The hall's vestibule is especially noteworthy for the gold leaf adorning its ceiling, while blue and amber stained-glass skylights punctuate the vaulting of the hall proper. At the rear of the hall stand glass cases containing a Gutenberg Bible and the Giant Bible of Mainz, one of the last hand-illuminated manuscript versions of the Bible. A grand staircase sculpted with elaborate bas-relief cherubs leads to the second-story colonnade, where a visitors' gallery overlooks the **Main Reading Room**. Occupying the vast rotunda under the library dome (height: 160ft from floor to lantern), the Main Reading Room is ringed by colossal Corinthian columns and arched windows, embellished with stained-glass state seals and eagles. In the lantern of the coffered dome is an allegorical mural entitled Human Understanding. The eight 11ft stone statues between the arches symbolize such subjects as commerce, law, poetry and science. Sixteen bronze statues along the balustrade of the galleries represent pivotal figures in the development of civilization. Rotating items from the library's permanent Americana and international collections are on view in the southwest and northwest galleries respectively.

Main Reading Room

FOLGER SHAKESPEARE LIBRARY★

201 E. Capitol St. SE.
Ⓜ Capitol South or Union Station.

The world's largest collection of Shakespeare's works is conserved behind this Art Deco exterior. Renowned as a research institution, the Folger also encourages a larger public appreciation of the traditions of Elizabethan England and the Renaissance through its program of exhibits, concerts, readings and theatrical performances.

Historical Notes

The Folger Bequest – The son of a Martha's Vineyard schoolmaster, Henry Clay Folger became a lifetime devotee of Shakespeare while attending Amherst College. There, in 1879, inspired by a lecture given by the aging Ralph Waldo Emerson, Folger bought a volume of Shakespeare's complete works.

Ten years later he made his first serious Shakespeare acquisition: a 1685 Fourth Folio edition purchased at an auction for $107.50. At the time, his finances were such that he was forced to request 30 days to raise the money. Through the years, however, his fortunes steadily increased, and he eventually became chairman of the board of the Standard Oil Co. of New York.

His wife and co-collector, Emily Jordan, was a schoolteacher and student of literature. She was particularly interested in acquiring different copies of the 1623 First Folio, the first collected edition of Shakespeare's plays, for the sake of scholarly comparison. In the 1920s the Folgers, who lived in New York state, began searching in both England and America for a site to establish a research library. They ultimately chose this nation's capital, and in 1930 the cornerstone was laid. Folger himself did not live to see the 1932 opening of the building that housed the 75,000 books, manuscripts, prints and engravings he and his wife had collected. Mrs. Folger continued to be active with the library until her death in 1936. The ashes of both are interred in the library, which today is administered by the trustees of Amherst College.

The Library's Holdings – *Research facilities are not open to the general public.* The Folger now owns some 275,000 books and manuscripts relating to the Renaissance period in England and other European countries. About a third of its holdings are considered rare, the most valuable being the only known copy of Shakespeare's early play *Titus Andronicus*. It was discovered in a cottage in Sweden and purchased for $10,000 by the Folgers in 1905.

The library holds 79 of the 240 first editions of the collected works of Shakespeare that are known to exist (Japan's Meisei University, the next-largest owner of first editions, owns only eight). The library also owns theatrical memorabilia—playbills, costumes, promptbooks, etc.—from 18C and 19C Shakespearean productions.

The Building – Paul Cret incorporated classical elements in this simple Art Deco marble facade, winning numerous accolades from fellow architects for the "traditional modernism" of his design. Nine long rectangular windows covered in a geometrical grillwork are offset by bas-relief underpanels depicting scenes from Shakespeare's plays. Chiseled into the facade, above the windows, are quotes about the Bard, and above the two entrances appear the masks of Tragedy and Comedy. Along the 2nd

Title Page of 1623 First Folio

Street side of the building is a free-standing marble statue of the character Puck from *A Midsummer Night's Dream*, inscribed with his famous quote "Lord, what fools these mortals be."

VISIT

Open year-round Mon–Sat 10am–4pm. Closed major holidays. Contribution requested. Guided tours (1hr) available Mon–Sat 11am (additional tour Sat 1pm). ♿ ☎ *202-544-7077. www.folger.edu.*

The 190ft-long **Great Hall**, with oak paneling and a barrel-vaulted ceiling reminiscent of a Tudor gallery, features a changing series of exhibits based on the books, manuscripts and memorabilia in the library's collection.

The east end of the building houses a reproduction of an **Elizabethan theater**, its stage flanked by wooden columns. The Folger Consort, a resident chamber music ensemble, holds scheduled performances in the theater and in the Great Hall. The library also sponsors a rich program of poetry and fiction readings.

Outside, the small Elizabethan garden features a knot garden and plants well known in Shakespeare's day *(guided tours available Apr–Oct the third Sat of the month)*.

UNION STATION★

50 Massachusetts Ave. NE.
Ⓜ Union Station.

Located north of the Capitol, this monumental granite building has long served as the hub of the city's rail travel. It is a formidable embodiment of the oft-quoted premise of its architect **Daniel H. Burnham**: "Make no little plans." More than 70,000 people pass through the station per day.

Historical Notes

When the first trains pulled into the mammoth terminal in 1907, it was the largest train station in the world, measuring 760ft by 344ft. Burnham designed the station with the colossal columns, arches and statues that characterize the Beaux-Arts style, of which he was a leading proponent. For half a century Union Station served as the city's main point of arrival, greeting soldiers, presidents, government representatives and royalty, as well as a steady flow of tourists.

With the demise of rail travel in the 1950s and 60s, the station steadily deteriorated. A renovation done in the 1970s met with much criticism, and an entirely new revamping was begun in 1986. The large-scale restoration project, which returned the station to its original splendor, was completed in 1988 at a cost of $160 million. In addition to being the main railway terminal for the metropolitan area, the station also houses scores of shops, eateries and a cinema complex.

■ **Station Specifics**

Original construction costs for Union Station exceeded $25 million. All woodwork, such as that for booths, counters and seats, is **solid mahogany**. Restoration of the hexagonal coffers, or recessed ceiling panels, required over 70lbs of **gold leaf**. The East Hall's columns consist of **scagliola**, an imitation ornamental marble made from ground gypsum, glue and colors. Can you spot the irregularity in the Main Hall's **large clock**? (It features "IIII" for Roman numeral "IV"—purposely retained during the restoration process.)

VISIT

Public areas open daily year-round. ✕ ♿ 🅿 📧 *202-371-9441. www.unionstationdc.com.*

A fountained plaza featuring a statue of Columbus and the Freedom Bell (a replica of the Liberty Bell) fronts the station, whose triple-arched, colonnaded entrance is modeled after Rome's Arch of Constantine. Another ancient Roman monument, the Baths of Diocletian, served as the inspiration for the station's cavernous **main hall**. A vaulted ceiling with gilded octagonal coffers soars 96ft, and 36 statues of Roman legionnaires look down from the second-story balcony rimming the hall.

Dining in Union Station

NATIONAL POSTAL MUSEUM★

Massachusetts Ave. and 1st St. NE.
Ⓜ Union Station.

Occupying part of the ground floor of the stately Beaux-Arts **City Post Office Building** next to Union Station, this Smithsonian Institution museum houses the world's largest philatelic collection and chronicles America's mail service from colonial times to the present.

Historical Notes

A gift of Confederate postage stamps in 1886 initiated the Smithsonian's philatelic collection. By 1908 the growing assemblage was housed on the Mall in the Arts and Industries Building; in 1964 it was transferred to the National Museum of American History. The landmark City Post Office Building (1914, Daniel H. Burnham) was chosen as the site for a new museum, which was established in 1990 by the joint efforts of the US Postal Service and the Smithsonian. It opened in 1993 after extensive renovation to the building, which also houses a large postal facility and other government offices. At present the museum comprises a research library, a theater and a discovery center, as well as six galleries, a stamp shop and a museum shop. The 16-million-item collection includes historic postal artifacts, personal letters, photographs and transport vehicles, in addition to rare stamps and premier covers.

National Postal Museum, Atrium Gallery

VISIT

📷 *Open year-round daily 10am–5:30pm. Closed Dec 25. Guided tours (1hr) available daily 11am & 1pm.* ♿ ☎ *202-357-2991. www.si.edu/postal.*

The lobby of the building, with its 40ft-high coffered ceiling, Ionic columns and marble floors, provides a grand passageway to the exhibit area *(located on the lower level)*, which is entered through a polished bronze and stainless steel **escalator arcade**. Three vintage mail planes, suspended from the ceiling, dominate the 90ft glass **atrium** gallery, where a walk-through railroad car with mail sorting bins, a Concord-style mail coach and a 1931 Model A Ford are also on view. The **Stamps and Stories** gallery contains changing selections of philatelic rarities from the museum's collection, such as the first prepaid stamps (1840), called "penny blues." Other galleries showcase little-known pockets of postal history and stamp collecting, from the annual Duck Stamp contest that since 1934 has raised $500 million to acquire natural habitat for US waterfowl to the more recent challenges posed by direct mail. Related activities like letter writing and envelope manufacturing may also be explored in exhibits complemented by novelties from the museum's far-ranging collection. A number of interactive videos, including an electronic souvenir postcard kiosk, invite visitor participation.

2 Eastern Market

7th St. between N. Carolina Ave. and C St. SE. ☎ *202-546-2698.* A nostalgically appealing market dating from the early 1870s, this brick building houses old-style butcher, produce and seafood stalls. On Saturdays it becomes the setting for a festive fair, when vendors selling everything from fresh flowers and potted herbs to ethnic artifacts and handicrafts set up outdoor stalls. By 10am the **Market Lunch** restaurant *(☎ 202-547-8444)* is typically edged with a long line of eager diners awaiting hearty pancake or waffle breakfasts. At noontime the queue is for local seafood lunches of crab cakes, fried fish and oysters.

Multilegged Mail Movers

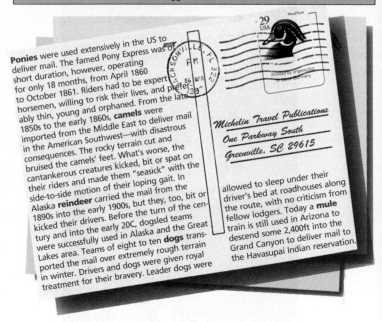

Ponies were used extensively in the US to deliver mail. The famed Pony Express was of short duration, however, operating for only 18 months, from April 1860 to October 1861. Riders had to be expert horsemen, willing to risk their lives, and preferably thin, young and orphaned. From the late 1850s to the early 1860s, **camels** were imported from the Middle East to deliver mail in the American Southwest—with disastrous consequences. The rocky terrain cut and bruised the camels' feet. What's worse, the cantankerous creatures kicked, bit or spat on their riders and made them "seasick" with the side-to-side motion of their loping gait. In Alaska **reindeer** carried the mail from the 1890s into the early 1900s, but they, too, bit or kicked their drivers. Before the turn of the century and into the early 20C, dogsled teams were successfully used in Alaska and the Great Lakes area. Teams of eight to ten **dogs** transported the mail over extremely rough terrain in winter. Drivers and dogs were given royal treatment for their bravery. Leader dogs were allowed to sleep under their driver's bed at roadhouses along the route, with no criticism from fellow lodgers. Today a **mule** train is still used in Arizona to descend some 2,400ft into the Grand Canyon to deliver mail to the Havasupai Indian reservation.

Michelin Travel Publications
One Parkway South
Greenville, SC 29615

CAPITAL CHILDREN'S MUSEUM

800 3rd St. NE.
Ⓜ Union Station.

Housed in a group of late-19C buildings on a 3-acre site, this privately funded learning playground conceived for children between the ages of 2 and 12 features "hands-on" exhibits that integrate the arts, sciences, humanities and technology.

VISIT

Ⓚ *Open Memorial Day–Labor Day daily 10am–5pm. Rest of the year Tue–Sun 10am–5pm. Closed Jan 1, Thanksgiving Day, Dec 25. $7.* ♿ 🅿 @ *202-675-4120.*
www.ccm.org.

The whimsical **Sculpture Garden**, situated at the museum's entrance, is inhabited by fantastic human and animal figures crafted out of tiles, rocks, broken bracelets and other scrap material by the Indian folk artist Nek Chand.
Inside, the flavor of Mexico is re-created in the International Hall *(2nd floor)*, where activities include preparing tortillas and petting a goat. You can also travel to Asia and pretend you are on board a Japanese *Shinkansen* bullet train. Other activities include performing your own science experiments or starring in a cartoon. Special exhibits and workshops are scheduled throughout the year.

SEWALL-BELMONT HOUSE

144 Constitution Ave. NE.
Ⓜ Union Station or Capitol South.

Reputedly one of the oldest buildings on Capitol Hill, this gracious house was erected in 1799 by Robert Sewall. Today it serves as the headquarters for the **National Woman's Party**.
The residence remained in the Sewall family for 123 years and served as one of Washington's first social centers. Among its noted tenants was Albert Gallatin, Secretary of the Treasury under Presidents Jefferson and Madison. According to certain sources, Gallatin worked out the financial arrangements for the Louisiana Purchase on the premises. Over the years the house has undergone major exterior and interior alteration. In 1929 the building was purchased by the National Woman's Party, which has maintained its head offices there ever since.

VISIT

Open early Jan–late Dec Tue–Fri 11am–3pm, Sat noon–3pm. Closed major holi-days. $3 contribution requested. Guided tours (1hr) available 11am, noon, 1pm & 2pm. ☎ 202-546-1210. www.natwomanparty.org.

Designated a National Historic Site, the building commemorates the women's movement with portraits and busts of the suffragists—those who fought for passage of the 19th Amendment (1920) granting women the right to vote.

The Mall

The Mall serves as the cultural heart of the capital and a political forum for the nation. Its imposing buildings and broad vistas underscore Washington's reputation as "the City Beautiful."

"A Vast Esplanade" – The city's designer, Pierre Charles L'Enfant, envisioned the Mall as a grand avenue extending from Jenkins Hill to the current site of the Washington Monument. L'Enfant's configuration of the Mall was determined in part by the courses of Tiber Creek and the Potomac, which at that time ran along present-day Constitution Avenue, 17th Street and Maine Avenue. Until the mid-19C little development took place here. Then in 1848 ground was broken for the Washington Monument and, a year later, for the Smithsonian Castle, paving the way for a growing institutional presence on the Mall. In 1850 Andrew Jackson Downing was commissioned to produce a landscape proposal for the Mall. Though his plan for intricate paths and gardens was not realized, his attempt at a cohesive design for the area influenced future plans.

After a severe flood in 1881, Congress appropriated funds for draining the Potomac flats south and west of the Mall and for dredging the Washington Channel. By the turn of the century, 621 acres had been reclaimed for the creation of Potomac Park, mandated by Congress "for the recreation and pleasure of the people." The Tidal Basin was formed to ensure a flow of fresh water through the Washington Channel.

Early-20C Development – By 1900 the original Mall area was a labyrinth of fashionable walks and drives bordering the Smithsonian Castle, the National Museum (now the Arts and Industries Building) and several other governmental structures. A railroad station stood on the present site of the National Gallery of Art. The McMillan Commission, appointed in 1901 to assess the future development of the city, called for transforming the Mall into a broad, tree-lined promenade.

Though the commission was unable to implement all of its improvements, it did succeed in negotiating the transfer of the railroad facilities to the newly proposed Union Station (1903). It also managed to protect the future 800ft-wide Mall greensward from encroachment by further construction and extended the boundaries of the Mall west by situating the planned memorial to Lincoln on the reclaimed flats of West Potomac Park. In 1917, to accommodate wartime exigencies, rows of barrackslike wooden structures known as "tempos" were constructed on and around the Mall. Although these temporary buildings were left standing until after World War II, the beautification of the Mall proceeded. In 1923 the Smithsonian opened the Freer Gallery of Art on the south side of the Mall, and in 1941 the National Gallery of Art rose on the north side of the Mall, near the new National Archives. The southwestern portion of the general Mall area was extended in the late 1930s when the Jefferson Memorial was built on the shores of the Tidal Basin.

A Dream Realized – Following World War II, gardens, monuments and museums gradually replaced the unsightly tempos. Since the mid-1960s the Smithsonian has added six museums, and the National Gallery of Art has constructed its widely acclaimed East Building. West Potomac Park has been further developed, and in 1982 "the Wall," an eloquent monument to Vietnam veterans, was erected. In 1995 the Korean War Veterans Memorial was dedicated, and a memorial to President Franklin D. Roosevelt was completed in the park in May 1997. Plans are under way for a new Smithsonian attraction in Washington, the **National Museum of the American Indian**. Projected to open in 2004, it will occupy the land east of the National Air and Space Museum, the last available building site on the Mall.

Traditionally a rallying point for political demonstrations, the Mall accommodated the enormous crowds in attendance at the 1963 March on Washington for Jobs and Freedom (at which Martin Luther King Jr. delivered his "I Have a Dream" speech), the 1979 visit of Pope John Paul II and the Million Man March in 1995 and a Promise Keepers rally in 1997. The Mall also hosts major national events, such as the annual Independence Day celebration on the Fourth of July.

Visiting the Mall

Orientation – Map pp 14-16. Known as the **East Mall**, the mile-long, tree-lined esplanade extending from the foot of Capitol Hill to 15th Street contains one of the world's densest concentrations of museums. The dominating presence here is the Smithsonian Institution, which operates nine museums on the Mall proper. The building on Jefferson Drive known as the Castle houses the Smithsonian Information Center. Comprising two structures, the independently administered National Gallery of Art dominates the northeast corner of the Mall. Just off the Mall are such governmental institutions as the National Archives, the Bureau of Engraving and Printing and the US Botanic Garden. The eastern end of the Mall is anchored by the Capitol Reflecting Pool, overlooked by an equestrian statue of President Grant that commemorates his leadership of Union troops in the Civil War. On the south side of the Reflecting Pool is a memorial to President Garfield, and on the north side there is an allegorical memorial to Peace.

Stretching from 15th Street to the Potomac River is the **West Mall**, an expansive greensward that contains the nation's best-known memorials. The monolithic Washington Monument is aligned on a north-south axis with the circular Jefferson Memorial, which overlooks the Tidal Basin. West of the Washington Monument stands the massive, rectangular Lincoln Memorial and the neighboring Vietnam Veterans Memorial to the northeast. South of the Lincoln Memorial, the panhandle between the Potomac and the Tidal Basin serves as the setting for West Potomac Park.

Helpful Hints – All museums and attractions on the Mall are free of charge. Smithsonian sights are open daily (except Dec 25) 10am–5:30pm. Street parking is allowed 10am–10pm, with a 3hr limit per car; spaces tend to be filled immediately after 10am, especially during the peak tourist seasons. Several Metro stations serve the Mall, making a visit here free of time restraints. Tourmobile shuttle buses loop through the entire Mall area, including West Potomac Park, allowing visitors to get on and off at various sights *(see Tourmobile)*. Old Town Trolley also serves sights on the Mall.

Due to the proximity of the Mall museums to one another, touring the area on foot is recommended. The Tourmobile (☎ 202-554-7950; see map pp 14-16) also makes stops at all major sites on the Mall.

The Smithsonian Information Center in the Castle building should be the first stop, as it is designed to help visitors plan their time on the Mall and elsewhere in the city. For a recorded schedule of daily events at Smithsonian museums, call Dial-a-Museum at ☎ 202-357-2020.

Cafes and cafeterias are located in many of the museums (indicated by the D symbol in the sight descriptions that follow). Lines can be very long, so eating an early or late lunch is suggested. Street vendors along Independence Avenue sell hot dogs, soft drinks and snacks. On the Mall there are a number of pleasant spots to enjoy a picnic lunch.

In early July the Smithsonian holds its annual Festival of American Folklife. From Memorial Day to Labor Day, concerts are presented by military bands and other musical groups several times weekly in the Sylvan Theatre, an outdoor stage situated to the south of the Washington Monument *(see Calendar of Events)*.

③ Museum shops on the Mall

Map p 14. Most DC museums have sales shops on the premises *(see Museum Shops)*. Especially fun are the shops in the **National Air and Space Museum** *(6th and Independence Ave. SW ☎ 202-357-1387).* Here you'll find a huge assortment of kites, space toys, model airplane kits and flight publications. Space-shuttle pens, science kits and novelties such as freeze-dried ice cream and other astronaut food are some of the most popular products. The **Arts and Industries Building** *(Jefferson Dr. at 9th St. SW ☎ 202-357-1369)* houses a sizable shop, brimming largely with Victoriana-motif stationery, jewelry, apparel and housewares. Books, international crafts and vintage recordings, especially jazz, are also well stocked. Next door, the **National Museum of African Art** *(950 Independence Ave. SW ☎ 202-786-2147)* displays handmade baskets, jewelry, musical instruments, toys and clothing from various African countries, plus a wide selection of books and African music—all for sale. A cornucopia of art books and reproductions fills the enormous ground-floor shop at the **National Gallery of Art** *(Madison Dr. between 3rd and 7th Sts. NW ☎ 202-842-6476).* In addition to a vast selection of prints, you will find a variety of videocassettes and art-emblazoned stationery, apparel, accessories and housewares.

THE CASTLE
Smithsonian Institution Building

Jefferson Dr. at 10th St. SW.
Ⓜ Smithsonian.

The turreted red sandstone "castle" on the Mall has become the symbol of the **Smithsonian Institution**, the nation's preeminent museum and research complex. The building functions as a visitor information center providing orientation to the Smithsonian's many museums and to other Washington sights.

Historical Notes

The Gift of an Englishman – The Smithsonian Institution is the brainchild of an Englishman who never visited America, **James Smithson** (1765-1829), an enlightened thinker and prominent Oxford scientist. As the illegitimate son of Elizabeth Macie and Hugh Smithson, the first duke of Northumberland, James Smithson spent the first 34 years of his life as James Macie. Eventually the British Crown granted his petition to bear the Smithson name.

Smithson wished to acknowledge blood ties before all else, and he consequently left his wealth to his only surviving relative, a nephew. When the nephew died in 1835 without descendants, the remaining money went, as Smithson's will had stipulated, "to the United States of America, to found at Washington, under the name of the Smithsonian Institution, an Establishment for the increase and diffusion of knowledge." In making this generous bequest, Smithson had prophesied, "My name shall live in the memory of men, when the titles of the Northumberlands...are extinct and forgotten."

> ### ■ Tolling Bell
>
> Created to commemorate the Smithsonian Institution's sesquicentennial, the Castle's bell weighs 821lbs and is 34in in diameter and 27in high. The $40,000 bronze bell was cast by the 576-year-old London foundry that cast America's first Liberty Bell. In 1996, on August 10 (the day the Smithsonian Institution was founded 150 years before), a 200ft hydraulic crane hoisted the bell 12 stories to the Castle's octagonal clock-tower roof. The bell tolls each hour in the key of D-flat.

A National Institution – In considering Smithson's unexpected bequest, some members of Congress opposed it, declaring it "beneath the dignity of the United States to receive presents of this kind." Thanks primarily to the efforts of John Quincy Adams, Congress finally passed a bill establishing the Smithsonian Institution in 1846, thereby ending years of heated debate. The bill called for the formation of a board of regents that would include the chief justice of the Supreme Court, the vice president, members of both houses of Congress and private citizens. Smithson's assets were converted into 105 bags of gold sovereigns, worth roughly $515,000 at the time.

In 1846 Congress appointed the respected American physicist Joseph Henry as the Smithsonian's first secretary. During his controversial 32-year tenure, Henry resolutely insisted on focusing the institution's role on scientific research rather than on museum development.

It was Henry's assistant secretary and successor, the biologist Spencer Fullerton Baird, who developed the Smithsonian as a federal institution of public exhibitions. Over the decades, the institution has grown through the generosity of major benefactors as well as the general public. Today it is the largest museum complex in the world, with an annual budget, from both private and federal appropriations, of more than $569.7 million. Its 16 museums in Washington, DC, of which 9 are located on the Mall, have total holdings of some 140 million artifacts, works of art and specimens. Exhibits range from Lindbergh's plane, the *Spirit of St. Louis*, to Picasso's paintings to a living coral reef. Such popular Americana as Michael Jordan's jersey, Archie Bunker's chair and the ruby slippers Judy Garland wore in *The Wizard of Oz* are also at the Smithsonian. In addition the institution administers the National Zoological Park.

Renwick's "Castle" – The Smithsonian's first building, a leading example of Romanesque Revival architecture, was designed by **James Renwick** in the late 1840s and completed in 1855. Inspired by 12C Norman architecture, the asymmetrical building is topped with nine towers that soar above a battlemented cornice. When it was first completed, the Castle housed research and administrative facilities, living quarters for scientists and Smithsonian personnel, and exhibit space. A renovation of the building's interior in 1989 restored the **Great Hall**, with its flanking columned arches, to its original appearance.

Peter Wrenn/MICHELIN

The Castle

VISIT

Open year-round daily 9am–5:30pm. Closed Dec 25. Guided tours (1hr) available Fri 10:15am, weekends 9:30am & 10:30am. ⚊ ☎ *202-357-2700. www.si.edu.*

The Castle's state-of-the-art **information center** features a series of interactive touch screens and wall maps, as well as three-dimensional maps and an orientation film *(20min)* that summarizes each Smithsonian museum.

A crypt containing the body of James Smithson, which was moved here in 1904, lies in the north foyer. Located at the south entrance, the **Children's Room**, commissioned in 1899 by Smithsonian secretary Samuel Pierpont Langley, contains the original turn-of-the-century ceiling mural depicting a vine-covered arbor. The Castle also houses administrative offices.

Recreation around the Mall

Map pp 14-16. The Mall offers two season-specific ways to appreciate its monuments and memorials.

4 In summer—and during the cherry blossom festival in spring—the Tidal Basin hosts a bevy of two-person **paddleboats**, which afford their pedaling passengers a unique perspective of the capital city *(rentals by the hour; photo ID required; Tidal Basin Boat House ☎ 202-479-2426).*

5 When winter settles in, **ice-skating** draws throngs of locals and tourists to the impressive National Sculpture Garden and Ice Rink, fronting the National Archives. *(☎ 202-289-3361)*

NATIONAL AIR AND SPACE MUSEUM★★★

Independence Ave. at 6th St. SW.

Ⓜ L'Enfant Plaza.

Plan pp 96-97

From Icarus' ill-fated flight to the far-flung space missions of recent decades, humans have attempted to conquer earth's relentless pull. This fascinating museum, commemorating man's aeronautical and astronautical achievements, welcomes more than nine million visitors annually, making it one of Washington's and the world's most popular museums.

Historical Notes

The Smithsonian in the Vanguard of Flight – The Smithsonian's interest in flight dates back to the early days of the institution. In 1861 the Smithsonian's first secretary, Joseph Henry, encouraged Thaddeus Lowe's balloon experiments, resulting in President Lincoln's decision to use balloons in the Civil War. Fifteen years later a group of kites brought from China for the Philadelphia Centennial Exposition was given to the Smithsonian and became the cornerstone of the national aeronautical collection, which evolved into the present National Air and Space Museum.

The appointment in 1887 of **Samuel Pierpont Langley** (1834-1906) as the third secretary of the Smithsonian was a key factor in the development of flight in the US. Though largely self-educated, Langley had gained renown as an astronomer, inventor, writer and researcher by the time he joined the Smithsonian. In May 1896 his *Aerodrome No. 5* proved that sustained mechanical flight with a device heavier than air was feasible. Although criticized during his lifetime for a series of unsuccessful flight projects, Langley prepared the way for manned flight and what he forecast as "the great universal highway overhead." The results of Langley's lifetime of research in the field of aeronautics are recorded in his influential work, *The Langley Memoir on Mechanical Flight* (1911).

In the 20C the idea for a museum dedicated to the history of flight evolved from the concern that the aircraft used by the US Air Force in World War II would be relegated to the scrap heap. With congressional support a conservation program was conceived, and in 1946 the National Air Museum was established by law "to memorialize the national development of aviation." In 1966 the museum's scope was enlarged to include space flight.

The Wright Brothers

A helicopter toy given as a present to young Wilbur (1867-1912) and Orville (1871-1948) Wright in 1878 sparked a passion for flight that remained with the brothers throughout their lives. As adults the self-taught engineers were among many in the US and abroad dedicated to making manned flight a reality. Drawing heavily from the experiences of Otto Lilienthal and other predecessors, they developed the 1903 *Wright Flyer*, an aircraft controlled by "wing warping," or changing the shapes of the wing tips to deflect the air.

On December 17, 1903, in Kitty Hawk, North Carolina, their efforts succeeded. The longest of their four flights that day was 852ft in 59 seconds, after which a sudden gust of wind smashed the craft. There was little publicity about the brothers'

Orville and Wilbur Wright

Courtesy National Air and Space Museum, Smithsonian Institution

breakthrough until 1905, but they patented their discovery and went on to build an airplane factory in Dayton, Ohio.

A Flight Chronology

Aircraft and spacecraft in the museum's collections appear in **bold**.

Beginnings

early 16C	Leonardo da Vinci studies bird flight and draws plans for flying devices—precursors of the airplane, helicopter and parachute.
1783	First manned balloon flight by the Montgolfier brothers in Paris.
1793	George Washington witnesses first US balloon flight in Philadelphia.
1861-65	Observation balloons are used in the Civil War.
1891-96	Otto Lilienthal makes 2,000 glides in weight-controlled monoplanes.
1896	The first successful engine-driven craft flight by Langley's *Aerodrome No. 5* in Washington, DC.

20C Innovations

1903	In Kitty Hawk, North Carolina, the Wright brothers successfully perform the first manned motorized flight in their **1903 Flyer**.
1909	Louis Bleriot crosses the English Channel in 36 minutes, flying a **Type XI monoplane**.
c.1910	Glenn H. Curtiss develops the first seaplanes, which are used subsequently by the US Navy.
1911	G.P. Rodgers makes the first coast-to-coast flight aboard the **Wright EX Vin Fiz**.
1918	Scheduled airmail service begins with a route between New York City and Washington, DC via Philadelphia.
1920	Beginning of regular passenger flights in Europe.
1923	The first nonstop coast-to-coast flight in the Dutch-built **Fokker T-2**.
1924	First round-the-world flight by two US Army **Douglas World Cruisers**.
1926	The first liquid propellant rocket is developed.
1927	Charles Lindbergh makes the first solo nonstop crossing of the Atlantic in the **Spirit of St. Louis**, covering 3,610 miles in 33 1/2hrs.
1932	Amelia Earhart is the first woman to make a solo nonstop transatlantic flight.
1944	The Germans begin launching the **V-2**, the world's first long-range ballistic missile.
1947	Air Force pilot Charles E. "Chuck" Yeager flies the **Bell X-1 Glamorous Glennis** faster than the speed of sound.

The Space Age

1957	The Soviets launch **Sputnik 1**, the first artificial satellite.
1958	The Boeing 707, the first US jet, begins commercial service. The National Aeronautics and Space Administration (NASA) is created.
1962	In **Friendship 7** John Glenn is the first American to orbit the earth.
1965	Traveling aboard the **Gemini 4** capsule, Edward White is the first American to walk in space.
1969	Astronauts fly **Apollo 11** to the moon and walk on its surface.
1970	Beginning of regular commercial service of the supersonic Concorde.
1973-74	The manned space missions of the **Skylab** orbital workshop conduct experiments and gather valuable data. *Pioneer 10* is the first spacecraft to reach Jupiter.
1977	**Voyager 1** and *Voyager 2* are launched to photograph outer planets.
1979	*Voyager 1* and *Voyager 2* reach Jupiter.
1981	*Voyager 2* reaches Saturn. Space shuttle *Columbia* is launched.
1986	*Voyager 2* reaches Uranus.
1989	*Galileo* space probe is launched toward Jupiter.
1990	*Magellan* space probe begins mapping the surface of Venus. **Hubble Space Telescope** is launched into orbit.
1991	First close-up views of an asteroid obtained by *Galileo* probe.
1993	The longest space-shuttle mission (14 days) to date is completed.
1996	US space shuttle *Atlantis* and Russian *Mir* space station form largest structure ever assembled in space. Astronaut Shannon Lucid remains in space for 188 days, longer than any American. The longest flight in space-shuttle history is achieved by *Columbia* (US)—a record 17 days, 15 hours, 54 minutes.

1997	The Pathfinder mission lands on Mars. *Sojourner*, the first robotic rover, successfuly collects and transmits data concerning the red planet's geological and chemical composition.
1998	John Glenn, the first American to orbit the earth, returns to space aboard the space shuttle *Discovery*, thirty-six years after his first mission aboard *Friendship 7*. A new era in space flight begins with the initial construction stages of the International Space Station, the largest scientific cooperative endeavor in history.
2001	Astronomers discover the first distant multiplanet system in which the planets have orbits similar to those in our own solar system.

The Building – Designed by the St. Louis-based architect Gyo Obata, the building, which took four years to complete, opened in July 1976 as a part of the nation's bicentennial celebration. The unadorned structure, measuring 635ft by 225ft and reaching nearly 83ft in height, comprises four massive rectangles connected by three glass "hyphens." The building is faced with Tennessee marble similar to that used on the National Gallery of Art across the Mall. The spacious structure contains 23 galleries, a theater, a planetarium, museum stores and a research library *(open by appointment only)*. A glass annex housing a large dining facility was added to the building's east end in the late 1980s.

The Collections – The museum possesses hundreds of aircraft and spacecraft, including manned vehicles, rockets, launching devices, space probes and satellites. As the museum has rights to all flown manned spacecraft from the US, its holdings constitute by far the most comprehensive collection of its kind in the world.

Authenticity is the keynote of the whole museum; nearly all the aircraft and most of the spacecraft in the galleries are genuine. As many spacecraft cannot be recovered once launched, the museum displays either the backup vehicle, a test vehicle, or a replica made from authentic hardware, as similar to the original as possible. Labels specifically note such distinctions.

VISIT

Kids *Open year-round daily 10am–5:30pm. Closed Dec 25. Guided tours (1hr 15min) available.* ✕ ☎ *202-357-2700. www.nasm.edu.*

Before beginning your visit of the museum, go to the **Langley Theater** box office **(C)** to reserve a seat for one or several of the popular **films** (including the classic *To Fly!*) that are shown on a rotating basis throughout the day *($6.50; recorded information on films and screening times* ☎ *202-357-1686)*. The theater's IMAX projection system and five-story screen create the illusion of being airborne.

The **Albert Einstein Planetarium** features regularly scheduled shows and special presentations during which the heavens are simulated on a 70ft overhead dome and discoveries of past centuries are re-created *(open year-round daily 11am–5pm; $3.75; recorded information* ☎ *202-357-1686)*.

The three vast glass halls on the 1st floor contain several suspended artifacts (aircraft and spacecraft), many of which are best viewed from the second floor which also contains suspended craft. Circled numbers on the floor plan indicate artifacts that are suspended from the ceiling.

First Floor

The spacious lobby is adorned with two spectacular murals. On the west wall, **Earthflight Environment (A)** by Eric Sloan depicts an ever-changing sky.

Courtesy National Air and Space Museum, Smithsonian Institution; photo: Eric Long

Space Hall, National Air and Space Museum

On the east wall, Robert McCall's **The Space Mural—A Cosmic View (B)** represents the artist's vision of the universe past, present and future.

Milestones of Flight – In the large hall that occupies the central part of the building, several epoch-making airplanes and spacecraft are displayed. Among the highlights are the Wright brothers' *1903 Flyer* **(2)**, Charles Lindbergh's Ryan NYP *Spirit of St. Louis* **(3)**, Chuck Yeager's Bell X-1 *Glamorous Glennis* **(4)**, John Glenn's *Friendship 7* **(5)** and *Apollo 11* **(6)**. The exhibit also features the rocket-powered X-15 NASA **(39)** that set unofficial speed and altitude records of 4,520mph (Mach 6.7) and 354,200ft (over 67mi), as well as a replica of the Soviet satellite *Sputnik* **(7)**, a surprisingly small (22.8in) polished sphere with four rod-shaped antennae. The Breitling Orbiter 3 **(38)** is the aircraft used in the first non-stop flight around the world. Visitors can touch a four-billion-year-old basalt moon rock **(8)** retrieved by the crew of Apollo 17 in 1972.

Air Transportation – Colorful aircraft fill this hall, illustrating the key stages of air transport. The sporty Pitcairn Mailwing **(9)** was designed to carry small loads for early mail routes in the eastern US. The all-metal Ford Tri-Motor **(10)** was a noisy but comfortable means of transport until the mid-1930s. Still used for passenger and cargo transport, the DC-3 **(11)**, inaugurated in 1935, supplanted Ford's "Tin Goose" as the airlines' favorite workhorse. Boeing's 247-D **(12)** led the familiar series whose later models, the Stratoliners, could cruise above turbulence on long flights.

■ The Physics of Flight

Flying is all about pressure and wing shape. To fly, an aircraft generates an upward force known as **lift**. To take off, lift must be greater than the aircraft's weight. An aircraft's **wings** are designed to be **curved** so that the air pressure at the top of the wing is different from the air pressure at the bottom of the wing. When the engines push the aircraft forward, air passes over the wings in such a way that a smaller pressure pushes down on the top of the wing and a higher pressure pushes up under the wing. This difference in pressure causes **lift**. The air coming off the wing is deflected downwards and the wing gets pushed upward. By varying this pressure difference, the pilot controls the altitude of the aircraft.

A pilot controls the amount of lift in two ways: by varying both the speed of the plane and the angle that the wing makes in relation to the plane's forward direction. In doing this, the pilot can make the aircraft climb, descend or fly level. Increasing speed increases lift. Increasing angle increases lift. This is why the angle of the wing is so important. Varying the angle of the wing to the oncoming air changes the wing shape (and as such an airplane can fly upside down). Parts of the wing, such as flaps located in the back of the wing, can also be deflected to change the wing shape. You might notice that at slower speeds, such as during climb or descent, the angle of the entire aircraft is high. The pilot is using angle to compensate for the lower speed. This allows the pilot to climb or descend at a controlled and desirable rate so as not to upset the passengers or to damage the aircraft.

© Brigitta L. House/MICHELIN

Wright Brothers' *Flyer*

The **Golden Age of Flight** highlights the history of aviation between the two world wars. Between these two galleries, the Curtiss P-40[E] **(13)**, a well-known World War II fighter plane, and an aerobatic Grumman Gulfhawk II **(14)** hang above a gallery that displays rotating exhibits of recently restored aircraft. In **Jet Aviation**, the mural **(D)** spanning the length of the wall depicts 27 planes, from the Heinkel HE (1939) to the Concorde (1971) and the Airbus Industry A300B (1972). Opposite the mural are three jet fighters: a Messerschmitt Me262 **(15)**, a Lockheed XP-80 **(16)** and a McDonnell FH-1 Phantom **(17)**. **Early Flight** displays craft in a facsimile of a 1913 indoor aeronautical exhibition. Among other planes located in this gallery are a glider (1894) designed by Lilienthal, the Wright 1909 Military Flyer **(18)**, which was the world's first military airplane, and a Bleriot Type XI monoplane **(19)**.

Cross the entrance hall to the east wing.

How Things Fly includes exhibits on gravity and air, stability and control, and other principles of flight. Visitors can man the controls of a Cessna 150, activate a supersonic wind tunnel and participate in many other interactive exhibits. The development of aerial photography and its practical applications is presented in **Looking at Earth**. A Lockheed U-2 is on display, along with interactive touch screens that show a Landsat view of each of the 50 states.

SECOND FLOOR

FIRST FLOOR

Space Hall – Large rockets, guided missiles and manned spacecraft are featured in the exhibit entitled **Space Race**. On display is the infamous V-2 rocket **(40)** as well as a replica of the Hubble Space Telescope **(37)**, a model of the *Columbia* space shuttle **(20)** and the *Apollo-Soyuz* spacecraft **(21)**, which was used for a joint docking-in-space experiment with the Russians in 1975. Visitors can walk through the Skylab Orbital Workshop **(22)** *(accessible from the 2nd floor)*.

The **Rocketry and Space Flight** gallery displays historic rockets, engines for missiles and spacecraft, some rocket engines and a variety of space suits. The adjacent area is occupied by **Lunar Exploration Vehicles**, largely unmanned lunar probes that photographed the moon's surface. Although the *Apollo* lunar module **(23)** was never sent into space, it was nevertheless used for ground testing.

Explore the Universe examines the evolution of humanity's ability to search the heavens. Islamic **astrolabes** and Danish astronomer Tycho Brahe's portable **mural quadrant** represent the first steps taken in charting the skies while William Herschel's telescope tube, Edwin Hubble's camera, turn-of-the-century spectrographs and the high-tech **Z machine** mark exceptional strides in the analysis of the ever-expanding frontier.

Second Floor

Pioneers of Flight – This open gallery houses planes that made historic flights. Among the artifacts displayed is Galbraith Perry Rodgers' Wright EX *Vin Fiz* **(24)**, named after a grape drink his sponsor was making at the time. This plane was the first to succeed in a coast-to-coast flight, albeit with many stops and repairs. Rodgers crossed the continent from September 17 to November 5, 1911, covering 4,321 miles in 82 hours with an average speed of 52mph. The Fokker T-2 **(25)**,

NATIONAL AIR AND SPACE MUSEUM

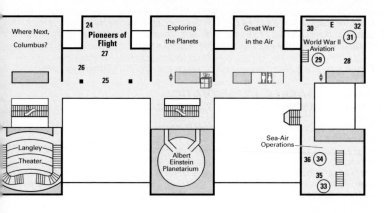

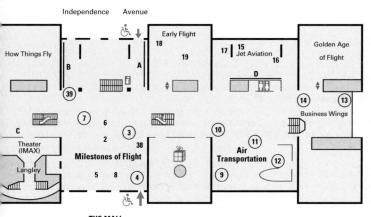

THE MALL

built in the Netherlands and modified in the US, was the first to fly nonstop coast-to-coast. On May 2 and 3, 1923, this plane, manned by two pilots, flew almost 27 hours at an average speed of 92mph. The Douglas World Cruiser *Chicago* **(26)** was one of two biplanes to fly around the world, logging 27,553 miles in 175 days from April 6 to September 28, 1924. **Amelia Earhart** (1898-1937), the legendary aviator who lost her life in the South Pacific while attempting an around-the-world flight, set two world records with her bright red Lockheed Vega 5B **(27)** in 1932. In May of that year, Earhart became the first woman to fly alone nonstop across the Atlantic, covering a total of 2,026 miles in less than 15 hours. Three months later (August 24 and 25), she flew solo the 2,448 miles between Los Angeles,California and Newark, New Jersey in 19 hours.

A replica of the *Voyager 1* probe is the main attraction of **Exploring the Planets,** which presents an introduction to the solar system. Some of the airplanes that determined the fate of nations can be viewed in **World War II Aviation**. Displays here include a Messerschmitt Bf 109 **(28)**, a Mitsubishi Zero **(29)**, a Supermarine Spitfire **(30)**, a Macchi MC.202 **(31)** and a North American P-51D Mustang **(32)**. The mural **(E)** was executed by Keith Ferris in 1976. **Sea-Air Operations** reproduces an aircraft-carrier hangar deck. Featured are some of the most important aircraft in US naval aviation, including the Boeing F4B-4 **(33)**, the Douglas SBD-6 Dauntless dive-bomber **(34)**, the Douglas A-4C Skyhawk **(35)** and the Grumman F4F Wildcat **(36)**.

Return to the Pioneers of Flight gallery and continue to the east side.

Where Next, Columbus? delves into the reasons people are driven to explore. Displays focus on 500 years of exploration, beginning with Columbus' trip to the New World. Visitors can join a mission to the "red planet" on a simulated Mars landscape, learn how to stay fit in space and see how the US signals other planets in the search for signs of life. The story of US manned spaceflight programs from Project Mercury to *Apollo 17* is retold in **Apollo to the Moon**.

Lunar samples are displayed along with a variety of space suits and lunar surface equipment such as a prototype of *Apollo 15's* Lunar Rover. **Beyond the Limits: Flight Enters the Computer Age** explores flight in the computer age, highlighting the importance of computers in such areas as aerodynamics, manufacturing and flight simulation. Here visitors will find the Cray Serial 14 supercomputer used from 1978 to 1986 at the National Center for Atmospheric Research. Rotating works in the **Flight and the Arts** gallery feature artists' interpretations of flight-related themes.

★PAUL E. GARBER PRESERVATION, RESTORATION AND STORAGE FACILITY

One of the Smithsonian's best-kept secrets, this facility has been used as a storage and restoration center since the 1950s. Today it also serves as a "no frills" **museum** where visitors can see skilled craftspeople at work as well as many of the holdings not on view at the National Air and Space Museum on the Mall.

Paul Garber joined the museum in 1920 and was a motivating force there for more than 70 years. It was his idea to send a cable to Charles Lindbergh in Paris before the pilot landed in that city, asking him to donate the *Spirit of St. Louis* to the nation's aircraft collection. Lindbergh agreed, and the following year the historic plane entered the Smithsonian's collection. Garber's artful machinations finally brought the Wright brothers' *1903 Flyer* to the Smithsonian in 1948, from the London Science Museum, where it had been on display for 20 years.

Visit

7mi from the Mall. Map p 259. 3904 Old Silver Hill Rd., Suitland, Maryland. From downtown, drive southeast on Pennsylvania Ave. One mile past I-295 turn right on Branch Ave. and continue to Iverson Mall. Turn left on Silver Hill Rd. and turn left on Old Silver Hill Rd. Visit by guided tour (3hrs) only, year-round Mon–Fri 10am, weekends 10am & 1pm (2-week advance reservation required). Closed Dec 25. ♿ 🅿 ☏ *202-357-1400.*

The Garber Facility will be closed for tours when the museum begins moving artifacts to the Steven F. Udvar-Hazy Center at Washington Dulles International Airport. Call ☏ 202-357-1400 or visit www.nasm.edu for the current status of tours.

Among the more than 100 artifacts on display are a Northrop P-61C Black Widow; a Curtiss JN-4D Jenny, the World War I trainer made famous by barnstormers in the postwar period; a Hawker Hurricane IIc, a World War II British fighter of the kind used in the Battle of Britain; and a J-2 engine, one of the power plants for the *Saturn* launch vehicles.

NATIONAL GALLERY OF ART★★★

Madison Dr. between 3rd and 7th Sts. NW.
Ⓜ Archives.
Plan pp 100-101

The National Gallery's world-class collection of masterpieces traces the development of Western art from the Middle Ages to the present. The original West Building concentrates primarily on European works from the 13C through the early 20C. Its contemporary counterpart, the East Building, highlights works of modern artists.

Historical Notes

One Man's Dream – The financier, industrialist and statesman **Andrew Mellon** (1855-1937) was the impetus behind the National Gallery of Art. Mellon began collecting art in the 1870s, traveling to Europe with his friend Henry Clay Frick, benefactor of the famed Frick Collection *(THE GREEN GUIDE New York City)*, for the purpose of acquiring 17C and 18C paintings. In the late 1920s, while serving as secretary of the Treasury, Mellon conceived of endowing a national gallery of art. From that time until his death in 1937, he became one of the world's foremost collectors of art. His intent was to amass masterpieces that would show the development of Western art from the 13C through the 19C. Among his acquisitions were 21 works from the Hermitage museum in Leningrad. They included paintings by such masters as van Eyck, Raphael, Titian and Rembrandt.

In 1937 Congress granted a charter to the new National Gallery of Art and pledged funds to support it. The stately building erected on the Mall was a gift from Mellon to the American people. Further, Mellon left the museum an endowment: 126 paintings and a collection of fine 15-16C Italian sculpture. The National Gallery's original building (today known as the West Building) opened to the public in March 1941.

Other Benefactors – Following Mellon's lead, other major American collectors have contributed to the gallery. Many of these collectors were active early in the 20C, when outstanding works of art were more readily available in the marketplace. Consequently, they were able to assemble private collections rich in the works of Old Masters and Impressionists. Joseph Widener offered the renowned Widener family collection of painting, sculpture and decorative arts to the National Gallery in the 1930s. Samuel Kress, a self-made business magnate, already had plans drawn up for a museum in New York City to house his superb Italian paintings and sculptures when he was persuaded in 1939 to donate his collection to the uncompleted National Gallery.

Works by French Impressionists and post-Impressionists were donated by financier Chester Dale. Lessing J. Rosenwald left the gallery 22,000 prints and drawings, and Edgar William Garbisch and his wife, Bernice Chrysler Garbisch, gave an important collection of 18C and 19C American naive paintings. More than 1,300 donors have contributed works of art to the National Gallery. Most recently, in 1995, Andrew Mellon's son, Paul, donated 85 works by Bonnard, Cézanne, Degas, Gauguin, Picasso and other masters.

A New Building – In only 30 years the expanding collections had outgrown the gallery's more than 100,000sq ft of floor space in the original building. **Paul Mellon** (1907-1999), Ailsa Mellon Bruce and the Andrew Mellon Foundation funded the

The East Building

NATIONAL GALLERY OF ART

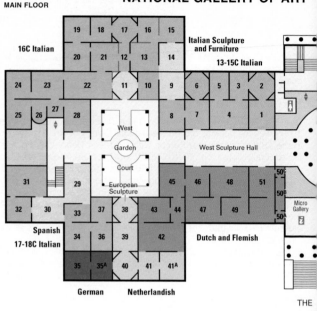

MAIN FLOOR

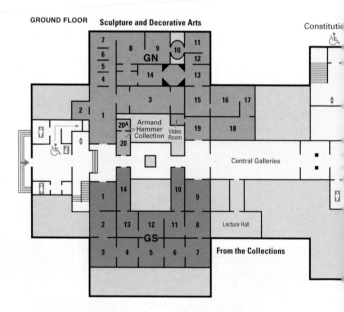

construction of a second building on the Mall just east of the original one. The $95 million East Building opened in 1978, establishing the National Gallery's reputation as a vital center for the presentation and appreciation of modern art.

The Collections – The gallery's collections include an estimated 3,200 paintings, 2,600 pieces of sculpture, 560 pieces of decorative art and more than 98,000 works on paper. Roughly 50 percent of these holdings are on display at any given time. The Italian works constitute one of the finest collections of its kind in the world. The gallery's *Ginevra de' Benci* represents the only portrait by Leonardo da Vinci in the Western Hemisphere. Federal funds support museum operations and maintenance. However, all of its acquisitions are made through private means.

Collection highlights appear in tan boxes roughly in order of visit.

West Building

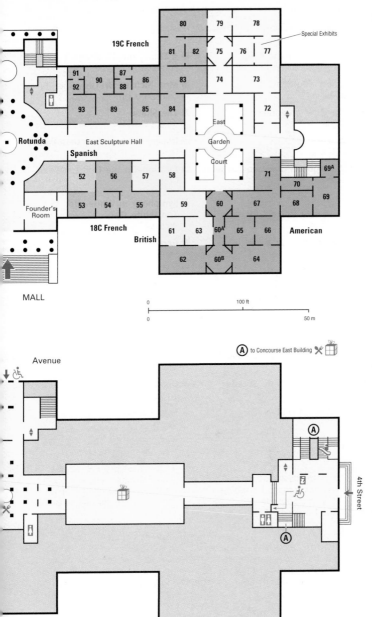

MALL

A to Concourse East Building

Visiting the Museum

West Building – *Open year-round Mon–Sat 10am–5pm, Sun 11am–6pm. Closed Jan 1 & Dec 25. Guided tours available. ✗ ♿ ☎ 202-737-4215, www.nga.gov. The West Building is undergoing long-term renovation. Some sections may be temporarily closed and some works of art mentioned below may not be on view. Check the Micro Gallery, accessible by the museum's web site or at terminals in the art information room, to find out the status of specific works and collections.* The main entrance to the West Building is located at the top of the steps on the Mall side between 4th and 7th streets. Wheelchair access is via the entrance at 6th Street. A checkroom is located to the right of the main entrance, beyond the Founder's Room. The art information room, with its state-of-the-art

Short on time?

If you have only two hours to visit the West Building, spend them seeing the following masterpieces. Begin by using the Micro Gallery to construct this personal tour:

- **Adoration of the Magi**
  Fra Angelico and Fra Filippo Lippi

- **Ginevra de'Benci**
  da Vinci

- **The Alba Madonna**
  Raphael

- **Laocoön**
  El Greco

- **Monsignor Francesco Barberini**
  Bernini

- **The Porta Portello, Padua**
  Canaletto

- **Two Women at a Window**
  Murillo

- **Portrait of a Lady**
  van der Weyden

- **Daniel in the Lions' Den**
  Rubens

- **Self-Portrait (1659)**
  Rembrandt

- **Woman Holding a Balance**
  Vermeer

- **Thérèse Louise de Sureda**
  Goya

- **Italian Comedians**
  Watteau

- **A Young Girl Reading**
  Fragonard

- **Mrs. Richard Brinsley Sherida**
  Gainsborough

- **The Skater**
  Stuart

- **Rubens Peale with a Geranium**
  Rembrandt Peale

- **Autumn–On the Hudson River**
  Cropsey

- **Symphony in White, No. 1: The White Girl**
  Whistler

- **Repose**
  Sargent

- **A Girl with a Watering Can**
  Renoir

- **The Boating Party**
  Cassatt

- **Fatata te Miti**
  Gauguin

- **Woman with a Parasol–Madame Monet and Her Son** Monet

- **Quadrille at the Moulin Rouge**
  Toulouse-Lautrec

- **Four Dancers**
  Degas

Micro Gallery, is to the left. The main floor of the West Building houses 13-19C European paintings and sculpture, and American art. Sculpture and decorative arts, prints and drawings and temporary exhibits are presented on the ground floor *(expected reopening late 2002)*. Artworks are displayed, for the most part, in chronological order by school.

We suggest you begin your visit at the art information room. Here you may obtain a list of current exhibitions, a schedule of docent-led tours and notices of temporary exhibits, lectures and special events. Spend 5-10min exploring the Micro Gallery, 13 touch-screen monitors that allow visitors to research artists and 1,700 works from the permanent collection. Along with historical commentary and analysis, this fascinating system provides the viewing status and location of specific works in the gallery. A random-access audio tour, *The Director's Tour*, offers curators' and conservators' perspectives on 130 works of art throughout the west building and is available for rental ($5) from the desk in the rotunda. A new audio tour, *Adventures in Art* Kids ($3), introduces the Dutch and Flemish collection to younger visitors.

East Building – *Open year-round Mon–Sat 10am–5pm, Sun 11am–6pm. Closed Jan 1 & Dec 25. Introductory guided tours (50min) available.* ⚒ ♿ *www.nga.gov* ☎ *202-737-4215.* The main entrance to the East Building is on 4th Street, across the plaza from the West Building. An underground concourse connects the two structures. Wheelchair access is to the left of the 4th Street entrance steps. All five levels of the East Building feature rotating exhibits drawn from the National Gallery's permanent collection of late-19C and 20C art. Works are not necessarily arranged in chronological order. The East Building's open interior space is easily adapted to changing exhibits; major traveling exhibits from all artistic periods are mounted here.

Begin your visit to the East Building at the ground-level art information desk, where you may obtain notices of current exhibitions and events as well as the day's schedule of guided tours.

Sculpture Garden – *Open year-round Mon–Sat 10am–5pm, Sun 11am–6pm. Closed Jan 1 & Dec 25.* ☎ *202-737-4215. www.nga.gov.* On the National Mall between 7th and 9th streets (across from the 7th Street entrance to the West Building), the Garden displays 20 major works of 20C sculpture in a pleasantly landscaped park.

Amenities – In the West Building the Garden Café *(ground floor, below the rotunda)*, serves lunch in a skylit atrium beside a fountain and numerous potted palms. Between the East and West buildings *(concourse level)* is the Cascade Café, a large food court and espresso bar with a view of the water wall, or *chadar*, beneath the plaza fountain. The Terrace Café *(East Building upper level)* serves coffee and light snacks on eye level with Alexander Calder's giant mobile. The sculpture garden's Pavilion Café is the museum's only outdoor offering; fancy pizzas, salads, and wrap sandwiches can be enjoyed indoors or outdoors at umbrella tables or on benches surrounding the reflecting pool and fountain.

The West Building's sizable museum shop *(ground floor, just east of the Garden Café)* has reproductions, calendars, stationery, art books, videocassettes and jewelry for sale. The concourse-level shop offers art books as well as exhibit catalogs and postcards for purchase. Posters and catalogs pertaining to special exhibits can be found in the East Building's museum shop *(concourse level)*.

Courtyards and galleries in both buildings offer seating for visitors. The Founder's Room in the West Building has comfortable chairs and writing desks for visitors' use. Flanking the steps of the Mall entrance to the West Building, twin gardens provide a shady respite, and both the Fourth Street Plaza and the sculpture garden have benches for taking a break.

WEST BUILDING

The capital's leading proponent of Classical Revival architecture, John Russell Pope designed this formidable domed structure. The West Building's appeal derives from the seven shades of glowing pink Tennessee marble incorporated in the facade. Its sober exterior is adorned only by simple blind windows and pilasters. Ionic porticoes highlight the north and south sides. The 785ft-long edifice ranks as one of the world's largest marble structures.

Main Floor

Flanking the entrance hall on the Mall side are the art information room, with its nifty **Micro Gallery** *(left)*, and the **Founder's Room** *(right)*, a lounge where portraits of major founding benefactors are prominently displayed. The hall leads to the **rotunda**, where green-black Tuscan marble columns surround a fountain whose centerpiece is a statue of Mercury. The broad sculpture halls of the building's two wings extend from the rotunda past the galleries, culminating in garden courts. The **East Sculpture Hall** features classically inspired marble statuary from the 17-19C, while works in bronze, including a selection of Italian busts, are displayed in the **West Sculpture Hall**.

13-15C Italian Painting – *Galleries 1-15.* Representing the evolution of Western painting from 1200 to the early 1500s, this section begins with the stylized Byzantine iconography that developed in Constantinople, capital of the Eastern Roman Empire and cradle of the Orthodox faith. The **icons**, or devotional images, are painted in egg tempera on wooden panels and enhanced with gold leaf. The Byzantine tradition transplanted in Italy gave rise to a more natural style. The Sienese school, whose most influential master was Duccio di Buoninsegna (1255-1318), is particularly well represented in the collection. In the late 13C, Florentine artists, notably Giotto (c.1266-c.1337), developed a realistic rendering of space that ushered in the Italian Renaissance.

National Gallery of Art

The Alba Madonna by Raphael

Gradually, the strict iconography was replaced with secular portraiture and more sensual paintings that depicted biblical scenes. In the quattrocento (15C), Florentine artists like Fra Filippo Lippi and Botticelli looked to classical antiquity for its scientific notions of anatomy and perspective.

Madonna and Child	Giotto	c.1330
The Adoration of the Magi	Fra Angelico and Fra Filippo Lippi	c.1445
Ginevra de' Benci	Leonardo da Vinci	c.1474
Giuliano de' Medici	Botticelli	c.1478

Italian Sculpture and Furniture – *Galleries 2, 5, 8, 11, 25-27 (The Cabinet Galleries)* The marble, bronze, wood, porphyry, and painted terra-cotta sculpture (13-16C) displayed here closely follows the evolution in Italian painting: the earlier pieces depict religious themes, while in later works, portrait busts, particularly of prominent Florentines, begin to appear. The Italian Cabinet Galleries *(25-27)* were designed to evoke the interior of an Italian Renaissance palace or villa. They contain 40 items from the Gallery's permanent collection. A fresco cycle by Bernardino Luini (c.1480-1532), along with other small paintings, provides a lustrous backdrop for bronze statuettes, glassware and porcelain.

Lorenzo de' Medici	Verrocchio and Benintendi	c.1478/1521

16C Italian Painting – *Galleries 16-28.* The Renaissance that began in 15C Florence spread to northern Italy, in part through the works of Andrea Mantegna (1431-1506). His bold lines and sense of perspective influenced artists in Ferrara and Venice. Another very different innovation in Venetian art of the 15C came from Giorgione (c.1478-1510), whose delicate use of color gave this period its characteristic style. Giorgione's teacher, Giovanni Bellini (c.1427-1516), preferred the three-quarter portrait to the traditional Renaissance profile, thus allowing more expression of emotion and character. The High Renaissance of the early 16C, the cinquecento, attained an unparalleled level of delicacy and grace, enhanced by the manipulation of light and shadow as expressed in the art of such masters as Leonardo da Vinci (1452-1519) and Raphael (1483-1520). Titian (c.1490-1576), the prolific master whose outstanding talent was sought after by the leading European rulers of the day, dominated the 16C. Tintoretto (1518-94) carried innovations of his predecessors further with his own impressionistic, emotionally charged paintings. The allegorical representation of religious figures and classical gods and goddesses against a pastoral setting became the predominant subject of northern Italian art, with sensuality and color as its hallmarks.

The Small Cowper Madonna	Raphael	c.1505
The Alba Madonna	Raphael	c.1510
The Adoration of the Shepherds	Giorgione	c.1510
The Feast of the Gods	Bellini and Titian	c.1514/1529
The Conversion of Saint Paul	Tintoretto	c.1545
Doge Andrea Gritti	Titian	c.1548
Venus with a Mirror	Titian	c.1555

17-18C Italian Painting – *Galleries 29-34.* Marked by the creative vision of Annibale Carracci (1560-1609), 17C Bologna was the birthplace of the exuberant art of the Baroque, which had its greatest flowering in papal Rome. In the next century Giovanni Battista Tiepolo (1696-1770) refined the Baroque's expansiveness into a lighter and more decorative style *(Gallery 32).* Tiepolo's frescoes adorned ceilings throughout Europe, but his genius marked the end of Italian dominance in art. Thereafter, the main innovations in art came from new centers in northern Europe. Also popular in 18C Italy were detailed cityscapes and architectural representations, such as those of Canaletto and Panini, that reflected fashionable interests in the grand tour of Italian antiquities. Featured in gallery 36 are works by French artists Nicholas Poussin and Claude Lorrain, both of whom lived and painted in Rome.

River Landscape	Carracci	c.1590
The Porta Portello, Padua	Canaletto	c.1741
Wealth and Benefits of the Spanish Monarchy under Charles III	Tiepolo	c.1762

Spanish Painting – *Galleries 28, 29, 34 and 52.* Restraint characterizes the work of most Spanish artists during the 16C, with the notable exception of El Greco (1541-1614). Born on the island of Crete and trained in Venice, El Greco is nonetheless considered a Spanish artist, whose elongated shapes and religious fervor distinguish his unique style.

The preeminent 17C Spanish artist Diego Velázquez (1599-1660) obtained in his later works "impressionistic" effects of color and light that foreshadow 19C stylistic trends. A court painter, Velázquez was renowned for his portraits of the Spanish royal family.

In the 18C Francisco de Goya (1746-1828) *(gallery 52)* was Madrid's most fashionable portraitist. His early works reflect the lighthearted Rococo spirit of the period, while his more probing later portraits anticipate the psychological Expressionism of the 20C.

Gallery 38 is devoted to European sculpture and painting from the 14C and 15C.

Laocoön	El Greco	c.1614
The Needlewoman	Velázquez	c.1650
Two Women at a Window	Murillo	c.1660
Thérèse Louise de Sureda	Goya	c.1804

German Painting – *Galleries 35 and 35A.* Albrecht Dürer (1471-1528), the preeminent German artist of the late 15C and early 16C, has been called the "Leonardo of the North." Renowned throughout Europe, Dürer was recognized as a master printmaker as well as an outstanding painter. Dürer's contemporary Matthias Grünewald (c.1475-1528) was a matchless interpreter of religious intensity, while Lucas Cranach the Elder (1472-1553) was renowned for both his religious works and his portraits. Hans Holbein the Younger (c.1498-1543) relocated to England and became a court painter to King Henry VIII. The artist was admired for his ability to convey a sense of nobility in the royalty he painted.

The Small Crucifixion	Grünewald	c.1520
Portrait of a Clergyman	Dürer	1516
Edward VI as a Child	Holbein	c.1538

Netherlandish Painting – *Galleries 39-41A.* Present-day Belgium, Holland, Luxembourg and even portions of France composed the Netherlands at the end of the Middle Ages. The wealthy regions of the Low Countries were a magnet for talented painters. During the 15C Flanders, in what is now part of Belgium, was a leading artistic center, thanks largely to Jan van Eyck (c.1390-1441). A technical virtuoso, van Eyck mastered the representation of interior space and, more importantly, is credited with having revolutionized painting by employing oil, as opposed to tempera, as the medium. This innovation, which allowed more subtlety in brushwork, attracted artists from throughout Europe to Flanders, among them Hans Memling (d.1494), whose delicate and serene paintings enjoyed great popularity. Rogier van der Weyden (c.1400-64), another Netherlandish master, achieved a virtuosity of brushstroke that influenced generations. François Clouet (c.1522-72) descended from a family of Flemish painters who lived in France. A celebrated court painter, Clouet is credited with popularizing bathing portraits.

The Annunciation	van Eyck	c.1436
Portrait of a Lady	van der Weyden	c.1460
A Lady in her Bath	François Clouet	c.1571

Dutch and Flemish Painting – *Galleries 42-51. The Dutch and Flemish Cabinet galleries 50 A-C feature small paintings from the permanent collection as well as temporary exhibits.* The robust vitality of Peter Paul Rubens (1577-1640) dominates the 17C Flemish Baroque. An artist of great versatility, Rubens enjoyed international renown for his allegories and portraits. His student Anthony Van Dyck (1599-1641) became one of Europe's most celebrated portrait painters *(Galleries 42 and 43).*

Among the numerous painters of the varied styles and genres developed in 17C Holland, Rembrandt van Rijn (1606-69) stands out as the abiding genius of this time. His mastery of chiaroscuro—the subtle play of light and shadow—influenced art for two centuries. *The Mill,* considered one of Rembrandt's finest landscapes, profoundly affected the work of 19C British artists such as J.M.W. Turner *(gallery 57)* and Sir Joshua Reynolds *(galleries 58 and 59).* Rembrandt's deeply psychological approach to portraiture takes the inventiveness of a slightly earlier Dutch artist Frans Hals (c.1583-1666), a step farther. Employing lively brushwork, Hals had broken with the staid portraiture of the past to show his sitters with striking informality.

Daniel in the Lions' Den	Rubens	c.1615
Willem Coymans	Hals	1645
The Mill	Rembrandt	c.1650
Self-Portrait	Rembrandt	1659
Woman Holding a Balance	Vermeer	c.1664

Johannes Vermeer (1632-75), another Dutch genius, used light and space in such a way that his scenes of the upper middle classes are infused with an ethereal quality. The numerous still lifes, landscapes and genre paintings that were produced by Dutch artists in the 17C often had allegorical meaning underlying their apparent realism.

17 and 18C French Painting – *Galleries 36-37 and 53-56*. During the reign of Louis XIV, the French Academy controlled all aspects of cultural life, and traditions of classicism prevailed in art. The most noted proponent of classicism, Nicolas Poussin (1594-1665) *(gallery 36)*, worked much of his life in Italy yet strongly influenced French art. His works depict harmoniously composed subjects set against an Arcadian backdrop. Claude Lorrain (1600-82) *(gallery 36)*, who also worked in Rome, shared Poussin's love of landscape but gave it a nostalgic interpretation. Louis Le Nain (1593-1648) and his two brothers *(gallery 37)* concentrated on realistic genre paintings. By the early 18C, Paris had become the cultural hub of Europe, and the French Rococo style was the fashion. This florid style is best exemplified in the work of Antoine Watteau (1684-1721), who created whimsically poetic images that emphasize color and depict the sophisticated manners of 18C French society. Later, François Boucher (1703-70) introduced new sensuous pastoral reveries, while Boucher's student Jean-Honoré Fragonard (1732-1806) focused on French subjects, representing them in quick, colorful brushstrokes. Portraits by Elisabeth Vigée-Lebrun (1755-1842) *(gallery 56)*, painter and confidante to Marie Antoinette, reflect her close ties to aristocratic French society. Traditional classicism persisted, however, in the works of Jacques-Louis David (1748-1825) and Jean-Auguste-Dominique Ingres (1780-1867).

Italian Comedians	Watteau	c.1720
Madame Bergeret	Boucher	1746
A Young Girl Reading	Fragonard	c.1776

National Gallery of Art. Collection of Mr. and Mrs. John Hay Whitney; photo: Philip A. Charles

Marcelle Lender Dancing the Bolero in "Chilpéric" (1895-1896) by Henri de Toulouse-Lautrec

19C French Painting – *Galleries 80-93.* In the early 19C the French Academy sanctioned the classicism of David and Ingres, but artists such as Eugène Delacroix (1798-1863) and Jean-Baptiste-Camille Corot (1796-1875) rebelled against such conventions, painting romantic landscapes in their own idiom. Gustave Courbet (1819-77), Honoré Daumier (1808-79) and Edouard Manet (1832-83) discarded romanticism in favor of an unsentimental realism that depicted everyday scenes. A group of young painters inspired by Manet's example broke from the state-sponsored Salon exhibitions in 1874 to show their works independently. Known as the **Impressionists** because of their unprecedented exploration of atmospheric light and color in natural landscapes and figure painting, the group was informally led by Claude Monet (1840-1926) and Pierre-Auguste Renoir (1841-1919). Edgar Degas (1834-1917) and Henri de Toulouse-Lautrec (1864-1901) depicted contemporary Parisian nightlife. Paul Gauguin (1848-1903), Paul Cézanne (1839-1906) and Dutch-born Vincent van Gogh (1853-90) each developed a highly personal style of modern art. American-born Mary Cassatt (1844-1926), known for her compositional structures and her evocative depictions of women and children, painted in Paris and exhibited with the Impressionists.

Agostina	Corot	c.1866
The Artist's Father	Cézanne	1866
The Railway	Manet	1873
Woman with a Parasol-Madame Monet and Her Son	Monet	1875
A Girl with a Watering Can	Renoir	1876
La Mousmé	van Gogh	1888
Quadrille at the Moulin Rouge	Toulouse-Lautrec	1892
Fatata te Miti	Gauguin	1892
The Boating Party	Cassatt	c.1894
Four Dancers	Degas	c.1899

British Painting – *Galleries 57-59, and 61.* British painting first achieved a distinctive voice in the mid-18C with William Hogarth (1697-1764), whose works depicted the London middle classes. Later in the century Thomas Gainsborough (1727-88) created his softly romantic portraits of English nobility, while his rival Sir Joshua Reynolds (1723-92) adopted the formal grandeur of the Baroque in his portraiture.

In landscape painting the works of J.M.W. Turner (1775-1851), executed in swirls of colored light, are dramatically charged. The landscapes of his contemporary John Constable (1776-1837) are executed with scientific realism but convey a pastoral tranquillity. Both artists influenced the work of the French Impressionists.

A Scene from The Beggar's Opera	Hogarth	1729
Lady Caroline Howard	Reynolds	1778
Miss Juliana Willoughby	Romney	1783
Mrs. Richard Brinsley Sheridan	Gainsborough	1787
Wivenhoe Park, Essex	Constable	1816
Keelmen Heaving in Coals by Moonlight	Turner	1835

American Painting – *Galleries 60-60B, 62, 71.* Like British painting of the 18C and early 19C, American art focuses on portraiture in the grand manner. Eminent artists of this period include Benjamin West (1738-1820), Thomas Sully (1783-1872), Charles Willson Peale (1741-1827), John Singleton Copley (1738-1815) *(Gallery 60B)* and Gilbert Stuart (1755-1828) *(Gallery 60A)*, who was sometimes called the "court portraitist to the young Republic" because of his many paintings of early leaders.

Watson and the Shark	Copley	1778
The Skater	Stuart	1782
Benjamin and Eleanor Ridgely Laming	Peale	1788
Autumn-On the Hudson River	Cropsey	1860
The White Girl	Whistler	1862
Breezing Up	Homer	1876
Siegfried and the Rhine Maidens	Ryder	1891
Repose	Sargent	1911

Breezing Up (1873-1876) by Winslow Homer

By the mid-19C landscape painting emerged as the dominant force in American art, with painters such as Thomas Cole (1801-48) *(gallery 60)* and Frederic Edwin Church (1826-1900) depicting the awe-inspiring natural wonders of the New World. Highly personal expression, as evidenced in the works of Winslow Homer (1836-1910) and the mystical paintings of Albert Pinkham Ryder (1847-1917), followed later in the century. European influences are seen in the works of James McNeill Whistler (1834-1903), Thomas Eakins (1844-1916) and John Singer Sargent (1856-1925), all of whom either lived or studied abroad.
Galleries 72-79 are devoted to special exhibits.

Ground Floor

The ground-floor galleries will be partially closed until Fall 2002 for a large-scale renovation and reinstallation. Consult the Micro Gallery to verify the location of works mentioned below. The Museum Shop and Garden Café will remain open.

Sculpture and Decorative Arts – Small sculpture and medals in the collection date from the 15C to the early 18C. Marble busts and statuary, primarily French and Italian, date from the 17C and 18C. Works, mainly terra-cotta or marble, of 18C French sculptors such as Clodion and Houdon and 19-20C sculpture by Degas, Rodin, Maillol, Bartholdi, Jo Davidson, Paul Manship and other masters round out the collection. Of special interest are Degas' *Dressed Ballet Dancer* (colored plaster, modeled 1881) and Rodin's *The Thinker* (bronze, 1880). Other noteworthy works include miniature bronze busts by Honoré Daumier titled *The Deputies* and four small bronze animals (1962) by Italian sculptor Giacomo Manzù (1908-91).
Decorative arts in the collection include 15C and 16C Flemish and 18C French tapestries, as well as Italian Renaissance and 18C French Rococo furnishings. Small ecclesiastical artworks, such as enamels and stained glass, of the Middle Ages and Renaissance, include a 12C bejeweled chalice of sardonyx and silver gilt.

Prints, Drawings and Photographs – The National Gallery owns more than 65,000 American and European works on paper and vellum, the vast majority of which were acquired in the postwar period. The **Armand Hammer collection** of drawings spans five centuries and includes the works of Leonardo da Vinci, Michelangelo, Dürer, Manet, Degas and Cézanne. The **Alfred Stieglitz collection**, donated to the museum by Stieglitz's wife, the artist Georgia O'Keeffe, represents the single largest holding of the photographer's work.

■ Art Show Attendance

The National Gallery of Art's biggest blockbusters:

Year	Exhibit	Total Attendance
1998	**Van Gogh's Van Goghs**	480,496
1996	**Johannes Vermeer**	330,000
1985-86	**Treasure Houses of Britain**	990,474
1985-86	**Ansel Adams: Classic Images**	651,652
1981-82	**Rodin Rediscovered**	1,053,223
1976-77	**Treasures of Tutankhamen**	835,924
1974-75	**Archaeological Finds of China**	684,238

American Naïve Paintings – Culled from the Gallery's renowned collection of 18C and 19C folk art, these 50 paintings by "naïve" artists, so called for their lack of formal training, abound with talent and imagination. Bold colors, skewed perspective and discrepancies in scale characterize these works, which range from bucolic landscapes such as Edward Hick's *The Cornell Farm* (1848) to the eerie, stylized portraits of Erastus Salisbury Field (1805-1900).

EAST BUILDING

Generally considered Washington's most impressive example of modern architecture, the East Building (1978, I.M. Pei) houses the gallery's growing collection of 20C art, as well as a selection of small-format 19C French paintings.

Because works are shown on a rotating basis, not all artists mentioned will be represented at one time. Inquire at the ground-floor art information desk for current exhibits.

The Architecture – The massive marble **building**★★ by I. M. Pei stresses line and angle over adornment. Pei's task was threefold: to design a structure that would showcase modern art, to harmonize with the West Building and to be monumental enough to anchor the northeast corner of the Mall. Given a trapezoidal lot formed by the intersections of Pennsylvania Avenue and the National Mall with 3rd and 4th streets, Pei chose a trapezoid formed of two distinct triangles. The northern isosceles triangle houses gallery space; the southern right triangle contains administrative and research facilities. Polygonal towers top the points of the isosceles triangle; each tower rises 108ft high, one foot less than the height of the West Building. The structure's marble facing came from the same Tennessee quarries as that of the West Building.

The 4th Street **plaza**, which fronts the East Building and links it visually to the West Building, is dominated by seven glass tetrahedrons, three-sided shapes that also serve as skylights for the underground concourse connecting the buildings. A fountain flows down a *chadar*, or water slide, that is visible from inside the concourse.

The Art – The gallery's stated goal is to "present the great European and American movements and masters of the century rather than to speculate on new trends." Works are displayed in large, fluid spaces on each of the building's five floors. Represented in the collection are the works of such 20C artists as Wassily Kandinsky, Henri Matisse, Constantin Brancusi, Pablo Picasso, Georgia O'Keeffe, Georges Braque, Joan Miró, Anselm Kiefer, Alberto Giacometti, Mark Rothko and Arshile Gorky.

Visit *Visiting the Museum p 101.*

Henry Moore's monumental Knife Edge Mirror Two Piece, situated outside the main entrance, softens the building's exterior angles. A skylit atrium opens from the low-ceilinged lobby and is dominated by an immense red, blue and black mobile by Alexander Calder, specially commissioned for this space. Another commissioned work, a sculpture titled National Gallery Ledge Piece, by Anthony Caro, is displayed over the door to the administrative wing *(located near the escalator)*. Two intimate ground-floor galleries feature rotating exhibits of smaller works, including

East Building, Atrium

American art, as well as French paintings from the collections of Ailsa Mellon Bruce and Mr. and Mrs. Paul Mellon. Works by Degas, Bonnard, Renoir, Corot, Vuillard, Manet, Morisot and other masters line the walls of these smaller galleries.

Mezzanine galleries are generally devoted to large traveling exhibits from all time periods. Primarily reserved for European paintings and sculpture, including monumental works, the upper-level galleries feature 20C artists such as Dubuffet, Derain, Mondrian, Picabia, Picasso, Miró, Gris, Brancusi, Modigliani, Giacometti, Magritte, Soutine and Gorky. The intimate tower gallery exhibits the museum's collection of **paper cutouts** by Matisse *(may be viewed Mon–Sat 10am–2pm, Sun 11am–3pm)*. The concourse galleries showcase predominantly American late-20C art, including works by Barnett Newman, Clyfford Still, Robert Motherwell, Andy Warhol, Agnes Martin, Louise Bourgeois, Roy Lichtenstein and Ellsworth Kelly.

Sculpture Garden

Opened in 1999, this attractive garden displays works from the National Gallery's collection of 20C sculpture amid trees, flowerbeds, and twisting paths. Its central reflecting pool and fountain, whose surrounding benches were carved out of the same pink Tennessee marble as the East and West buildings, is used as an ice-skating rink in winter. In summer, the fountain's spray tempers the muggy weather. Besides providing a relaxing outdoor escape from museum crowds, the six-acre space presents a who's-who in contemporary sculpture: Louise Bourgeois, Claes Oldenburg and Coosje van Bruggen, Isamu Noguchi, and Roy Lichtenstein are just a few of the 20 or so artists with work on display.

National Archives seen from National Gallery of Art Sculpture Garden

NATIONAL ARCHIVES★★

Constitution Ave. between 7th and 9th Sts. NW.
Ⓜ Archives or Federal Triangle.

This imposing Classical Revival "temple" just off the Mall holds the nation's documentary treasures, including the Declaration of Independence, the Constitution and the Bill of Rights.

Historical Notes

A Strongbox for the Nation – Completed in 1937, the National Archives filled a pressing need for a central repository of official and historical records. Before this institution's establishment, each department of the federal government stored its own archival material. Important documents were frequently lost or damaged due to haphazard treatment. In 1921 a fire destroyed all of the 1890 census records. That loss, coupled with the Public Building Act of 1926, finally precipitated plans to construct a fireproof federal archives building. Today the National Archives and Records Administration, as it is officially designated, safeguards 5 billion paper documents, 9 million aerial photographs, 6 million still photographs and 300,000 video, film and sound recordings. The collection includes such varied items as letters from private individuals to US presidents, Commodore Matthew Perry's journals from his historic 19C mission to Japan, Civil War photographs by Mathew Brady and the photo albums of Hitler's mistress, Eva Braun.

The Building – The massive rectangular limestone building, designed by John Russell Pope to engender a sense of awe, occupies an entire city block. Corinthian colonnades embellish its four facades, and elaborate bas-relief pediments top the entrance porticoes on the north and south sides of the building.

Inside, a sweeping staircase leads visitors up to the entrance of the National Archives' **rotunda**. Popularly known as "the Shrine," the cavernous, 75ft-high, half-domed space with its coffered ceiling inspires reverence. Its centerpiece is an altarlike marble dais where the nation's most revered documents are permanently enshrined.

VISIT

The Rotunda – *The Rotunda will be closed for renovation until 2003. Enter from Constitution Ave. Open Apr–Labor Day daily 10am–9pm. Rest of the year daily 10am–5:30pm. Closed Dec 25. Guided tours (1hr 30min) available Mon–Fri 10:15am & 1:15pm; 3-week advance reservations required.* ♿ ▥ ☎ *202-501-5000. www.archives.gov.* On view are the country's esteemed documents known as the **Charters of Freedom★★★**: the **Declaration of Independence**, two pages of the **Constitution** (preamble page and signature page) and the **Bill of Rights**. Sealed in helium-filled cases that are covered with a green ultraviolet filter, the fragile parchments are lowered each night into a vault 20ft below the rotunda.

Two 34ft-long murals, painted in the 1930s by Barry Faulkner, adorn the walls on either side of the dais. The left mural, *The De-*

S. Brown/National Archives

Charters of Freedom

claration of Independence, is Faulkner's fictitious depiction of Thomas Jefferson presenting a draft of the Declaration to John Hancock, while the Continental Congress looks on. *The Constitution*, on the right, shows another imagined scene of James Madison offering the final document to George Washington at the Constitutional Convention. Displayed in a separate case is a 1297 version of England's **Magna Carta**, on indefinite loan to the National Archives from the Texas billionaire Ross Perot. A circular gallery *(access from the rotunda)* features changing exhibits from the permanent collection.

Research Facilities – *Enter from Pennsylvania Ave. Open year-round Mon–Fri 8:45am–5pm (Tue, Thu, Fri til 9pm), Sat 8:45am–4:45pm. Closed major holidays. Guided tours (1hr 30min) available Mon–Fri 10:15am & 1:15pm; 3-week advance reservations required. Photo ID required to enter facility. Children under 16 must be accompanied by an adult.* ✗ ♿ ☎ *202-501-5400.* The National Archives functions as a major source of historical material for researchers from the US and abroad. The ornately paneled **Central Research Room** *(2nd floor)* serves visitors engaged in scholarly research. Among the holdings are the papers of the Continental Congress, court and congressional records, historic correspondence and records of federal agencies deemed to be of "enduring value."

The **Microfilm Research Room** *(4th floor)* serves persons engaged in genealogical research. It contains such materials as census, military service and pension records and ship passenger arrival lists. A film, pamphlets and staff offer instruction on how to trace family histories.

As of 1978 certain presidential papers were declared federal property and came under archival jurisdiction. Most are housed in separate presidential libraries administered by the National Archives. The **Nixon Watergate tapes**, kept in an archives facility in College Park, Maryland, are accessible to the public *(shuttle buses to the facility leave from the Archives Mon–Sat on the hour 9am–4pm)*

NATIONAL MUSEUM
OF NATURAL HISTORY★★

Constitution Ave. at 10th St. NW.
Ⓜ Smithsonian
Plan p 114

The National Museum of Natural History, part of the Smithsonian Institution, ranks as one of the most visited museums in the world. Two floors of exhibits and two large-format cinemas explore life on earth through clues nature has left behind—among them dinosaur skeletons, prehistoric fossils and glittering gemstones, as well as artifacts of human cultures past and present.

Historical Notes

Soon after the completion of the Arts and Industries Building (1881), designed to complement the Castle and to house the exhibits from the 1876 Centennial Exposition, more space was needed to accommodate the rapidly expanding Smithsonian collections. In 1903 Congress authorized the construction of the Smithsonian's third building, today known as the National Museum of Natural History. Designed by Hornblower and Marshall in the Classical Revival style, the original four-story granite structure faced with a seven-column entrance portico was completed in 1910. Its octagonal rotunda is 80ft in diameter and rises to a height of 1241.5ft. The addition of the six-story east and west wings in 1963 and 1965 brought the building's footprint up to 16 acres. Today the museum encompasses 300,000sq ft of exhibition space and two large-format theaters, conserves more than 124 million specimens and provides laboratory facilities for 500 geologists, zoologists, botanists, anthropologists and paleontologists.

VISIT

Kids *Enter from the Mall (Madison Dr.). Open year-round daily 10am–5:30pm. Closed Dec 25. Guided tours available Mon–Fri 10:30am & 1:30pm.* ♿ ☎ *202-357-2700. www.mnh.si.edu. To select an itinerary best suited to your interests and schedule, start your visit in the first-floor rotunda. An information desk to the left of the mall entrance provides a free map and guide, and posts notices on guided tours and special events. At the rear of the hall is the box office for the IMAX and Immersion theaters. Both 2-D and 3-D movies are shown on the 60ft-by-60ft flat screen. In the Immersion Cinema, audience members can manipulate the onscreen action with their very own control panels. Tickets for either theater may be purchased up to two weeks in advance; to buy tickets or get information on prices and show times ☎ 202-633-7400 or 877-932-4629. The museum is undergoing long-term renovation. Some exhibits listed below may be temporarily relocated or not on view.*

Amenities – Lunch and snacks are served in the Atrium Cafe located on the ground floor (10am–5:15pm). The museum also maintains museum shops on the ground and second floors.

First Floor

The rotunda is dominated by a 13ft-tall **African bush elephant**, which weighed nearly 12 tons at its death in 1955 at the age of 50. Surrounding exhibits describe the sights and sounds of the savanna, home to creatures ranging from tiny, industrious dung beetles to giant elephants like this one.

Dinosaurs – Say hello to "Hatcher," the most recent resident of the collection. This new **triceratops** skeleton was made thanks to 3-D computer modeling technology, which allowed scientists to show the 65-to70-million-year-old dinosaur in a more natural pose than did the original mount. The skeleton was discovered in Wyoming by bone collector John Bell Hatcher in 1891 and nicknamed by the grade-school winner of a recent essay contest. Shown doing battle with **Tyrannosaurus Rex**, Hatcher is also kept company by a 90ft **Diplodocus skeleton**, a life-size model of a **pterosaur**, a **stegosaurus stenops** and four new casts of bone-headed dinosaurs, or **pachycephalosaurs**.

Fossil Galleries – Circling the Dinosaur Hall is a chain of galleries that describe the parade of life from the big bang 4.6 billion years ago through the Cenozoic era, which began 65 million years ago and extends through the present. Evidence for many of the theories presented here lies in the fossil record. Stone imprints of microorganisms and stubby shoreline plants chart the first four billion years on earth, after which emerged a wild panoply of animals. In the Fossil Mammals gallery, a re-created 5ft **eryops** skeleton from the Permian era, a 50-million-year-old rhinocerous-like **uintatheres** skeleton and a large array of Oligocene mammals, including a *mesohippus* (tiny horse), are on view. The giant sea turtle and the massive *mosasaur* are highlights in the **Life in the Ancient Seas** gallery.

Ice Age Mammals – A brief presentation of glacial history precedes this impressive display of fossilized mammal skeletons from the Pleistocene epoch, also known as the Ice Age. The woolly mammoth and the mastodon are both "cousins" of the elephant. The saber-toothed cat was recovered from Los Angeles' La Brea tar pits, where it met its sticky end along with more than one million other animals.

Mammals – *(The Mammals Hall is closed due to renovation. Expected date of completion: fall 2003.)* A trail of window cases and dioramas offers the visitor an overview of the mammal class in all its diversity. Along with more familiar animals, the exhibit includes specimens of such exotic creatures as the jaguar, kinkajou, jerboa, tapir, wallaby, Chinese civet, and dik-dik. Several dioramas illustrate habitats and survival mechanisms, such as food gathering, migration and defense strategies, that either led these mammals to their present stage of development or caused them to perish.

African Bush Elephant in the Rotunda

National Museum of Natural History, Smithsonian Institution

African Voices – This new, large-scale exhibit uses film clips, recorded narratives, poetry excerpts and music, along with 400 artifacts from the museum's permanent collection, to explore African history. Starting from the west entrance, a path leads through the millennia, as human life takes form, the Nile cultures rise and fall, and tribal cultures spread across the continent, producing a wealth of traditions and arts. An *aqal*, or a Somalian portable house, is on display, as is a stunning 8ft-tall antelope mask made of corn husks by the Chewa people of Malawi. Exhibits on more recent history tell African stories of survival and protest: the slave revolts of the 1800s; the 1960s independence movements in Congo, Nigeria, Senegal and Kenya; the successful fight against apartheid in South Africa; and the ongoing struggle against the AIDS epidemic.

Mighty Marlin – This small exhibit at the rear of the museum describes the fascinating, mighty and potentially very large marlin. Black marlin can swim at speeds of up to 70mph, weigh up to 1,560lbs and push their stomachs out of their mouths to expel indigestible items such as squid beaks and fish hooks. Once emptied, the stomach is then swallowed, apparently with no harm done to the fish.

Discovery Room – *Open year-round Tue–Fri noon–2:30pm, weekends 10:30am–3:30pm.* This hands-on educational exhibit offers visitors the opportunity to touch and examine various objects and artifacts (fossils, minerals, and animals both living and preserved) that are representative of those found in the museum.

Cultural Exhibits – Dioramas and murals in **Native Cultures of the Americas** depict the indigenous inhabitants of North and South America, from Point Barrow, Alaska, to Cape Horn and include a fine collection of North American Indian art objects. In the nearby halls are dioramas and display cases devoted to **Asian and Pacific Cultures**. They contain fishing and hunting equipment as well as masks and spears (Pacific Islands); Samurai armor, folk crafts and musical instruments (Japan); and contemporary Korean ceramics. Examples of calligraphy illustrate the Chinese writing system, which incorporates eight basic strokes into nearly 4,000 characters.

NATIONAL MUSEUM OF NATURAL HISTORY

SECOND FLOOR

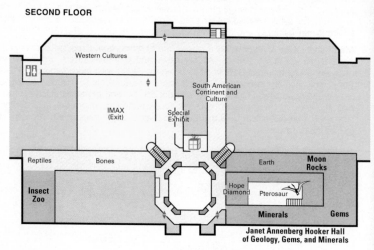

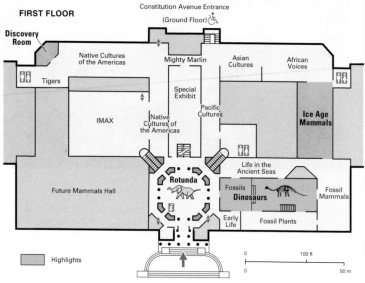

Second Floor

Geology Hall – The museum's most popular attraction is the fabulous **gem and mineral collection**★★★ housed in the Janet Annenberg Hooker Hall of Geology, Gems and Minerals. As visitors enter the exhibit, the largest blue diamond in the world at 45.5 carats, the legendary **Hope Diamond** celebrated for its exquisite color and clarity, draws immediate attention. The 330-carat **Star of Asia** sapphire from Sri Lanka and the 138.7-carat **Rosser Reeves Ruby** are among the finest in the collection. Set in a brooch containing 138 diamonds is the 75-carat **Hooker Emerald**. A display of the jewelry of royalty includes a flawless emerald necklace of 15C Spanish origin and a diadem studded with 950 diamonds given by Napoleon to Empress Marie-Louise at their wedding in 1810.

A flawless 127.88in Burma **quartz ball** and a headlight-size **golden topaz** from Brazil, the largest cut gemstone in the world at 22,892.5 carats, highlight the impressive array. **Diamonds** on view show a remarkable range of sizes and colors, from the 253.7-carat **Oppenheimer Diamond**, which is uncut and unpolished, to the 2.9-carat pink beauty from Tanzania. An extremely rare red diamond of 5.03 carats is one of only five publicly documented.

Large mineral samples as well as smaller interesting specimens are on view in many shapes, colors and consistencies. Smithsonite, or zinc carbonate, was first identified by James Smithson, founder of the Smithsonian. The State of California donated the large piece of neptunite, which resembles snow peppered with black crystals, as well as gold flakes from the Eureka mine. Minerals are largely grouped in families of increasing chemical complexity or arranged by their places of origin. Interactive displays offer insight into subjects ranging from mining to plate tectonics in the next two exhibits. Actual crystal pockets and ore veins are re-created in the **mine gallery**, and how earthquakes, mountain chains and volcanoes result from the movement of the earth's plates is illustrated in **plate tectonics**.

The exhibit continues with the **moon, meteorites and the solar system.** Moon rocks have contributed greatly to our understanding of the solar system and its origins. Samples in the collection were brought to earth by astronauts on four different *Apollo* flights *(Apollo 14-17)* and constitute the world's largest public display of lunar rocks. Also on view are pieces of more than 150 meteorites, including a fragment of the 4.6 billion-year-old Allende meteorite, one of the oldest mineral specimens ever found.

Insect Zoo – The arthropod group comprises 90 percent of animal life on earth. Many of the living and preserved insects in the O. Orkin Insect Zoo exemplify the adaptations that have enabled arthropods to survive for 475 million years. Most are contained in low cases, enabling children to see natural habitats as well as physical details. Video monitors installed on a re-created 18ft African termite mound show a colony of the tiny builders at work. A bustling ant farm forms a complete, small-scale society, and a buzzing beehive is equipped with an exit tube to the outdoors, allowing inhabitants to forage for food. *Tarantula feedings Tue–Fri 10:30am, 11:30am & 1:30pm; weekends & holidays times vary.*

Giant Squid – No one has ever seen a giant squid alive in its natural habitat, but museum scientist Clyde Roper has tried. The exhibit charts his search for *Architeuthis dux*, the world's largest invertebrate. This eight-armed, two-tentacled monster can measure up to 60ft in length and weigh up to one ton. Its eyes are thought to be about the size of human heads. By comparison, the 9ft specimen on view here, which washed ashore in Massachusetts, is a mere baby.

Other Exhibits – A series of dioramas in the **South American Continent and Culture** exhibit show the effects of diverse climactic conditions on the development of South American cultures. The remainder of the exhibit space is devoted to dioramas illustrating aspects of Western civilization and prehistoric North America, as well as to bones of mammals and reptiles.

NATIONAL MUSEUM
OF AMERICAN HISTORY★★

Constitution Ave. between 12th and 14th Sts. NW.
🅼 Federal Triangle or Smithsonian.
Plan p 117

The repository for such popular national icons as the Star-Spangled Banner, Archie Bunker's chair and various First Ladies' gowns, this unique museum captures the essence of America by presenting the objects and ideas that have figured prominently in the nation's material and social development.

Historical Notes

Totaling some 3 million objects, the museum's collection traces its origins to 1858, when the models from the US Patent Office were transferred to the Smithsonian Institution. Beginning in 1881, selections from this collection were exhibited in the Arts and Industries Building. To provide adequate space for the rapidly expanding collection of diverse artifacts illustrating America's scientific, cultural, political and technological achievements, the current marble structure was opened in 1964 as the National Museum of History and Technology. Renamed the National Museum of American History in 1980, this institution has in recent years committed itself to presenting issue-oriented exhibits that explore key events and social phenomena in American culture.

VISIT

🄺 *Enter the museum from Constitution Ave. Open year-round daily 10am–5:30pm. Closed Dec 25. Guided tours (1hr) available.* 🍴 ♿ ☎ *202-357-2700. http://americanhistory.si.edu. To see the popular "American Presidency" exhibit, obtain a free timed-entry pass immediately upon arrival at the museum, as time slots can fill up early. Passes are available at the 3rd-floor ticket booth, adjacent to the exhibit entrance, or in advance through Ticketmaster ☎ 800-551-7328. The museum is undergoing long-term renovation. Some sections may be temporarily relocated, and some exhibits mentioned below may not be on view. Call or check the web site for up-to-the-minute information. To check out the museum's cyber-displays log on to http://historywired.si.edu.*

115

Amenities – Take a break in the Palm Court *(first floor, opposite the Constitution Avenue entrance)*, with its late-19C decor. Lunch and snacks are served in the ice cream parlor to the rear *(11am–4pm)*. The museum also maintains a cafeteria *(lower level, West Wing)*, and museum shops on the lower level *(below the rotunda)* on the second floor *(Mall entrance)* and on the third floor *(outside the "American Presidency" exhibit entrance)*.

First Floor

The authentic **post office-general store** *(closed weekends)* situated to the left of the entrance was constructed in Headsville, West Virginia and transferred to the museum in 1971. Visitors can buy stamps and mail letters that will be canceled with a special museum postmark.

A Material World, the exhibit occupying the central gallery, explores the evolution of the materials used to produce everyday objects and their impact on American lifestyles over the last two centuries. The enlightening exhibit comprises numerous artifacts ranging from a 19C handcrafted wooden washing machine to Tupperware to an industrially designed aluminum and steel bicycle of recent vintage. On prominent display toward the East Wing is the *Swamp Rat XXX* **(1)**, a dragster whose remarkable aerodynamic qualities are attributed to the combination of synthetics and alloys used in its design. Note the 10ft-long section of test cable from the George Washington suspension bridge in New York City; the section alone weighs 34,000lbs.

East Wing – The galleries in this wing illustrate the extent to which agriculture, transportation and power machinery made the "good life" possible in America.
Resting on a section of an 1845 iron bridge from the Philadelphia and Reading Railroad, the **John Bull** (1831) is the nation's oldest operable steam locomotive. This type of locomotive replaced the likes of the buckboard, the Concord coach, and the riverboat, all of which were too slow and too labor-intensive to satisfy the demands put upon them. Farm implements on display reflect the importance of **Agriculture** throughout the nation's development. Around the turn of the 20C, the wooden plow, the cradle scythe and the Holt combine gave way to internal combustion tractors, which led to dramatic transformations in rural America. The advent of **"Old Red" (2)**, the International Harvester mechanical cotton picker, marked the end of the labor-intensive cotton industry and improved the lot of the average farmer by paving the way for modern large-scale farming. The 1913 Model T Ford **(3)**, displayed in **Road Transportation**, inevitably sent the horse-drawn wagon into retirement by ushering in the automobile age. Built between 1908 and 1927, some 15 million Model T cars set the American way of life into perpetual motion.

The **American Maritime Enterprise** retraces the evolution of sailing ships and offers a look at new forms of motive power—such as steam- and, later, gasoline-operated vessels—that navigated lakes, rivers and canals to move people and products from farm to market. One of nearly 7,000 such engines built between 1905 and 1930, the 280-

Facts about the Flag

(the Star-Spangled Banner on view on the second floor)

Size: 30ft by 34ft (originally 30ft by 42ft).

Design: Fifteen hand-sewn white cotton five-pointed stars (approximately 24in wide) on blue field of English wool bunting. 15 handsewn stripes (8 red, 7 white, approximately 24in wide) of wool bunting.

Weight: 40-50lbs (without backing).

Crafted by: Mrs. Mary Pickersgill of Baltimore.

Date: July-August 1813.

Features: The red V is of unknown origin and date. The irregular "fly edge" has resulted from the flag's snapping in the wind and from the cutting of pieces during the 1800s.

National Museum of American History, Smithsonian Institution

Star-Spangled Banner

NATIONAL MUSEUM OF AMERICAN HISTORY

THIRD FLOOR

SECOND FLOOR

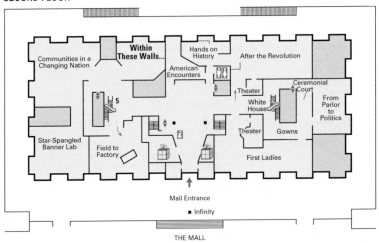

FIRST FLOOR

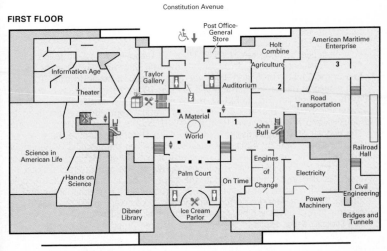

ton Pacific-type locomotive 1401 in the **Railroad Hall** was used by the Southern Railway between 1926 and 1951, when the age of steam came to its close. The large-scale model (1949) of the E-8 series diesel locomotive is representative of a later generation of motive power. The **Electricity** exhibit gives prominent coverage to Thomas Edison's inventions (his 1879 lightbulb is on display) and presents the new motors and engines that sparked the industrialization process. **Engines of Change: The American Industrial Revolution, 1790-1860** gives an overview of not only the machines but also the work habits and ideas that provided the impetus for the evolution from manual to industrial labor. Exhibits on bridge and tunnel construction, power machinery and timekeeping are also located in the East Wing.

West Wing – Just outside the entrance to the West Wing stand three unassuming glass cases that nonetheless contain some of the most popular artifacts in the museum: **TV objects** such as Mr. Rogers' zippered red cardigan, Archie Bunker's threadbare armchair and the Fonz's leather jacket. **Science in American Life** highlights the country's scientific history from 1876 to the present. On display are over 1,000 instruments and appliances, many of which reflect science's expanded influence on society. Completing the exhibit are interactive videos, a hands-on science center and a biotechnology unit where a DNA game introduces children to the origin of life.

The **Information Age** explores the history of information transfer and its effects on American economy and society. Telegraphs dating from the 1840s, Alexander Graham Bell's induction telephone (1876) and one of Thomas Edison's early lightbulbs (1883) can be seen here. The exhibit also traces the rapid development of computers and emphasizes the impact of these technologies, which expand the horizon while shrinking the world.

Second Floor

Opposite the National Mall entrance stands the exhibit **American Encounters**, which traces the mingled histories of American Indians, Hispanics and Anglo-Saxons in New Mexico. The only museum exhibit to deal specifically with the West, it tackles such thorny issues as the Christianization of natives by Catholic missionaries starting in the 1500s, the place of ceremony and rituals in modern life, and how tourism affects tribal cultures. The adjacent exhibit **Hands-on History** invites children ages five and up to participate in tactile activities involving museum objects and themes *(open Tue–Sun noon–3pm)*.

East Wing – The **Ceremonial Court** at the center of the East Wing replicates White House interiors as they appeared in the early 20C. Some authentic White House and presidential artifacts from different administrations have been incorporated in the period rooms. **First Ladies: Political Role and Public Image** profiles the lives of White House wives, chronicles the changing interpretations of the job (from hostess to political partner) and displays some of the inaugural gowns worn by them. The adjacent exhibit, **From Parlor to Politics**, shows how ordinary women changed history between 1890 and 1925 by fighting for better working conditions, bringing about the passage of child-labor laws, and securing women's right to vote. **After the Revolution** presents characteristic features of rural and urban life in the early days of the new Republic. Its sections illustrate the wide disparity among the lifestyles of a Virginia planter, a black slave, a Seneca Indian and a Philadelphia artisan.

West Wing – In the hallway leading to this wing stands a highly evocative piece of civil rights history: the turquoise Woolworth's **lunch counter** where in 1960 four African-American students sat and demanded to be served, despite the Jim Crow laws that segregated people by race in public accommodations. The action brought about six months of protests and a boycott of the Greensboro, North Carolina store that led to the counter's desegregation on July 25, 1960, and to similar demonstrations across the South.

Commissioned by Congress in 1832, Horatio Greenough's majestic **sculpture (5)** of George Washington looms at the end of the hall. Unfortunately, after its installation in the Capitol rotunda in 1841 the floor beneath it began to sink. The piece was moved to the Capitol gardens and then, in 1908, the sculpture was presented to the Smithsonian. **Field to Factory**, the exhibit to the left of the statue, is a dramatic chronicle of the African-American migration from the rural South to the industrialized North between 1915 and 1940, and its impact on American cities. The popular **Star-Spangled Banner★**, exhibit allows visitors to observe the enormous flag (originally 30ft by 42ft) that was "still there" on the morning of September 14, 1814, after an intensive British bombardment of Fort McHenry in Baltimore during the War of 1812. In British custody during the attack, Francis Scott Key saw this flag still waving through the haze of battle and penned the poem that was later set to music and, in 1931, proclaimed the national anthem of the United States of America. After conservation is complete in 2002, the flag will become part of a new exhibit, For Which It Stands. The adjacent exhibit **Communities in a Changing Nation** explores the evolution of three American communities during the 19C and their influence in shaping a national identity. Opened in 2001,

Within These Walls showcases the largest object in the museum's collection: a 240-year-old house from Ipswich, Massachusetts. Five families who once lived in the Georgian-style structure are profiled in the exhibit, which charts the course of history as it was experienced by ordinary working people.

Third Floor

This floor has a little something for everyone—ceramics, coins, musical instruments, military memorabilia, even a dollhouse—as well as the large new exhibit, **The American Presidency★**. *For the presidency exhibit, free timed-entry passes are available on day of visit at 3rd-floor ticket booth or in advance through Ticketmaster ☎ 800-551-7328. A free family guide* 🖼 *is also available.* Just outside the exhibit entrance, a colorful jumble of campaign buttons, hats, shirts, posters and novelties such as bubblegum, cigars, pipes and china, demonstrates the lengths to which presidential candidates will go to procure votes. Inside, 900 objects illustrate the winners' personalites: John Quincy Adams' chess set, Abe Lincoln's top hat, Warren Harding's silk pajamas, Teddy Roosevelt's chaps, and Bill Clinton's saxophone are some of the quirkier objects. Yet the star of this exhibit is the office itself, deemed by various holders "A Hell of a Job," "A Glorious Burden" and everything in between. A series of cases illustrating the history of money highlights the **Money and Medals** exhibit. The cases contain ancient coins (7C BC) from Asia Minor and some 15-16C Japanese gold and silver coins that were a gift to President Grant. In the Gold Room **(8)**, do not miss the $20 high-relief gold coin (1907), which was designed by Augustus Saint-Gaudens at the request of President Theodore Roosevelt. Only 11,000 were minted before the design was changed to low relief.

East Wing – The massive gunboat **Philadelphia (7)** is the oldest existing American gunboat. It sank while under the command of Benedict Arnold in 1776, the same year it was built. **A More Perfect Union** presents a case study of the American constitutional process by chronicling the Japanese-American internment experience during World War II. The artifacts, photographs and personal accounts attest to the US government's violation of the constitutional rights of some 120,000 American citizens of Japanese ancestry. The story of American servicemen and women, the development of military weapons and the evolution of fighting ships are presented in the **Armed Forces History** exhibit nearby. Memorabilia left at "the Wall" can be found at the display on the Vietnam Memorial.

West Wing – In the hallway between the East and West wings, a changing display of American textiles is on display, drawn from the museum's 50,000-piece collection of quilts, coverlets, looms and other sewing paraphernalia. Adjacent to it are several gigantic dollhouses. The **Popular Culture★** exhibit preserves in humble glass cases objects that have been immortalized by artists and athletes. These include the jersey worn by basketball legend Michael Jordan during the 1996-97 NBA Championships, the red-sequined shoes worn by Judy Garland in the 1939 classic *The Wizard of Oz*, Dizzy Gillespie's B-flat trumpet case and a baseball signed by Babe Ruth. **Printing and Graphic Arts** presents the history and technology of printing and printmaking. A noteworthy collection of presses and four period print shops includes the early-19C shop with the 1720 press **(6)** on which journeyman Benjamin Franklin may have worked in London. Jazz legend **Ella Fitzgerald**, "the first lady of song," is honored in a tribute that includes photographs, sheet music, concert posters, clothes and written remembrances surrounding a television showing performances and interviews.

Noteworthy collections of **musical instruments** and ceramics are also on display in the West Wing.

HIRSHHORN MUSEUM AND SCULPTURE GARDEN★★

Independence Ave. at 7th St. SW.
Ⓜ L'Enfant Plaza or Smithsonian.

An unmistakable architectural statement on the Mall, this cylindrical building houses one of the finest collections of modern art in the country. Its sculpture holdings, ranging from the realistic to the monumental and abstract, make up the world's most comprehensive collection of 20C works in that medium.

Historical Notes

The Benefactor – Born in Latvia on the eastern coast of the Baltic Sea, **Joseph Hirshhorn** (1899-1981) immigrated to Brooklyn with his widowed mother and 10 siblings when he was six years old. At age 13 he left school to help support his family, and at 18 he was a broker on Wall Street. He eventually became a wealthy financier and uranium magnate.

Hirshhorn traced his first interest in art to a series of paintings by Salon masters he saw reproduced in an insurance calendar. His early collecting followed in that vein, but by the late 1930s his tastes had turned to the works of French Impressionists and post-Impressionists. That interest also passed, as he increasingly focused his collecting on contemporary American and European painting and on modern sculpture from around the world.

In 1962, with the first major public exhibition of his art treasures at the Solomon R. Guggenheim Museum in New York City, his collection drew international attention. Representatives from several foreign countries approached Hirshhorn, offering to establish museums for the collection in their respective countries. However, in the mid-1960s, President Johnson and Smithsonian secretary S. Dillon Ripley convinced Hirshhorn to donate his collection to the Smithsonian. In 1966 Congress established the Hirshhorn Museum and Sculpture Garden, to which the benefactor contributed more than 6,000 works. He continued to be an avid collector until his death in 1981. At that time, he bequeathed another 6,000 works to the museum.

Lee Stalsworth/Hirshhorn Museum and Sculpture Garden/Smithsonian Institution

The Burghers of Calais (1953-1959) by Auguste Rodin

A "Doughnut" on the Mall – Almost every new addition to the Mall has met with a certain degree of controversy, but the so-called "doughnut" by architect **Gordon Bunshaft** incited harsh criticism, since it was the first unabashedly modern building erected on the prestigious national showplace. Dillon Ripley said of Bunshaft's design, "If it were not controversial in almost every way, it would hardly qualify as a place to house contemporary art." Elevated on four piers, the drum-shaped, unadorned concrete building wraps around a fountain plaza that extends beneath the raised building, serving almost as a first floor. Gallery windows along the interior circumference overlook the plaza.

The Collection – Some 5,000 paintings, 3,000 pieces of sculpture and mixed media and 4,000 works on paper compose the collection, roughly five percent of which is on view at any one time. The core collection is continually being refined and updated by an active acquisition program.

VISIT

Open year-round daily 10am–5:30pm. Closed Dec 25. Guided tours (45min) avail-able Mon–Fri 10:30am & noon, weekends noon & 2pm. Sculpture garden tours May–Oct daily 12:15pm. ⚓ (outdoors, summer only) ♿ ☎ 202-357-2700. www.hirshhorn.si.edu.

Paintings – The paintings in the collection are organized chronologically, begin-ning with early-20C American works on the third floor. Among the artists featured here are such renowned painters as George Bellows and John Sloan, adherents of the Ashcan school; and prominent 20C artists Edward Hopper, Marsden Hartley, Max Weber, Stuart Davis and Georgia O'Keeffe, among others. The third-floor gal-leries devoted to European and American modernism feature paintings and three-dimensional works by Constantin Brancusi, Alberto Giacometti, Jean Arp, Joan Miró, Isamu Noguchi, Jean Dubuffet, Francis Bacon, Willem de Kooning, Mark Rothko, and Richard Diebenkorn and others.

Also on this floor is a gallery titled **Directions**, devoted to rotating exhibits that high-light the work of emerging contemporary artists.

The second-floor galleries are reserved for major special exhibits and a variety of small, changing exhibits of art from the permanent collection.

Contemporary art is housed on the underground level. Featured are works by pro-ponents of Pop Art (Jasper Johns, Robert Rauschenberg, Andy Warhol and others), and representative works of more recent tendencies by a rotating group of artists, including Bruce Nauman, Anselm Kiefer and Damien Hirst.

Sculpture Ambulatories – On the second and third floors, continuous galleries fol-lowing the interior circumference of the building feature small sculptural works. The display begins on the second floor with such 19C European artists as Maillol, Rodin, Degas and Renoir. The Hirshhorn's collection of sculptures by **Henri Matisse** is particularly rich. The third-floor ambulatory is devoted to 20C sculpture by such masters as Pablo Picasso, Alberto Giacometti and Alexander Archipenko. The Hirshhorn possesses one of the country's most extensive collections of **Henry Moore** (1898-1986), with some 60 sculptures and 20 works on paper that represent the entire career of the celebrated British sculptor.

Outdoor Sculpture – The **plaza** on which the building stands is a showplace for monumental contemporary sculpture, including works by Alexander Calder, Claes Oldenburg, Tony Cragg and Juan Muñoz.

Smaller figurative works are featured in the sunken and walled **Sculpture Garden** *(across Jefferson Dr.)*. Prominent among these are the works of Rodin, including his monumental *Burghers of Calais*, and Maillol. Also on display are sculptures by Gaston Lachaise and Henry Moore, as well as a series of rare relief plaques by Matisse *(Backs)*.

SMITHSONIAN QUADRANGLE★

Independence Ave. between 9th and 12th Sts. SW.
Ⓜ Smithsonian or L'Enfant Plaza.

Topped by a street-level garden, this handsome underground complex occupies a prime site in the shadow of the venerable Castle building. Opened in September 1987, the quadrangle comprises two Smithsonian museums—the National Museum of African Art and the Arthur M. Sackler Gallery—and an education center, the S. Dillon Ripley Center.

Historical Notes

The Smithsonian Quadrangle is the brainchild of S. Dillon Ripley, secretary of the Smithsonian from 1964 to 1984. During his tenure the noted collector Dr. Arthur M. Sackler pledged a significant portion of his Asian and Near Eastern artifacts to the Smithsonian, but the institution lacked a suitable space for their display. Ripley also faced the problem of finding a larger facility for the Museum of African Art, which had outgrown its cramped quarters in a row of Capitol Hill town houses. Appreciating the institution's need to enlarge its focus to international fields of research and to house the two art collections, Ripley spearheaded a major development program for an "international center of advanced study." Ripley's project neatly addressed these needs while bringing a more international flavor to the cultural offerings on the Mall. In October 1982 Congress appropriated $36.5 million (approximately half of the total cost) for the project. In the following year, construction of the complex began on the quadrangular site bordered by the Castle, the Freer Gallery, the Arts and Industries Building and Independence Avenue.

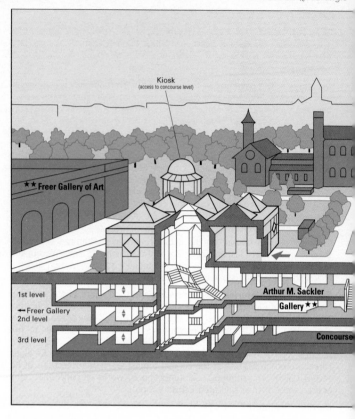

Kiosk
(access to concourse level)

★★ Freer Gallery of Art

1st level

← Freer Gallery
2nd level

3rd level

Arthur M. Sackler

Gallery ★★

Concourse

VISIT

Enid A. Haupt Garden – *Open year-round daily 7am. Closing times are deter-mined seasonally. Closed Dec 25. Guided tours available mid-Apr–Sept.* ♿ ☎ *202-357-2700. www.si.edu.* This 4-acre garden, named after its New York benefactor, is a peaceful, contemplative haven replete with antique benches, urn planters, walkways and 19C-style lampposts. The centerpiece of the garden is the ornamental parterre, adorned in 19C fashion with changing seasonal plantings. The iron and red sandstone gate opening onto Independence Avenue is based on designs by James Renwick, architect of the Castle.

On either side of the gate stand attractive entrance pavilions that lead to the two underground museums. Though similarly proportioned, these structures are adorned with motifs intended to create a visual link with the surrounding land-marks: The pyramidal roof and diamond shapes of the Sackler pavilion echo the lines of the Arts and Industries Building, while the domes and rounded arches of the Museum of African Art pavilion complement the exterior of the Freer Gallery. Behind the Sackler Gallery entrance pavilion is an intimate garden with a circle-in-square fountain, based on the Temple of Heaven in Beijing, and two 9ft pink granite "moon gates." Adjacent to the Museum of African Art pavilion is a series of fountains and canals terminating in a *chadar*, or water wall, inspired by the Alhambra gardens in Granada, Spain.

Concourse – *3rd underground level; accessible through the street-level kiosk situated between the Freer Gallery and the Castle. Open year-round daily 10am–5:30pm. Closed Dec 25.* ☎ *202-357-2700. www.si.edu.* Visitors enter the glass-enclosed kiosk and descend one floor down a circular staircase, flooded with streams of light from above. An escalator ride completes the descent to the third level Ripley Center, where a passageway leads to an open concourse complete with trees and a fountain. A trompe-l'œil mural by Richard Haas dominates the eastern wall. Classrooms and offices, which include the Smithsonian Institution Traveling Exhibition Service and the Smithsonian Associates, line both sides of this broad, airy concourse.

Museums – The showpieces of the Smithsonian Gardens complex are the National Museum of African Art and the Arthur M. Sackler Gallery. The two museums, which are administered separately, each feature approximately 20,000sq ft of exhibit space situated principally on the first and second underground levels. Upon entering the naturally lit entrance pavilions, from which the descent to the museums begins, the visitor can appreciate the fine building materials, the elegant detailing and the fluid interior space, all of which greatly enhance the display of the exquisite objects within.

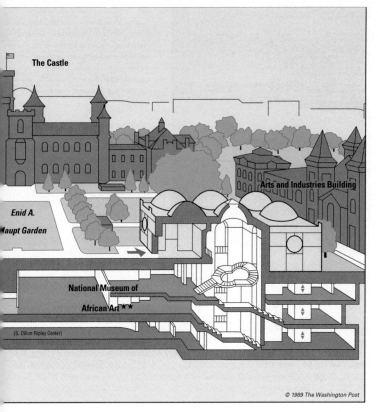

The Castle

Arts and Industries Building

Enid A.
Haupt Garden

National Museum of
African Art★★

(S. Dillon Ripley Center)

© 1989 The Washington Post

NATIONAL MUSEUM OF AFRICAN ART★★

The Smithsonian Quadrangle at 950 Independence Ave. SW.
Ⓜ Smithsonian or L'Enfant Plaza.

Originally located in a row of Capitol Hill town houses, the National Museum of African Art today occupies more spacious quarters in the underground Smithsonian Gardens complex. Devoted to the research, acquisition and display of traditional African arts, especially those of the sub-Saharan regions, the museum possesses a permanent collection of over 7,000 items.

Only a small selection of this expanding collection is exhibited at any particular time. Pieces in bronze, copper, wood, ivory and fiber are exhibited on a rotating basis. The sculptures, utilitarian objects, architectural elements, decorative arts and textiles on display are organized by regions, thereby emphasizing how geography determines the selection of materials, as well as form and style.

To complement the museum's permanent collection, temporary exhibits of African art are arranged from private and public collections in the US and in other countries.

VISIT

Open year-round daily 10am–5:30pm. Closed Dec 25. Guided tours available. ♿
☏ 202-357-4600. www.si.edu. Obtain a floor plan from the information desk. Check the wall boxes in some of the galleries for brochures on exhibits. The following is a description of highlights of the permanent collection, selections of which are displayed in five of the level-one galleries:

■ Notes on African Art

Given the pervasive role of religion in African culture, most objects created for utilitarian, economic, aesthetic or ritual purposes bear religious significance. Unlike most cultures throughout the world, which keep written documents, many African cultures rely on sculptured works and other artifacts to pass down values and beliefs from generation to generation. These objects are generally infused with symbolic meanings. An enlarged head, for example, is a symbol of power and wisdom.

Mask (Pwo), Chokwe Peoples, Zaire

Franko Khoury/National Museum of African Art, Smithsonian Institution

The museum's collection of **Royal Benin Art** from the historic West African kingdom of Benin (present-day Nigeria) includes several cast-copper alloy sculptures on permanent display. The ceremonial figures, heads, pendants and plaques were created between the 15C and 19C and reveal the elaborate rituals and ornate regalia of the Benin *oba* (king) and his entourage. Note especially the figure of an *oba* (19C); his regalia symbolizes his role as a divine ruler. A 16-17C carved ivory spoon, produced specifically for export, illustrates foreign influences on the style of Benin art.

Objects on display evidence the tremendous variety of shapes, proportions and designs present in African sculpture. Among the fine pieces that may be on display are initiation masks, woman-and-child figures created as icons of human perfection and fertility, and reliquary guardian figures. The permanent collection also includes a number of **ritual objects** that are believed to be conduits of communication with spirits. Medicinal figurines, arranged in a Chokwe fiber divination basket, play a significant role in the healing process. Finely sculpted Sherbo Bullom stone figures, like those owned by the museum, are still used by the Mende people of the Guinea coast to assure a good harvest. An Igala shrine figure was part of an altar created as an intermediary space between the spiritual and physical worlds.

ARTHUR M. SACKLER GALLERY★★

The Smithsonian Quadrangle at 1050 Independence Ave. SW.
Ⓜ Smithsonian or L'Enfant Plaza.

The Sackler Gallery is dedicated to the study and exhibition of the arts of Asia from the Neolithic period to the present. Major strengths of the expanding collection are Chinese jades and bronzes, ancient Near Eastern gold and silverwork and a collection of 11-19C Islamic manuscripts. Selections from the permanent collection are complemented by international loan exhibits offering a comprehensive study of the breadth and beauty of Asian art and culture.

An underground gallery links the Sackler to the adjacent Freer Gallery, with which it is associated.

Historical Notes – The core of the museum's holdings was donated by **Dr. Arthur M. Sackler** (1913-87), the New York psychiatrist, medical researcher and publisher, who donated 1,000 objects from his personal collection to the Smithsonian Institution in 1982. Sackler began acquiring Asian art in the 1950s to supplement his already extensive collection of Western art. The avid collector was the principal benefactor of Harvard University's Arthur M. Sackler Museum, and he contributed generously to the Eastern art holdings of the Metropolitan Museum of Art *(THE GREEN GUIDE New York City)*. Since its inception, the gallery has sought to expand the core collection donated by Sackler.

VISIT

Open year-round daily 10am–5:30pm. Closed Dec 25. Guided tours available. ♿
☎ *202-357-2700, www.asia.si.edu.*

Highlights of the Chinese Collections – Ancient Chinese culture placed particular importance on tradition: Laws and customs were passed through the generations, and ancestor worship was a common practice, which explains in part the presence of ancestor figures in the decoration of ritual bronzes and jades. The economy was largely agricultural, and the attributes of nature became a powerful force in ancient Chinese religion. Clouds, rain, wind and stars appear frequently as symbolic ornamentation on vessels and objects, which the Chinese used presumably to deflect evil spirits and to invoke the protection of particular deities.

Jade Collection – The mountains of the Chinese provinces contained rich veins of nephrite jade, a gemstone so prized by the Chinese that they associate it with the five cardinal virtues of charity, modesty, courage, justice and wisdom. The Sackler's jade collection of more than 450 decorated objects dates from about 3000 BC. Artifacts from the Neolithic period include ax blades (c.3000 BC) produced in most cases as ceremonial burial objects. The jades of the Shang dynasty (1700 BC) were ornamental and used for ceremonial functions. Many of the Shang images and forms reappear in art of later periods.

Chinese Bronzes – The gallery's bronzes date from the Shang through the Han dynasties (1700 BC-AD 220). Many of these objects are generously inscribed, providing a wealth of information about this period, which has long remained obscure to historians.

Ancient Near Eastern Gold and Silver – The civilizations that developed in ancient Iran, Anatolia (present-day Turkey) and the region around the Caucasus Mountains are credited with introducing metalwork as early as 7000 BC. Over the ensuing millennia the craftspeople of these regions produced exquisite objects in copper, silver, gold and lead, employing a wide range of metallurgical techniques. Many of the gold and silver vessels and ornaments in the Sackler collection are gilded or inlaid with niello (an enamel-like alloy) and date from 3000 BC to 8C AD. These objects, which were used principally for ceremonial occasions, offer glimpses of often sumptuous court life in the nations that developed in the Tigris-Euphrates Valley.

FREER GALLERY OF ART★★

Jefferson Dr. at 12th St. SW.
Ⓜ Smithsonian.

The Smithsonian's first museum on the Mall devoted exclusively to art, the Freer Gallery possesses an outstanding Asian collection and one of the world's largest collections of works by James McNeill Whistler (1834-1903).

Historical Notes

The Connoisseur – A successful railroad car manufacturer, Charles L. Freer (1854-1919) became, like Arthur Sackler, a keen collector of Asian art. From his first purchase in 1887 of a Japanese fan, he gradually amassed thousands of objects, many of which were acquired during his trips to Japan, India and China. In 1887 he also bought several Whistler prints, his initial acquisition of works by the artist who would become his good friend. Retiring at age 45, Freer became a full-time collector and world traveler, expanding both his Asian and American holdings. In 1904 he revealed plans to bequeath a significant portion of his collections to the Smithsonian Institution and to finance the construction of a building to house the art. At his death his bequest totaled some 9,000 works. Today the museum's Asian properties have grown to over 27,000 works (Freer stipulated that his American collection not be expanded).

The Building – After the announcement of his proposed gift, Freer embarked on a search for a suitable building design, visiting American and European museums to gather ideas as to gallery size, ventilation and lighting. In 1912 he hired New York architect Charles A. Platt, who employed Neoclassical symmetry in the marble and granite Renaissance-style structure that is built, as Freer had specified, around a central courtyard. The building's two entrances on Jefferson Drive and Independence Avenue are distinguished by triple arches. The arch motif is repeated in the bronze-framed Palladian windows and glass doors surrounding the 60sq ft fountained courtyard, which is faced with white Tennessee marble. The stone balustrade of the exterior parapet appears again above the courtyard's arches. The museum was officially opened in 1923. After extensive renovation, begun in 1988, the museum reopened in 1993 with 19 galleries on the first level and study rooms, an auditorium, a conference room and a gallery shop on the lower levels. An underground exhibition gallery permits passage between the Freer and the Sackler Gallery.

VISIT

Open year-round daily 10am–5:30pm. Closed Dec 25. Guided tours available. ♿
☎ *202-357-2700. www.asia.si.edu. A floor plan can be obtained from the information desk.*

Asian Collection – Highlights of the Chinese holdings include ornamental implements of the emperors of the Ming (1368-1644) and Qing (1644-1911) dynasties; 15C blue and white porcelain bowls from the imperial workshop in Jingdezhen in southeast China; and bronzes, jades and lacquerware from the Ancient Chinese collection, which dates from 3500 BC to the first century AD. Traditional Japanese

painting and calligraphy can be seen on hanging scrolls (ink and color on silk or paper); 15-19C *byobu*, or folding screens; late-16-19C porcelain pieces and lacquered wooden boxes; and 13-17C stone and earthenware tea bowls. Korean ceramics from the 10C to the 14C, Indian 16-19C court paintings and Islamic manuscripts are showcased in separate galleries.

American Collection – Paintings by prominent American artists include Whistler's *Caprice in Purple and Gold: The Golden Screen* (1864) and John Singer Sargent's *Breakfast in the Loggia* (1910). Of special interest are Whistler's "Notes," miniature oils depicting Chelsea shops and English landscapes c.1882, and "Nocturnes," dramatic paintings of the Thames River at night, inspired by Japanese prints. Full of light and grace are his "Six Projects" of the late 1860s—varied compositions of figures against the backdrop of the sea *(All six paintings may not be on view)*. Oil portraits and landscapes by Abbott Hen Thayer, Thomas Dewing's paintings of women in fields and Dwight Tryon's large oil and pastel landscapes adorn other galleries devoted to the American collection.

Glazed Stoneware,
Southern Song Dynasty,
China 12C

Permanently installed in Gallery 12 is the **Peacock Room★**, Whistler's only extant interior design (1876-77). Freer purchased the room in 1904 from a London art dealer; prior to the museum's opening, it was transferred from his Detroit home to the premises. Asked by English shipping tycoon Frederick Leyland to redecorate portions of his 20ft-by-32ft London dining room, the artist began what evolved into a major (ostensibly unauthorized) overhaul. The result was a highly original, gilded setting for Leyland's blue and white Chinese porcelain collection. Intricate paintings of golden peacocks and peacock motifs embellish the walls, shutters and ceiling. Dominating the mantel is Whistler's painting *The Princess from the Land of Porcelain*, which Leyland had purchased. In the mural depicting two fighting peacocks *(south wall)*, the artist immortalized his dispute with Leyland over payment for his interior work. The porcelain pieces on view are similar to those in Leyland's collection and were acquired for the room's 1993 restoration.

Harmony in Blue and Gold: The Peacock Room by James McNeill Whistler

US HOLOCAUST MEMORIAL MUSEUM★★

South of Independence Ave. between 14th St. and Raoul Wallenberg Pl. SW.
Ⓜ Smithsonian.

A deeply moving, wholly absorbing history lesson awaits visitors to this large museum-research complex, conceived "to commemorate the dead and to educate the living." Occupying nearly 2 acres of land adjacent to the Bureau of Engraving and Printing, just off the Mall, the striking edifice houses a compelling permanent exhibit that focuses on the Nazi extermination of millions of Jews and others during World War II.

Historical Notes

The Museum Takes Shape – In 1980 Congress chartered the United States Holocaust Memorial Council—the museum's governing body—and the federal government donated a museum site just south of the Washington Monument. Soon thereafter, the council began extensive fund-raising and international artifacts-collecting efforts. In 1986 the New York firm of I.M. Pei & Partners was chosen, with James Freed as principal architect, to design an appropriate structure. Construction commenced on the $90 million building project in the spring of 1989, and the museum formally opened in April 1993.

An Unconventional Building – Given the museum's highly charged subject matter, the challenge to design a suitable structure, able to match its powerful message with dignity and sensitivity, was immense. The main five-story brick and limestone building is a post-Modern "penitentiary," with its series of "watchtowers" lining the north and south walls. The exposed metal beams, railings and metal-framed glass doors of the building's 7,500sq ft glass-roofed central atrium, the **Hall of Witness**, amplify the feeling of imprisonment. The contrasting hexagonal, 6,000sq ft beige limestone annex *(located on the west side)* houses, on the second floor, the 60ft high **Hall of Remembrance**, an unadorned, natural-light-filled space provided for quiet contemplation and commemorative ceremonies. Four nonrepresentational works by prominent artists were commissioned for the museum: Wall art by Ellsworth Kelly and Sol LeWitt graces transition rooms between the floors of the permanent exhibit; Richard Serra's steel monolith anchors the atrium's lower staircase; and Joel Shapiro's monumental sculpture fronts the west entrance. The 250,000sq ft complex also contains an auditorium, a theater, museum shop, education center and learning center as well as temporary exhibit space.

Hall of Witness

© Mark Wieland Photography

VISIT

Open year-round daily 10am–5:30pm. Closed Yom Kippur & Dec 25. Timed passes, available at the box office, may be required for the permanent exhibit; advance passes obtainable from Tickets.com (☎ 800-400-9373) carry a service charge. ✗ ♿ ☎ 202-488-0400. www.ushmm.org.

In lieu of the permanent exhibit, a special exhibit entitled "Daniel's Story: Remember the Children" is available for young visitors. The permanent exhibit covers three floors. Visitors take an elevator to the 4th floor and then walk down to the 2nd floor.

Before entering the elevator, visitors are given a keepsake photo identification card containing the background and fate of a Holocaust victim.

In the darkened surroundings of the fourth floor, visitors are confronted with photographs, archival films and artifacts in the exhibit entitled "Nazi Assault 1933-1939." Informative panels begin the tragic story of the calculated deprivation of the property, human rights, dignity and eventually the lives of nearly six million European Jews, and some five million others, including three million Soviet POWs, as well as Slavs (Czechs, Poles and Russians), Gypsies, communists, homosexuals, Jehovah's Witnesses and people with disabilities. The exhibit is augmented by documentaries, newspaper headlines, vintage newsreels, documents, letters and architectural casts. Two small theaters offer continuous showings of films on anti-Semitism *(14min)* and on the Nazi regime's rise to power *(13min)*.

Ghetto and concentration camp life is evoked on the third floor in "Final Solution: 1940-1944." Personal articles, food bowls and work implements are interspersed with an actual railcar, which visitors can walk through, and a scale model of a gas chamber. Especially sensitive topics are presented discreetly, for optional viewing, by way of sunken video monitors surrounded by chest-high walls. In "Voices of Auschwitz" visitors can listen in a glass-paneled sitting area to survivors' stories. In "Aftermath 1945 to the Present" on the final floor of the permanent exhibit, the valor and success of various rescue and resistance efforts are hailed. Here, resistance fighters' weapons and hundreds of photos of rescuers, prison martyrs and survivors are on view, as are photos of "death" marches. Shown continuously is film footage recording the liberating armies' arrival at the camps, and the Nuremburg trials. A display is devoted to **Raoul Wallenberg**, the Swedish diplomat stationed in Budapest who led the War Refuge Board's mission to save Hungarian Jews. Near the exit a small, open theater presents recently filmed interviews with Holocaust survivors.

BUREAU OF ENGRAVING AND PRINTING★

14th and C Sts. SW.
Ⓜ Smithsonian.

This nondescript 20C building at the foot of the 14th Street Bridge calls itself, justifiably, "the nation's money factory." Here, paper currency, postage stamps and many of the official documents issued by the US government are produced.

Historical Notes

Early Exchange – The most widely circulated currency during the colonial period was the Spanish *peso de 8 reales*, or "piece of eight." During the Revolution the hoarding of reales and other coins led to a shortage and consequently to the Continental Congress' issue of its own currency. Backed by no reserves, this currency gave rise to the expression "not worth a Continental." Under the Articles of Confederation enacted after the war, the dollar was adopted as the unit of currency, but paper money was not issued until 1861 when non-interest bearing "demand notes" were first issued by the United States government as an emergency measure to help pay the costs of the Civil War. Gradually, more issues of paper currency became necessary until a national currency system was established. These first issues of paper money led to the eventual growth and establishment of the Bureau of Engraving and Printing.

Growth of the Bureau – Functioning as a division within the Treasury Department, the Bureau initially consisted of four women and two men who, working in the basement of the Treasury Building, sealed and separated notes printed by private companies. After a year the bureau began printing some notes on its own, and by 1878 it was responsible for all currency printing. The green ink, chosen for one side of these bills because of its resistance to physical and chemical change, earned the notes the name "greenbacks."

The bureau's expanding operations warranted more space; in 1880 it moved into its own building at the corner of Independence Avenue and 14th Street. Known as the Auditor's Building, the brick structure, crowned by a slim tower, is now part of the Department of Agriculture. In 1914 the Bureau moved to its current building, slightly south on 14th Street, and in 1938 the annex building was constructed across 14th Street. Engraving facilities are now housed in the annex *(not open to the public)*. The total floor space of bureau operations encompasses 30 acres. In addition to bills and postage stamps, these facilities also produce Executive and Treasury seals, official engravings of presidents and governmental buildings, presidential invitations and military certificates.

Currency Confections

The Bureau of Engraving and Printing produces 37 million notes a day with a face value of approximately $696 million. About 95 percent of the bills are intended as replacement for worn-out currency already in circulation. A dollar bill, for example, has a life span of 22 months, while a $100 note lasts approximately 9 years. The Federal Reserve Board regulates the number of bills to be printed and their denominations. Typically, half of the bureau's production is devoted to manufacturing $1 bills, 20 percent to $20s, 12 percent each to $5 and $10 bills and 2 percent each to $50 and $100 notes. The $100 bill is the largest denomination produced since 1947. The cost to manufacture each bill is approximately 4 cents.

VISIT

Open year-round Mon–Fri 9am–2pm (visitor center 8:30am–3:30pm). Closed major holidays. Same–day free tickets available from the kiosk (open 8am) on the bureau's west side (R. Wallenberg Pl.) are required. It is advisable to pick up tickets before 11:30am during peak season. Congressional visits available (p 255). ♿ 〰〰〰
☎ *202-874-3188. www.moneyfactory.com.*

The entrance hall contains displays and a film *(15min)* on the history of currency and US paper-money production. The remainder of the self-guided tour leads past three processing rooms. In the first room, bills are printed by a process called intaglio printing, whereby impressions are made by pressing inked engravers' plates into the currency fabric, a blend of 75 percent cotton and 25 percent linen. Each fabric sheet holds 32 bills.

In the second area, sheets are trimmed and examined for imperfections. Any defective sheets, called "muts"—an abbreviation of mutilated—are shredded. However, 99.9 percent of the printed bills are without defect. The third processing room is devoted to printing Treasury seals and serial numbers on the bills. After this final printing the bills are cut, stacked and banded in preparation for their dispersal to the 12 Federal Reserve banks throughout the country. The tour ends in an exhibit hall displaying stamps, bills and historical materials.

ARTS AND INDUSTRIES BUILDING

Jefferson Dr. at 9th St. SW.
Ⓜ Smithsonian or L'Enfant Plaza.

This 19C brick and Ohio sandstone building has long served the Smithsonian Institution as a storehouse for various collections and as a showcase for art, history, science, and culture.

Historical Notes

In 1876 the US celebrated its centennial by hosting the nation's first world's fair, known as the International Exhibition, in Philadelphia. When it ended, 60 freight cars full of centennial exhibits were shipped to the Smithsonian. As the institution's only building at that time, the Castle was unable to accommodate these acquisitions. Congress authorized the construction of a national museum, now called the Arts and Industries Building, on the Mall. Adolph Cluss designed the elaborate structure with four turreted wings radiating from a skylit fountained rotunda.

Arts and Industries Building

A sculptural trio entitled *Columbia Protecting Science and Industry* by Casper Buberl ornaments the gable above the main entrance. Completed in 1881, the museum was the setting for President Garfield's inaugural ball. The building housed artifacts and specimens that are today part of the collections of other Smithsonian museums.
A restoration undertaken for the 1976 Bicentennial celebration returned the building to its former glory and reinstated exhibits from the Philadelphia Centennial, which celebrated the coming of the industrial age.

VISIT

Open year-round daily 10am–5:30pm. Closed Dec 25. & ☎ *202-357-2700. www.si.edu.*

Today the museum displays rotating exhibits from the Smithsonian Institution's museums as well as those from other museums and galleries. A museum store in the north wing offers books, crafts, jewelry and items related to the temporary exhibits. In the west wing, the Discovery Theater presents live theater performances for children.

US BOTANIC GARDEN

1st St. SW.
Ⓜ Federal Center.

Situated at the foot of Capitol Hill, this lush conservatory serves as the nation's living plant museum and provides a pleasant respite from the activity of the Mall.

Historical Notes – This federally owned institution was chartered by Congress in 1818. The first greenhouse was established in 1842 to conserve the collection of exotic specimens brought from the South Seas by a team of US explorers. Originally located on the premises of the Patent Office Building, the collection was transferred to the Mall in 1850. The present conservatory, begun in 1931, has just completed a four-year renovation. The garden features a skillful blend of two building types traditionally used for storing and displaying plants: the 19C iron and glass greenhouse and the stone orangerie of French palace gardens, with its characteristic full-length arched windows.

VISIT

Mall entrance on Maryland Ave. Open year-round daily 10am–5pm. & ☎ *202-225-8333. www.aoc.gov.*

The entrance hall, the setting for resplendent seasonal floral exhibits, leads into a large glass pavilion with towering subtropical plants. The two smaller pavilions flanking this central space house exotic plants: flowering orchids; coffee, chocolate and banyan trees; and a collection of cycad trees similar to those existing on earth 200 million years ago.
The park situated across Independence Avenue blooms with myriad seasonal flowering plants that provide a colorful setting for the cast-iron **Bartholdi Fountain**, executed by Frédéric-Auguste Bartholdi (1834-1904), sculptor of the Statue of Liberty.

THE MEMORIALS★★★

Map pp 11-12

The portion of the Mall west of 15th Street is the setting for the nation's most venerated monuments. Offset by the graceful **Tidal Basin** and the Potomac River, the landscaping in this area lends both grandeur and contemplative beauty to the memorials to Presidents Washington, Jefferson and Lincoln. Skillfully positioned at major focal points of the city's monumental axes, these three memorials command striking vistas that further enhance their tremendous emotional impact. By contrast, the design of recent memorials often seeks to blend in with the existing landscape, making more subtle yet equally powerful statements.

Historical Notes

The centerpiece of **West Potomac Park** is the impressive **Reflecting Pool**, which stretches 350ft beyond the east facade of the Lincoln Memorial. Created in the 1970s, **Constitution Gardens**, with its 45 acres of landscaped grounds surrounding a pleasant pond, borders the pool to the north. The small island in the pond provides a placid setting for the semicircular memorial to the signers of the Declaration of Independence, which was dedicated in 1984. Discreetly positioned in the northwest corner of Constitution Gardens is "the Wall," a simple but revered black granite monument to America's soldiers who were killed or captured or remain missing in Vietnam. A classically inspired memorial (1924) to DC veterans graces the green expanse on the south side of the Reflecting Pool. The new Korean War Veterans Memorial, also located south of the Reflecting Pool, was dedicated in 1995, and the Franklin D. Roosevelt Memorial was completed in 1997. Three additional memorials—honoring Virginia statesman George Mason, World War II veterans, and Civil Rights leader Martin Luther King Jr.—have been approved by Congress and are in various stages of planning; a memorial to the nation's first father-and-son presidents, John and John Quincy Adams, remains under serious discussion.

Encircling the Tidal Basin are the city's famous **Japanese cherry trees★★** *(generally in bloom late March or early April)*, which originated as a gift from the mayor of Tokyo to Washington, DC in 1912. In 1958 the Japanese presented the city with two additional gifts: a 17C granite lantern to commemorate Commodore Perry's voyage to Japan (1853-54) and a stone pagoda. Both objects now stand among the cherry trees on the west bank of the Tidal Basin.

East Potomac Park, the peninsula projecting southeast from the Tidal Basin, is also bordered by cherry trees. The park is devoted to general recreational uses.

WASHINGTON MONUMENT

The Mall at 15th St. NW. Ⓜ *Smithsonian. Map p 12.*

The capital's most conspicuous landmark, and the world's tallest freestanding stone structure, this austere white marble obelisk rises from a knoll in the middle of the Mall. Though it took nearly four decades to complete, the monument, ringed by US flags, now stands both as a commanding memorial to the man who was "first in the hearts of his countrymen," and as an indelible symbol of the city that bears his name.

Military Commander – Soldier, statesman and leader, **George Washington** (1732-99) began his long service to this country while in his early 20s, distinguishing himself as a commander during the French and Indian War in the 1750s. Following the war Washington served as a loyal British member of the Virginia House of Burgesses in Williamsburg, Virginia. However, as tension over British taxation grew among the colonists, Washington became increasingly disenchanted with the mother country. In 1774 he served as one of seven Virginia delegates to the Continental Congress in Philadelphia. A year later, at the second Continental Congress, he was unanimously elected head of the Continental Army. For eight years Washington spearheaded the fight against Britain, frequently keeping the war effort alive through the strength of his own convictions. In addition to battling the superior forces of the British, Washington had to contend with his own poorly trained, often unenthusiastic troops, as well as with the vicissitudes of a Congress frequently reluctant to provide neces-

■ Washington Monument Statistics	
Height:	555ft 5 1/8in
Weight:	90,854 tons
Thickness at base:	15ft
Thickness at top:	18in
Width at base:	55ft 1 1/2in
Width at top:	34ft 5 1/2in
Depth of foundation:	36ft 10in
Cost:	$1,187,710

sary funds or moral support. After countless setbacks and lost battles, the Continentals, thanks to Washington's military brilliance and the help of French allies, won a decisive victory against Lord Cornwallis' troops on October 19, 1781, at Yorktown, Virginia.

Father of the Nation – For six years, from 1783 to 1789, Washington enjoyed a respite from public life at his plantation, Mount Vernon, near Alexandria, Virginia. But in 1787, when growing anarchy and lack of centralized government threatened the new confederation of states, he presided over the Constitutional Congress in Philadelphia. Judicious and nonpartisan, Washington served as a stabilizing force that allowed the contentious delegates to arrive at a mutually acceptable Constitution for the young Republic. Two years later, in 1789, the new electoral college unanimously voted Washington the first president of the nation. On April 30, 1789, he took the oath of office on the steps of Federal Hall in New York City. Faced with defining the presidency, Washington proceeded cautiously. He managed to keep the young country out of European wars, and to establish federal authority over individual states and presidential authority over issues of foreign policy. He argued (unsuccessfully) against the adoption of a partisan political system, and he set a standard of ceremonial decorum for his office. He also approved and began construction of the new federal city that would bear his name. After eight years and two terms as president, he refused a third and in 1797 retired for a final time to Mount Vernon.

A Monument to the Man – In 1783 the Continental Congress passed a resolution to erect an equestrian statue honoring the hero of the Revolution. Washington approved L'Enfant's plan to position the statue at the center of the Mall, where the east-west axis, originating at the Capitol, intersected the north-south axis aligned with the White House. Lack of funds delayed the project for decades. Finally, in 1833, a group of prominent citizens formed the Washington National Monument Society. In a public drive to raise money, the society solicited each

Washington Monument seen from Jefferson Monument

American for $1. Having raised $28,000 by 1836, the group held a contest to choose a design for the monument. The well-respected architect **Robert Mills** won with his concept of a "grand circular colonnaded building...from which springs an obelisk shaft." The cornerstone was laid July 4, 1848, though not at the site originally intended by L'Enfant, as that proved too marshy to bear the weight. Instead the site was moved 360ft east and 120ft south to higher ground. Mills' design was also altered to become, as one congressman put it, "a simple shaft...free from anything tinsel or tawdry."
Progress was slow due to the chronic problem of insufficient funding. To speed construction, the Monument Society invited citizens, states, and even foreign countries to contribute embellished memorial stone blocks for the interior. Work ceased when the funds finally ran dry in 1853, leaving the monument a truncated 152ft shaft that languished in unsightly neglect for nearly 25 years, until President Ulysses S. Grant approved an act authorizing the federal government to complete the project. Stone from the same Maryland quarry used for the original shaft was used for the later work; it was extracted from a different stratum, however, causing a change in shading still clearly visible about a third of the way up the structure. Dedicated on February 21, 1885, the monument opened to the public in 1888. During the 20C some 75 million people have visited it.

Visit

Open Memorial Day-Labor Day daily 8am–11:45pm. Rest of the year daily 9am–4:45pm. Closed Dec 25. Timed tickets (free) are required year-round and can be obtained from the 15th St. kiosk. Advance tickets obtainable from Spherix ☎ 800-388-2733 carry a service charge. Guided tours (1hr) available weekends 10am & 2pm (phone the day of your tour). During summer hours, we strongly recommend visiting the monument at night; entry lines are generally shorter and the view of the lighted city is spectacular. ♿ 🅿 ☎ *202-426-6841. www.nps.gov/nacc.*

Visitors to the nation's capital in the late 1990s saw a Washington Monument encased in scaffolding, as exterior stonework was cleaned and repaired during a four-year restoration project. Interior renovations focused on the installation of state-of-the-art elevator systems, including a new cab with windows which permit riders to view some of the restored commemorative stones. The elevator makes a 70-second ascent from the ground to the observation room at the summit of the monument. Eight small windows, two on each side of the pyramidal apex of the obelisk, afford the best **panorama★★★** available of the capital city. The south-facing windows overlook the Tidal Basin and the Jefferson Memorial; the western view highlights the Reflecting Pool and the Lincoln Memorial; the north faces the Ellipse and the White House; and the east overlooks the long stretch of Mall ending at the Capitol. Photographs above the windows reproduce the views and identify major landmarks. Visitors exit one level below the observation room.
On the "Down the Steps" tour *(1hr)*, guides explain some of the 193 embellished memorial stones given as gifts by individuals, groups, cities, states, and foreign nations.

JEFFERSON MEMORIAL

South bank of Tidal Basin. Map p 11.

In a peaceful shaded spot on the south shore of the Tidal Basin, the nation's third president is commemorated with a 20C adaptation of the ancient Roman Pantheon. Inscribed on its marble walls are Jefferson's own writings concerning the role of government in safeguarding human liberties.

The Man – Statesman, architect, musician, inventor, horticulturalist, philosopher and president, **Thomas Jefferson** (1743-1826) was one of the country's greatest geniuses. He brought his talents to bear on many of the issues facing the new nation, helping to formulate its system of government, assisting in the planning of its capital city and developing such fundamental principles as public education and religious freedom. In 1962 President Kennedy paid Jefferson a lasting homage when he greeted a group of Nobel Prize winners by saying that they were "the most extraordinary collection of talent, of human knowledge, that has ever gathered together at the White House—with the possible exception of when Thomas Jefferson dined alone."

Early Years – Born into a well-respected Virginia family, Jefferson spent his boyhood on the edge of what was then the Western frontier, in Albemarle County. His father, Peter, was a civil engineer and prominent local figure, serving as a justice of the peace, a colonel of the local militia and a member of the House of Burgesses. While a student at the College of William and Mary in Williamsburg, Virginia, young Tom turned his prodigious intellect to the study of the natural sciences, the arts and especially law, which he believed shaped the social and political conditions of man. During his college years he also became acquainted with a number of Virginians who, like Jefferson himself, would become Revolutionary leaders.

Jefferson Memorial

After studying law for five years with the famous Virginia jurist George Wythe, Jefferson practiced on his own for another seven years. In 1769 he was elected to the House of Burgesses and, while serving, participated in the colonists' protests against British taxation. In 1774 he was elected to the first Continental Congress in Philadelphia. At the second Continental Congress a year later, he was appointed to a five-man committee charged with drafting a statement to the British Crown that justified the colonists' stand on independence. Noted for his eloquent writings, Jefferson was encouraged by his fellow committee members to draft the document himself. On July 4, 1776, his Declaration of Independence was signed by the Continental Congress.

Serving the New Nation – In 1790 President Washington appointed Jefferson as the first secretary of State. Jefferson's architectural interests and talents were invaluable during this period. Along with Washington, he was a major force behind implementing plans for the new federal city. It was also at this time that he became embroiled in his historic conflict with Secretary of Treasury Alexander Hamilton. Their strident opposition to one another's views on the power of state versus federal governments under the Constitution led to the formation of a two-party political system. From 1797 to 1801 Jefferson served as vice president under John Adams before becoming the third US president, as well as the first to be inaugurated in Washington. During his two terms in office (1801-09), the US negotiated the Louisiana Purchase, effectively doubling the size of the young country and strengthening its position in the international arena. The accession of this vast territory, which included lands west of the Mississippi purchased from France for $27,267,622, led to the country's westward expansion. Jefferson's administration also sponsored the Lewis and Clark expedition, which explored and charted this new land.

The Final Years – In 1809 Jefferson retired to his beloved Monticello, the domed plantation house he had designed in his elegant and sober brand of Neoclassicism, outside Charlottesville, Virginia. Here, he pursued his long-cherished dream of founding an institution of public education. Jefferson personally conceived both the architecture and the educational approach for the University of Virginia in Charlottesville, which opened in 1825. On July 4, 1826—the 50th anniversary of the signing of the Declaration of Independence—Thomas Jefferson died at Monticello.

A Controversial Monument – In 1934 Congress enacted a resolution authorizing this memorial, which became the last in the city's triumvirate of presidential monuments along with those honoring Lincoln and Washington. From the beginning, the project was beset by controversy. **John Russell Pope**, the designer of numerous federal buildings in the capital city, planned the structure as an adaptation of the Pantheon in Rome, in deference to Jefferson's love of classical architecture. Critics alternately demanded that a more contemporary architectural plan be used or that a utilitarian building, such as a national auditorium or stadium, be built instead of a monument. Ultimately Pope's design, though scaled down to half its initial size, triumphed.

The first site chosen for the memorial, 450ft north of its present location, also met with public protests. It would have required reshaping the Tidal Basin and destroying many of the site's cherry trees given as a gift by the mayor of Tokyo in 1912. The current site lies on an axis with the White House, thus creating a monumental north-south perspective consistent with the spirit of L'Enfant's original plan for the city.

134

Visit

Enter on the Tidal Basin side. Visitor facilities open year-round daily 8am–11:45pm. Closed Dec 25. Guided tours (20min) available on request. ♿ 🅿 ☎ *202-426-6841. www.nps.gov/nacc.*

The wide, paved plaza in front of the monument along the Tidal Basin offers a sweeping **view** of the capital's famous cherry trees, which bloom resplendently around late March and early April. Stairs lead from the plaza to the monument's entrance portico, which supports a sculpted marble pediment depicting Jefferson surrounded by the four other members of the committee chosen to draft the Declaration of Independence (from left to right: Benjamin Franklin, John Adams, Jefferson, Roger Sherman and Robert Livingston).

Encircled by an Ionic colonnade, the open-air interior of the monument is dominated by a 19ft bronze **statue** of Jefferson by Rudulph Evans. Standing on a 6ft pedestal, the likeness of a middle-aged Jefferson, in knee breeches and a fur-collared coat, clutches a rolled parchment on which the Declaration of Independence is written. The four wall panels surrounding the statue are inscribed with Jefferson's writings, including portions of the Declaration of Independence, admonitions against slavery, and statements promoting religious freedom and flexibility in government.

LINCOLN MEMORIAL
The Mall at 23rd St. NW. Map p 11

From this stately memorial the famous marble likeness of a seated, brooding Lincoln stares across the Reflecting Pool to the Washington Monument and to the Capitol beyond. On the southwest side of the monument, Arlington Memorial Bridge serves as a symbolic link between Lincoln and the South's great hero, Robert E. Lee, whose home, Arlington House, overlooks the monument from the Virginia bluffs. Along the same axis is positioned the eternal flame marking the Arlington gravesite of President John F. Kennedy (the flame is visible from the rear of the memorial).

Preserver of the Union – Born in Kentucky in 1809 to a poor farming family, **Abraham Lincoln** (1809-65) was a self-educated, self-made man who became this country's 16th president and perhaps its most admired political hero. He is remembered by an affectionate public as "Honest Abe," the down-home, commonsensical statesman; as the Great Emancipator who ultimately freed the country of slavery; and as the president who fought a protracted civil war in order to keep the nation intact. Catapulted from state politics to the presidency, Lincoln was faced with a nation in turmoil even before he took the oath of office in March 1861. South Carolina, knowing Lincoln to be an opponent of slavery, seceded from the Union shortly after he was elected. Other southern states quickly followed suit. The month after Lincoln's inauguration, Confederate and Union troops exchanged fire at Fort Sumter, South Carolina. For the next four years, Lincoln waged a war to bring the Southern states back into the Union.

In 1863 he issued his renowned **Emancipation Proclamation**, decreeing that slaves in the Confederate states would thereafter be free. Though this was more a symbolic gesture than a real reversal of slavery nationwide, it helped set the stage for the eventual passage in 1865 of the 13th Amendment to the Constitution, which did in fact abolish slavery.

In April of 1865, at the start of Lincoln's second term, Robert E. Lee surrendered to Ulysses S. Grant at Appomattox, Virginia. With the long war over, the president turned his thoughts to the reconstruction of the South, but his plans of reconciliation were never realized. On April 14, 1865—five days after Lee's surrender—he was shot at Ford's Theatre by the actor John Wilkes Booth. The following day, at age 56, President Abraham Lincoln died of his wounds.

An Anchor for the Mall – A congressional commission was established two years after Lincoln's death to plan a monument in his memory, and for several decades various proposals were made concerning the monument's design and location. It was not until 1901 that the McMillan Commission, with the backing of the Commission of Fine Arts, endorsed a memorial at the western end of the recently extended Mall. Inspired by Greek architecture, the monument's designer, Henry Bacon, produced his version of a Doric temple, reminiscent of the Parthenon in Athens. Unlike the builders of antiquity, however, Bacon positioned the main entrance on the long side of the structure, overlooking the Mall. Work began on the memorial in 1914; it was dedicated in 1922 in a ceremony attended by Robert Todd Lincoln, the president's only surviving son.

A National Forum – Over the years this monument epitomizing Lincoln's ideals has served on many occasions as the forum for public protests and demonstrations. The acclaimed black opera singer Marian Anderson gave a historic outdoor concert here in 1939, after being refused permission to perform at the DAR's Constitution Hall. It was here in 1963 that Martin Luther King, Jr. inspired a crowd of 200,000 with his famous "I Have a Dream" oratory. During the Vietnam War, President Richard Nixon paid an unofficial late-night visit to the protesters gathered here.

Visit

Visitor facilities open year-round daily 8am–11:45pm. Closed Dec 25. Guided tours available on request.   202-426-6841. www.nps.gov/nacc.

Reproduced on copper pennies and $5 bills, the facade of this building is easily identifiable. Thirty-six Doric columns form a continuous colonnade ringing the edifice and symbolize the states in the Union at the time of Lincoln's death. The names of the 36 states are inscribed in the entablature above the columns. The parapet crowning the structure is adorned with a frieze sculpted with bas-relief swags and bearing the names of the 48 states that existed at the time the monument was completed.

Lincoln's craggy aspect comes into view as you ascend the long flight of marble stairs of the memorial. **Daniel Chester French** collaborated with Bacon to create a statue of Lincoln that would harmonize with the architecture. French's powerful and massive marble **statue★★★**, 19ft high, depicts a contemplative Lincoln and captures the force of the man himself. Lincoln's own words adorn the memorial. The right wall is inscribed with his second inaugural address and a mural by Jules Guerin, allegorically portraying the freeing of slaves. The Gettysburg Address (1863), the celebrated oratory that begins with the oft-quoted words "Four score and seven years ago," is chiseled into the left wall and topped by a similar Guerin mural showing the unity of the North and South.

The monument steps afford a grand **view★★** of the Mall extending the length of the Reflecting Pool to the Washington Monument.

VIETNAM VETERANS MEMORIAL

Constitution Gardens at Constitution Ave. and 22nd St. NW. Map p 11

Though it was conceived in controversy, this long, solemn black wall has become one of the nation's most cherished and moving memorials. Tucked away in the sylvan setting of Constitution Gardens, it bears the names of all those killed or missing in the Vietnam War.

"Serenity, Without Conflict" – The impetus for this monument came from a small group of Vietnam veterans living in the capital. Troubled by the public's indifference toward those Americans who served in the Southeast Asian conflict, they formed the Vietnam Veterans Memorial Fund in 1979, soliciting congressional support and contributions from individuals and corporate donors. In July 1980, President Jimmy Carter signed a joint congressional resolution authorizing the placement of the monument on a 2-acre plot in Constitution Gardens just northeast of the Lincoln Memorial.

The fund then held a national design competition for the memorial and appointed an eight-member jury of internationally- known artists and designers to judge the entries. The following criteria had to be met: that the memorial be reflective and contemplative, that it harmonize with its site, that it bear the names of the dead and missing and that it make no political statement about the Vietnam War. The competition attracted 1,421 entries. The winning design, characterized by one juror as "a simple solution of serenity, without conflict," was submitted by **Maya Ying Lin**, a 21-year-old architectural student at Yale University. Lin's wall was conceived as a symbol of healing. As she explained, "Take a knife and cut open the earth, and with time the grass would heal it."

The Wall – Begun in March 1982, the monument, known as "the Wall," was completed and dedicated by November of the same year. Its abstract simplicity aroused some controversy, and in an attempt to quell the dissatisfaction, a realistic sculpture

Lincoln Memorial

by Frederick Hart was added nearby in 1984. The life-size work, portraying three young soldiers of different ethnic origins, is intended to commemorate all US military men who served in the conflict. However, the Wall quickly became accepted as the moving shrine it was intended to be, a place of healing where family and friends could touch the names of loved ones lost in battle.

Visit

Open year-round daily. Closed Dec 25. Guided tours (20min) available on request 8am–11:45pm. ♿ *202-426-6841. www.nps.gov/nacc. Directories specifying the memorial panels on which names appear are located at the approaches to the Wall.*

IN THIS TEMPLE
AS IN THE HEARTS OF THE PEOPLE
FOR WHOM HE SAVED THE UNION
THE MEMORY OF ABRAHAM LINCOLN
IS ENSHRINED FOREVER

Fred Sieb Photography

© Norman Nokleby

Vietnam Veterans Memorial

Inset in a low hill, the memorial is actually two triangular walls that join at a 125° angle, with their ends pointing toward the Washington Monument and the Lincoln Memorial. Composed of granite from Bangalore, India, they are intended to reflect the surroundings in their polished surface. The memorial extends 493.5ft in length and rises to a height of 10ft at its apex. The names of the more than 58,000 men and women incised in the Wall are arranged chronologically, beginning with the first casualty in 1959 and ending with the last in 1975 *(more than 200 names were added in 1996)*. Those who died in the war are indicated by a diamond; those missing or imprisoned are denoted by a cross.

A grove of trees just south of the Wall is the site of the **Vietnam Women's Memorial**. Dedicated in 1993, it features a bronze statue (1992, Glenna Goodacre) nearly 7ft high depicting three military women tending a wounded male soldier. In 1989 President George Bush authorized its construction as a memorial to the more than 265,000 women who served in the US armed forces in Vietnam.

KOREAN WAR VETERANS MEMORIAL
Independence Ave. at French Dr. SW. Map p 11

Located southeast of the Lincoln Memorial, this compelling ensemble of statues, freestanding wall and circular pool honors the members of the US armed forces who served in the Korean War (1950-53). A recent addition to the Mall's commemorative places, the $18 million memorial was funded by private contributions and dedicated in 1995 by President Bill Clinton and Kim Young Sam, president of the Republic of Korea.

"The Forgotten War" – American veterans of the Cold War conflict attached this sobriquet to a war they felt was overshadowed by the magnitude of World War II and the controversy of Vietnam. In 1986 Congress authorized the American Battle Monuments Commission to oversee the design of a memorial, and in 1988 the current 2-acre site on the Mall was approved. A team of architects from Pennsylvania State University won the design competition in 1989 but withdrew from the project when reviewing agencies requested alterations. Washington, DC firm Cooper-Lecky Architects completed the project. The human figures were sculpted by Frank Gaylord and the granite "mural" was crafted by Louis Nelson. At the groundbreaking ceremony in 1992, President George Bush stated that the memorial's realization would assure that "no American will ever forget the test of freedom" faced by US troops. Of the 1.5 million Americans serving in the Korean War, more than 54,000 died, over 110,000 were captured or wounded and some 8,000 were declared missing.

Visit

Open year-round daily. Closed Dec 25. Guided tours (20min) available on request 8am–11:45pm. ♿ ☏ *202-426-6841. www.nps.gov/nacc.*

Nineteen larger-than-life stainless-steel statues (each about 7ft tall) of men wearing combat raingear stand in patrol formation within a triangular plot of junipers. One side of this "field" is lined with a 164ft-long wall of polished black granite, etched with the faces of more than 2,500 servicemen and women. The wall recalls the neighboring Vietnam Memorial, but it provides no written identification of those who lost their lives in the war. Mounted in the granite apex, an American flag stands guard over the dedicatory inscription: "Our nation honors her sons and daughters who answered the call to defend a country they never knew and a people they never met." A circular pool behind the flagpole is interrupted by a lower, separate wall bearing the words "Freedom is not free." Etched on the rim of the pool, the statistics of the war's toll bear witness to this poignant summary.

FRANKLIN DELANO ROOSEVELT MEMORIAL

Tidal Basin, west of the Jefferson Memorial. Map p 11

Situated on 7.5 acres bordering the Tidal Basin, this memorial to the nation's 32nd president combines sculpture, water and natural landscape to forge a dramatic setting for recounting the lifetime events and terms of office of **Franklin D. Roosevelt** (1882-1945).

In 1955 Congress authorized a commission to oversee the construction of a memorial to Roosevelt. The present site in West Potomac Park was set aside in 1959. After years of rejecting design submissions, the Commission of Fine Arts approved a design by Lawrence Halprin in 1978. In the 1980s Congress authorized construction and partial funding. The groundbreaking ceremony was held in September 1991, followed by a fund-raising drive to raise an additional $10 million from private sources for construction, which began in the fall of 1994. The memorial opened to the public in May 1997.

Visit

Visitor facilities open year-round daily 8am–11:45pm. Closed Dec 25. Guided tours (20min) available on request. & ☎ *202-426-6841. www.nps.gov/nacc.*

Ornamental plantings, trees, waterfalls and quiet pools lend a sense of tranquility and seclusion to this expansive memorial. Four outdoor galleries constructed of red South Dakota granite contain sculptured figures and cascading water walls designed to symbolize each of FDR's terms as president (1933-45). The First-Term Room (1933-37) symbolizes the dedication of the president and his determination to overcome the nation's economic problems with optimism and courage. A country in the depths of the Great Depression is represented in the Second-Term Room (1937-41). World War II's destruction and devastation is symbolized by strategically placed, rough-hewn granite blocks in the Third Term Room (1941-45). In the Fourth-Term Room (1945), a bronze bas-relief, *Funeral Cortege*, depicts the president's death and testifies to its impact on the country, while a statue of Eleanor Roosevelt honors and commemorates her role as First Lady, champion for human rights, and first delegate to the United Nations.

President Bill Clinton dedicated an addition to the memorial in January 2001. A bronze statue, sculpted by Robert Graham and sited at the memorial's entrance, depicts FDR sitting in the wheelchair he designed and used daily after his crippling bout with polio in 1921. While the depiction of FDR in his wheelchair was met with great controversy, it was decided that the statue's demeanor emphasizes his indomitable spirit. As Eleanor declared, "Franklin's illness gave him strength and courage he had not had before."

■ Memorials In The Works

To be sited along the Tidal Basin southwest of the Jefferson Memorial, the **George Mason Memorial Garden** will commemorate the author of the first document in America to call for freedom of the press, religious tolerance, and other rights which citizens take for granted today. George Mason (1725-92) wrote the Virginia Declaration of Rights in 1776, and refused to put his name to the Constitution because it did not contain a Bill of Rights—a document added, largely due to his steadfast urging, in 1791. The memorial garden plans to feature a statue of Mason seated beneath an arbor and flanked by stone walls inscribed with appropriate quotes. A project of the regents of Gunston Hall Plantation *(see entry heading)*, the garden could be completed as early as spring 2002.

Located adjacent to 17th Street on the east-west axis between the Lincoln Memorial and the Washington Monument, the Rainbow Pool anchors the eastern end of the Reflecting Pool. It is also the approved site of the future **National World War II Memorial**, which was authorized by Congress and signed into law by President George W. Bush on Memorial Day 2001. (A symbolic groundbreaking took place on Veterans Day, November 11, 2000, with President Bill Clinton, former Senator Bob Dole and others in attendance.) Though its location has been hotly contested by those who believe it will mar the open spaces and vistas of the Mall, the memorial itself is not under debate. Encompassing 7.4 acres, the approved design intends to maintain 70 percent of the area as a parklike setting of water, grass and trees, with the remaining 30 percent as hard surface.

The **Martin Luther King Jr. National Memorial** aims to evoke the spirit and fundamental themes of King's life and his mission: democracy, justice and hope. The approved site, a four-acre plot on the northwest edge of the Tidal Basin, will create a visual "line of leadership" from the Lincoln Memorial, site of Dr. King's famous "I Have a Dream" speech, to the Jefferson Memorial.

3

White House Area

Inspired by the stately presence of the Executive Mansion, this area maintains a decorous gentility, with manicured parks, elegant row houses and grandly conceived public structures.

Lafayette Square – In L'Enfant's plan the "President's house" was to be surrounded by an 80-acre park. However, Jefferson felt that this was too large an area to be held only for presidential enjoyment. In the early 19C, he ordered Pennsylvania Avenue extended in front of the still incomplete White House. The 7-acre plot to the north of it became a public park known as President's Square.

Around 1815 St. John's Church took its place on the north side of the park, and three years later the square's first private home, Decatur House, was built on the northwest corner. Before long some of the nation's most prominent citizens took up residence in dignified homes facing the square. In 1824 the park was renamed Lafayette Square to honor America's French ally in the Revolution, the Marquis de Lafayette, then on a triumphal second visit to America. That same year **Blair House** *(no. 1651)*, another celebrated historic dwelling, was erected within view of the White House on Pennsylvania Avenue. Restored in 1988, the house serves as an official guest house for foreign dignitaries *(not open to the public)*.

In the early 1850s an equestrian statue of Andrew Jackson was placed in the center of the park. The installation led to the later erection of four statues to foreign heroes who aided in the American Revolution: Lafayette (1891, southeast corner); Jean-Baptiste Rochambeau (1902, southwest corner); Friedrich von Steuben (1910, northwest corner); and Thaddeus Kosciuszko (1910, northeast corner). During the Civil War, troops were quartered on the square, and following the war the first major landscaping of the park was carried out in keeping with an 1850s design prepared by Andrew Jackson Downing.

Today many of the remaining Federal row houses bordering Lafayette Square serve as offices. Except for frequent demonstrations outside the White House by protesters of government policies, most of the square itself is a tranquil park. The tranquillity has been heightened by the closing of Pennsylvania Avenue between 15th and 17th Streets to traffic in 1995 for security reasons. Lafayette Square and the Ellipse *(below)* are being integrated into a **President's Park**, which will include plazas, paved walkways, plantings and outdoor seating.

Grandiose Buildings – Though work began on the White House in 1792, the building evolved gradually and has been continually enlarged. On its east side is the stately Treasury Building, which was erected between 1836 and 1869. To the west of the White House is the colossal Old Executive Office Building, completed in 1881.

In the late 19C and early 20C, the 17th Street corridor south of the White House witnessed the construction of several dignified buildings, including the Corcoran Gallery of Art, the headquarters for the American Red Cross, the Daughters of the American Revolution complex and the Organization of American States.

From "White Lot" to Ellipse – South of the White House, the open expanse of ground now called the **Ellipse** was once marshy lowland. During the Civil War, military livestock was enclosed here behind a whitewashed fence that, by tradition, gave rise to the designation "white lot." In the late 19C the area was reclaimed. At the corner of Constitution Avenue and 17th Street, a stone **lock keeper's house** still stands as a reminder of the Washington Canal. Across the avenue, on either side of the Ellipse, are a pair of gatehouses, designed by Charles Bulfinch, that once stood on the Capitol grounds.

For decades the Ellipse expanse served as a recreational area. Then in the mid-20C, it became a ceremonial grounds for the White House. On its north side is the **Zero Milestone**, from which all distances in the federal city are computed. Also on this side is the **National Christmas Tree**, a blue spruce planted during the administration of President Jimmy Carter. Just east of the Ellipse, on E Street at 15th in the Commerce Building, is the **White House Visitor Center**.

WHITE HOUSE★★★

1600 Pennsylvania Ave. NW.
Ⓜ McPherson Square, Metro Center, or Federal Triangle.

For almost two centuries, the White House has been the home of America's First Families. More than just an official residence, the stately structure has become a universally recognized symbol of the US presidency. Today its public rooms house an exemplary collection of Americana, both furnishings and historic memorabilia, reflecting the tastes of the nation's leaders.

White House

The President's Palace – L'Enfant had envisioned the "President's house" as a grand palatial structure, some five times its current size, but after the Frenchman's acrimonious departure in 1792, the city commissioners announced a public design competition for the official residence. Among the drawings submitted was an anonymous entry executed by Secretary of State Thomas Jefferson, who, as a self-taught architect, was involved in the planning of the new federal city. The $500 prize went to **James Hoban**, a young Irish builder. His plan called for a three-story stone structure reminiscent of a Georgian manor, with a hipped roof surrounded by a balustrade. The main facade featured a columned portico with an eagle carved in the pediment. Jefferson considered the proposed size "big enough for two emperors, one Pope and the grand Lama."

The cornerstone was laid on October 13, 1792, but due to a lack of skilled labor, particularly stonemasons, and a shortage of public funds, the work proceeded slowly. Faced with financial challenges, the three city commissioners approached President Washington with a plan to reduce the mansion's dimensions. In October 1793 Washington compromised by agreeing to omit the third floor, and Hoban redrew plans for a two-story building. (It was not until 1927 that a third floor was actually added to create additional living quarters.)

First Occupants – The structure was not completed during Washington's presidency; while serving his two terms in office, the first president lived in private homes in New York and Philadelphia, both of which served as temporary capitals while the federal city was being built. The house was complete enough for the second President, **John Adams**, to move in a few months prior to the end of his term (1797-1801). In November 1800 Adams became the first president to occupy the mansion. Though conditions in the still incomplete house were drafty and unpleasant, Adams nonetheless left a lasting benediction on it. After his first night there, he wrote, "May none but honest and wise men ever rule under this roof!"

> ■ **Christmas on the Ellipse**
>
> Every year during the first week in December, the president presides over the lighting of the National Christmas Tree *(check local newspapers for specific time)*. A permanent fixture on the Ellipse, this enormous Colorado blue spruce serves as a seasonal centerpiece for the 56 other trees that represent the states, the District and US territories. Enticed by the festive holiday atmosphere complete with burning Yule logs and occasional performances, the public celebrates the holidays here nightly throughout December.

Thomas Jefferson, the mansion's first long-term resident (1801-09), turned his architectural attentions to the design of the White House, as the whitewashed sandstone building had come to be known. Collaborating with his surveyor of public buildings, **Benjamin H. Latrobe**, Jefferson designed colonnaded wings on the east and west sides to house domestic and office spaces. Latrobe also replaced the mansion's heavy slate and mortar roof with a lighter one of steel.

Historical Notes

Conflagration and Reconstruction – James Madison's stay in the Executive Mansion (1809-17) was marked by disaster. In August 1814, during the War of 1812, the British entered the city and set fire to several public buildings, among them the White House. Thanks to the forethought of Mrs. Dolley Madison, many important documents, as well as a Gilbert Stuart portrait of George Washington that now hangs in the East Room, were saved from destruction. Had a summer rain not put out the fire, the mansion probably would have burned to the ground.

The city commissioners called on James Hoban to salvage the mansion he had initially begun. Finding that many of the stone walls were seriously weakened, Hoban had them demolished and began rebuilding. In 1818 President James Monroe was able to occupy the house. During the Monroe administration (1817-25) the south portico was added, and the elaborate French Empire pieces that remain at the core of the White House's historic furniture collection were acquired.

Throughout the 19C, architectural changes and redecorating occurred as funds were available. In order to customize the house to his own taste, a new president frequently resorted to raising funds by selling old furnishings at public auction. Congressional appropriations for the upkeep and refurbishing of the Chief Executive's home were generally dependent on the political and economic climate. During the popular administration of Andrew Jackson (1829-37), for example, bountiful funds allowed for the purchase of new china and glassware, the installation of indoor plumbing and the completion of the north portico. In other administrations, however, furnishings became seriously dilapidated.

During James Polk's tenure (1845-49), gas lights were added and long-term interior transformations were initiated. Chester A. Arthur (1881-85) undertook a major refurnishing of the mansion in 1882. According to contemporary reports, he had 24 wagonloads of old furniture carted away for public auction. He then called on the celebrated New York designer Louis C. Tiffany to redecorate the interior. Electricity was installed in the White House in 1891.

20C – In 1902 vast changes were again wrought on the mansion by Theodore Roosevelt (1901-09), who entrusted the prominent architectural firm McKim, Mead and White with large-scale renovation. The extensive greenhouses that had flanked the west and south sides of the house for decades were demolished. The west wing was added and an expansive carriage porch built on the east. The interior, whose old plumbing, wiring, heating and flooring were in dangerous disrepair, was revamped and modernized. The Roosevelt renovation began the process of restoring the White House to its original appearance—a process that has been continued by succeeding presidents. In 1942, while Franklin D. Roosevelt was in residence (1933-45), the current east wing was built. Under Roosevelt's successor, Harry S. Truman (1945-53), another major structural renovation was undertaken to shore up and replace the weakened flooring, walls and foundations. The second-story balcony was added to the south portico during the Truman presidency.

During her stay in the White House (1961-63), Jacqueline Kennedy began a campaign to acquire items of historic and artistic interest. Following her precedent, in 1964 President Lyndon Johnson (1963-69) established the Committee for the Preservation of the White House, which provided for a permanent curator. The curatorial staff today continues to expand and document the White House collection.

> *"Tonight took a long look at the President's house.*
> *The white portico—the palace-like, tall, round columns,*
> *spotless as snow—the walls also—tender and soft moonlight,*
> *flooding the pale marble, and making peculiar faint languishing*
> *shades, not shadows—everywhere a soft transparent, hazy, thin,*
> *blue moonlace, hanging in the air—the brilliant and extra-plentiful*
> *cluster of gas, on and around the facade, columns, portico, etc.—*
> *everything so white, so marbly pure and dazzling, yet soft—*
> *the White House of future poems, and of dreams and dramas,*
> *there in the soft and copious moon—the gorgeous front,*
> *in the trees, under the lustrous flooding moon, full of reality,*
> *full of illusion—the forms of the trees, leafless, silent,*
> *in trunk and myriad angles of branches under the stars and sky—*
> *the White House of the land, and of beauty and night...."*

Walt Whitman, *Specimen Days* (24 February 1863), 1882

Visiting the White House

White House Visitor Center – *15th and E Sts. NW. Open year-round daily 7:30am–4pm. Closed Jan 1, Thanksgiving Day, Dec 25.* ♿ ☎ *202-208-1631. www.whitehouse.gov.* Make this the first stop of your visit. Housed in the spacious, ground-floor Baldrige Hall in the Commerce Building, the new center, opened in 1995, features an information booth staffed by National Park Service rangers, displays and a souvenir sales area. White House tour tickets *(below)* are available here. Obtain a map of the White House area to familiarize yourself with the grounds and entrance gates. If you have time, see the 30min film titled *Within These Walls.*

Tours – Due to the large number of visitors to the White House, timed **tickets** *(free)* are required mid-Mar–Labor Day for the **self-guided tours**. Tours are permitted Tues–Sat 10am–noon. Tickets are issued at the White House Visitor Center on the day of the tour only on a first-come, first-served basis beginning at 7:30am. Tours in peak season *(mid-Mar–mid-Sept)* start at the bleachers on the Ellipse, the large grounds located south of the White House. From mid-Sept–mid Mar, visitors may go directly to the southeast visitor entrance of the White House. **Congressional visits** *(p 255)* are available. As the White House may close without advance notice to accommodate official functions, we recommend calling the 24hr tour line the morning of your visit for current tour information ☎ 202-456-7041.

Special Events – The White House organizes a series of public annual events, all of which traditionally attract immense crowds. An **Easter Egg Roll**, customarily held the Monday after Easter on the White House's south lawn, is open to children three to six years of age. Activities for older children are staged on the Ellipse at the same time. Spring and fall **garden tours** are held twice a year on designated Saturdays and Sundays in April and October. **Christmas candlelight tours** take place on three evenings in late December. As these events are free of charge and do not require tickets or reservations, entry lines are often very long. For further information, call ☎ 202-456-7041.

■ Presidents of the United States of America

George Washington	1789-1797	Grover Cleveland	1885-1889
John Adams	1797-1801		1893-1897
Thomas Jefferson	1801-1809	Benjamin Harrison	1889-1893
James Madison	1809-1817	William McKinley	1897-1901
James Monroe	1817-1825	Theodore Roosevelt	1901-1909
John Quincy Adams	1825-1829	William H. Taft	1909-1913
Andrew Jackson	1829-1837	Woodrow Wilson	1913-1921
Martin Van Buren	1837-1841	Warren G. Harding	1921-1923
William Henry Harrison	1841	Calvin Coolidge	1923-1929
John Tyler	1841-1845	Herbert Hoover	1929-1933
James K. Polk	1845-1849	Franklin D. Roosevelt	1933-1945
Zachary Taylor	1849-1850	Harry S. Truman	1945-1953
Millard Fillmore	1850-1853	Dwight D. Eisenhower	1953-1961
Franklin Pierce	1853-1857	John F. Kennedy	1961-1963
James Buchanan	1857-1861	Lyndon B. Johnson	1963-1969
Abraham Lincoln	1861-1865	Richard M. Nixon	1969-1974
Andrew Johnson	1865-1869	Gerald R. Ford	1974-1977
Ulysses S. Grant	1869-1877	James Carter	1977-1981
Rutherford B. Hayes	1877-1881	Ronald Reagan	1981-1989
James A. Garfield	1881	George Bush	1989-1993
Chester A. Arthur	1881-1885	William J. Clinton	1993-2000
		George W. Bush	2001-

State Dining Room

Red Room

Blue Room

North Entrance H

South Portico

Diplom
Recept
Roo

Adapted from drawing by R. W. Nicholson
© White House Historical Assoc.

VISIT

Open year-round Tue–Sat 10am–noon. ♿ ⅡⅢ ☏ *202-208-1631. www.white house.gov.*

The White House is set off by 18 acres of flower gardens, lawns and trees *(grounds not included on tour)*. A balustraded roofline, Ionic pilasters and windows with alternating rounded and triangular pediments adorn the rectangular facade of the main structure. The columned and balconied south portico extends out in an expansive bay overlooking the sweep of the south lawn and the Ellipse beyond.

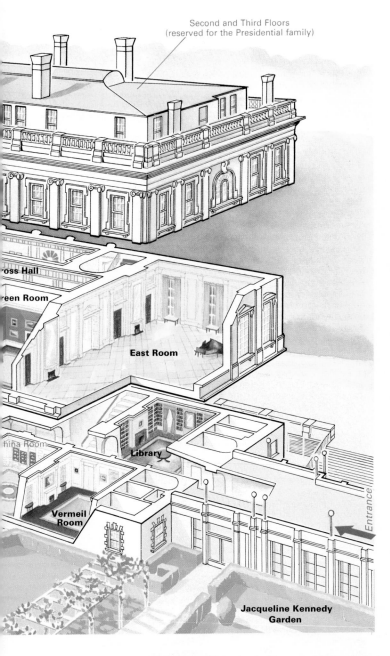

Second and Third Floors
(reserved for the Presidential family)

oss Hall

een Room

East Room

hina Room

Library

Vermeil
Room

Entrance

Jacqueline Kennedy
Garden

The colonnade of the north portico facing Pennsylvania Avenue and Lafayette Park supports an unadorned pediment. Elaborate carvings grace the area above the fan-light of the double entrance doors. Pavilions connect the one-story east and west wings to the main mansion. The west wing *(not open to the public)* houses the Cabinet Room, several staff and reception rooms, and the president's Oval Office, which opens onto the Rose Garden.

In the mansion, the ground-floor and first-floor rooms function as formal state reception areas, while the First Family's private living quarters are located on the second and third floors.

Ground Floor – *Visitors first enter a security building on East Executive Ave.* In the paneled entrance hall of the east wing, as elsewhere in the mansion, portraits of first ladies and presidents adorn the walls. A glassed colonnade overlooking the intimate **Jacqueline Kennedy Garden** displays exhibit panels explaining the history of the White House.

Just beyond the White House souvenir sales area is an elegant vaulted marble corridor. Portraits of recent first ladies also hang here, and a large Sheraton breakfront holds an assortment of presidential porcelains. The **library**, which opens off the right side of the hall, is decorated in late Federal style and contains some 2,700 volumes. The **Vermeil Room**, situated directly across the hall, is so named for its collection of French and English gilded silver, or vermeil, dating from the 17C to the early 20C. The China Room and Diplomatic Reception Room, situated on the ground floor, are included on congressional visits only *(p 255)*.

First Floor – The vast and ornate **East Room**, the setting for White House concerts, dances and official ceremonies, contains elaborate plaster ceiling decorations and entablatures, fluted pilasters, Bohemian cut-glass chandeliers and four marble mantels. Because it is used for a variety of purposes, the gold and white room is sparsely furnished. The legendary 1797 **portrait of George Washington** that Dolley Madison saved hangs in this room. The small drawing room off the East Room is known as the **Green Room**, owing to the color scheme it has retained since the days of President John Quincy Adams (1825-29). An intricately patterned Turkish Hereke carpet complements the room's green watered-silk wall coverings and the tones of the upholstered Sheraton-style chairs and settees, many from the early-19C workshop of Duncan Phyfe. On the dropleaf sofa table is the silver-plated coffee urn that John Adams considered one of his "most prized possessions."

The French Empire furnishings in the elliptical **Blue Room** include seven of the original Bellange gilded armchairs ordered from Paris by James Monroe. The gilded wood chandelier and Carrara marble mantel contain classical motifs mirrored in the wallpaper frieze that forms a border around the wainscoting and entablature. Portraits of the first presidents to live in the house are among the paintings hanging in this reception room. The three long casement windows afford a striking **view** of the Washington Monument and the Jefferson Memorial beyond. From this standpoint, the visitor can easily discern the extent to which the Washington Monument is positioned off the axis that links the White House with the Jefferson Memorial. The small parlor known as the **Red Room** also contains French Empire-style furnishings prevalent from 1810 to 1830, including gilded chairs upholstered in red and gold damask. Displayed on the wall between the windows is a bust by Hiram Powers of President Martin Van Buren (1837-41). Above the fireplace hangs a painting depicting Van Buren's daughter-in-law and official hostess, Angelica. Note that the bust is featured in the painting.

In the gold and white **State Dining Room**, the Neoclassical pilaster, wall paneling and ceiling molding are modeled on decor found in late-18C English estates. Gold upholstered Queen Anne-style chairs surround the long mahogany dining table, which holds the gilded plateau from a service ordered by James Monroe.

Over the mantel is the Lincoln portrait executed by George P.A. Healy in 1869. Marble-topped side tables with gilded eagle pedestals rim the room. When prepared for a state dinner, this room can seat 140 people. Marble columns separate the long **Cross Hall** from the North Entrance Hall. Both halls are hung with portraits of recent presidents. The carpeted marble staircase, connecting the state rooms to the first family's private quarters, is frequently used by the president and first lady to make ceremonial entrances.

The tour exits through the north portico.

© White House Historical Assn.; photo by National Geographic Society

Red Room

CORCORAN GALLERY OF ART★★

In a city now dominated by federal museums, the Corcoran Gallery of Art can claim to be the capital's oldest institution and its most venerable private gallery. Although it houses a fine collection of European art, the Corcoran is primarily known as a showcase for American art.

Historical Notes

The Benefactor – A self-made man, self-educated connoisseur and respected philanthropist, **William Wilson Corcoran** (1798-1888) began constructing a museum to house his private collection in 1859. That original building, now the Renwick Gallery, was almost complete when Corcoran halted the project in 1861. As a Southern sympathizer, Corcoran found himself unwelcome in wartime Washington, and he left for Europe in 1862. He returned in 1865, his patriotism still in question, and resumed his museum project, in part to prove his goodwill toward the nation. In 1870 he formed a board of trustees to govern the new museum, which was to be used "for the purpose of encouraging American genius." Corcoran generously donated his personal collection, the building and grounds, and a $900,000 endowment.

One of the nation's first major galleries of art, the Corcoran opened in 1874. From the outset it enjoyed great popularity, both with the public and with American artists, who considered it a great honor to be exhibited there. In order to further the cause of the arts in America, Corcoran made another endowment of $100,000 in 1879 for an art school, to function as an adjunct to the museum.

The "New" Corcoran – William Corcoran died in 1888 and so never saw the elegant Beaux-Arts building that now bears his name. In 1897 this new, larger Corcoran opened several blocks south of the old building, which was no longer big enough for its school and its expanded, 700-work collection.

Faced with a trapezoidal plot, the building's architect, Ernest Flagg, designed the new museum with a semicircular amphitheater at the lot's acute angle, where 17th Street and New York Avenue intersect. The facade of white Georgia marble is set off by a green copper roof, ornate grillwork, and a frieze inscribed with the names of 11 great artists, among them Dürer, Raphael and Rembrandt. Above the entrance is W.W. Corcoran's motto: "Dedicated to Art." The prominent 20C architect Frank Lloyd Wright considered the Corcoran "the best designed building in Washington."

In 1925 Sen. William Andrew Clark of Montana bequeathed to the Corcoran his noted European collection of works by such masters as Rembrandt, Turner, Corot and Degas. The **Clark Bequest** also includes tapestries, rugs and stained glass, as well as an 18C French salon. A gift of $700,000 from Clark's family went to build a wing to house his bequest. This addition, off the southwest end of the original building, was designed by Charles A. Platt, architect of the Freer Gallery. In 1937 Edward and Mary Walker donated their collection, which includes the paintings of such pivotal French Impressionists as Renoir, Pissarro and Monet. Recent acquisitions include the Olga Hirshhorn collection, comprised of works by notable artists such as John Singer Sargent, Willem de Kooning, Pablo Picasso and Alexander Calder, and a gift of African-American art donated by Thurlow Evans Tibbs Jr. in 1996. The Evans-Tibbs collection includes paintings by Aaron Douglas, Henry O. Tanner, Raymond Saunders and Sylvia Snowden as well as photographs by James Van Der Zee and Addison Scurlock. Today the Corcoran Gallery has more than 14,000 works in its permanent collection.

Tea and history

Map pp 14-15. Three historic hotels in the vicinity of the White House feature formal afternoon tea, complete with traditional finger sandwiches, raisin scones—perhaps even toasted crumpets and clotted cream—plus a selection of tarts, pastries and fine teas.

6 At the exclusive **Hay-Adams Hotel** *(16th and H Sts. NW ☎ 202-638-6600)*, an extensive tea is served amid the tasteful, parlorlike setting of the dining room.

7 Teatime at the famous **Willard Hotel** *(1401 Pennsylvania Ave. NW ☎ 202-628-9100)* takes place on weekdays in either Peacock Alley, where such luminaries as Mark Twain once strutted, or Cafe Espresso. On weekends the venue becomes the formal Willard Room.

8 The airy Cafe Promenade in the grand **Renaissance Mayflower Hotel** *(1127 Connecticut Ave. NW ☎ 202-347-3000)* provides a gracious milieu for full tea service, complemented on occasion by the music of a harpist.

VISIT

Open year-round Wed–Mon 10am–5pm (Thu 9pm). Closed Jan 1, Thanksgiving Day, Dec 25. $5. Guided tours (45min) available. ✗ ♿ ☎ *202-639-1700. www.corcoran.org. Because only a small portion of the museum's vast collection can be displayed at any one time, exhibits change frequently, as do the specific locations of pieces of art within the museum.*

First Floor – Just beyond the museum entrance are a pair of two-story atriums. The pillared, skylit galleries display 19C marble portrait busts by American Neoclassical sculptors, notably Hiram Powers, as well as contemporary pieces.

One of the Corcoran's best-known works, Powers' famous nude sculpture **The Greek Slave** (1846) *(second floor)*, scandalized Victorian audiences when it was first shown in the old Corcoran Gallery (now the Renwick Gallery).

Gallery 1, a small space opening onto the south atrium, is devoted to rotating exhibits featuring the works of contemporary American artists. The first two in a series of connected galleries off the far end of the south atrium display 18-19C American art, primarily portraiture. Rembrandt Peale's historical painting *Washington Before Yorktown* (1825), a heroic depiction of the general on horseback, dominates an entire wall. The remainder of these galleries contains 17-19C European paintings, sculpture and decorative arts, many of which are from the Clark collection.

The **Salon Doré** was bequeathed to the Corcoran by Senator Clark, who had the room and its furnishings transplanted from an 18C Parisian mansion to his own New York residence. Richly appointed with gilded woodwork moldings and paneling, the salon is considered one of the finest late French-Rococo interiors in this country.

Located on the steps to the spacious landing between the floors is **The Veiled Nun**, an enigmatic marble bust by Giuseppe Croff, which was purchased by Corcoran himself. The Clark Landing presents landscape and genre paintings as well as sculpture by predominantly 19C French and American artists.

The rotunda gallery, visible from the atrium hall and connected to it by a marble stairway, showcases the *Hope Venus*, a replica of a work executed by the Italian sculptor Antonio Canova (1757-1822). The sculpture was commissioned by Thomas Hope, a descendant of the owner of the famous Hope Diamond. Paintings from the museum's permanent collection are displayed here when the gallery is not devoted to special exhibits.

Second Floor – The four main galleries flanking the atrium chronicle American art predominantly from the mid-19C to the mid-20C. The far left gallery includes several portraits by the popular 19C painter George Peter Alexander Healy (1813-1894) of men who served as US president, including a beardless Abraham Lincoln (1860). The largest gallery features American art from the early days of the Republic *(left side)*, including Powers' *The Greek Slave*, to the late 19C *(right side)*. The large historical painting *The Old House of Representatives* (1822) by the inventor of the Morse code, Samuel F.B. Morse, realistically portrays the original House chamber and each of the 80-some members of the 17th Congress. Most prominent of the mid-19C landscapes are the works of such Hudson River school painters as Thomas Cole, Frederic Edwin Church and Albert Bierstadt. Notable works displayed here include Church's **Niagara** (1857), considered America's most popular 19C landscape rendering, and Bierstadt's *Mount Corcoran* (1877), a painting that created controversy because the artist named it after a nonexistent American peak, in order to curry favor with Corcoran. The works of late-19C and early-20C masters are on exhibit in the third gallery, including Thomas Eakins' compelling genre painting **The Pathetic Song**. John Singer Sargent's painting of **Madame Edouard Pailleron** (1879) was instrumental in establishing his reputation as a portraitist in Paris in the 1880s. A different kind of portrait, *Susan on a Balcony Holding a Dog* characterizes Mary Cassatt's artistic style of juxtaposing well-defined

Niagara (1857) by Frederic Edwin Church

figures against an impressionistic background. Winslow Homer's *A Light on the Sea* (1897) echoes the artist's theme of mankind's precarious flirtation with the forces of nature.

In the fourth gallery the works of John Sloan, Robert Henri and George Bellows reflect the **Ashcan school** of early-20C realism. Other American artists whose works are mounted here include Childe Hassam, Thomas Hart Benton and Edward Hopper. *Into Bondage* by Aaron Douglas is part of the Corcoran's recently acquired Evans-Tibbs collection of African-American art.

The two galleries off the south end of the atrium normally display 20C art from the museum's impressive and constantly growing collection, which includes works such as the large canvases of Abstract Expressionists Hans Hofmann, Mark Rothko and Helen Frankenthaler. Andy Warhol and other Pop artists are also represented in the collection.

The remainder of the second-floor galleries features photographs, prints and drawings from the permanent collection, as well as temporary exhibits and new acquisitions typifying the most current movements in American art.

RENWICK GALLERY★

Pennsylvania Ave. and 17th St. NW.
Ⓜ Farragut West or Farragut North.

The earliest major example of the Second Empire style in America and an embodiment of Victorian tastes, this ornate brick building adds a touch of quiet elegance to the bustling corner of Pennsylvania Avenue and 17th Street. Inside, its galleries highlight the best works of contemporary and traditional American craftsmanship.

Historical Notes

The City's First Art Museum – In 1858 the wealthy financier William Wilson Corcoran commissioned one of the period's most influential architects, **James Renwick**, to design a building to house his private art collection. Impressed by the innovative contemporary architecture he had seen on a recent visit to Paris, Corcoran requested that Renwick adopt the fashionable Second Empire style. Renwick's use of that style influenced architectural tastes in America; many of the public buildings constructed in the later Grant administration, such as the Old Executive Office Building, situated across the street, embodied this style.

In 1874, after a hiatus brought on by the Civil War, the Corcoran Gallery of Art, as the building was then called, opened as Washington's first art museum. Exhibiting the paintings and sculpture of its founder, the museum also displayed, in Victorian fashion, plaster copies of classical sculpture in its statuary hall. Because these works were nudes or seminudes, separate visiting hours were maintained for men and women.

 Georgia Brown's
Map p 15. 950 15th St. NW.
☎ *202-393-4499*. This trendy, well-appointed restaurant has made a splash with its nouvelle Southern cuisine, which takes Dixie cooking to new heights by combining standard Southern ingredients in unusual ways and presenting them with a decidedly artistic flair. For starters, try the crab and okra soup with tomato and roasted corn or the fried Mississippi catfish fingers. Entrées include "head-on" shrimp with spicy sausage and creamy grits, frogmore stew, and peach-barbecued Cornish game hen.

The Corcoran School of Art had its inception here in 1879. By 1897 the collection and school had outgrown the original building and were moved down 17th Street to the building they occupy today.

Renewal and Rebirth – Sold to the government for $300,000, the old building was used by the US Court of Claims until 1964, the year in which demolition was proposed. The successful campaign to preserve the threatened landmark was championed by the Kennedy and Johnson administrations. Renamed the Renwick Gallery, it became part of the Smithsonian Institution in 1965. To return the building to its original appearance, restoration architects used old drawings and the photographs of Mathew Brady. The refurbished Renwick opened as a department of the Smithsonian American Art Museum in 1972.

VISIT

Open year-round daily 10am–5:30pm. Closed Dec 25. ♿ ☎ *202-357-2700. www.americanart.si.edu.*

Exterior – The brick facade is embellished with sandstone pilasters, vermiculated quoins, garlands and window trim. Filigreed ironwork caps the ridges of the building's distinctive mansard roof. On the long western facade, niches hold statues of

Courtesy Smithsonian American Art Museum

Portal Gates by Albert Paley

Rubens and Murillo, replicas of two of the original eleven statues of artists that once adorned the facades. With American flair, the capitals of the two pilasters flanking the entrance feature sculpted tobacco fronds and ears of corn. Above the entrance bay is a medallion profile of Corcoran, inscribed with his monogram and motto: "Dedicated to Art."

Interior – A red-carpeted staircase leads from the entryway to the second-floor **Grand Salon**. Decorated in the style of a Victorian picture gallery, the 90ft-long room is furnished with red velvet "poufs"—circular settees—and brocade sofas and chairs. Paintings, hung in tiers, cover its raspberry walls from the wainscoting to the ceiling molding. Among the 170 paintings and sculptures on view from the Smithsonian American Art Museum *(currently closed for renovation)* are a suite of three stunning views of Yellowstone and the Grand Canyon by Thomas Moran. Other artists represented include George Catlin, George Inness, Edmonia Lewis, Rembrandt Peale, Hiram Powers and John Twachtman.

The **Octagon Room**, a smaller Victorian gallery *(directly opposite the Grand Salon)*, was initially designed to showcase Hiram Powers' daring nude sculpture *The Greek Slave* (1846), now in the Corcoran Gallery. Today 19C furnishings adorn the room, a blue pouf at its center. The Octagon Room showcases several works by Winslow Homer, Albert Pinkham Ryder and Thomas Wilmer Dewing, also part of the Smithsonian American Art Museum's permanent collection.

The remainder of the museum is devoted to **American crafts**. The galleries on both sides of the Octagon Room feature selected pieces from the Renwick's permanent, comprehensive collection of outstanding 20C crafts, ranging from traditional basketry to abstract works in glass, wood, clay, metal and fiber. A highlight of the collection is the elaborate metalwork of Albert Paley's *Portal Gates*. The five first-floor galleries are devoted to temporary exhibits—either traveling shows or exhibits mounted by the museum itself. The Renwick's exhibits are renowned for their innovative arrangement and sophisticated content.

DAUGHTERS OF THE AMERICAN REVOLUTION★

17th and D Sts. NW.
Ⓜ Farragut West.

This stately complex occupies an entire city block and is reputedly the world's largest group of structures owned and maintained exclusively by women. The national headquarters of the Daughters of the American Revolution (DAR), it houses an extensive collection of genealogical materials and artifacts relating to the colonial and early Republic periods through the mid-19C.

Historical Notes

The DAR was established in 1890 by a group of women who were descended from Revolutionary War patriots. In the last century the organization has achieved a national reputation for perpetuating "the memory and spirit of the men and women who achieved American independence" and for fostering "true patriotism and love of country." Today it is supported by more than 170,000 members belonging to chapters throughout the 50 states and abroad.

The Beaux-Arts edifice known as **Memorial Continental Hall** was designed at the turn of the century by Edward Pearce Casey, who also collaborated on the construction of the Library of Congress. Facing the gracious expanse of the Ellipse, the original entrance is dominated by a monumental porte-cochere, or carriage entry, covered by a pedimented roof. The semicircular portico that rises from the balustraded terrace on the C Street side features 13 columns, representing the 13 colonies. In the 1920s, having outgrown its original building, the DAR commissioned the prolific architect John Russell Pope to design **Constitution Hall**, a colossal structure whose columned, pedimented entrance faces 18th Street. The building contains a U-shaped, 3,800-seat auditorium, where the Daughters meet for their annual convention. In addition, the hall functions as a public auditorium where a variety of concerts and lectures are held.

VISIT

Open year-round Mon–Fri 8:30am–4pm, Sun 1pm–5pm. Closed major holidays. Guided tours available Mon–Fri 10am–2:30pm, Sun 1pm–5pm.   ♿ ☎ *202-879-3241. www.dar.org.*

Memorial Continental Hall houses 33 **period rooms** depicting scenes of early American life including a colonial home, tavern, church and other historical interiors dating from the late 17C to the mid-19C. Of note are the Georgia Room, portraying the late-18C Peter Tondee Tavern in Savannah; the brick-floored Oklahoma kitchen; and the Virginia room, reproducing an 18C dining room.

The original meeting hall, an enormous room overhung by a vaulted skylight and elaborate Neoclassical trim, is now the DAR library, a renowned repository of genealogical material. (Author Alex Haley used these facilities while researching his 1970s classic, *Roots*.) The **DAR Museum** regularly displays ceramics, silver, glass and textiles. Additional pieces from the permanent collection of more than 30,000 objects are placed on view in changing exhibits. Unless it is reserved for DAR or other functions, Constitution Hall is visited on the tour.

DECATUR HOUSE★

748 Jackson Place NW.
Ⓜ Farragut West or Farragut North.

For almost a century and a half, this sedate brick town house on the northwest edge of Lafayette Square figured prominently in the social and political life of Washington. The first home built on the square and the last to remain in private ownership, it served as the residence of military heroes and renowned statesmen.

Historical Notes

The Decatur Years – Stephen Decatur, a 19C naval hero, had the house built in 1818. Substantial prize money from his military successes against the Barbary pirates off the coast of North Africa and against the British in the War of 1812 enabled him to commission the eminent architect **Benjamin H. Latrobe** to design a home in elegant style. The three-story structure, 51ft wide and 45ft deep, cost Decatur $11,000. He and his wife, Susan, entertained lavishly here, but only for a brief 14 months. At the age of 41, the young commodore was killed in a duel with a discredited naval captain who believed Decatur responsible for his disgrace. Bereft, Mrs. Decatur moved to a Georgetown town house and rented the Lafayette Square house to a succession of dignitaries. In the 1820s Secretary of State Henry Clay, the "Great Compromiser," lived in Decatur House, calling it "the best private dwelling in the City." After Clay, Martin Van Buren, then secretary of State and soon to be president, occupied the house. In 1836 the hotelier John Gadsby purchased it from Mrs. Decatur. During the Civil War Decatur House was appropriated by the government as a commissary facility.

The Beale Era – Edward Fitzgerald Beale, a renowned Western adventurer, became owner of the house after the Civil War. In 1847 Beale, accompanied by his cohort Kit Carson, brought back word of California's accession to the Union. A year later Beale again crossed the country, in a record-breaking 47 days, to officially report the discovery of gold in California.

When Beale and his wife, Mary, took possession of Decatur House in 1872, it was in disrepair from wartime use. Following the fashion of his day, Beale added such Victorian embellishments as sandstone trim around the entrance and windows. He also had the Latrobe fanlight and side lights around the front door removed and the first-floor windows lengthened. For two decades the Beales were prominent members of the capital's social circles. President Grant frequently crossed Lafayette Square to visit Beale, who was one of his closest friends.

In 1902 the house passed to the Beales' son, Truxtun. He and his second wife, Marie, made Decatur House a focal point of Washington society. One of the capital's most important annual events, a dinner following the White House Diplomatic Reception, was given here for three decades. Mrs. Beale, considered the city's premier hostess, continued to entertain diplomats, royalty and statesmen after her husband's death in 1936.

In the early 1940s, recognizing the historic significance of her home, Mrs. Beale engaged the noted restoration architect Thomas Tileston Waterman to recover the Latrobe character of the house. In 1956 she bequeathed it to the National Trust for Historic Preservation, which operates it today.

VISIT

Visit by guided tour (30min) only, year-round Tue–Fri 10am–3pm, weekends noon–4pm. Closed Jan 1, Thanksgiving Day, Dec 25. $4. ♿ ☎ *202-842-0920. www.decaturhouse.org.*

Latrobe's vestibule combines domes, arches and recesses to achieve an effect of understated elegance. Off the vestibule to the left lies the parlor, which, like the dining room adjacent to it, is decorated with furnishings appropriate to the Decatur period. Among the parlor furnishings is a *secrétaire à guillotine*, so called for its sliding front panel. The room off the right side of the vestibule was recently discovered to be the original kitchen of the house. Curving double doors, fit to the contours of the vestibule's rear wall, lead to a separate hallway and the main staircase.

The second floor is devoted to the Beale period. A small family sitting room is decorated as it was in Truxtun Beale's day, with informal furnishings and family photographs. In the two formal Victorian drawing rooms, the Beales held their famous soirees. Note the seal of California, composed of a dozen different woods, inlaid in the floor of the north drawing room.

Decatur House (1882) by E. Vaile

DWIGHT D. EISENHOWER
EXECUTIVE OFFICE BUILDING★

17th and G Sts. NW.
Ⓜ Farragut West or Farragut North.

The massive granite pile that rises like a tiered wedding cake to the west of the White House is one of Washington's foremost architectural treasures. Having survived years of derision and neglect, it has been restored to its former grandeur and houses several key government offices of the Executive branch, including the Executive Office of the President.

Historical Notes

Second Empire Landmark – Erected as headquarters for the Departments of State, War, and Navy, this grand building (1888) symbolized the renewed vitality of the post-Civil War government. Its chief architect was Alfred Mullett, who had recently designed the north wing of the Treasury Building, flanking the opposite side of the White House. Rather than adopt the Neoclassical vocabulary used in his earlier building, Mullett opted for the French Second Empire style, following the example of the Corcoran Gallery (now the Renwick Gallery) that was completed 20 years earlier

Dwight D. Eisenhower Executive Office Building

on a site just across Pennsylvania Avenue. Known in the US as the General Grant style because of the popularity it enjoyed during the Grant administration (1869-77), this style is characterized by mansard roofing and prominent corner and central pavilions. Although the Executive Office Building lacks the elaborate sculpture and ornamental detailing generally adorning Second Empire edifices, its exterior is noteworthy for its vigorous play of surfaces, lines and recesses. With 900 exterior columns, 1,572 windows, more than 550 rooms, nearly 2 miles of corridors and 4 1/2ft-thick granite walls, this construction was Washington's largest and most lavish office building and is generally considered to be the finest surviving example of the Second Empire style in the country.

A Threatened Monument – Like many 19C works of architecture that did not fit the capital's predominant Neoclassical mold (e. g., the Pension Building and the Old Post Office), the Executive Office Building has evoked more scorn than admiration. By the time the edifice was completed in 1888, the Second Empire style had already passed out of fashion. In the period between the two world wars, plans were drawn up to transform the facade to resemble the numerous Neoclassical edifices throughout the city. Owing to insufficient funds, these projects were never carried out; however, the building was allowed to deteriorate, and demolition seemed inevitable.

Gradually the original occupants moved to more modern quarters in various sites around the city. The Navy Department led the way soon after World War I, followed by the War Department in 1938. After the State Department's move in 1947, the Executive Office of the President appropriated the building as an annex to the adjacent White House (hence the structure's name).

The Kennedy administration was instrumental in promoting the building's subsequent rehabilitation. The exterior was cleaned in the 1960s and finally, in 1983, a large-scale restoration project was begun to refurbish the spectacular interior. In addition to the president's office, among the most influential divisions of the Executive branch housed in the building today are the Office of Management and Budget, the National Security Council, and the Office of the Vice President.

VISIT

Visit by guided tour (1hr 30min) only, year-round Sat 9am–11:30am. Closed major holidays. Minimum 2-week advance reservations suggested. ♿ ☎ 202-395-5895. www.whitehouse.gov/history.

Interior Highlights – The sumptuous halls, stairways and offices, designed primarily by Mullett's successor, Richard von Ezdorf, have provided a splendid workplace for scores of noted government figures over the 20C. Theodore Roosevelt, Franklin D. Roosevelt, Taft, Hoover, Eisenhower, Johnson, Ford and George H. Bush all maintained offices here at some point in their careers before moving into the executive mansion next door. The **cast-iron detailing**, employed throughout the building for fire protection, is an outstanding decorative feature.

Executive Office of the President Libraries – Four stories of alcoves enclose the library's central reading area, crowned by an elegant vault pierced by a skylight. The upper three stories are adorned with intricately designed white cast-iron balconies, resembling marvelous pieces of lacework.

Similar in layout to the above-mentioned room, the three-story law library features dark cast-iron balconies. The floors of both libraries are laid with Milton tiles arranged in elaborate geometric patterns.

Indian Treaty Room – Originally the Navy's library and reception room, this graceful hall contains a lacy cast-iron balcony featuring eagles, anchors, shells and other nautical motifs.

Office of the Secretary of the Navy – The original fireplace, mirrors and elaborately stenciled walls of this spacious suite have been restored to their former splendor. Note the four **corner domes** and two **central rotundas**, especially the skylight of the **west rotunda**, covered in gold leaf and tinted in soft yellow, peach and pale green colors.

ORGANIZATION OF AMERICAN STATES

17th St. and Constitution Ave. NW.
Ⓜ Farragut West.

Conceived as a symbolic amalgam of North and South American architecture, this white marble building with a terra-cotta roof has the gracious ambience of a Spanish Colonial villa. As the headquarters for the Organization of American States (OAS), the building serves as a forum for discussions and conferences affecting the political and economic climate of the Western Hemisphere.

Historical Notes

Established in 1890 as the International Union of American Republics, this organization is the oldest such alliance of nations in the world. It was created to engender peaceful relations and economic cooperation among the independent countries of the Americas. In its more than 100-year history, it has grown from 24 member nations to 35, the most recent to join being Canada, in 1990. The US was a charter member of the organization.

In the early 20C Washington was chosen as the site for this headquarters building because it was the only city in which all member nations maintained permanent legations. Congress donated the tract of land, which then became international territory. In addition to housing the offices of the permanent staff, the building serves as headquarters of the General Secretariat, the 700-member body responsible for OAS administration and policy implementation.

Political Americana
1331 Pennsylvania Ave.
☎ *202-737-7730 or Union Station 202-547-1685.* For mounds of political memorabilia—buttons, hats, license plates, banners, mugs and more—from recent and past campaigns, stop in these interesting shops or in the ❿ **Capitol Coin & Stamp Co.** *(Map p 15; 1100 17th St. rm. 503* ☎ *202-296-0400).*

⓫ **Counter Spy Shop**
Map p 15. 1027 Connecticut Ave. NW. www.spyshop.com ☎ *202-887-1717.* Visit this unique store for high-tech, high-ticket espionage paraphernalia, including the latest in bulletproof clothing, antibugging devices, video equipment, lie-detector telephones and night-vision goggles.

VISIT

Open year-round Mon–Fri 9am–5:30pm. Closed major holidays. ♿ ☎ *202-458-3760. www.oas.org.*

Headquarters Building – For their innovative blending of classical elements and traditional Latin motifs, Paul Cret (designer of the Folger Shakespeare Library) and Albert Kelsey won the architectural competition to design this "House of the Americas," as it is frequently called. A gracious plaza fronts the triple-entry arches, which are flanked by allegorical statues, one depicting North America *(right)*, by Gutzon Borglum (best known for his presidential profiles at Mount Rushmore), and the other, South America *(left)*, by Isidore Konti.

The lobby is dominated by the **tropical patio**, designed after a Spanish Colonial courtyard. A fountain bearing motifs occupies the center of the patio, whose lush vegetation includes the now enormous "peace tree," a grafted fig and rubber tree planted at the building's dedication in 1910 to symbolize the peaceful coexistence of North and South America. The coats of arms of the member nations embellish the entablature around the roofed overhang. A gallery behind the patio features changing exhibits, generally from the collection of the OAS museum *(below)*.

On the second floor the columned **Hall of the Americas**, an ornately trimmed and vaulted auditorium, contains three Tiffany rock-crystal chandeliers and Tiffany stained-glass windows. The adjacent Old Council Room is adorned with bronze bas-relief friezes depicting scenes in the histories of the Americas.

Museum and Grounds – Behind the main building, the Aztec Gardens display contemporary and traditional sculpture. The stuccoed loggia fronting the garden pool is the rear of a building designed by Cret and Kelsey to serve as the residence of the OAS secretary-general. In 1976 it was converted to the **Art Museum of the Americas** *(open year-round Tue–Sun 10am–5pm; closed major holidays; guided tours available Tue–Fri, reservations required;* ☏ *202-458-6016; www.museum.oas.org).* In addition to hosting occasional traveling art shows, the museum mounts rotating exhibits devoted to the works of the modern Caribbean and Latin American artists represented in its permanent collection of some 700 pieces.

At the north corner of the complex is a small stuccoed building originally designed by Benjamin Latrobe as the stables for the private estate that first occupied the site.

ST. JOHN'S CHURCH

Lafayette Square at 16th and H Sts. NW.
Ⓜ McPherson Square.

Occupying a prominent corner of Lafayette Square since 1815, this elegant structure is one of the most historic and prestigious churches in Washington. It enjoys the sobriquet "the church of Presidents," because every chief executive since the church's inception has worshiped here at some time while in office.

Historical Notes

In the early 19C parishioners of the capital's only Episcopal church, Christ Church on Capitol Hill, began to consider creating a new parish in the area that was then developing around the White House. In 1815 the eminent architect **Benjamin H. Latrobe** was engaged to draft plans for the building. Latrobe's church took the shape of a Greek cross, and the finished product so pleased him that he wrote his son after the church's opening in 1816, "I have just completed a church that made many Washingtonians religious who were not religious before."

Throughout the church's history, its vestry has attempted to maintain the integrity of Labrobe's design even as the building has been expanded and altered. A pillared porch was added to the west side in 1822; thereafter this side replaced Latrobe's south entrance as the main entrance. The bell tower was also added at this time, and the west transept extended, changing the church's shape to a Latin cross.

In 1883 another prominent architect, James Renwick, oversaw further renovation to the church, including the addition of a Palladian window behind the altar and stained-glass windows designed by Madame Veuve Lorin, curator at Chartres Cathedral in France.

VISIT

Open year-round Mon–Sat 9am–3pm, Sun 8am–3pm. Closed major holidays. ♿ ☏ *202-347-8766.*

Latrobe's graceful, saucered dome and lantern draw the eye to the midpoint of the low-ceilinged church. A brass plate on **pew 54** indicates the president's pew, where attending chief executives are seated. The kneeling stools in this and nearby pews are covered in needlepoint patterns bearing the presidential seals and the names of presidents.

Adjoining the church on H Street is Ashburton House, a Federal-style structure (1836) that now functions as the parish house.

TREASURY BUILDING

15th St. and Pennsylvania Ave. NW.
Ⓜ Metro Center.

Pictured on the back of the $10 bill, the stately Treasury Building, which flanks the executive mansion on the east, is the seat of government finances and a prominent architectural landmark in its own right.

Historical Notes

The Department of the Treasury – Established in 1789 as a department of the Executive branch, the Treasury has monitored many of the financial and quasi-financial functions of the federal government throughout the nation's more than 200-year history. The Postal Service, General Land Office (now the Department of the Interior), Departments of Commerce and Labor, and the Coast Guard all initially began as arms of the Treasury.

Today the Treasury Building houses executive and support offices for the secretary of the Treasury and other high-level administrators. A number of bureaus administered by the department are housed elsewhere in the city. Among these are the Bureau of Engraving and Printing, where currency is printed; the Customs Service; the Internal Revenue Service; and the Secret Service.

The Building – The first Treasury Building, designed by George Hadfield, was one of the few official buildings completed when Congress and the president officially moved to Washington in 1800. A compact Georgian structure, it stood on the site of the current building. During the British invasion of 1814, the building was burned to the ground but was quickly replaced with a new structure designed by White House architect James Hoban. This structure, too, was destroyed, in a fire set by arsonists in 1833. The current building was begun in 1836, with the construction of the T-shaped east wing, designed by **Robert Mills**, who also created the Washington Monument and the Old Patent Office Building. Mills employed brick vaulting to fireproof the interior and, in compliance with the wishes of Congress, used Aquia Creek sandstone, an ill-suited material that was also used in the construction of the White House and the Capitol. His plan ultimately envisioned additional wings on the north and south, forming an E-shaped building with the ends open to the White House. The colossal size of the structure, and particularly the addition of the south wing, broke with the original city plan, which called for an unobstructed view along Pennsylvania Avenue between the White House and the Capitol.

In 1851, due to political wrangling, Mills was dismissed and eventually replaced by Thomas U. Walter, best known as the designer of the Capitol dome. Walter modified Mills' E-shaped structure by adding a west wing that would enclose the E in a square and create two interior courtyards. The south, west and north additions took 14 years to complete and were supervised by the following architects who added their own embellishments to the interiors: Ammi Young (south wing, 1860); Isaiah Rogers (west wing, 1864); and Alfred Mullett (north wing, 1869). Shortly after completing the Treasury Building, Mullett began work on his most celebrated project, the Dwight D. Eisenhower Executive Office Building, positioned on the west side of the White House. The granite building (the Aquia Creek sandstone exterior and east colonnade were replaced in 1909) covers two blocks and reflects the Greek Revival style prevalent in the 1830s and 40s. The building's most distinctive feature is the Ionic colonnade of 30 monolithic columns, each 36ft high, that adorns the east facade. The

Treasury Building, detail

© Brigitta L. House/MICHELIN

south, north and west entrances are approached by wide plazas. The south plaza contains a statue of Alexander Hamilton, first secretary of the Treasury (1789-95), and the north plaza, one of Hamilton's successor, Albert Gallatin (1801-14). Both statues were designed by James Earle Fraser. Broad staircases lead from the plazas to columned and pedimented porticoes. Pediments also cap the ends of the east and west facades, interrupting the roofline balustrade.

VISIT

Visit by guided tour (1hr 30min) only, year-round Sat 10am, 10:20am, 10:40am & 11am. Closed major holidays. 2-week advance reservations required; visitor's name and date of birth and social security number must be provided when making reservations. Photo ID required for building entry. ♿ ☎ 202-622-0896. www.ustreas.gov/curator.

The tour follows the chronological construction of the building. The hallways in the original T-shaped east wing were conceived by Mills with Doric columns and groin- and barrel-vaulted ceilings. The more elaborately ornamented hallways of the south, north and west wings exemplify the Greek Revival style. Cast-iron pilasters lining the hall feature eagles and a hand holding the Treasury key. Ornate cast-iron balustrades adorn the circular staircases.

⓬ McCormick & Schmick's
Map p 15. 1652 K St. NW.
☎ *202-861-2233.* This upscale (but not pricey) restaurant, with a score of establishments nationwide, is renowned for its exceptionally fresh and varied seafood. The menu typically features a dozen kinds of shellfish—clams, oysters, mussels and crabs from both coasts—as well as a wide array of fish. Request menu items grilled or sautéed to your taste, or choose one of the mouth-watering specials such as panfried flounder or sole with Parmesan crust and lemon-caper butter.

The third-floor corridors serve as a portrait gallery hung with paintings of the secretaries of the Treasury, arranged in chronological order. The **Secretary's Conference and Reception Rooms** have been created to reflect the decor popular in public buildings in the late 1860s through the 1880s. The conference room features a painting of George Washington attributed to the eminent portraitist Gilbert Stuart and one of Salmon Chase (Treasury secretary under Lincoln from 1861 to 1864) attributed to Thomas Sully.

The **Andrew Johnson Suite** has been restored to its appearance in 1865, when the suite served as the Executive Office for President Andrew Johnson following Lincoln's assassination. Johnson maintained his office in the Treasury building until Mrs. Lincoln vacated the White House.

The walls and ceilings of the **Secretary Salmon Chase Suite** are lavishly decorated with stenciling, allegorical figures and gilt detailing that dates from Chase's tenure.

The second floor is notable for the Treasurer's Office, where a decorative cast-iron **vault wall**, designed by Isaiah Rogers in 1864, is visible. Incised with seals and medallions, the wall was obscured behind other vault extensions and forgotten about for 80 years. The wall has now been restored, and its interior lining of steel balls, intended to prevent burglary, can be viewed through a wall cutaway.

The north lobby, fronting Pennsylvania Avenue, opens onto the opulent **Cash Room★**, designed by Alfred Mullett. The site of Ulysses S. Grant's inaugural reception in 1869, the impressive 72ft-by-32ft chamber features immense bronze chandeliers, a coffered ceiling, and walls and floors faced in seven different kinds of marble. A mezzanine with ornate pilasters and an elaborate bronze railing rims the room. Intended to inspire public trust in paper money, which the government first issued in 1862, the Cash Room functioned to redeem government-issued certificates and to supply commercial banks with coins and currency. It ceased operations in 1976 and is now used for official functions.

4

Downtown

Traditionally the commercial heart of Washington, Downtown reflects the flavor of the city's past and present. Large office buildings and retail complexes tower above 19C shopfronts, and the process of revitalization is everywhere.

19C – Conceived by planner L'Enfant to link the White House and the Capitol, **Pennsylvania Avenue** was the capital's first major thoroughfare, and as such it gave rise to the city's commercial district. In 1801 President Jefferson authorized the building of a central market on the avenue between 7th and 9th streets, and in 1807 construction began on the ill-fated Tiber Creek canal, which was eventually covered over in the 1870s. For much of the 19C, Pennsylvania Avenue was lined with hotels, boardinghouses and theaters, in keeping with L'Enfant's intent that this be a thoroughfare "attractive to the learned and affording diversion to the idle." Among the diversions were the **National Theatre**, an institution still in operation between 13th and 14th streets, and the **Willard Hotel**, for decades Washington's premier hostelry. Established in the 1850s, the Willard has occupied several buildings on the same site. The present building (1901) was designed by H.J. Hardenberg, architect of Manhattan's celebrated Plaza Hotel.

As the city grew, F Street became the site of major government buildings and fashionable residences. North-south growth occurred along 7th Street, where two- and three-story brick buildings housed shops and residences. In the 1830s 7th Street was chosen as the site for the Patent Office and became an enclave for German immigrants working in the dry-goods trade. By the turn of the century, their businesses had made this street the commercial hub of Downtown.

A Century of Change – During the first half of the 20C, Downtown continued to thrive, with major new development occurring in the land bordered by Pennsylvania and Constitution Avenues. Known as **Federal Triangle**, this cluster of Classical Revival government buildings was designed by a group of eminent architects working in collaboration. On the last available site looms the 3 million sq ft **Ronald Reagan Building** (1997, Pei Cobb Freed & Partners, and Ellerbe Becket). This new international trade center houses federal offices and conference rooms, restaurants, exhibit spaces and the Washington, DC Visitor Information Center.

After World War II Downtown declined as it lost business to suburban malls. When John F. Kennedy's inaugural parade moved down Pennsylvania Avenue, the thoroughfare was described by one cabinet member as "a vast, unformed, cluttered expanse." A cabinet committee established by Kennedy in 1960 began a redevelopment process that has gradually revitalized the avenue. At the core of this rebirth was the renovation of the Old Post Office while other landmark construction includes the 53,879sq ft **Navy Memorial** dedicated in 1987.

In recent years such mixed-use complexes as Hartman-Cox's Market Square (1984), near the site of the old city market, have risen on the avenue. The Landsburgh complex *(7th, 8th and E Sts.)*, home of the **Shakespeare Theatre** (1992), was the result of the overhaul of several buildings. Both Market Square and the Landsburgh are part of **Pennsylvania Quarter**, the designation for Pennsylvania Avenue's north side between 6th, 9th and E streets. Today a refurbished Willard Hotel overlooks Pershing Park, a pleasant square with an outdoor cafe. Nearby **Freedom Plaza**, designed by the prestigious architectural group, Venturi, Rauch and Scott Brown, has a large-scale copy of **L'Enfant's city plan** incised in its pavement. Anchoring the northern portion of Downtown is the **Washington Convention Center**, which has encouraged the development of major hotel-office complexes. The area has also become a testing ground for the innovative rehabilitation of 19C commercial architecture, as seen in the Gallery Row complex at F and D streets. On G and 9th streets is the **Martin Luther King Memorial Library** (1972), an austere building designed by Mies van der Rohe, one of the 20C's most influential architects. **Chinatown**, a small stretch of restaurants and shops on H Street between 6th and 7th streets, is recognizable by its ornate Friendship Archway. Chinatown's newest and biggest neighbor is the **MCI Center**, a 20,000-seat sports arena for the city's basketball and hockey teams. Other renovation projects include revitalizing the old Atlas and Le Droit buildings at 8 F Street to become the new home of the **International Spy Museum**.

NATIONAL PORTRAIT GALLERY★★

Sharing the elegant interior of the Old Patent Office Building with the Smithsonian American Art Museum since 1968, this museum might be thought of as the nation's family album. Modeled after its namesake in London, the National Portrait Gallery conserves some 15,000 paintings, sculptures, photographs, engravings and drawings of "men and women who have made significant contributions to the history, development and culture of the people of the United States." To be accepted into the permanent collection, portraits must be original works of art, preferably taken from life.

Historical Notes

Home for the Arts – In the mid-1830s Congress authorized a "temple of the useful arts"—a patent office—to be constructed on this site equidistant from the Capitol and the White House. In 1836 construction began on the Greek Revival edifice designed by William Parker Elliott. Monumental and severe, the stone **Old Patent Office Building★★** features a pedimented Doric portico on each of its four sides and encloses a spacious central courtyard. The distinguished architect Robert Mills oversaw construction of the south wing, which was finished in 1840. (The golden sandstone used in this wing contrasts markedly with the granite employed throughout the rest of the building.) Throughout the almost 30 years of ensuing construction, Thomas U. Walter, designer of the Capitol dome, and Edward Clark were involved in the building project.

The War Years – During the Civil War, the broad corridors of the building served as a hospital for Union soldiers. Clara Barton, a Patent Office copyist and founder of the Red Cross, ministered to the wounded, as did poet Walt Whitman, who read to them from his works. In 1865 Lincoln's second inaugural reception was held here, just five weeks prior to his assassination. A benefit to raise funds for the families of Union soldiers, the gala attracted some 4,000 people and took place in the immense 264ft-long, marble-pillared hall—now called the Lincoln Gallery—on the third floor of the east wing.

Structure Preserved – When completed in 1867, the building was the largest structure in Washington. In addition to housing the patent office, it was also home, at various times, to the Department of the Interior and the Civil Service Commission. In 1958 Congress saved the building from threatened demolition and gave it to the Smithsonian Institution, which now uses it to house two museums—the National Portrait Gallery and the Smithsonian American Art Museum—as well as the Archives of American Art. The two museums are connected by hallway galleries. The building's interior **courtyard**, with its cast-iron fountains and monumental pieces of sculpture, including Alexander Calder's *The Spiral*, is one of the most pleasant and tranquil spots in Downtown.

Self-Portrait by John Singleton Copley

Courtesy National Portrait Gallery, Smithsonian Institution

VISIT

The gallery will close for renovation until 2004. Entrance on F St. Open year-round daily 10am–5:30pm. Closed Dec 25. Guided tours (45min) available Mon–Fri 10am–3pm, weekends 11:15am & 1pm. ✗ ♿ ☎ 202-357-2700. www.npg.si.edu. Begin the visit on the 2nd floor.

Second Floor – The panorama of American history unfolds on the second-floor landing, which is dominated by Gilbert Stuart's celebrated **Lansdowne portrait★ (A)** of George Washington (another version by Stuart hangs in the East Room of the White House). The wall to the right **(B)** is reserved for other major works by Stuart—his celebrated **Athenaeum Portraits** of George and Martha Washington (which are co-owned with the Museum of Fine Arts in Boston) are alternated every three years with Stuart's **Thomas Jefferson portrait** (co-owned with Monticello, Jefferson's estate near Charlottesville, Virginia). The Athenaeum portrait is the most widely known representation of the first president, since it served as the model for the portrait that appears on the $1 bill.

The handsome, groin-vaulted Hall of Presidents *(to the right of the landing)* provides a stately setting for the museum's series of **presidential portraits**, featuring representations in various media of the Americans who have occupied the nation's highest office. Note George P.A.Healy's oil painting of a pensive Abraham Lincoln. Adjacent to the hall, room 202 contains numerous engravings, paintings and busts of George Washington.

Fourteen galleries on the opposite side of the landing present a chronological overview of prominent people and events in American history. Half of this section's L-shaped central corridor features portraits of illustrious Americans who have made noteworthy contributions to fine arts and literature. Among those depicted here are the painters John Singleton Copley and **Mary Cassatt** (by the 19C French artist Degas); renowned 19C writers such as Hawthorne, Thoreau, Longfellow and Emerson; as well as actors such as Edwin Booth (brother of President Lincoln's assassin) and Ira Aldridge.

At the end of the corridor, photographs by Mathew Brady of Abraham and Mary Todd Lincoln, Jefferson Davis, industrialist Peter Cooper and explorer John C. Fremont highlight the Meserve Collection, an array of 5400 glass-plate negatives.

The survey of the country's historical figures begins in the south corridor in **Colonial America** *(gallery 204)* and **The Age of Revolution** *(gallery 206)*, which feature a selection of Founding Fathers and notable settlers, including a portrait of Pocahontas and a terra-cotta cast of Benjamin Franklin. Among the works exhibited in **The Early Republic** *(gallery 208)* are a marble bust of Whig presidential candidate Winfield Scott and portraits of the Naval officers Oliver Perry and Stephen Decatur, both heroes from the War of 1812. In the adjoining gallery *(gallery 210)*, portraits of *New York Times* correspondent Grace Greenwood and antislavery activist Lucretia Mott attest to women's involvement in the issues pertinent to **Jacksonian America**.

Continue the visit in gallery 205 at the other end of the corridor.

The **Native Americans** exhibit *(gallery 205)* presents watercolors, photographs and paintings, including four oils by George Catlin, a renowned painter of the nation's indigenous peoples. **The Expanding Frontier** *(gallery 207)* shows the adventurer David Crockett, better known as Davy Crockett. Portraits in the next room highlight **Pre-Civil War Science and Invention** *(gallery 209)*. Of note is the group portrait titled *Men of Progress* (1862), which depicts 19 Americans who made important contributions in the field of technology. The figures portrayed were painted separately and then regrouped on one canvas.

⑬ 7th Street feasting

Map p 15. Chinatown and its restaurants once dominated the 7th Street corridor, but in recent years two tapas restaurants have become the biggest draws (tapas are small side-dish servings that Spaniards munch on). The trendsetting, always-crowded **Jaleo** *(480 7th St. NW ☎ 202-628-7949)* specializes in classic Spanish tapas, including Jaleo's famous fried calamari with aioli, and all kinds of mushroom dishes. On Wednesday night Flamenco dancers weave among the tables. **Coco Loco** *(810 7th St. NW ☎ 202-289-2626)* offers Mexican-style tapas, such as cold seafood salads or stuffed cheese dishes. Also featured are a traditional Brazilian *churrasqueria* (selection of rotisserie meats) and a great antipasti bar. Coco Loco's nightclub, which presents Latin music, gets going at about 11pm Thursday, Friday and Saturday.

The galleries along the 7th Street hallway are filled with portraits of Americans prominent in history, literature and the arts in the last 60 years, including Carl Sandburg, Robert Frost, Martha Graham and George Gershwin. **Industry, Change and Reform** *(galleries 211 and 212)* introduces late-19C inventors, tycoons and agents of social change: inventor Thomas Edison, steel magnate Andrew Carnegie, and financial giants J.D. Rockefeller and J.P. Morgan; suffragists Susan B. Anthony and Elizabeth Cady Stanton; Chicago social worker and 1931 Nobel Peace Prize recipient Jane Addams; and Tuskegee Institute founder Booker T. Washington.

The Twenties *(gallery 213)* in the east corridor features personalities from this turbulent period in American history such as Andrew Mellon, secretary of the Treasury and founder of the National Gallery of Art; and John Pershing, the first military leader since Ulysses S. Grant to hold the rank of General of the Armies of the US. **Modernism: Literature and the Arts** *(gallery 214)* showcases Gertrude Stein, T.S. Eliot and other artistic trailblazers.

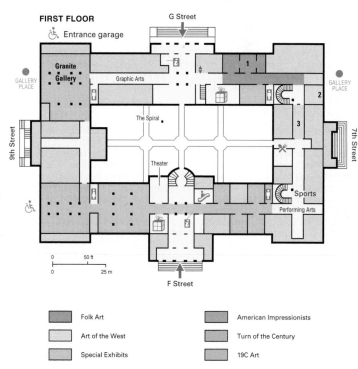

SECOND FLOOR

**NATIONAL PORTRAIT GALLERY/
AMERICAN ART MUSEUM**

World War II *(gallery 215)* commemorates public figures who shaped American international policy in the early 20C, such as Douglas MacArthur and George C. Marshall. Gallery 216 features Franklin D. Roosevelt and **The New Deal**. Cesar Chavez and Thurgood Marshall are among those remembered in **Civil Rights and Liberties** *(gallery 217)*, and **Exploration and Discovery** *(gallery 218)* pays tribute to creative achievers such as Albert Einstein and George Washington Carver. Gallery 219 is devoted to a rotating selection of portraits by the noted sculptor **Jo Davidson** (1883-1952), who immortalized in bronze, stone or terra-cotta many prominent figures of his period including Clare Boothe Luce, Robinson Jeffers and Fiorello La Guardia.

Return to the main landing. Take the twin staircases to the 3rd floor; note the finely crafted bronze balustrade.

Third Floor – The entire south wing of the museum on this floor is occupied by the **Great Hall**, whose decor of multicolored Milton tiles, carved ceiling medallions, and a yellow and blue central skylight reflects eclectic, late-19C tastes. The frieze of six relief panels illustrating sources of technology (fire, electricity, water, agriculture, metal fabrication, mining) is a reminder that the hall was originally designed to display miniature patent models. On its long sides the hall is flanked by mezzanines with cast-iron balustrades. An exhibit devoted to the **Civil War Period** begins on the east mezzanine *(take the elevator to the left)*, which is dominated by a full-length portrait of Abraham Lincoln. Renowned figures from this period include Harriet Beecher Stowe, author of *Uncle Tom's Cabin*; the abolitionist John Brown; and generals William Tecumseh Sherman and Ulysses S. Grant. Particularly moving is the famous **"cracked plate" photograph of Abraham Lincoln** taken on February 5, 1865, just two months before his assassination. Completing this historical survey of the Civil War is a portrait of the dashing commander of the Confederate forces, Gen. Robert E. Lee.

First Floor – The east corridor is lined with paintings and photographs of **Champions of American Sport** (Arthur Ashe, Ty Cobb, Jack Dempsey, Joe Louis and others) and popular figures in the **Performing Arts**, including great names in American theater, film and music, such as Aaron Copland, Marilyn Monroe, Marian Anderson, Benny Goodman, Grace Kelly and Will Rogers. Galleries in the adjacent corridor are reserved for changing exhibits.

The vaulted galleries situated on the opposite side of the lobby are also devoted to special exhibits.

SMITHSONIAN AMERICAN ART MUSEUM★

Old Patent Office Building at 8th and G Sts. NW.
Ⓜ Gallery Place.
Plan p 161

Housed in the landmark Old Patent Office Building, this museum contains the country's oldest federal collections of art. Its holdings run the gamut of American art from early-18C portraiture and 19C landscapes to the free-form sculpture and large, abstract canvases of contemporary artists.

Historical Notes

The museum traces its beginnings to the efforts of a Washingtonian named John Varden. In 1829 he began a collection of art, artifacts and natural history specimens, which he displayed in his own "Washington Museum." In 1841 his collection was joined with that of the congressionally mandated National Institute. The combined collections were exhibited in the completed south wing of the Patent Office Building, alongside cases displaying inventions, including Benjamin Franklin's printing press and an assortment of historic treasures, among them the Declaration of Independence (now in the National Archives).

In 1862 the collection was donated to the Smithsonian Institution, which exhibited selected pieces at various times and in several buildings throughout the city, including the Castle, the Corcoran Gallery and the National Museum of Natural History. In 1906 the collection was officially designated the National Gallery of Art, but it still had no permanent home or cohesion. Even its title was short-lived, since the new museum being built on the Mall to house the Mellon Collection was officially named the National Gallery of Art in 1937.

The National Collection of Fine Arts, as it was then called, remained in the Museum of Natural History until 1968, when it was permanently installed in its original quarters—the Old Patent Office Building. Since then, the collection has increased fivefold and now includes more than 34,000 objects. It received its previous name, the National Museum of American Art (NMAA), in 1980, to reflect its mandate to display exclusively the works of US artists. The NMAA was also the repository for art created under federal patronage, including the works commissioned by the Federal Art Projects. On October 27, 2000 President Bill Clinton signed into law a bill renaming the museum the Smithsonian American Art Museum.

VISIT *Floor plan p 161.*

The museum will be closed for renovation until 2004. Entrance on G St. Open year-round daily 10am–5:30pm. Closed Dec 25. Guided tours (1hr) available Mon–Fri at noon, weekends 2pm. ✕ ♿ ☎ 202-357-2700. www.nmaa.si.edu. The museum displays roughly 1,000 objects from its permanent collection at any one time.

First Floor – Not to be missed in the **Folk Art** section is James Hampton's **Throne of the Third Heaven of the Nations' Millennium General Assembly (1)**. This astounding three-dimensional work depicts the throne of God surrounded by altarlike pulpits and offertories. While employed as a Washington janitor from 1946 to 1960, Hampton created this monumental piece from discarded furniture, bottles and other items that he wrapped in aluminum and gold foil. The remaining galleries in this section showcase other works from the museum's 600-piece collection of 19C and 20C American folk art.

A section **(2)** at the end of the east corridor features works by Frederic Remington, John Stanley Mix and other 19C artists who portrayed life in the **American West**. The corridor **(3)** is devoted to the early-19C paintings of American Indians by artist-anthropologist **George Catlin** (1796-1872). The museum's collection includes 445 works by Catlin.

Rotating exhibits of graphic arts are displayed in the west corridor of this floor. The low-ceilinged **Granite Gallery**, which takes its name from the massive stone pillars that support the room's elegant vaulting, is devoted to special exhibits.

Second Floor – American art produced in the 19C and early 20C is displayed on this floor. The three **Western scenes** by Thomas Moran *(The Chasm of the Colorado* and two views of *The Grand Canyon of the Yellowstone)* that hang in the lounge **(4)** exemplify the monumental landscape painting of the period, a genre continued in the works displayed in the east corridor. Gallery 2-D **(5)** features the haunting, visionary scenes of Albert Pinkham Ryder (1847-1917), while the gallery diagonally across the corridor **(6)** highlights the paintings of Ryder's contemporary

14 Red Sage
Map p 15. 605 14th St. NW. ☎ *202-638-4444.* This two-story restaurant and chili bar has roped in the crowds with its singular Southwestern fare and decor since it opened to rave reviews in 1992. Mock cowhide seating, faux adobe walls, buffalo-blazoned ceiling lights and deer-antler sconces create the warmth of an upscale, multiroomed Rio Grande hacienda. The street-level chili bar serves light border food—signature chilies (Texas red ostrich or steak and black bean), sandwiches and specialty grill entrées (BBQ brisket quesadilla or BBQ chicken tostada with *guajillo* and *queso cotija*). Menu selections from the cozy downstairs dining rooms include wood-roasted quail and grilled rabbit sausage, Virginia buffalo and pepper-smoked wild shrimp, red chili-pecan-crusted chicken breast and duck pot pie.

Winslow Homer (1836-1910), whose use of color and light prefigures the Impressionists. The east corridor contains later-19C art, including the paintings of John Singer Sargent and Thomas Eakins.

The three galleries at the end of the east corridor **(7)** display works by John La Farge, Abbott Thayer, Augustus Saint-Gaudens and other artists of the Gilded Age. *Eve Tempted*, a Neoclassical sculpture by prominent 19C artist Hiram Powers, graces the hallway.

Among the paintings on view in the galleries devoted to art of the **Turn of the Century** and **American Impressionists** are the lyrically romantic works of Childe Hassam, Thomas Wilmer Dewing, John Henry Twachtman and Julian Alden Weir, all members of The Ten, a group of renowned American Impressionists. Also shown are works by Mary Cassatt, Romaine Brooks and Maurice Prendergast.

At the end of the west corridor, the works of prominent **18C and early-19C portraitists** Gilbert Stuart, Charles Willson Peale and Thomas Sully are presented, as are portrait miniatures.

Third Floor – Galleries in the east corridor display American art from the 1900s to the 1940s, including pieces from the museum's extensive Federal Art Projects holdings. The cavernous **Lincoln Gallery** highlights major schools and trends in mid-to-late-20C art. The Ashcan school (Robert Henri and John Sloan) is represented, as are Abstract Expressionism (Hans Hofmann and Franz Kline), Color Field (Morris Louis and Kenneth Noland) and Pop Art (Jasper Johns, Robert Rauschenberg, Andy Warhol). The west corridor is reserved for special exhibits.

"Washington is not a nice place to live in.
The rents are high, the food is bad, the dust is disgusting,
the mud is deep, and the morals are deplorable."
Horace Greeley, *New York Tribune*, July 13, 1865

FORD'S THEATRE AND PETERSEN HOUSE★

10th St. between E and F Sts. NW.
Ⓜ Metro Center.

In the heart of Downtown, amid a stretch of 19C structures, stands old Ford's Theatre, where Abraham Lincoln was shot by an assassin, and Petersen House, where he died of his wound.

Historical Notes

A Tragic Gala – On the evening of April 14, 1865, President and Mrs. Lincoln attended a performance of the popular comedy *Our American Cousin* at Ford's Theatre. The capital was in a festive mood as, only five days before, Confederate Gen. Robert E. Lee had surrendered to Union Gen. Ulysses S. Grant at Appomattox, Virginia. Grant and his wife had, in fact, been in Washington on April 14 and were to have attended the theater with the Lincolns, but they made the decision to leave town earlier in the day. In their stead, Clara Harris, daughter of Sen. Ira Harris, and her fiancé, Maj. Henry Rathbone, attended. That night the theater was full of Washingtonians hoping for a glimpse of Grant, who had rarely visited the city. In preparation for the president's arrival, boxes no. 7 and no. 8 had been draped with flags and the partition between them removed to allow the presidential party more space. The Lincoln party was engrossed in the third act of the play when **John Wilkes Booth** silently entered the box and shot the president at close range. The bullet from the small, single-shot derringer entered behind Lincoln's left ear and lodged behind his right eye. Major Rathbone immediately tried to subdue the attacker, but Booth defended himself with a large knife, stabbing the major in the left arm. Booth leaped over the balustrade of the box, but as he did so, his feet got tangled in the draped flags. He landed off balance on the stage 12ft below, breaking a small bone in his leg. Most accounts claim that Booth then stood and flourished his knife, declaring "Sic semper tyrannis!" ("Thus always with tyrants"). The audience, believing that Booth's appearance was part of the play, was slow to respond. In the theater alley Booth mounted a horse he had sequestered and escaped.

Lincoln's Final Hours – Three army surgeons in the audience immediately attended the stricken Lincoln. Recognizing the seriousness of the wound, they ordered him moved to the nearest bed; the president was carried across the street to a boarding house owned by a tailor named Petersen. He was laid in a first-floor back room then being rented by a young man in the Union Army. Due to Lincoln's height, he had to be placed diagonally across the bed. As the night passed, Cabinet ministers, physicians and other prominent people gathered in the back parlor, while Mrs. Lincoln was consoled by friends in the front parlor. Lincoln never regained consciousness. At 7:22am the following morning, he died.

After official ceremonies in Washington, Lincoln's body was taken by train to Springfield, Illinois, for burial. Along the route he lay in state in several large cities. Abraham Lincoln was buried at Springfield's Oak Ridge Cemetery on May 4.

The Assassination Plot – A successful actor who appeared several times on the stage of Ford's Theatre, John Wilkes Booth apparently sought to achieve lasting fame for himself by what he considered his "heroic" act on behalf of the Confederacy. He was the ringleader of a band of conspirators who had initially plotted the kidnapping of Lincoln. When logistics prevented this approach, Booth hatched a plot in which he would kill Lincoln and his accomplices would assassinate other high government officials. Only Booth was successful.

Once he had inflicted the mortal wound, Booth made for the home of Dr. Samuel Mudd in the southern Maryland countryside. Mudd set his leg, and Booth continued his flight, accompanied by a fellow conspirator, David Herold. The two men crossed into Virginia and were apprehended the night of April 26 by a cavalry detachment in Port Royal, Virginia. Herold surrendered, but Booth refused, forcing his pursuers to set on fire the barn in which he was hiding. As the building burst into flames, the assassin was fatally shot through the neck by one of the soldiers.

FORD'S THEATRE

Open year-round daily 9am–5pm. Closed Dec 25 and during rehearsals & performances. Guided tours (30min) available. ☎ 202-426-6924. www.nps.gov/foth.

When John Ford opened the doors of this brick structure in 1863, it was one of the grandest theaters in the country, with an advertised seating capacity of 2,500. Though its facade was adorned only with arched door bays, window trim, pilasters and an undecorated pediment, its interior was lavishly appointed. A cantilevered "dress circle," or balcony, flanked by private boxes, sloped toward the stage.

After Lincoln's assassination, the theater was ordered closed by the federal government. John Ford's announced intention to continue dramatic productions in the theater met with threats, so the War Department leased the building from Ford and began converting it into office space, ultimately purchasing it a year later for $100,000.

In 1893 another tragedy occurred here when collapsing floors killed 22 office workers. Thereafter the building was used only for storage until 1932, when the government opened it as a Lincoln museum, displaying memorabilia relating to the life of the 16th president. In the mid-1960s Congress authorized a restoration of the building to its 1865 appearance. Ford's Theatre reopened in 1968 as both a memorial and an active playhouse.

The **box** where Lincoln sat is decorated as it was on the night of April 14, 1865, with upholstered Victorian period pieces, including the settee that had been specially placed there for the president and his guests. On the balcony level is an imposing **bronze head of Lincoln** by Carl Tolpo, which was presented to Ford's Theatre in 1965.

In the basement, the refurbished **Lincoln Museum** *(same hours as the theater)* displays such artifacts from the assassination as Booth's derringer and the clothes Lincoln was wearing.

Presidential Box, Ford's Theatre

© Fred J. Maroon/FOLIO, Inc.

PETERSEN HOUSE

Across the brick-paved street from the theater at 516 Tenth St. Open year-round daily 9am–5pm. Closed Dec 25. ☎ 202-426-6924.

The simple three-story brick row house where Lincoln died on April 15, 1865, was built in 1850 by William Petersen, a tailor. Its three first-floor rooms, a front and back parlor and bedroom, decorated in Victorian period furnishings, are open to the public.

FEDERAL BUREAU OF INVESTIGATION★

E St. between 9th and 10th Sts. NW.
Ⓜ Federal Triangle.

Officially known as the J. Edgar Hoover FBI Building, this immense, fortresslike structure bordering Pennsylvania Avenue houses the national headquarters of the Federal Bureau of Investigation (FBI).

Historical Notes

An arm of the Justice Department, the FBI traces its beginnings to 1908, when a permanent investigative force of special agents was placed under the control of the attorney general. In 1935 this force was designated the Federal Bureau of Investigation and its powers broadened in an effort to combat rampant gangsterism. Under the 48-year leadership (1924-72) of director **J. Edgar Hoover**, the bureau became the supreme federal authority in matters of domestic crime.

Begun in 1963, the headquarters building was completed 12 years later in 1975, at a cost of over $126 million. Stanley Gladych's design exemplifies the New Brutalism school of architecture, which features exposed concrete and little embellishment. Covering a city block, the building wraps around an interior courtyard. An exterior arcade along the perimeter is lined with rows of massive pillars. According to the FBI's own literature, the design of the structure "retained the idea of a central core of files." The building houses nearly 8,000 workers. In addition, the FBI maintains 56 field offices and over 400 resident agencies, employing more than 11,000 agents.

Fingerprinting Firsts

- **1686:** Using the newly invented microscope, a University of Bologna professor observes the "loops and spirals" on the ends of fingers.

- **1858:** A British chief administrator in Bengal, India, requires the native residents to affix their fingerprints to contracts, the first known official use of fingerprints on a large scale.

- **1880:** A medical doctor in Toyko recommends, in a published scientific journal, the use of printer's ink as a transfer medium for fingerprints.

- **1882:** To prevent forgery, a US Geological Survey official uses his own fingerprint on a commissary document, the first authenticated record of official use of fingerprinting.

- **1883:** A noted British anthropologist devises the first scientific method for classifying fingerprint patterns.

- **1902:** The first known systematic use of fingerprinting begins in the US—on New York civil service applicants, to prevent cheating on tests.

- **1903:** New York introduces the first systematic use of fingerprints in the US to identify criminals.

- **1924:** An act of Congress establishes the FBI's Identification Division to serve as a national repository of fingerprint files for criminal identification.

VISIT

🧒 *Visit by guided tour (1hr) only, year-round Mon–Fri 8:45am–4pm (congressional visits available—p 255). Closed major holidays.* ♿ ▥ ☎ *202-324-3447.*

The FBI tour is one of Washington's most popular attractions. A small exhibit hall contains displays on the history of the bureau and its procedures. The remainder of the tour is devoted to various research facilities housed here, such as the labs where bullet, firearm and fiber analyses are conducted. A live firearms demonstration often concludes the tour.

NATIONAL MUSEUM OF WOMEN IN THE ARTS★

1250 New York Ave. and 13th St. NW.
Ⓜ Metro Center.
Plan p 12

Behind this Beaux-Arts exterior is the world's only major museum devoted exclusively to the works of women artists. The 2,700-piece permanent collection includes works from the 16C to the present, covering every medium from native American pottery to abstract sculpture.

Historical Notes

Local philanthropists Wilhelmina and Wallace Holladay founded the museum in 1981 as a private institution "to encourage greater awareness of women in the arts and their contributions to the history of art." The Holladays donated their own collection to form the core of the museum's holdings, which today comprise works from more than 800 women artists.

The edifice housing the museum was a Masonic temple constructed in 1908. Its architect, Waddy B. Wood, designed the stately limestone and granite trapezoid to be "in keeping with the classic public buildings" of the capital city. Designated a National Historic Landmark in the early 1980s, the building has set the style for urban renewal in this area, influencing the architecture of such structures as the nearby office buildings at nos. 1212 and 1201 New York Avenue.

In 1983 the newly founded museum purchased the building from the fraternal order of Masons and formally opened at this new location in 1987. An $8 million renovation transformed the interior into three levels of exhibit space, a library and research center and a 200-seat auditorium, where public lectures, workshops, films and concerts are held. The Kasser Wing, which houses additional exhibit space, a conference room and an expanded museum shop, was completed in 1997.

VISIT

Open year-round Mon–Sat 10am–5pm, Sun noon–5pm. Closed Jan 1, Thanksgiving Day, Dec 25. $5. ✗ ♿ ☎ 202-783-5000. www.nmwa.org.

The main floor is dominated by the extensively remodeled **Great Hall**, a two-story expanse of rose, white and gray Turkish marble (and *faux marbre*) overhung by three crystal and gold-leaf chandeliers. The mezzanine level, which was added during the renovation, is rimmed with a heavy marble balustrade that extends along the twin staircases on opposite sides of the hall. The gilded lions' heads topping the columns on this level and the ornate ceiling are the only features from the building's original interior. Light is admitted through the mezzanine's large arched windows.

Lady with a Bowl of Violets (c.1910) by Lilla Cabot Perry

Courtesy The National Museum of Women in the Arts, Gift of Wallace and Wilhelmina Holladay

Selected works from the permanent collection are hung in the Great Hall and on the mezzanine on a rotating basis, while the second floor is generally devoted to major temporary exhibits.

The museum's third-floor galleries, arranged chronologically, are devoted to works from its **permanent collection** *(take elevator to 3rd floor)*. The earliest works (displayed in the 16-18C gallery) are primarily still lifes and portraits, characteristic of the subject matter of early women artists. The oldest work in the collection is the *Portrait of a Noblewoman* (c.1580) by Lavinia Fontana, a 16C Italian painter from Bologna who is considered the first professional woman artist. *Still Life of Fish and Cat* by Clara Peeters, a 17C Flemish artist, highlights her contributions to the development of that genre. Two still lifes of flowers are representative of the work of Rachel Ruysch, a 17C Dutch artist. This gallery also contains a portrait by the court painter of Marie Antoinette, Elisabeth Vigée-Lebrun (1755-1842).

The 19C gallery displays works by the well-known animal portraitist Rosa Bonheur and *The Cage*, a still life by the famous French Impressionist Berthe Morisot, as well as the sculpture *Young Girl With a Sheaf* by Camille Claudel. Among the 19C American works are an early portrait by Cecilia Beaux, and *The Bath*, from a renowned series of graphics by the acclaimed Impressionist Mary Cassatt. Lilla Cabot Perry, who introduced the work of Monet to Americans, is represented by her *Lady with a Bowl of Violets* and *Lady in Evening Dress*.

The museum's notable collection of **19C sculpture**—a rare medium for female artists of that period—includes the works of Malvina Hoffman, Anna Vaughn Hyatt Huntington, Bessie Potter Vonnoh and Evelyn Beatrice Longman.

The 20C galleries feature paintings by Helen Frankenthaler, Elaine de Kooning, Lee Krasner, Nancy Graves and others. Mexican artist Frida Kahlo's *Self-Portrait*, painted in homage to Trotsky, reflects her revolutionary zeal and introspection.

Inter-American Development Bank Cultural Center and Art Gallery
Map p 10. 1300 New York Ave., NW. Open year-round Mon–Fri 11am–6pm. ☎ *202-623-3774.* Latin American art lovers should not miss a visit to this welcome respite from the crowds of the National Mall. For over three decades, the Bank has collected works reflective of the multicultural and ethnic diversity of its member countries. Drawing from its own collection as well as works on loan, the gallery showcases four exhibits a year that celebrate the artistic and intellectual life of Latin America and the Caribbean.

NATIONAL BUILDING MUSEUM

401 F St. NW (north side of Judiciary Square).
Ⓜ Judiciary Square.

Formerly known as the Pension Building, the colossal brick edifice bordering the north side of Judiciary Square was long considered one of the capital's most monumental eyesores. Painstakingly refurbished, this extraordinary example of 19C eclecticism now houses a museum devoted to America's achievements in the building arts.

Historical Notes

"Meigs Old Red Barn" – In the 1880s US Army engineer Gen. **Montgomery Meigs** (1816-92) was commissioned to design a permanent workplace for the 1,500 employees of the Pension Bureau, the federal agency responsible for distributing government pensions to wounded veterans and survivors of persons killed in American military conflicts. Earlier in his career, Meigs had supervised the mid-19C extension of the Capitol and the construction of the Arts and Industries Building. Nicknamed "Meigs Old Red Barn," the **Pension Building★**, impressive in both its scale and design, has been a subject of controversy since its completion in 1887. Referring to the building, Union Gen. William Tecumseh Sherman reputedly commented, "The worst of it is, it is fireproof."

Occupying an entire city block, the massive rectangular edifice (400ft by 200ft) contains more than 15 million bricks and stands almost 160ft tall (the height of a 15-story modern building). The exterior design, with its prominent overhanging cornice and three stories of pedimented and linteled windows, is a double-scale version of the Palazzo Farnese in Rome—the 16C architectural masterpiece partly designed by Michelangelo. The outstanding decorative feature on the building's exterior is the 3ft-high terra-cotta **frieze** that extends around the entire structure above the ground-floor windows. Created by 19C sculptor Casper Buberl, the 35 panels making up this memorial to the Civil War dead depict Union infantry, cavalry, artillery, naval and medical troops on the march.

New Features, New Tenants – The oversized "palazzo" is crowned by a curious roof structure consisting of intersecting gable-ended clerestories, specially designed to provide abundant light within and to conserve heat in winter. Concerned with providing healthy conditions for the office workers, Meigs incorporated other technical innovations into his design, such as a sophisticated ventilation system that afforded an excellent crosscurrent between the roof, windows and the small openings below each window. The structure was made fireproof by the use of brick and metal.

Since the transfer of the Pension Bureau to more spacious accommodations in the 1920s, the building has housed various government agencies. In the 1950s demolition was considered, but the building's survival was ensured during the following decades, thanks to its designation as a National Historic Landmark and the decision to convert it into a museum devoted to the building and arts trades. The Pension Building is now the home of the National Building Museum (NBM), created in 1980 by congressional mandate to commemorate American architecture and to encourage the study and appreciation of the building arts.

National Building Museum

VISIT

Open year-round Mon–Sat 10am–5pm, Sun noon–5pm. Closed Jan 1, Thanksgiving Day, Dec 25. Guided tours (45min) available Mon–Wed 12:30pm, Thur–Sat 11:30am, 12:30pm & 1:30pm, Sun 12:30pm & 1:30pm. $5. ✗ ♿ ☏ 202-272-2448. www.nbm.org. For information on exhibits and activities, consult the website or the NBM's calendar of events, published monthly.

At present, the museum's main attraction is the building itself. Upon entering the vast interior court known as the **Great Hall**, the visitor is impressed by its staggering proportions. Measuring 116ft by 316ft, this monumental space is punctuated by eight 75ft Corinthian columns made of brick and painted to resemble Siena marble. Out of scale with the rest of the interior, these colossal pieces of solid masonry support the central roof structure, which admits abundant light. The court is flanked by two stories of elegant galleries lined with 72 Doric and 72 Ionic columns, evoking the graceful courtyards of Renaissance palaces. The third-floor parapet is ornamented by plaster replicas of the terra-cotta urns originally designed for the building. In the cornice of the hall's central section high above the colossal columns, 244 niches *(best seen from the upper floors)* contain life-size busts symbolic of American builders and craftsmen. Roaming through the spacious building *(the 1st and 2nd floors are open to the public)*, you will discover a wealth of fine architectural detail, including deep-set brick stairways covered by pure-lined barrel and groin vaulting.

Since 1885 the Great Hall has been the setting of **inaugural balls** for 13 presidents, including Theodore Roosevelt, Richard Nixon, Jimmy Carter, Ronald Reagan, George Bush and Bill Clinton.

On the second floor, a presentation of the building's construction and restoration is permanently displayed. The exhibit entitled "Washington: Symbol and City," featuring models of several prominent monuments, offers an overview of the development of architecture in the nation's capital *(under renovation until summer 2002)*. In addition to organizing temporary exhibits, the museum sponsors numerous walking tours, lectures and programs on various aspects of building.

OLD POST OFFICE

Pennsylvania Ave. and 12th St. NW.
Ⓜ Federal Triangle.

Saved from the wrecker's ball at the eleventh hour, this rejuvenated Pennsylvania Avenue landmark has been converted into a "festival market" that attracts numerous residents and tourists throughout the year.

Historical Notes

The massive granite structure, which was built as the headquarters of the US Postal Service, met with public disfavor almost immediately after its completion in 1899. Designed in the then-outmoded Richardsonian Romanesque style—replete with rough-faced masonry, gabled dormers, corner turrets and an imposing tower—the building was facetiously nicknamed "Old Tooth." The structure greatly deteriorated in the decades following the postmaster general's move to new quarters in 1934.

In 1971, the year in which the building's demolition was officially approved, various preservation groups spearheaded a popular movement that ultimately led to the building's resurrection. A $30 million, federally funded restoration project (1978-83) transformed the Old Post Office into a multifunctional complex with office and commercial space. This widely acclaimed adaptive-use project served as a catalyst for the rehabilitation of the blighted Pennsylvania Avenue area.

VISIT

Open Easter Sunday-Labor Day daily 8am–10:45pm (closed Thu 7pm–9pm for bell ringing). Rest of the year daily 10am–5:30pm. Closed Jan 1, Thanksgiving Day, Dec 25. Guided tours (30min) available. ✗ ♿ ☏ 202-606-8691.

Capitol Steps
Map p 15. Friday and Saturday nights at the Ronald Reagan Building & International Trade Center. 1300 Pennsylvania Avenue, NW. ☏ 202-312-1555. www.capsteps.com. Billed as "musical political satire," this two-hour comedy show, performed by current and former congressional staffers, evolved from an office Christmas party skit in 1981. The popular political satirists have kept audiences (including several presidents) roaring with irreverent, boisterous spoofs of Washington politics and offbeat impressions of politicians. Musical parodies such as "We Arm the World," "For He's a Jolly Good Felon" and "Fools on the Hill" make for unforgettable fun. Tickets available through Ticketmaster ☏ 202-432-7328.

Interior – The outstanding architectural feature is the central glass-roofed **courtyard** (99ft by 184ft; 160ft high) surrounded by seven floors of offices for various federal agencies. The courtyard's first three levels accommodate a variety of restaurants, cafes, fast-food stands, souvenir shops and a stage for live entertainment. Called the Pavilion, this popular spot has been the setting for several annual festivities, including a New Year's celebration.

Tower – Ascending the 315ft clock tower by means of the glass elevator *(situated in the northwest corner of the courtyard)* allows visitors to appreciate the vastness of the courtyard. Near the summit are the **Congress bells** donated to the US government by the Ditchley Foundation of Great Britain in 1983 to commemorate the end of the American Revolution. Cast in London in 1976, the 10 bells are played for state occasions and to mark the opening and closing of sessions of Congress. The observation deck, the area's second highest public vantage point (surpassed only by the Washington Monument), offers a **view** of the surroundings.

NATIONAL AQUARIUM

Department of Commerce Building,
14th St. and Constitution Ave. NW.
Ⓜ Federal Triangle.

This small aquarium is the nation's oldest. Established in 1873 under the auspices of the Federal Fish Commission, it has occupied various locations, including a series of ponds on the grounds of the Washington Monument. In the early 20C the Fish Commission came under the direction of the Department of Commerce, and in 1932 the aquarium was moved to its present location in the basement of the Department of Commerce Building. Since 1982 the aquarium has functioned independently of the government as a private, nonprofit organization.

15 Pershing Park
Map p 15. Pennsylvania Ave. and 14th St. NW. Offering shade and serenity amid the bustling streets of Downtown, this small park is situated opposite the Willard Hotel. Take a break on a bench or get a quick bite to eat from the cafe. The park's ponds attract ducks in the fall and ice-skaters in winter *(skates available for rent; Pershing Park Ice Rink ☎ 202-737-6938).*

VISIT

🄺 *Open year-round daily 9am–5pm. Closed Dec 25. $3. Shark feeding Mon, Wed & Sat 2pm, piranha feeding Tue, Thu & Sun 2pm.* ♿ ☎ *202-482-2825.*

The aquarium's tanks house some 1,500 specimens of aquatic life, including sea turtles, lemon sharks, piranhas, moray eels and lungfish. A touch tank allows visitors to handle such marine life as sea urchins and hermit crabs, and a theater features presentations on the underwater world.

5

Foggy Bottom

Once industrialized riverfront, this bottomland lying west of the White House was transformed after World War II into an administrative quarter. Today it houses private institutions, government departments, a celebrated performing arts complex and the city-styled campus of **George Washington University**.

Breweries and Gasworks – Prior to the founding of the federal city, a small German settlement called Hamburg was located on the present site of the State Department Building. In L'Enfant's city plan *(p 30)* little was stipulated for this end of town except a circle—now Washington Circle—and a battlement, to be constructed on Camp Hill between what are now 23rd and 24th streets. In the early 19C a glassworks and brewery attracted more Germans here, but the area called Foggy Bottom—presumably because of the mists that hovered over its marshy ground—developed slowly. One of the earliest and finest homes in the area was The Octagon, built a few blocks west of the White House. On higher ground, along the K Street corridor, well-heeled Washingtonians built substantial dwellings. In 1844 a naval observatory was constructed atop Camp Hill. The original building still stands on the grounds of the Navy Bureau of Medicine and Surgery *(not open to the public)* on 23rd Steet. In 1856 the Washington Gas Light Storage Facility was built in Foggy Bottom and became a major employer, particularly for the Irish immigrants who lived in Connaught Row, south of Virginia Avenue.

The growing black population in the area amassed the funds to commission the renowned architect James Renwick to design **St. Mary's Episcopal Church**. Established in 1886, the brick Gothic Revival church still stands at 728 23rd Street.

Two breweries—the Heurich Brewery, established by Christian Heurich *(p 198)*, and the Abner Drury Brewery—employed many of the neighborhood's German residents. Waterfront warehouses and wharves added to the industrial character of this malarial bottomland, and rows of narrow brick tenements constituted its residential core.

Transformation – In 1912 George Washington University moved to the northern end of Foggy Bottom, lending a collegiate air to the streets southeast of Washington Circle. Nonetheless, throughout the first half of the 20C, the lowlands near the Potomac remained an industrial area of steadily declining fortunes and substandard housing. Then in 1947 the State Department moved into a large, graceless new headquarters building at 23rd and D streets. At the same time the century-old gas plant ceased operations, and Foggy Bottom took on a new respectability.

Throughout the 1950s the neighborhood shifted from low-income industrial to middle-class professional. A series of office-residential medium-rise buildings were constructed, and in the 1960s the Potomac shoreline became the site of the John F. Kennedy Center for the Performing Arts. Beside it, the exuberant curves of the exclusive **Watergate complex** of condominiums and shops further enhanced the riverfront. In the 1970s the complex gained national notoriety as the site of the Democratic National Committee break-in that ultimately led to President Richard Nixon's resignation. Offsetting this modern construction, pleasant pockets of 19C row houses can still be found in the vicinity of George Washington University *(18th–25th Sts. and E-K Sts.)*.

In Foggy Bottom's southern quarter are the administrative headquarters of such international organizations as the **World Bank** *(1818 H St.)* and the **Pan-American Health** and **World Health Organizations** *(both at 523 23rd St.)*, as well as numerous government departments. The north side of Constitution Avenue is lined with the dignified facades of the **Department of the Interior** (1937), the **Federal Reserve** buildings (1937), the **American Pharmaceutical Assn.** (1934), and the **National Academy of Sciences** (1924). A compelling monument to physicist Albert Einstein is located on the grounds of the academy.

JOHN F. KENNEDY CENTER
FOR THE PERFORMING ARTS★★

New Hampshire Ave. at Rock Creek Parkway.
Ⓜ Foggy Bottom.

Its gleaming horizontal mass dominating Foggy Bottom's riverfront, the Kennedy Center today ranks as one of the country's leading cultural institutions. Its designation as the capital's official memorial to the 35th president of the US has greatly contributed to the center's popularity as a tourist attraction.

Historical Notes

"A Living Memorial" – Although the idea of establishing a national cultural center in Washington dates back to the early days of the capital, it was only in 1958 that such an undertaking received congressional approval. In that year President Eisenhower signed the National Cultural Center Act authorizing the creation of a national showplace for the arts.

A prime Foggy Bottom site comprising just under 10 acres of government property was chosen for the facility's location, and architect Edward Durell Stone was commissioned to design the complex. Due to a lack of sufficient private funds, the project lagged until early 1964, when Congress unanimously voted to designate the center as the capital's only monument to assassinated President John F. Kennedy. Unlike the other presidential memorials erected in Washington, the John F. Kennedy Center for the Performing Arts, as the complex was renamed, was to be "a living memorial." To hasten construction of the privately funded project, Congress appropriated $23 million in federal matching funds. In the groundbreaking ceremony that took place in December 1964, President Lyndon Johnson wielded the same gold-plated shovel used by two of his predecessors to initiate the construction of two other presidential monuments: the Jefferson Memorial and the Lincoln Memorial. Over 40 foreign governments offered gifts—primarily works of art—to adorn the presidential memorial.

To mark the Center's official opening on September 8, 1971, the world premiere of Leonard Bernstein's *Mass* was performed in the Opera House by a cast of 200 performers before an audience that included numerous personalities in the arts and government.

Operation of the Center – Headed by a board of trustees appointed by the US president, the Kennedy Center operates as a nonprofit institution supported by private gifts and ticket sales. As a presidential memorial, the building and its property (excluding theater and administrative facilities) are maintained by the National Park Service.

The complex houses under the same roof six theaters of varying sizes with a total seating capacity of over 7,000, as well as an educational resource center. Home of the National Symphony Orchestra, the Kennedy Center schedules a wide spectrum of world-class entertainment in music, dance and theater, including hit Broadway shows. Selected performances are broadcast on national television and radio. Among the acclaimed artists who have performed here are Bill Cosby, Placido Domingo, Duke Ellington, Ella Fitzgerald, Rudolf Nureyev, Jason Robards, Arthur Rubenstein, Beverly Sills, Frank Sinatra, Isaac Stern and Elizabeth Taylor.

Grand Foyer

Distinguished orchestras and opera and ballet companies, such as the Berlin Philharmonic, La Scala, the Vienna State Opera, the Metropolitan Opera and the Bolshoi Ballet, are regularly invited to perform here. The overwhelming success of the Kennedy Center has been instrumental in propelling the capital into the forefront of the national and international cultural scene, thereby belying Washington's long-held reputation as a cultural backwater.

VISIT

Open year-round daily 10am–11pm. Guided tours (1hr) available. ☎ 202-416-8340 or 800-444-1324. Tickets must be purchased for most performances. ✕ ♿ ⅌ ☎ 202-467-4600. www.kennedy-center.org. Free shuttle service to/from Foggy Bottom Metro station and Kennedy Center Mon–Sat 9:45am–midnight, Sun noon–midnight every 15min via the center's burgundy and white minibuses.

Exterior – The low rectangular structure (630ft by 300ft) is surrounded on all sides by a colonnade of metal piers supporting a roof terrace, above which rises the building's central section. Clad in white Carrara marble (a gift from Italy), the stark structure seems to echo the overall design of the Lincoln Memorial, situated just a half mile downstream.

Interior – The two principal entrances, situated on the east facade, lead to a pair of lofty galleries clearly designed to inspire awe. The dizzying effect experienced upon entering is created by the relative narrowness of these spaces. The **Hall of States** *(north side)* displays flags of the 50 states, while the **Hall of Nations** *(south side)* is decked with flags of all foreign countries diplomatically accredited by the US. These parallel halls traverse the building's width, separating the three main auditoriums and ultimately connecting with the **Grand Foyer**, reputedly one of the largest rooms in the world (630ft long, 40ft wide, 60ft high). Occupying the entire length of the river facade, this awesome space is lined with 60ft-high mirrors (a gift from Belgium) that reflect the river terrace outside the foyer's floor-to-ceiling windows. Eighteen Orrefors crystal chandeliers (donated by Sweden) illuminate the gigantic expanse. In the central section of the foyer, note the expressive bronze **bust** of President Kennedy by Robert Berks.

The foyer serves as a vestibule to the three main auditoriums: the **Opera House** (2,318 seats), flanked by the **Concert Hall** (2,759 seats) and the **Eisenhower Theater** (1,142 seats). Renowned for their excellent acoustics, these theaters are appointed in color schemes of red, ivory and gold and contain gifts, in the form of stage curtains, chandeliers and artwork, from foreign countries that contributed to the project. The **American Film Institute Theater** (224 seats), situated off the Hall of States, shows more than 600 movies annually and organizes festivals of film classics.

The roof level *(accessible by elevators in the Hall of States and Hall of Nations)* houses two additional theaters, the educational resource center, restaurants and exhibit spaces. A gift from Japan, the **Terrace Theater** *(off the north gallery)* was designed by noted architects Philip Johnson and John Burgee. This 512-seat performing space hosts concerts of chamber music as well as recitals and small-scale dance and theatrical performances. The **Theater Lab** (350 seats), designed for experimentation in sound research, is often the setting for children's entertainment.

DIPLOMATIC RECEPTION ROOMS★★
DEPARTMENT OF STATE

23rd St. between C and D Sts. NW.
Ⓜ Foggy Bottom.

Housed in an undistinguished 1960s government office building, these reception rooms have been transformed into architectural masterpieces of 18C interior design. They are furnished with one of the most impressive collections of American decorative arts in the country.

Historical Notes

When the State Department headquarters building opened in 1961, its eighth-floor rooms, used for official functions in honor of visiting dignitaries, were furnished in a stark, streamlined decor in keeping with the building's concrete and glass modernism. Before long, an effort called the **Americana Project**, under the direction of the Fine Arts Committee of the State Department, was begun to upgrade these reception areas. Spearheaded by Clement E. Conger, then the department's deputy chief of protocol and curator of the White House, the project solicited private donors for contributions of funds and furnishings. Over the past three decades, it has amassed a collection of **American decorative arts★★** from the period between 1725 and 1825 valued at approximately $90 million.

Edward Vason Jones, a Georgia architect, dedicated the last 15 years of his life to redesigning the rooms in the style of great 18C American manor houses. The ornately plastered ceilings, pilasters, paneling, entablatures and pediments complement the fine furnishings.

Bombé Desk and Bookcase (1753)

W. Brown/Diplomatic Reception Rooms, US Department of State

VISIT

Visit by guided tour (45min) only, year-round Mon–Fri 9:30am, 10:30am & 2:45pm. Closed major holidays. 2-4 week advance reservations required year-round (in summer 3–month advance reservations suggested). Tour is not recommended for children under 12. ♿ ☏ 202-647-3241.

From the austere modernism of the building lobby, elevators ascend to the Edward Vason Jones Memorial Hall. Originally a nondescript elevator hall, it now serves as an elegant **foyer** appointed with marbelized pilasters and entablatures and rare King of Prussia gray marble floors.

Adjoining it, the **Entrance Hall** contains the Chippendale furnishings, oriental rugs, ornate paneling and English cut-glass chandeliers characteristic of the 18C American decor seen throughout most of the reception rooms. The mahogany bombé secretary-bookcase in this hall is the oldest dated and signed piece of bombé furniture in North America. It was made by Benjamin Frothingham of Boston in 1753.

A short passageway opens onto the **Gallery**, a long, narrow room that was effectively lightened and enlarged by adding Palladian windows at either end. Among the **Chippendale and Queen Anne furniture** is a bombé chest of drawers made in Boston about 1765 and considered one of the finest examples of its kind in the world. Also made in Boston about the same time, the mahogany secretary belonged to Robert "King" Hooper, an 18C colonial shipping magnate of Marblehead, Massachusetts. A portrait of his daughter, Alice, by a young John Singleton Copley, and a later Copley of Mrs. John Montresor hang here. The five-part breakfront holds a set of Chinese Export porcelain in the Fitzhugh pattern. Ordered from England about 1800, the 65-piece set arrived in Philadelphia with an incorrect family monogram and was never used. It remained packed in its original shipping boxes until put on display here. In the large 18C-style **John Quincy Adams State Drawing Room**, official guests are greeted by secretaries of State and other dignitaries in receiving lines. Wall paneling, door and window cornices, an elaborate mantelpiece and oriental rugs ornament this formal room. Portraits of Mr. and Mrs. John Quincy Adams hang on the walls. The original **portrait of John Jay** (1784) by Gilbert Stuart is considered the finest painting in the collection. The English Sheraton tambour, or desk, where Jay signed the Treaty of Paris, Britain's formal acceptance of American Independence, is among the room's furnishings, as is the simple architectural desk on which Thomas Jefferson may have drafted the Declaration of Independence.

The Neoclassical proportions and Doric entablature of the **Thomas Jefferson State Reception Room** reflect Jefferson's own architectural tastes. A copy of the David Anger statue of Jefferson that stands in the US Capitol occupies a pedimented niche at the end of the room. Several

⑱ 2000 Pennsylvania Ave. NW *Map p 14.* Chef Bob Kinkead's innovative combination of sauces and ingredients makes his award-winning, self-proclaimed American brasserie, **Kinkead's** (☏ 202-296-7700. *www.kinkead.com*), perhaps the premier seafood restaurant in the city. Portuguese-style mussels with chorizo and tomato, tuna carpaccio with fennel salad, and roasted monkfish with artichokes are just a sampling of the enticements on the menu. Meat (lamb shanks, pork medallions) and chicken (grilled paillard) dishes are memorable as well.
Two capacious floors full of tapes and CDs at **Tower Records** (☏ 202-331-2400) boast a comprehensive selection of rock, jazz, blues, classical and country recordings as well as pop and music-related magazines and newspapers.

Jefferson portraits, including Thomas Sully's 1822 work, are on display. A fine pastel portrait of Benjamin Franklin by Jean-Baptiste Greuze also hangs here. The Savonnerie carpet, measuring roughly 39ft by 21ft, is a reproduction of one originally made for the palace at Versailles.

The cavernous **Benjamin Franklin State Dining Room**, the most recently renovated room, was redesigned by John Blatteau and completed in 1985. Red-veined scagliola columns are set off by gilded capitals and entablatures. An 8,000-pound **Savonnerie rug** in rose and gold covers the floor, and eight cut-glass chandeliers flank a gilded Great Seal of the US in the ceiling. Above the mantel hangs Benjamin Franklin's favorite portrait of himself, painted by David Martin.

THE OCTAGON★

1799 New York Ave. NW.
Ⓜ Farragut West.

One of Washington's earliest and finest residences, this many-sided architectural gem played a decided role in the history of the young Republic. Still retaining its Federal appearance *(illustration p 34)*, the Octagon houses period rooms and a gallery devoted to architecture and design exhibits organized under the auspices of the American Architectural Foundation, which also administers the property.

Historical Notes

Historical Role – In the 1790s George Washington, anxious to spur development of the new federal city, convinced his friend Col. John Tayloe to build a town house several blocks west of the planned President's Park (now Lafayette Square). A wealthy Virginia planter, Tayloe commissioned Dr. William Thornton, the first architect of the Capitol. Thornton's task was complicated by the fact that Tayloe's lot was triangular, formed by the intersection of New York Avenue and 18th Street. In order to harmonize the house with its setting, Thornton conceived an ingenious, multisided structure that became known as the Octagon, considered one of the burgeoning city's finest homes. The Tayloes used it as their winter residence after its completion in 1801, entertaining the capital's most influential figures here. During the August 1814 burning of Washington by the British, French Minister Louis Seurier was in residence at the house, and at his request, the British spared the Octagon. The White House, however, was gutted by fire, and while it was being repaired, President Madison lived in several different private homes, including the Octagon. During the Madisons' stay, from September 1814 to March 1815, peace was negotiated, ending the War of 1812. The **Treaty of Ghent**, signed by the British in Ghent, Belgium, on December 24, 1814, was brought to Washington and signed by James Madison at the Octagon, on February 17, 1815.

Decline and Revival – By the time of Mrs. Tayloe's death in 1855, the house and surrounding neighborhood had deteriorated. Tayloe's heirs leased the property for the remainder of the century to various groups, including the Federal Hydrographic Office. By the late 19C it had become an ill-kept tenement, but its architectural integrity attracted the interests of the **American Institute of Architects** (AIA). In 1902 the institute purchased the building from the Tayloe family for $30,000, moved its headquarters here and began a meticulous restoration. In 1972 the AIA built the modern structure that wraps around the rear of the Octagon to house its offices, library facilities and bookstore. The attractive courtyard that separates the contrasting buildings features a free-form stainless steel sculpture by James Rosati titled *Triple Arc 1* (1984).

VISIT

Open year-round Tue–Sun 10am–4pm. Closed Jan 1, Thanksgiving Day, Dec 25. $5. Guided tours (45min) available. ☎ 202-638-3105. www.archfoundation.org.

Though its name suggests eight sides, this brick structure is actually six-sided, with a rounded front pavilion that serves as a large entrance foyer. Beyond the foyer the main hall is dominated by a graceful oval staircase. Opening off the main hall are two large public rooms, furnished in Federal style. The drawing room is notable for its rare mantel of Coade stone, an artificial material produced in England from the late 18C until the mid-19C. In the symmetrical, Adam-style dining room hang portraits of Col. and Mrs. Tayloe by Gilbert Stuart.

The circular study on the second floor is known as the Treaty of Ghent Room. Madison is believed to have signed the historic document at the round mahogany table in the center of the room. The two flanking rooms are devoted to changing exhibits on architecture.

The brick-floored basement houses a kitchen and wine cellar.

DEPARTMENT OF THE INTERIOR MUSEUM

Department of the Interior Building at C St. between 18th and 19th Sts. NW.
Ⓜ Farragut West.

This small museum, located on the first floor of the Interior Department building, has retained the flavor of the late 1930s, when it first opened to the public.

Historical Notes

In 1849 Congress created the Department of the Interior primarily to conserve and manage the country's natural resources, including public lands, mineral resources, forests and wildlife. The department was also given responsibility for American Indian reservations and the US island territories. Today it comprises 10 bureaus: Reclamation, Indian Affairs, Land Management, Mineral Management, Surface Mining, US Geological Survey, US Fish and Wildlife, National Park Service, Office of the Secretary, and Policy, Budget and Administration.

In 1935 Secretary of the Interior Harold Ickes suggested that space for a museum be included in the Interior building, which was completed in 1936. Opened in 1938, the museum contained a gallery for every bureau to display its equipment, documents, maps, models, natural history specimens and other artifacts. The museum became such a popular attraction that opening hours had to be extended into the evening and maintained even during World War II.

VISIT

Open year-round Mon–Fri 8:30am–4:30pm. Closed major holidays. Photo ID required to enter the building. Guided tours (1hr) available (2–week advance reservations requested). ⅏ ☎ 202-208-4743.

Seven of the 10 bureaus have gallery space in the museum. Their exhibits include artifacts, drawings, documents, diagrams, photos and paintings. A former Interior Department agency, the Bureau of Mines closed in 1996, but its exhibit continues to be on display. Throughout the museum visitors can view the attractive **dioramas** depicting historic or characteristic scenes from the nation's past, such as the meeting of generals Washington and Lafayette at Morristown in 1780, a 19C Indian trading post in 1835, fur traders of the upper Missouri River, the land rush in Oklahoma in 1889 and a mine disaster. The dioramas and the delightful **metal cutouts** crowning the displays of the first two sections were executed by artists in the 1930s.

The **Native American section**—featuring a canoe and a variety of pottery and baskets—presents only a small fraction of the department's rich collection. In the passageway leading to the other exhibits hang four paintings by artist William H. Jackson depicting some of the earliest survey teams on assignment in the West during the second half of the 19C. Working from authentic period photographs, Jackson executed these paintings in 1938 when he was in his 90s.

Surveying equipment such as zenith and meridian telescopes used at the turn of the century, as well as facsimiles of early documents granting land to homesteaders and to military personnel, are on display in the section devoted to the Bureau of Land Management.

Artifacts from various Pacific islands, such as Micronesia, the Marshall Islands and American Samoa include models of watercraft and a wooden Palauan storyboard. Storyboards are carved and painted rafters, taken from traditional clubhouses, that depict a legend or commemorate a historic event.

Upon leaving the museum, stop in at the shop across the hall, where contemporary Indian crafts and specialized publications are on sale *(open year-round Mon–Fri 8:30am–4:30pm; closed major holidays; ⅏ ☎ 202-208-4056).*

⑲ Indian Craft Shop
Map p 14. In Department of Interior Building, 1849 C St. NW. ☎ 202-208-4056.
Opened in 1938, this shop—two tiny rooms opposite the Department of the Interior Museum—teems with authentic American Indian arts and crafts from over 35 of the nation's tribes or pueblos. Baskets, pottery, jewelry, beaded bags, kachinas, weavings, sculpture, clothing, and Alaskan and fetish carvings are for sale, along with related books and stationery. Note the entry-room wall murals depicting a buffalo hunt by Apache artist Allan Houser, and a deer hunt by Navajo artist Gerald Nailor.

6

Georgetown

Washington's choicest neighborhood, Georgetown today is an amalgam of popular nightspots, restaurants and shops surrounded by quiet residential streets. Predating Washington itself, this historic quarter functions as a well-preserved village, bounded on the south by the Potomac and on the east by Rock Creek. Congressional representatives, foreign dignitaries and the capital's intelligentsia live in many of its fine late-18C and 19C homes.

A Rock and a Knave – In 1703 Ninian Beall, a Scottish immigrant who acquired enormous landholdings throughout the state of Maryland, patented a 795-acre tract on which most of present-day Georgetown now stands. Beall named the tract the Rock of Dunbarton, after a geologic formation in his native Scotland. Thirty years later George Gordon acquired an adjacent tract of land known as Knave's Disappointment. Gordon changed the name to Rock Creek Plantation and established a tobacco inspection house on it, near the confluence of Rock Creek and the Potomac River.

A small settlement, predominantly of Scottish immigrants, began to grow up here, and in 1751 the inhabitants petitioned the Maryland Provisional Assembly to establish a town. The assembly agreed, appointing six commissioners to negotiate the sale of lots on a 60-acre tract encompassing the lands of George Gordon and those of George Beall, who had inherited the holdings of his father, Ninian. Though both owners were dissatisfied with conditions surrounding the sale, the lots were parceled out and the new town formed. To this day no clear consensus on the town's namesake—the former owners George Gordon and George Beall or King George II—has been reached by historians.

The Golden Age – Positioned at the head of the Potomac's navigable waters, Georgetown thrived in the late 18C as a port of entry for foreign goods and as an exporter of products from the fertile Ohio Valley in the West. Even during the Revolution the town prospered, as a base of supplies and munitions.

After the war, when the site for the new federal city was being chosen, local landowners requested that George Washington consider the "lands owned by them in the vicinity of Georgetown." Though Washington did not choose the area, the town thrived during the building of the capital. Well established and respected, Georgetown was considered the "court end" of the still rough federal city.

During this golden age, such grand manors as Evermay *(1623 28th St.)* and Tudor Place dotted the hills of upper Georgetown, and elegant Federal-style town houses lined its lower residential streets. In 1789 the first Catholic institution of higher learning in the country, Georgetown College—now **Georgetown University**—was founded at the western edge of the town.

Decline and Rebirth – By the late 1820s Georgetown found itself being eclipsed by Washington. In 1828 construction on the Chesapeake and Ohio Canal, with its eastern terminus in Georgetown, was begun in an attempt to stimulate commerce and westward migration. Ironically, just as the canal was being built, so too was the Baltimore and Ohio Railroad. The efficiency of train travel gradually brought an end to barge transport. At the same time, the advent of steam navigation, which required deeper ports than the town could provide, spelled doom to Georgetown's shipping business. By midcentury, as the town continued its decline, residents began a movement to consolidate Georgetown and Washington, but those plans were waylaid by the coming of the Civil War.

Since Georgetown counted both Union and Confederate sympathizers among its residents, sentiments ran high among its citizenry during this period. Many of its churches and public buildings were used as hospitals for the Union wounded, and as elsewhere in Washington, the area was generally consumed with the war effort.

In 1871, with the war over, Georgetown was consolidated with the District of Columbia. In order to incorporate it into Washington's gridiron street plan, its original street names were changed to the letters and numbers used elsewhere in Washington.

Washington Harbour

From the late 19C through the first half of the 20C, Georgetown fell into decline. Though its great houses remained in the hands of the wealthy, many of its old row houses were divided into apartments and rooming houses and adorned with Victorian flourishes. Only in the last 30 years has the neighborhood in general regained its prestige. Under the Old Georgetown Act of 1950, the area was declared a National Historic District. Demolition, new construction and renovation now are subject to review by the Commission of Fine Arts.

Today Georgetown's residential streets, with their carefully restored Federal-style and mid-19C houses, exude refinement and respectability. At the exclusive private parties held in these homes, much of the business of government, politics and private enterprise is conducted. Georgetown's commercial district is concentrated almost exclusively on Wisconsin Avenue and M Street, which are lined with numerous restaurants and small trendy boutiques. **Georgetown Park**, a popular large-scale urban mall, is situated at the intersection of these two streets. Anchoring the intersection of those two main thoroughfares is the golden dome of Riggs National Bank, Georgetown's most prominent landmark. Along the canal and the waterfront, redevelopment has generally taken the form of large brick office complexes. An exception is the riverfront showcase **Washington Harbour** (1986), a glittery complex of condominiums, offices, shops and restaurants. Its elaborately terraced and fountained courtyard affords a fine **view** down the Potomac.

The old towpath along the canal, saved through the efforts of conservationists, remains a quiet walker's thoroughfare reminiscent of the town's historic past.

Access – *Georgetown is not served by Metrorail. Due to the scarcity of parking garages and available street parking (particularly in the evening), visitors may find it most convenient to reach this area by bus. The bus line (nos. 32, 34, 36, and 38) linking central Washington to Georgetown runs along Pennsylvania Ave., M St. and Wisconsin Ave.*

WALKING TOUR

Distance: 1 1/2 miles. Map p 181

Begin at the corner of the towpath and 30th St. NW.

★**C&O Canal and Towpath** – Georgetown is the terminus for the old **Chesapeake and Ohio Canal**, which runs 185 miles through 75 lift locks to Cumberland, Maryland. In 1971 the entire canal was designated a national park. Here, at lift lock no. 3, a **bust (1)** of Supreme Court Justice William O. Douglas commemorates his work in spearheading the movement to preserve the canal as a recreation area. *Mule-drawn boats on the canal depart from 1057 Thomas Jefferson St. Apr–Oct Wed–Sun 11am–4pm. Round–trip 1hr. Commentary. $8. ☎ 202-653-5190. www.nps.gov/choh.*

Continue down the towpath.

At the intersection with Thomas Jefferson Street, the brick Federal structure (c.1810) at **no. 1058** originally housed the Potomac Masonic Lodge, whose early members were present at the ceremonies for the laying of the Capitol cornerstone. The quaint **row houses** just past it along the towpath were built after the Civil War as residences for artisans and laborers.

Turn right on 31st St. and then right on M St., one of Georgetown's main thoroughfares.

Old Stone House – *3051 M St. Open year-round Wed–Sun 10am–4pm. Closed major holidays. Guided tours (30min) available. ☎ 202-426-6851. www.nps.gov/rocr.* The front of this small, two-story house, one of the oldest structures in Washington, was built by Christopher Layman around 1765. Since 1960 the National Park Service has maintained it as a museum house characterizing colonial life. Note the paneling in the dining room. A large garden in the rear offers a respite from the bustle of M Street.

Continue east on M St.

The twin buildings at nos. 3037 and 3039 (known as the Nathan Loughborough houses) date from the turn of the 19C. The Junior League of Washington, a women's civic organization, restored them in 1963 and now uses them as its DC headquarters. The late-18C buildings at **nos. 3001** and **3003** were the home of Thomas Sim Lee, an ardent Revolutionary, governor of Maryland and friend of George Washington. In 1951 the buildings were saved from demolition under the strictures of the newly established Old Georgetown Act.

Turn left on 29th St., then right on N St.

★**N Street** – This handsome street contains some of the finest Federal-style architecture in the city. The elegant brick residence at **no. 2812** was built in the early 19C. Susan Decatur is said to have lived here after her departure from Decatur House on Lafayette Square.

Return to the corner of N and 29th Sts. and continue to 30th St.

The **3000 block of N Street** boasts many of Georgetown's most distinguished town houses. During the Civil War it was a bastion of Southern support.

At the corner of N and 30th Streets stands the **Laird-Dunlop House** *(no. 3014)*, a brick building constructed in 1799 by John Laird, a wealthy tobacco merchant, who apparently modeled his sprawling home after residences he had seen in Edinburgh,

Chesapeake and Ohio Canal

© Norman Nokleby

Georgetown Architecture

Scotland. Laird's daughter Barbara married James Dunlop, a law partner of Francis Scott Key, who penned "The Star-Spangled Banner." In 1915 Abraham Lincoln's son Robert Todd, who had been a secretary of War and minister to Britain, bought the house from Dunlop heirs. He added the attached dwelling at no. 3018.

The large house across the street at **no. 3017** was built in the 1790s by Thomas Beall, descendant of original Georgetown landowner Ninian Beall. **Jacqueline Kennedy** briefly lived here in 1963, after President Kennedy's death. The dwelling at no. 3038, with its elegant doorway and shingled dormers, is a particularly fine example of the smaller town houses built during the early 19C.

Turn right on 31st St. and left on Dumbarton Ave.

Surrounded by a lush garden and a white picket fence, the imposing residence at **3123 Dumbarton Avenue** was built by Henry Foxall, a prominent Georgetown businessman, for his daughter Mary Ann McKenney. Dating back to the early 19C, the house is considered one of the most architecturally pristine structures in the area. According to local legend it also houses a famous Georgetown ghost—a maiden lady who came to luncheon at the McKenneys' and never left.

The yellow-brick **Dumbarton United Methodist Church** *(no. 3133)* was constructed in 1849 in the Romanesque Revival style. During the Civil War the church was used as a hospital, and poet Walt Whitman, serving as a nurse, ministered to the Union wounded here. The current facade was added in an 1894 renovation.

Continue across Wisconsin Ave. and turn left on O St.

Note the remnants of the old trolley track embedded in this brick-paved street.

St. John's Church – *3240 O St. Open Jun–Aug Mon–Fri 9am–4:30pm, Sun 9am–noon. Rest of the year Mon–Fri 9am–4:30pm, Sun 8:30am–1:30pm. Closed major holidays except Thanksgiving Day & Dec 25.* & ☎ *202-338-1796.* Built between 1796 and 1804, the interior walls of this Federal-style stucco structure make it the oldest Episcopal church in Georgetown. Thomas Jefferson donated money for its building, and Francis Scott Key served as one of its vestrymen. In 1831 the church was abandoned due to lack of funds. Financier and art patron William Wilson Corcoran purchased it as a philanthropic gesture in 1837 and gave it back to the church two years later.

The 3300 block of O Street has a typical Georgetown mix of Federal and late-19C structures.

Bodisco House – *3322 O St.* Built about 1815, the handsome, porticoed Federal dwelling was home to Robert E. Lee's mother after she left Alexandria. The residence is most renowned, however, for the romantic tale surrounding another of its former occupants—Baron Alexander de Bodisco, the Russian minister to the US in the mid-19C. At that time the structure housed the Russian legation. After the 62-year-old baron married a 16-year-old Georgetown belle, Harriott Beall Williams, he and his new bride used the house as the setting for lavish parties that became legendary. For years it was a focal point of Georgetown society.

Turn left on 34th St. and left again on N St.

★**Cox Row** – This handsome group of five Federal houses *(nos. 3339-3327)*, adorned with swags and high, graceful dormers, was built in 1805 by Col. John Cox. Georgetown's first mayor elected by popular vote, Cox held that office for 22 years (1823-45). No. 3339 was Cox's residence for a time. In 1824 he entertained the Marquis de Lafayette in no. 3337.

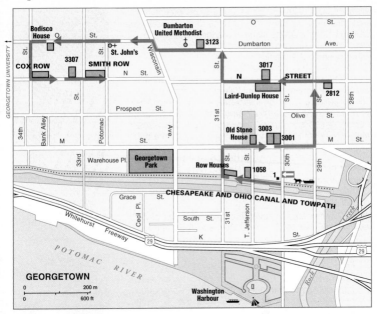

GEORGETOWN

Sen. **John F. Kennedy** purchased **no. 3307** in 1957 as a present for his wife, Jacqueline. The Kennedys lived here until moving into the White House in 1961. This house and its twin at no. 3311 were built in 1811.

Like a number of Georgetown homes dating from the Federal period, the facade of no. 3311 has been embellished with 19C Italianate detailing (elaborate cornice and door frame, hooded window crowns with brackets).

★**Smith Row** – An unbroken, manicured block of Federal row houses extends from no. 3267 to no. 3255. Their exteriors have been little altered since they were built by Clement and Walter Smith in 1815.

DUMBARTON OAKS★★

1703 32nd St. NW.

Renowned for its outstanding collection of Byzantine and Pre-Columbian art, this gracious museum and research institution is situated at the heart of what has been called "America's most civilized square mile." The 16-acre estate set on a ridge above Rock Creek Park is graced with a harmonious ensemble of buildings surrounded by beautifully landscaped gardens.

Historical Notes

The Oaks – In 1800 and 1801 Sen. William Dorsey of Maryland purchased 22 acres on the northern edge of Georgetown from Thomas Beall, a descendant of Ninian Beall, whose vast, 795-acre Rock of Dunbarton tract had once encompassed much of present-day Georgetown. Dorsey constructed the brick Federal-style home still standing at Dumbarton. He and his family lived here for only a year before personal and financial problems forced Dorsey to sell. In the ensuing decades the property passed through a succession of prominent owners, among them Edward Linthicum, a self-made businessman who, in the 1860s, added substantial wings to the original structure, Victorianized its appearance and renamed it "The Oaks," because of the fine stand of white oaks surrounding it.

A Marriage of Taste and Wealth – In 1920 Robert and Mildred Bliss purchased the estate. From adolescence the Blisses had known each other, because their separate, widowed parents had wed, making them stepbrother and sister. Cultured, widely traveled and independently wealthy, the Blisses transformed Dumbarton Oaks, as they renamed it, into an elegant "country house in the city." With the help of the prominent architectural firm McKim, Mead and White, the interior was restructured and the exterior restored to its original Federal style. In 1929 a large music room was added. Working closely with Mrs. Bliss, Beatrix Jones Farrand, the noted landscape architect and a personal friend of the couple, designed the extensive gardens.

Robert Bliss' career in the foreign service prevented the couple from living here until 1933. During their years abroad, they had begun to acquire important Byzantine

181

artifacts, and once settled at Dumbarton they continued collecting, amassing at the same time an extensive research library. A west wing was added with two pavilions and an enclosed courtyard to function as a museum open to the public.

In 1940 the Blisses gave the house, grounds, their Byzantine collection, a library of some 14,000 volumes and an endowment to **Harvard University**, which maintains the estate as a research institution and museum. They also donated an adjacent 27-acre tract known as Dumbarton Oaks Park *(open year-round daily dawn-dusk)* to the National Park Service to be enjoyed by the public. In 1944 the famous **Dumbarton Oaks Conferences**, involving representatives from the US, the United Kingdom, China and the Soviet Union, were held at the Blisses' former home. The accords reached among the participants ultimately resulted in the creation of the United Nations.

Access – **By bus:** *take any even-numbered 30s bus, or D 2, D 4, or M'2 bus to Wisconsin Ave. and R St. and walk one block east on R St.*

MUSEUM

Open year-round Tue–Sun 2pm–5pm. Closed major holidays and during inclement weather. Contribution requested ($1). ♿ ☎ *202-339-6401. www. doaks.org.*

★★Byzantine Collection – After their initial donation of artifacts, the Blisses continued to enrich the collection, as did other donors. Today the collection comprises some 1,500 artifacts—all valuable examples of the refined artistic production of the Byzantine empire,

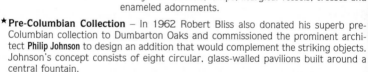

Pebble Garden

Byzantine Collection/Dumbarton Oaks

Gold Medallion
of Constantine I (c.326)

the empire that held sway over the eastern Mediterranean region from the 4C to 15C. The museum's collection of 12,000 Byzantine coins is one of the most complete and extensive in the world.

The columned interior courtyard is devoted to artifacts predating, or created on the periphery of, the Byzantine empire. Displays include late Roman and early Byzantine bas-reliefs, Roman glass and bronze (1-5C), textiles from Egypt and the eastern Mediterranean (6-12C) and a 6C Syrian floor mosaic. The adjacent gallery displays 6C ecclesiastical silver from the Sion Treasury, found in present-day Turkey, and Byzantine icons, lamps, liturgical vessels, crosses and enameled adornments.

★Pre-Columbian Collection – In 1962 Robert Bliss also donated his superb pre-Columbian collection to Dumbarton Oaks and commissioned the prominent architect **Philip Johnson** to design an addition that would complement the striking objects. Johnson's concept consists of eight circular, glass-walled pavilions built around a central fountain.

Arranged by cultures, the pavilions house Olmec figurines and masks *(gallery II)*; Mayan architectural reliefs and ceramics *(III-IV)*; stone yokes and axes from Veracruz *(V)*; gold jewelry from Central America *(VI)*; pottery, gold and tapestries from ancient Peruvian and Bolivian cultures *(VII)*; and Aztecan carvings, frescoes, masks and vessels *(VIII)*.

★Music Room – This stately hall is dominated by a large stone chimney piece from the Château de Thébon (16-17C) in France's Bordeaux region. The ornately painted wooden ceiling beams are modeled on those in the 17C Château de Cheverny in the Loire Valley. Flemish and German tapestries hang on the walls, as does El Greco's *Visitation* (c.1610) *(left wall)*. The frescoes adorning the arched stair alcove *(far wall)* were painted by Allyn Cox, who executed many of the murals in the Capitol. During the Blisses' residency in the house, a number of famous musicians performed here, including Ernest Schelling, Ignace Paderewski, Nadia Boulanger and **Igor Stravinsky**, whose *Concerto in E-flat*, also known as the *Dumbarton Oaks Concerto*, was commissioned by the Blisses for their 30th anniversary.

© Fred J. Maroon

A rotating selection of rare books from the permanent collection of the garden library is displayed in the hall to the right of the entrance pavilion.
The original brick Federal-style residence now houses research and administrative offices *(not open to the public)*.

★★GARDENS

Entrance at 31st and R Sts. Open mid-Mar–Oct daily 2pm–6pm. Rest of the year daily 2pm–5pm. Closed major holidays and during inclement weather. $5 (mid-Mar–Oct only). ☎ *202-339-6401. www.doaks.org. In the flowering season, a map is available at the garden gate.*

Following the natural slope of the land, Beatrix Jones Farrand planned "a series of broad terraces leading from the strictly formal architectural character of the house through various transitions to the delightful informality of the lower garden with its loose plantings of flowering trees, shrubs and naturalized bulbs." In addition, several "garden rooms" function as extensions of the house itself.
Today the meticulously tended grounds include 10 acres of formal terraces devoted to such plantings as rose and herb gardens. Paths lead to secluded fountains, pools, terraces and arbors, offset by flowering trees and shrubs. The centerpiece of the lovely **Pebble Garden**, added in the 1960s, is a shallow pool framed by Rococo borders of moss and paved with a mosaic of Mexican stones arranged to represent a wheat sheaf.

To appreciate the ever-changing landscapes of Dumbarton Oaks Gardens, visit them at different times of the year.

■ Some seasonal highlights:

Mid-March through April – Cherry blossoms, forsythia, wisteria, azaleas, dogwood, lilacs, akebia, star magnolia
May – Lilacs, clematis, roses, peonies, fringe tree
June – Clematis, roses, grandiflora, magnolia, canna
July through August – Daylilies, fuchsia, gardenias, agapanthus, oleanders
Late September through October – Chrysanthemums

TUDOR PLACE★

The landmark mansion and stately grounds of Tudor Place have dominated this block of Georgetown for some 180 years. Home to the prominent Peter family for six generations, the estate now functions as a house museum and a monument to old Washington traditions.

Historical Notes

Tudor Place was built as the home of Thomas Peter and his wife, Martha Custis Peter, the granddaughter of Martha Washington and the sister of George Washington Parke Custis and Nelly Parke Custis Lewis *(table p 191)*. In 1805, with the $8,000 inheritance Martha Peter received from her stepgrandfather, George Washington, the Peters purchased an 8-acre city block in Georgetown Heights with sweeping views of the growing capital city and the Potomac River. Dr. William Thornton, a family friend and the first architect of the Capitol, was commissioned to design a home befitting the Peters' status as Washington descendants (Thornton also participated in the building of Nelly Lewis' home, Woodlawn). Thornton's project called for a two-story central structure to be joined to the preexisting east and west wings by means of one-story hyphens. Construction proceeded slowly, but the stuccoed brick mansion was finally completed in 1816.

At her death in 1854, Martha Peter left the estate to the youngest of the three Peter daughters, Britannia Wellington Peter Kennon, who had been widowed after only a year of marriage. During the Civil War years, Britannia, a staunch Southern sympathizer and relative of Robert E. Lee, allowed Union officers to use Tudor Place as a boardinghouse, stipulating only that "affairs of war not be discussed" in her presence. According to legend, the mistress of Tudor Place refused to receive Mrs. Ulysses S. Grant as a boarder. However, Britannia willingly agreed to temporarily store the belongings of Mrs. Robert E. Lee when she was forced to flee Arlington House. Other illustrious 19C visitors to this respected Washington residence include the Marquis de Lafayette, Henry Clay, Andrew Jackson, Daniel Webster and John C. Calhoun.

The estate remained in the family until the death of Armistead Peter III, in 1983. It then passed to the Tudor Place Foundation, which opened the property to the public in 1988.

Access — By bus: *take any no. 30s bus to Wisconsin Ave. and Q St. Walk east on Q St. and then turn left on 31st St.*

VISIT

Mansion visit by guided tour (45min) only, Feb–Dec Tue–Fri 10am, 11:30am & 1pm, 2:30pm (advance reservations required), and Sat 10am–3pm hourly (no reservations required). Grounds open year-round Mon–Sat 10am–4pm. Closed major holidays. Contribution requested $6 (grounds only $2). Holiday tours available mid-Dec. $10. ☏ 202-965-0400. www.tudorplace.org.

Bistrot Lepic
1736 Wisconsin Ave., NW. ☏ *202-333-0111.* After a day of enjoying the historic homes and museums of Georgetown, repose yourself and restore yourself at this cozy bistro located within walking distance of Dumbarton Oaks. Commence with the favorite *parmentière de moules et poireaux* (mussel soup with leeks and potatoes), then savor the flavors of the French countryside with dishes such as *risotto de trompettes noires aux escargots* (risotto of black trompette mushrooms with fresh snails) and *truite grillée, petits légumes et sauce carotte* (grilled boneless rainbow trout with carrot sauce and julienne of vegetables). Reasonable prices, inventive daily specials and a nice selection of wines round out the menu.

The simple Federal-style north facade fronts a boxwood-edged carriage drive. The centerpiece of Thornton's distinctive design is the circular south portico, which stands like a columned "temple" overlooking Georgetown. The recessed semicircular wall of the portico projects into the interior, creating a striking convex glass wall in the central salon. A number of furnishings come from Mount Vernon, having been purchased by the Peters when that estate's belongings were auctioned off in the early 19C. The first-floor rooms as well as the bedrooms on the upper story contain memorabilia from various eras in the family's history and do not reflect any one time period. The 5 1/2 acres of **grounds** surrounding the house are devoted on the north side to more formal plantings, including a flower "knot," a circular garden and a bowling green. The south lawn slopes in a broad green expanse. Against the south facade of the house is a border of old roses, a few dating from Martha Custis Peter's occupancy.

DUMBARTON HOUSE

2715 Q St. NW.

This brick Federal-style house is a fine example of the imposing residential architecture that predominated in upper Georgetown during the community's golden age. Today it serves as a house museum and the headquarters of a national women's organization.

Historical Notes

Built in the last years of the 18C, the house quickly passed through several owners, until 1804, when it was purchased by Joseph Nourse, registrar of the US Treasury. When Charles Carroll became owner of the house in 1813, he named it Bellevue, a name it retained for more than a century.

In the early 20C, Georgian Revival quoins, balustrades and other embellishments were added, and in 1915 the house was moved 100 yards north to accommodate the eastward extension of Q Street. After the move, the present east and west wings were added to the house. In 1928 the **National Society of the Colonial Dames of America**, a women's organization dedicated to historic preservation and education, bought the property and renamed it Dumbarton House, after the original Rock of Dunbarton tract that once included much of present-day Georgetown. With the consultation of the eminent architectural preserver Fiske Kimball, the Dames had the house restored to its Federal appearance.

Access – By bus: *take D 2, D 4, D 6 or D 8 bus to 27th or 28th St. Dumbarton House is on Q St. between 27th and 28th Sts.*

VISIT

Visit by guided tour (45min) only, Jan–Jul & Sept–Dec Tue–Sat 10:15am, 11:15am & 12:15pm. Closed Thanksgiving Day & weekend, Dec 25–Jan 3. $3. & 🅿 ☎ *202-337-2288. www.dumbartonhouse.org.*

The exterior features a columned portico with a fanlight over the doorway and stone lintels above the windows. A sweeping staircase dominates the wide interior entrance hall, flanked by a formal library, a dining room, a music room and a parlor. The rooms, furnished in the Federal period, display a number of pieces originally from Woodlawn Plantation. Among these are china, crystal, quilts and clothing that belonged to Martha Washington and her granddaughter Eliza Custis Law *(table p 191)*. Also notable is a 1789 painting by Charles Willson Peale. It portrays the children of Benjamin Stoddert, first secretary of the Navy, with a view of old Georgetown and the Potomac River in the background. The second floor contains four bedrooms, also furnished predominantly in the Federal style.

Benjamin Stoddert's Children by Charles Willson Peale

Georgetown Heritage Trust

185

OAK HILL CEMETERY

One of the city's oldest and most venerable cemeteries, Oak Hill occupies a wooded, rolling 25-acre tract of land along the west bank of Rock Creek.

William Wilson Corcoran, financier and founder of the Corcoran Gallery of Art, donated the original 15 acres of ground to the cemetery company, incorporated by Congress in 1849. James Renwick, the architect of the Castle and the first Corcoran Gallery (now the Renwick Gallery), designed the picturesque **Gothic Revival chapel** (1850) and the cast-iron gate that encloses the cemetery along R Street.

Access – By bus: take any no. 30s bus to Wisconsin Ave. and R St. Walk east on R St. to 30th St.

VISIT

Entrance at R and 30th Sts. Open year-round Mon–Fri 10am–4pm. Closed during funeral services and inclement weather. ☎ 202-337-2835. A brochure with a detailed map of the grounds is available at the superintendent's lodge.

The grounds are fashioned as a garden cemetery. Most graves date to the 19C, and the tombstones and monuments are characteristic of that period. Corcoran's own grave is marked by a replica of a Doric temple, designed by 19C Capitol architect Thomas U. Walter. Among the many other prominent citizens buried here are John Howard Payne, composer of "Home, Sweet Home"; Dean Acheson, secretary of State under Truman; and descendants of George Washington.

7

Arlington
Across the River

Arlington is a mixture of high rises, middle-class neighborhoods and ethnic enclaves. Along its Potomac shoreline, a network of pleasant parkways, dotted with memorials and statues, connects Arlington to the capital.

The Beginnings – The first accounts of the lands along the Potomac came from Capt. John Smith, who made an exploratory expedition up the river in 1608. He recorded an Indian village along what is now the Arlington shoreline. By the mid-17C, much of the present county had been claimed by absentee landholders. Chief among them were members of the Alexander family, after whom the town of Alexandria, established in 1748, is named.

Throughout the colonial period and into the 19C, the Arlington region was inextricably bound, both administratively and economically, to Alexandria, which served as the urban focus for the area's scattering of small farms.

Part of the Capital City – By a 1789 act of the Virginia General Assembly, land along the Potomac was ceded for the formation of the new federal city. Amounting to 34 acres and encompassing parts of what are now Arlington and Alexandria, these former Virginia lands officially became the County of Alexandria of the District of Columbia. For the first half of the 19C, the current jurisdiction of Arlington was part of the capital, and yet it retained its rural character. In 1846, disillusioned with their association with the nation's capital, the county's residents voted by public referendum to retrocede to Virginia.

War and Devastation – During the Civil War, Arlington's lands were occupied by Union forces guarding the southern flanks of the capital city against Confederate incursions. Forests were felled, fortresses built and earthworks erected, all of which had a devastating effect on the land of this agrarian community. Robert E. Lee's own home, Arlington House, became the headquarters for various Union commanders.

Shortly after the war ended, Virginia's adoption of a new constitution added to the community's troubles. Under the 1870 law, cities with populations of 5,000 or more became independent units, completely separate from any county jurisdiction. Alexandria thus became an entity altogether divorced from the County of Alexandria, leaving Arlington, which had come to be called "the country part of the county" to fare on its own. It took 30 years to recover from the war, but by the turn of the century, truck farms and nurseries were flourishing here. During the decade between 1910 and 1920, Arlington's population grew by 60 percent, in large part due to an influx of workers in the World War I years. In 1920 the Virginia General Assembly recognized the county's growing prominence by changing its name from the County of Alexandria to Arlington County, named in honor of General Lee's Arlington home.

Arlington Today – In the last six decades, Arlington has continued its phenomenal growth, largely as a bedroom community for government workers. World War II saw Arlington grow from 57,000 people in 1940 to 120,000 in 1944. Federally funded housing projects for this white-collar work force sprouted up in the southern part of the county, as did military buildings, including the enormous Pentagon. More recent additions to the city's attractions include **Newseum**, an interactive museum of world-wide media, and its adjoining Freedom Park.

Some 171,000 people now live in Arlington's 25.7sq mi. While its affluent northern neighborhoods retain their traditional suburban character, the neighborhoods of south Arlington are home to many Hispanics and South Asians, some of whom operate small specialty food stores or restaurants in the area.

ARLINGTON NATIONAL CEMETERY★★

On the Arlington side of Memorial Bridge – Map p 189

A sylvan retreat situated just minutes from the hubbub of the Mall, Arlington National Cemetery is the country's most revered burial ground and one of the capital's most poignant sights. This vast military cemetery, lined with endless rows of gleaming white headstones, contains the graves of a host of distinguished Americans.

Historical Notes

An Act of Vindication – At the outbreak of the Civil War, Arlington House was established as the headquarters for the defense of Washington, and military installations were erected in various locations around the 1,100-acre estate. As much of the early fighting took place around the capital, the need for burial space soon became evident. In 1864 Quartermaster-General of the Army Montgomery Meigs (architect of the Pension Building), who was responsible for overseeing the appropriation of government land for military purposes, recommended that the grounds of Arlington House be used to inter war casualties. With the approval of Secretary of War Edwin Stanton, 200 acres of the estate were designated as a burial ground, and on May 13, 1864, the first soldier, Pvt. William Christman from Pennsylvania, was laid to rest there. Showing considerable vindictiveness toward Lee, whom he viewed as a traitor, Meigs ensured that the first graves were situated in the immediate vicinity of the mansion as a deterrent to the return of the Lee family. In Mrs. Lee's rose garden, located just south of the mansion, a large vault was constructed to hold the remains of 2,111 unidentified soldiers. Meigs himself, who died in 1892, was eventually buried at Arlington.

In 1883, following a Supreme Court decision that the Arlington estate should be returned to the Lees, the family accepted a financial compensation of $150,000 rather than demanding the restitution of the estate, which by that time contained the remains of some 16,000 war casualties. In that same year, Arlington became the official national cemetery of the US.

A National Shrine – The cemetery now comprises 612 acres and contains the graves of more than 240,000 military personnel and their dependents. Among those laid to rest in the cemetery's rolling hills are veterans of every armed conflict in which the US has participated since the Revolutionary War.

Access – *The cemetery is located on the Arlington side of Memorial Bridge, about 3/4mi from the Lincoln Memorial.* **By Metro:** Ⓜ *Arlington Cemetery.* **By foot:** *The short walk across Memorial Bridge can be very pleasant in nice weather.* **By car:** *cross Memorial Bridge to the parking lot (hourly charge) situated adjacent to the visitor center.* **By Tourmobile:** *The cemetery is included on the standard Washington tour – p 58.*

Touring the cemetery – The cemetery is situated on a tract of hilly terrain crisscrossed with meandering paved routes. Car traffic is permitted only for disabled visitors and for relatives of persons interred in the cemetery. The cemetery grounds can be explored on foot *(allow half a day and wear comfortable walking shoes)*. If you are pressed for time or do not feel up to walking, we recommend riding the special Tourmobile shuttle that operates within the cemetery, making stops at the most popular sights (Kennedy gravesites, Tomb of the Unknowns and Arlington House). Tickets for the cemetery tour *($5.25)* can be purchased at the visitor center, in front of which shuttles depart continually from opening time to a half hour prior to closing.

Headstones

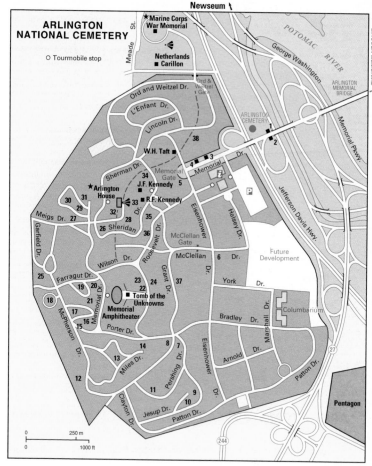

Newseum

ARLINGTON NATIONAL CEMETERY

○ Tourmobile stop

1 Seabees Memorial

2 United Spanish War Veterans Memorial

3 Admiral Richard E. Byrd Memorial

4 101st Army Airborne Division Memorial

5 Women in Military Service for America Memorial

6 Memorial to service personnel killed in Beirut, 1983

7 USS Serpens Memorial

8 Mary Roberts Rinehart: mystery writer, war correspondent

9 William Jennings Bryan: Secretary of State

10 US Coast Guard Memorial

11 John P. Pershing: General of the Armies

12 Argonne Cross (dedicated to Americans killed in France during WWI)

13 Virgil Grissom and Roger Chaffee: *Apollo I* astronauts

14 Walter Reed: instrumental in combating yellow fever

15 Nurses Memorial

16 John Foster Dulles: Secretary of State

17 Rough Riders Memorial

18 Confederate Monument

19 USS Maine Memorial

20 Shuttle *Challenger* Astronauts Memorial

21 Memorial to service personnel killed in the attempt to rescue US hostages in Iran, 1980

22 Frank Reynolds: broadcast journalist

23 Joe Louis: heavyweight boxing champion

24 George C. Marshall: General, Secretary of State

25 James Parks: Arlington House slave

26 Claire L. Chennault: Commander of the WWII Flying Tigers

27 Montgomery Meigs: Quartermaster--General, engineer, architect

28 Johnny Clem: youngest soldier in the US Army

29 Lockerbie, Scotland, Pan Am 103 Memorial

30 Anita Newcomb McGee: first female Army surgeon

31 Tomb of the Unknown Dead of the War of 1812

32 Tomb of the Unknown Civil War Dead

33 Pierre Charles L'Enfant: planner of Washington DC

34 Oliver Wendell Holmes, Jr.: Supreme Court Justice

35 Richard E. Byrd (grave): polar explorer

36 George Westinghouse: inventor

37 Dashiell Hammett: detective novelist

38 Medgar Evers: civil rights leader

CEMETERY GROUNDS

Open Apr–Sept daily 8am–7pm. Rest of the year daily 8am–5pm. ♿ 🅿
☎ *703-697-2131.*

At the entrance to the cemetery, the new **Women in Military Service for America Memorial**
is a testament to all US women who have served in the armed forces from the
Revolutionary War to the present. Two US presidents are buried in Arlington
Cemetery: President **William H. Taft** (1857-1930); and President **John F. Kennedy**
(1917-63), whose simple grave is marked by an eternal flame. The grave of **Robert
F. Kennedy** (1925-68), marked by a white cross, lies close to that of his older
brother.

Designed by Carrère and Hastings, the 5,000-seat **Memorial Amphitheater** (1920) is
used for special ceremonies such as Memorial Day and Veterans Day services. As
the country's most prestigious burial ground, Arlington Cemetery has been chosen
to house numerous **memorials** dedicated to special groups or particular events in the
nation's history. Scattered throughout the cemetery, these memorials include group
headstones, statues, plaques and even trees. Especially moving is the **Tomb of the Unknowns** *(located behind the
Memorial Amphitheater).*
The remains of these sol-
diers represent symbolically
all the men and women
who lost their lives in those
conflicts. Not to be missed
at the tomb is the **Changing
of the Guard**, whereby visitors can witness the preci-
sion and skill of the military
sentries *(daily in summer
on the half-hour; rest of the
year daily on the hour).* The
cemetery's most prominent
memorial, Arlington House,
occupies a hilltop site overlooking the cemetery.

■ Burial in the National Cemetery

Service personnel eligible for interment at
Arlington include those who:

■ died on active duty;

■ had a minimum of 20 years active
duty or reserve service;

■ were honorably discharged for disabil-
ity before October 1, 1949; or

■ held the country's highest military
decorations (e.g., Medal of Honor,
Silver Star, Purple Heart).

Also eligible are spouses or unmarried
children (under 21) of any of the above.

★ARLINGTON HOUSE/THE ROBERT E. LEE MEMORIAL

Map p 189.

The mansion is situated on the grounds of Arlington National Cemetery. Access p 188.
Surrounded by the white headstones of Arlington Cemetery, the dignified mansion
that has been designated the official Robert E. Lee Memorial tops a high bluff overlooking Washington. Lee, hero of the Confederacy, called this his home for
30 years. Here, he wrote, "my affections and attachments are more strongly placed
than at any other place in the world."

The Custises – Arlington House, as the mansion is commonly known, was built
by George Washington Parke Custis, whose father, John, was the son of Martha
Washington by her first husband. When John Custis died during the Revolution,
George and Eleanor (Nelly), the youngest of his four small children, were brought
to Mount Vernon and raised by the Washingtons. Young George Custis spent his
childhood among the Washingtons' illustrious circle of acquaintances.

Washington died in 1799 and Martha in 1802. Mount Vernon passed to Bushrod
Washington, a nephew of George Washington, and the 21-year-old Custis moved
to a 1,100-acre tract of land his father had left him across from the newly established federal city.

At once Custis began planning a mansion worthy of housing what he called
the "Washington Treasury"—the Mount Vernon memorabilia he had acquired
through inheritance or by purchase. The architect chosen to draw up the plans
was George Hadfield, who supervised part of the construction of the early Capitol.
Hadfield's building, incorporating the lines of a Doric temple, was the area's
first example of the Greek Revival style, which gained considerable popularity
in the early 19C. Though he had limited funds, Custis proceeded with construction, using bricks made from clay on the estate and timber from its forests.
By 1804 he had completed the south wing, and in the same year he married Mary
Lee Fitzhugh. About this time he also renamed his estate Arlington, after a Custis
family property in Northhampton County, Virginia. The mansion was completed in
1818.

Sophisticated and talented, Custis was a poet, playwright and painter. Much of his
skill and enthusiasm went to perpetuating the memory of his guardian and idol,
George Washington. A gregarious and gracious gentleman, Custis opened the
grounds of the estate to picnickers coming by ferry from Washington.

The Lees – Robert E. Lee, a distant relative of the Custises, grew up in nearby Alexandria and visited their home often as a boy. In 1831 he and Mary Anna Randolph Custis, the Custises' only surviving child, were married at Arlington House. For the next 30 years, the Lees were posted to various locations as Robert pursued his military career. During this time they considered Arlington House their true home and spent many winters here. Arlington House was the birthplace of six of the seven Lee children. At the Custises' death, title to the house passed to the Lees. In January 1861, fearing the consequences of mounting hostilities between the North and South, Lee wrote to a friend, saying "There is no sacrifice I am not ready to make for the preservation of the Union, save that of honour." Three months later, on April 18, he was called to Blair House and offered the command of the Union troops. He refused, and on April 20 at Arlington House, he wrote his letter of resignation from the US Army. On April 22, he left Arlington House for Richmond, Virginia, where he accepted command of the Virginia forces. He would never return to his beloved home again.

Confiscation – In May 1861 Union troops crossed the river to Virginia and quickly made the strategically located Arlington House into the headquarters for the Army of the Potomac. Throughout the war the estate grounds were turned into fortifications and earthworks, and ultimately into a national cemetery for the Civil War dead (Arlington National Cemetery).

In 1864 Arlington House was claimed by the federal government due to a dubious tax law that required Mrs. Lee to pay a $92 property tax in person. Mrs. Lee, in poor health, chose not to travel to Washington, sending a cousin instead. The government refused payment from the cousin, seized the property, and offered it up for public auction. As no bidders were forthcoming, the government bought it for $26,800. After a legal battle that was decided by the Supreme Court, the Lees' eldest son, George Washington Custis Lee, won a suit for the return of the property. In 1883 Lee accepted the congressional appropriation of $150,000, based on the estate's market value, rather than reclaiming the land, which by then had the character of a cemetery. Congress designated the house a national memorial to Robert E. Lee in 1925, and the National Park Service began administering it in 1933.

Visit

Open Apr–Sept daily 9:30am–6pm. Rest of the year daily 9:30am–4:30pm. Closed Jan 1 & Dec 25. ▯ ☎ *703-557-0613. www.nps.gov/arho.*

The mansion commands an exceptional **view★★** of Washington, with Memorial Bridge stretching to the Lincoln Memorial in the near distance and the whole panoply of the city beyond it. The main facade, with eight large Doric columns supporting an unadorned pediment, provides a gracious entrance to the off-white stucco structure.

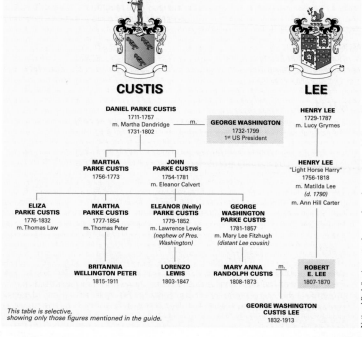

National Park Service; coats of arms redrawn by permission of Arlington House

Interior – Off the entrance hall to the right is the family parlor, where the Lees were married. Over the simple mantel is a portrait of a young Mary Custis painted by Auguste Hervieu just prior to her marriage. The room, and most of the rest of the house, is furnished with period pieces from the first half of the 19C.

In the dining room, adjacent to the family parlor, the table setting includes pieces of the Lee family porcelain and silver. Across the hall the spacious "white parlor" holds crimson-upholstered Victorian chairs and settees chosen by the Lees. Copies

Courtesy National Park Service

Robert E. Lee

of portraits of a dashing young Lee and his wife, done in 1838, hang over the room's mantels. Beyond the parlor is the well-lit room that served as an artist's studio for George W.P. Custis and for Mary Lee, who, like her father, was a painter. On an easel rests Custis' *Battle of Monmouth, New Jersey*, which hung in the US Capitol for several years. The five bedrooms and two dressing rooms on the upper floor housed the Lees and their seven children. It was in his bedchamber that Lee drafted his resignation from the Union Army.

On the lawn in front of Arlington House is the **tomb of Pierre L'Enfant**, whose remains were moved here in 1909. A marble plaque incised with his original city plan for Washington commemorates his unique contribution. A small museum *(behind the house and to the north)* features exhibits highlighting Lee's career.

MARINE CORPS WAR MEMORIAL★
Iwo Jima Memorial
Off N. Meade St.
Map p 189

This striking sculpture, honoring all US Marines who have lost their lives in military duty, ranks as one of the nation's most famous war memorials. Its prominent location across the Potomac in near-perfect alignment with the Mall's principal axis visually links the memorial to the heart of Washington.

Access – **By Metro:** Ⓜ *Arlington Cemetery or Rosslyn.* **By car:** *Leave Washington via Memorial Bridge heading toward Rte. 50 West and follow signs to the memorial and Fort Meyer. To reach the memorial from the grounds of Arlington Cemetery, exit by the Ord and Weitzel Gate.*

VISIT

Open daily year-round. The **US Marine Corps Sunset Parade** *is held here Jun–Aug Tues 7pm–8:30pm. For parade information* ☎ *703-289-2500.*

The sculpture depicts six Americans raising the Stars and Stripes on Mount Suribachi in 1945 during the assault of the Japanese-controlled island of Iwo Jima (hence the memorial's popular name). The capture of this strategically located island is considered one of the Marines' greatest victories and marked a turning point in the American campaign in the Pacific. Based on the Pulitzer Prize-winning war photograph by **Joseph Rosenthal**, the memorial was designed by Horace W. Peaslee and sculpted by Felix de Weldon. The work's poignancy is further intensified by the incessant waving of the US flag that rises from the bronze statue group.

The nearby tower, known as the **Netherlands Carillon**, is a gift from the Dutch people in appreciation of American assistance during and after World War II. Reminiscent of the pure geometrical style of the 20C Dutch masters Rietveld and Mondrian, this lofty metal structure contains 50 bells of various dimensions. **Carillon concerts** are given here from May to September. *For concert information, call* ☎ *703-289-2550.*

W. Clark/Courtesy National Park Service

Marine Corps War Memorial

The grounds of the US Marine Corps Memorial and the Netherlands Carillon afford spectacular **vistas★★** of the Mall area. The eye is drawn across the Potomac past the Lincoln Memorial and the Washington Monument to the dome of the Capitol in the distance.

1 **Clarendon eats**
Map p 258. Wilson and Clarendon Blvds., between Garfield and Highland Sts. Ⓜ *Clarendon (yellow line).* This compact section of Arlington became a popular place for Vietnamese restaurants in the 1980s. Since then, it has expanded its offering to all kinds of cuisine. Local favorites include **Little Viet Garden** *(3012 Wilson Blvd.* ☎ *703-522-9686)*, where the decor is jungly and the spring and garden rolls and caramelized, clay-pot dishes are memorable. Next door is **Red Hot & Blue** *(3014 Wilson Blvd.* ☎ *703-243-1510)*, which offers both eat-in and carryout Memphis pit-style barbecues of pork and chicken with the traditional cole slaw or potato salad trimmings. At **Hard Times Cafe** *(3028 Wilson Blvd.* ☎ *703-528-2233)* you can sample spicy Texas, Cincinnati and vegetarian chilies. For traditional Greek salads, spanakopita, moussaka and more, try the **Aegean Taverna** *(2950 Clarendon Blvd.* ☎ *703-841-9494)*.

PENTAGON

I-395 at Washington Blvd.
Ⓜ Pentagon.

The heart of the American military establishment, this enormous pentagonal building houses the offices of the highest authorities of the armed services—the secretary of Defense and the joint chiefs of staff (Army, Navy, Air Force and Marines)—all of whom answer to the commander in chief, the president of the US.

Conceived during World War II, the Pentagon combined for the first time all of the branches of the Department of War, as it was called, under one roof. Army engineers were given one weekend in July 1941 to design the building, which was to be situated on the Arlington shore of the Potomac. Since the lot was five-sided, they devised a pentagonal shape for the building. Though the new structure was not ultimately constructed on the original lot, the five-sided shape was retained. Built of reinforced concrete faced with limestone, the five-story Pentagon was constructed in a relatively short 16 months and was completed on January 15, 1943.

On September 11, 2001 the west wall of the Pentagon was struck by a hijacked commercial airliner resulting in the loss of over 180 lives. This event, coupled with the attack, on the same day, on New York City's World Trade Center, was the worst terrorist attack on US soil in the nation's history.

VISIT

Visit by guided tour only. year-round Mon–Fri 9am–3pm. Closed major holidays. Visitors must show a photo ID.   ($2.50/day)   ☎   703-695-3325. *www.defenselink.mil/pubs/pentagon/#tour.*

■ **Pentagon Profile**

The Pentagon contains 6 1/2 million sq ft, making it one of the world's largest single-structure office buildings. Its interior comprises five concentric circles that enclose a 5-acre central courtyard. Each of its five sides is larger than the Capitol, and together they contain 17 1/2 miles of corridors. Some 23,000 personnel, about half of whom are military, work here in round-the-clock shifts.

An introductory film *(12min)* explains the history of the construction of the Pentagon. The remainder of the tour walks visitors through office corridors displaying military art (battle scenes, portraits of high-ranking officers) and the **Hall of Heroes**, where the names of those who have received the Congressional Medal of Honor are listed.

★
Dupont Circle

A t the beginning of the 20C, this neighborhood was the preferred address of Washington's moneyed elite. Back in vogue, the Dupont Circle area today boasts many of the city's finest boutiques, galleries, restaurants and cafes.

From Swamp to Swank – During the city's early history, this area was known as the "Slashes," a tract of swampland dotted with shanties and separated from the rest of the city by a tributary of Rock Creek called Slash Run. It was during the public works projects overseen by Alexander "Boss" Shepherd in the early 1870s that the Dupont Circle area developed. Shepherd diverted Slash Run into an underground sewer system and, in compliance with L'Enfant's original city plan, laid out streets radiating from Pacific (now Dupont) Circle.

The improvements attracted the interests of an informal group of real estate investors that included Sen. William Stewart of Nevada. In 1873 he began constructing an elaborate home on the circle between Massachusetts and Connecticut avenues. Stewart's Castle (sometimes called Stewart's Folly because it stood alone in this undeveloped area) was an extravagant Second Empire estate, complete with a stable of thoroughbreds. The mansion was razed in 1901; since 1924 a branch of Riggs Bank has stood on the site. In 1874 the British legation constructed its own impressive Second Empire structure at the corner of N Street and Connecticut Avenue. For the next decade and a half, however, few other substantial structures were built, and the side streets in the area developed as a modest working-class neighborhood. Not until the 1890s did the area become a "millionaires' colony," peopled mostly by Americans who had made fortunes elsewhere and chose to settle in the nation's capital. Typical of these millionaires was Levi Leiter, a Chicago department store magnate who in 1891 built a 55-room mansion on the circle's north side.

In the early 20C, Massachusetts Avenue became a corridor of elegant Beaux-Arts palaces. The Virginia architect Waddy B. Wood designed more than 30 mansions in this area and in **Kalorama**, another prestigious neighborhood just northwest of Dupont Circle. As the mansions rose along the avenue, the working-class houses on the side streets gave way to stylish brick row houses. In addition to private residences, a number of foreign missions were built in the area.

20C Vicissitudes – In the 1920s the character of Dupont Circle gradually began to shift toward the commercial, and a number of the fine homes were torn down in order to build offices and stores. With the Great Depression, the flamboyant lifestyle of the old Massachusetts Avenue residents reached an end, and in the following decades the area gradually lost its cachet as a neighborhood of the fabulously rich. By the 1950s many of the mansions were occupied by private clubs and businesses, and the row houses had been converted into boardinghouses. During the 1960s these dwellings became the homes of student activists and "hippies," as Dupont Circle became a haven of the counterculture.

The Tax Reform Act of 1969 encouraged the demolition of old buildings and led to the loss of many of the area's surviving grand structures. To counter the razing, citizen groups petitioned the city to provide legal protection for the Dupont Circle environs.

In 1978 the streets around the circle and north to T Street were designated a historic district. Now the neighborhood's renovated 19C row houses are once again home to professionals, and great efforts have been made to preserve the elegant old mansions that still grace Massachusetts Avenue. Galleries, cafes, shops and museums make this area attractive to visitors.

The annual **Dupont-Kalorama Museum Walk Weekend,** held on the first Saturday and Sunday in June, is a neighborhood festival featuring musical performances, special exhibits and activities, and tours of local museums and cultural institutions. Sights open to the public free of charge on that day include the Historical Society of Washington, DC, the Society of the Cincinnati Museum, and the Phillips Collection. For information ☎ 202-667-0441.

WALKING TOUR

Ⓜ Dupont Circle-19th St. exit.

Distance: 1 1/3 miles. Map p 197

Begin the tour at the circle.

Dupont Circle – Situated at the junction of five thoroughfares—Massachusetts, Connecticut and New Hampshire avenues, and 19th and P streets—this bustling intersection has become a focal point of the city's Northwest quadrant, true to the vision of planner Pierre Charles L'Enfant. It is here that the Frenchman's proposed arrangement of streets and avenues converging on a central green with a monument at its center can best be appreciated.

Originally known as Pacific Circle, owing to its location in the western section of the city, it was renamed in 1884 to honor Rear Adm. Samuel F. Du Pont (1803-65), the Civil War hero who directed Union naval operations along the south Atlantic coast. A bronze statue of Du Pont stood in the center of the circle until 1921, when the hero's family transferred the memorial to Wilmington, Delaware. Shortly thereafter, the Du Ponts replaced the statue with the marble **fountain** that now occupies the center of the circle. Designed in 1921 by Daniel Chester French, sculptor of the celebrated statue of Abraham Lincoln in the Lincoln Memorial, the fountain consists of a wide basin resting atop a central pillar adorned with figures symbolizing the sea, wind and stars—references to Du Pont's naval career.

During the 1960s and 70s, Dupont Circle gained prominence as a major gathering place for the counterculture and political activists. Today this busy urban park is frequented by a representative cross section of Washington's diverse residential population, making it one of the capital's best outdoor spots for people watching.

Cross over to Massachusetts Ave. south of P St. on the east side of the circle.

© Catherine Karnow/FOLIO, Inc.

Dupont Circle

Sulgrave Club (Wadsworth House) – *1801 Massachusetts Ave. NW. Not open to the public.* This buff brick mansion, with a semidetached bow window overlooking the circle, was the residence of Herbert and Martha Wadsworth, wealthy landowners from upstate New York. Constructed around 1900 (architect unknown) on a choice triangular lot, this elegant two-story structure is crowned by a roof balustrade and features a Palladian window above the principal entrance *(on Massachusetts Ave)*. A gilded ballroom on the second floor was the scene of lavish social gatherings attended by prominent Washington personalities.

In 1918 Wadsworth donated his residence to the Red Cross, which occupied the mansion until 1932. At that time it was sold to a group of Washington women who established the Sulgrave Club, one of the city's private social clubs.

Continue on Massachusetts Ave. to the corner of 18th St.

The 1700 block of Massachusetts Avenue contains four buildings by **Jules Henri de Sibour** (1872-1938). Born into an aristocratic French family and trained at Yale and at the École des Beaux-Arts in Paris, de Sibour settled in Washington, where he designed several palatial residences for the capital's moneyed classes.

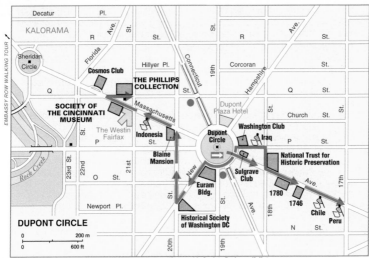

National Trust for Historic Preservation (McCormick Apartments) – *1785 Massachusetts Ave. NW. The lobby is open to the public year-round Mon–Fri 9am–5pm. Closed major holidays.* & ☎ *202-588-6000. www.nationaltrust.org.*
The five-story edifice that dominates the intersection of Massachusetts Avenue and 18th Street was the city's most luxurious apartment building and perhaps de Sibour's finest commission.

Completed in 1917, the building takes its name from the original owner, Stanley McCormick, son of Cyrus McCormick, inventor of the reaper and founder of the International Harvester Co. The two principal facades, gracefully articulated by means of the rounded corner entrance, are accented by a rusticated first story, bas-relief panels and a balcony with cast-iron railings that crowns the cornice. The steep mansard roof is lined with chimneys and pedimented dormers adorned with characteristic Beaux-Arts ornamentation.

The building's original interior reflected the fabulous lifestyle of the early-20C millionaires. Each floor was occupied by a single apartment (except the ground floor, which was divided into two). The average apartment contained six bedrooms and measured 11,000sq ft, with ceilings over 14ft high. Among the numerous amenities were a wine closet, a silver vault, a central vacuuming system and a laundry chute leading to individual washing machines in the basement. The building could accommodate more than 40 live-in servants.

The building's most illustrious occupant was financier and Secretary of the Treasury Andrew Mellon, who rented the fifth-floor apartment in the 1920s and 30s. In 1936 the art dealer Joseph Duveen leased the apartment below Mellon's and filled it with Old Master paintings and sculptures in the hopes of selling the works to Mellon, whose own quarters already housed some of the finest works of European painting in this country. Duveen gave his upstairs neighbor an apartment key so that the avid collector could appreciate the art at his leisure. Mellon eventually agreed to purchase 24 paintings and 18 sculptures for a total of $21 million. The masterpieces that once graced the walls of these apartments formed the core of the world-renowned collection of the National Gallery of Art, which Mellon founded in Washington, DC in 1937.

Among the other privileged tenants to have enjoyed these sumptuous quarters were Robert Woods Bliss, founder of Dumbarton Oaks; and Mrs. Perle Mesta, US ambassador to Luxembourg and leading Washington hostess.

Since the 1950s the building has housed the offices of various public and private organizations. Today the landmark building is the headquarters of the National Trust for Historic Preservation.

Continue east on Massachusetts Ave.

■ **National Trust Properties**

Of the 19 historic sites the National Trust for Historic Preservation owns in the US, the following are located in Washington, DC and Mount Vernon, Virginia:

Decatur House

Pope-Leighey House

Woodrow Wilson House

Woodlawn Plantation

Across the street stands **no. 1780**, built by de Sibour in 1922 for the Ingalls, another wealthy Washington family. The building has been remodeled to accommodate the Yater Clinic, which has occupied the site since the 1950s.

The five-story limestone and brick mansion at **no. 1746** was commissioned in 1906 by Clarence Moore, a West Virginia tycoon who perished on the ill-fated *Titanic* (1912). The building housed the Canadian diplomatic mission from 1927 until 1988, when the embassy moved into more spacious quarters in the colossal limestone building opposite the National Gallery of Art at 501 Pennsylvania Avenue NW.

The unadorned brick and sandstone building (1889), now the **Chilean chancery** *(no. 1732)*, was constructed as a private residence by local architect Glenn Brown. It served as the headquarters of the Washington chapter of the Daughters of the American Revolution (DAR) from 1940 to 1973.

The dignified mansion at the corner of Massachusetts Avenue and 17th Street, now the **Peruvian embassy** *(no. 1700)*, was designed by de Sibour in 1910 for the widow of Beriah Wilkins, a congressman from Ohio and editor and publisher of the *Washington Post*. Its imposing facade, composed of a slightly projecting central section flanked by a pair of wings set at oblique angles, is reminiscent of a Renaissance palazzo.

Walk back up Massachusetts Ave. toward Dupont Circle, turn right on 18th St. and left on P St.

On the corner of P and 18th streets, note the **embassy of Iraq** (1801 P St.), a tan brick structure with Richardsonian detailing. Completed in 1893, this former residence was designed by the architectural firm Hornblower and Marshall.

Continue on P St. to Dupont Circle.

Washington Club (Patterson House) – *15 Dupont Circle NW. Not open to the public.* This ornate white marble and terra-cotta mansion, which resembles a Mannerist palazzo, was built in the early years of the 20C by Stanford White of the noted New York firm McKim, Mead and White.

Commissioned by the Chicago socialite Mrs. Robert Patterson, this opulent residence was yet another setting for lavish entertaining in the capital. The Pattersons' daughter, Cissy (1884-1948), publisher of the *Washington Times-Herald*, assumed the role of the capital's premier hostess during the 1930s and early 40s.

During the renovation of the White House in the summer of 1927, Patterson House served as the temporary residence of President and Mrs. Coolidge. In the course of their stay, the Coolidges hosted the nation's hero, Charles Lindbergh, just back from his historic transatlantic flight. For three days immense crowds gathered in Dupont Circle to hail the young aviator, who greeted them from the first-floor loggia. In accordance with the terms of Cissy Patterson's will, the family's Washington residence was donated to the Red Cross after her death in 1948. Three years later the mansion was sold to the Washington Club, the elite women's organization that now occupies the building.

R. Corbel/MICHELIN

Washington Club

Walk clockwise along the circle.

Note the **Euram Building** at 21 Dupont Circle. Designed in 1971 by the Washington architectural firm Hartman-Cox, this glass, brick and concrete office building enclosing a handsome courtyard is one of the capital's most innovative works of contemporary architecture.

Turn left on New Hampshire Ave. and continue one block to the intersection of New Hampshire Ave., 20th St. and Sunderland Pl.

Historical Society of Washington DC (Heurich Mansion) – *1307 New Hampshire Ave. NW. Open year-round Mon–Sat 10am–4pm. Closed major holidays. $3.* ♿ ☎ *202-785-2068. www.hswdc.org.* This landmark Richardsonian Romanesque building is one of the city's best-preserved house museums and a resource center for the study of the capital's history.

The imposing mansion (1894) was commissioned by Christian Heurich, the German-born founder of a prosperous brewery that stood on the present site of the Kennedy Center in Foggy Bottom. The house remained in the Heurich family until 1956, when Heurich's descendants donated the building along with its furnishings to the Columbia Historical Society (later renamed the Historical Society of Washington DC). The society, founded in 1894 "to preserve, collect and teach the history of the nation's capital," established its headquarters here and maintains the property as a house museum.

Exterior – The building's exterior features—massive brownstone and brick walls, rounded arches and a prominent corner tower—are characteristic of the Richardsonian Romanesque style. The entrance is highlighted by a stone carriage porch supported by squat coupled columns with elaborately carved capitals. Two fanciful gargoyles projecting from the porch's crowning balustrade stand guard over the entrance driveway. Constructed of poured concrete, the building is one of the earliest fireproof residences in the city, owing to the insistence of Heurich, whose brewery had been seriously damaged by fire.

Interior – The ornate period rooms, designed by a New York decorator, reflect the eclectic tastes of its owners. Carved oak and mahogany woodwork abounds alongside a profusion of painted, plastered and stenciled decoration.

The entrance foyer features a staircase with onyx risers, marble treads and a cast-bronze balustrade. A charming musicians' loggia opens onto three of the adjoining rooms: a sitting room and two formal parlors with late-19C French-style furniture. Beyond the parlors are the intimate music room, the formal dining room (note the remarkable coffered oak ceiling) and a spacious conservatory. The breakfast room in the basement, resembling a *Ratskeller*, or German tavern, was the homey setting where the Heurichs gathered for informal meals. The bedrooms on the second floor contain many original furnishings and fixtures, numerous family portraits and personal objects.

The third and fourth floors accommodate the society's research collections *(accessible to the public)* numbering over 100,000 manuscripts, books, photographs, prints, maps and other materials pertaining to the social history of the capital. Small changing exhibits on local history are presented in galleries on the first and third floors. In the warm season the mansion's tranquil garden *(accessible from Sunderland Pl.)* is a pleasant urban oasis, where many of the neighborhood's office workers relax during their lunch hour.

Upon leaving the building, cross over to 20th St. and continue north to the corner of Massachusetts Ave.

16 Connecticut Avenue
Map p 14. A longtime favorite with literature lovers and cafe-goers, **Kramerbooks & Afterwords** *(1517 Connecticut Ave. NW ☎ 202-387-3825)* combines a well-stocked bookstore with a bar and cafe/restaurant. Enjoy "comfort foods" like quesadillas or designer sandwiches, and a changing selection of microbrewery draft beers. If you're in the mood for simply kaffeeklatsching, the coffee and dessert menu is extensive. Try the death by chocolate or the Kahlua walnut pie. As you climb the stairs to **Taj Mahal** *(1327 Connecticut Ave. NW ☎ 202-659-1544)*, the smells of curry assail you. This pleasant, second-floor restaurant offers a great lunch buffet on white tablecloths, including several curry selections and all the chutneys and condiments that accompany a typical Indian meal. **Marvelous Market** *(1511 Connecticut Ave. NW ☎ 202-332-3690)* is a great place to put together your own carryout meal of homemade soup, gourmet pâtés, cheese and spreads, fresh fruits and the market's own superb breads and pastries. Over thirty farmers bring their goods to producer-only **FRESHFARM Market** *(Apr-Dec Sun 9am-1pm; Dupont Circle at Massachusetts Ave & 20th St. NW. www.farmland.org ☎ 202-331-7300)* where you can find fresh fruit, vegetables, dairy products, meat, homemade jams, jellies, flowers and soaps. Chef at the Market *(call or check web for schedule)* gives visitors an opportunity to explore the market with a local chef.

Blaine Mansion – *2000 Massachusetts Ave. NW. Not open to the public.* Erected in 1881, this severe brick edifice with an elaborate roof design is Dupont Circle's oldest surviving mansion. It was built as the Washington residence of **James G. Blaine** (1830-93), cofounder of the Republican Party, member of Congress, secretary of State under two administrations (Garfield and Harrison) and unsuccessful Republican candidate in the 1884 presidential election (against Grover Cleveland). Displeased with the vastness and high maintenance costs of their home, the Blaines leased it to the Chicago businessman and real-estate baron Levi Leiter in 1883 for the record annual sum of $11,500. Leiter remained in the mansion until the early 1890s, when he moved to a stately residence he had built on the north side of Dupont Circle (demolished in 1947). The prolific inventor George Westinghouse purchased the Blaine mansion in 1901 and lived there until his death in 1914.

Over the years the building's interior and exterior have been considerably altered. Originally a freestanding structure with entrances on the three surrounding streets, the building is now flanked on its P Street side by an unattractive row of one-story shops, and today the wooden carriage porch (slightly transformed) on Massachusetts Avenue serves as the main entrance. Since the late 1940s professional offices have occupied the building.

Continue west on Massachusetts Ave.

Indonesian Embassy (**Walsh Mansion**) – *2020 Massachusetts Ave. NW. Visit by guided tour (45min) only, year-round Mon–Fri 9am–5pm. Closed Indonesian and major holidays. As this sight is often closed for special events, it is advisable to phone before visiting.* & ☎ *202-775-5200. www.kbri.org.* This fabulous turn-of-the-century mansion was built by Thomas Walsh, an Irish immigrant who struck it rich in the Colorado goldfields. After moving his family to Washington, Walsh commissioned Henry Andersen, a Danish-born architect, to design a mansion befitting his vast wealth. He had made about $45 million from the sale of his Camp Bird Mine in Colorado.

During the Theodore Roosevelt administration, the Walshes were prominent social figures, using their palatial home as the setting for parties whose lavishness became legendary. At Mrs. Walsh's death in 1932, the house passed to her daughter Evalyn. Married to Edward Beale McLean, whose family owned the *Cincinnati Enquirer* and the *Washington Post*, Evalyn Walsh McLean was a Washington socialite, now remembered as the last private owner of the celebrated Hope Diamond (on view in the National Museum of Natural History). In 1951 she sold the home to the Indonesian government.

17 Restaurant corner

Map p 15. Clustered at the corner of 17th and P streets NW are several inexpensive eateries: **Bua** (☎ *202-265-0828*), known for its well-prepared Thai cuisine; **Skewers** (☎ *202-387-7400*), longtime mecca for lovers of Middle Eastern appetizers and specialties; and **Cafe Luna** (☎ *202-387-4005*), a casual, low-key sidewalk cafe with Italian and American cuisine.

Visit – A balustraded terrace, a second-story loggia, ornate limestone trim, bay swells and a red-tiled mansard roof adorn the tan brick exterior of the mansion. The carriage porch extending from the west side of the house is balanced on the east by a semicircular conservatory with stained-glass trim.

The arched double doors of the entrance portico open onto a sumptuous hall three stories high and topped by a stained-glass skylight. An Art Nouveau banister of mahogany sweeps up from floor to floor, its ornate woodwork repeated in the balustrades that line the open promenades on each level.

In the Louis XVI drawing room, now partially filled by a stage for embassy functions, rose damask walls are embellished with gilt and white pilasters and arched woodwork. Elaborate plaster flourishes ornament the ceiling, in the center of which is a mural entitled *Eternity of Angels*.

The adjoining music room contains dark mahogany wainscoting and trim that is echoed in the woodwork of the pipe organ. Inset wall cabinets now display traditional Indonesian crafts, such as shadow puppets and Balinese wood carvings.

The building at 2100 Massachusetts Ave., across 21st Street, houses the Westin Fairfax Hotel.

Continue west on Massachusetts Ave.

★Society of the Cincinnati Museum (**Anderson House**) – *2118 Massachusetts Ave. NW. Open year-round Tue–Sat 1pm–4pm. Closed major holidays. Guided tours (1/2hr) available.* & ☎ *202-785-2040.* This distinguished edifice is the headquarters of the venerable Society of the Cincinnati. A bastion of tradition, the society displays an impressive collection of Revolutionary artifacts and preserves its opulent building as a house museum reflecting the era of early-20C grandeur.

The Society – Founded in 1783 by former officers of the Revolution, this patriotic organization can claim George Washington as its first president-general. Named for Lucius Quinctius Cincinnatus, a 5C Roman military hero and farmer, the society extols the ideal of the soldier returning to productive civilian life and spearheaded the establishment of military pensions in America. Membership passes, by tradition and charter, through the line of eldest sons.

The Andersons – Larz Anderson, who had the house built, was descended from a founding member of the Society of the Cincinnati and was a member himself. A career diplomat, Anderson served as minister to Belgium and ambassador to Japan. He shared with his wife, Isabel Weld Perkins, a Boston heiress, an interest in travel and collecting, as reflected in the furnishings of this impressive 50-room residence.

Designed by the firm of Little and Brown, the mansion was completed in 1905 at a cost of $800,000. After his retirement Anderson and his wife entertained here, often hosting official state dinners. At Anderson's death in 1937, Mrs. Anderson donated the house to the Society of the Cincinnati.

Visit – Arched carriage gates lead into a walled courtyard dominated by the elegant rounded portico. Flag and pennant motifs adorn the tympanum of the roof-level pediment. Inside the front hall is a bust of Washington by Thomas Crawford, who designed the statue of Freedom that tops the dome of the Capitol. The small room to the right is lined with late Renaissance choir stalls. On the wall above is a frieze by Henry Siddons Mowbray that depicts awards bestowed on the Andersons and on the society. In the billiard room hang military portraits by such eminent 18C and 19C American artists as Gilbert Stuart, John Trumbull and George Catlin. The great stair hall contains cases with battle dioramas, detailed French miniatures of soldiers and other memorabilia. A late-19C painting, *The Triumph of the Dogaressa Anna Maria Foscari in the Year 1424*, by Jose Villegas y Cordero, dominates the staircase landing. On the second floor, the reception room is notable for its Siena and white marble floor bearing the pattern of the Greek key. The allegorical wall and ceiling friezes in this room were also painted by Mowbray. An ornately paneled, Louis XV-style parlor displays jade trees from the Andersons' Ching dynasty collection. Among the furnishings in the adjoining English parlor are Hepplewhite pieces, English portraiture and Chinese porcelains from the 16C to the 19C. The long corridor known as the Olmsted gallery contains Asian antiques and Italian paintings, while the formal dining room is decorated with early-17C Belgian tapestries. This room opens onto a musicians' gallery, overlooking the grand **ballroom** and supported by twisted columns of Verona marble. Over the ballroom mantel is a portrait of Gen. Henry Knox, considered the society's founder. Arched doors lead from the ballroom into a charming solarium that overlooks a gracious walled sculpture garden. A reflecting pool faced by an 18C statue of a Japanese Buddha gives the garden an Oriental appearance.

Cross Massachusetts Ave.

Cosmos Club (**Townsend House**) – *2121 Massachusetts Ave. NW. Not open to the public.* Set behind a landscaped entrance driveway, this dignified limestone mansion is the headquarters of one of the country's most exclusive social clubs. In 1899 Richard Townsend, the president of the Erie and Pittsburgh Railroad, and his wife, Mary, heiress to the Pennsylvania Railroad fortune, commissioned the renowned architectural firm Carrère and Hastings to design a palatial residence appropriate to their social position and grand lifestyle. The architects received strict instructions to integrate the site's preexisting brick house into their plan because Mrs. Townsend had been warned by a fortune-teller that calamity would strike if she were to settle into a brand-new house. Despite the precautions taken, Mr. Townsend died from a riding accident in 1902, the year following the house's completion. In accordance with the Townsend's request for a house in the style of the 18C Petit Trianon at Versailles, the architects designed a central facade composed of three bays separated by colossal pilasters and crowned by a roof balustrade. A mansard roof punctuated by dormer windows constitutes the fourth floor. The two-story wings that flank the central section lend balance to the design.

Mrs. Townsend gained fame among the capital's affluent circles for the extravagant manner in which she entertained in her splendid Massachusetts Avenue residence.

---

⑳ Gabriel

Map p 14. Radisson Barcelo Hotel, 2121 P St. NW. ☎ 202-956-6690. While the menu here offers well-prepared Salvadorean *pupusas* (corn tortillas stuffed with pork and cheese) and entrées seasoned with cumin or jalapeños, the real deal in this relaxed, inviting restaurant is the tapas table. At lunch and at happy hour *(5pm-8pm)*, this help-yourself buffet features redolent bean-and-beef dishes, quesadillas, all kinds of legume salads and the pungent cheese, crisp olives and de rigueur almonds that accompany any true tapas repast.

㉑ Brickskeller

Map p 14. 1523 22nd St. NW. ᪲ ☎ 202-293-1885. Even before microbreweries were the rage, this simple bar with checkered tablecloths was well known to beer aficionados. Its libations menu—really a booklet—is broken down by countries, with all available beers from a particular nation listed. The hundreds of brews available range from Belgium Trappist ale to Lebanese Almaza.

In the 1930s the mansion was home to the Townsends' daughter, Mathilde, and her second husband, Sumner B. Welles, under secretary of State during most of the Roosevelt administration. The Welleses hosted President and Mrs. Roosevelt for several weeks in January 1933 before the first family moved to the White House. In 1950 the residence was purchased by the Cosmos Club, a social club founded in 1878 for men of distinction in the fields of science, literature and the fine arts. Inscribed in its prestigious register are the names of three US presidents and more than 80 Nobel and Pulitzer Prize recipients.

Continue one block east on Q St. to the corner of 21st St.

★★THE PHILLIPS COLLECTION

On a quiet corner a few steps from the bustling shops and restaurants along Connecticut Avenue stands a small museum of great distinction. The Phillips Collection, the nation's first museum of modern art, exhibits outstanding works by prominent American and European artists in an intimate setting.

The Collector – The grandson of one of the cofounders of the Jones and Laughlin Steel Co., **Duncan Phillips** (1886-1966) developed an interest in art during his studies at Yale and in the course of his numerous travels abroad. In 1908 Duncan and his brother, James, began expanding the small private collection that hung in the family's unpretentious brick and brownstone home built by the firm of Hornblower and Marshall in 1896. Following James' death in 1918—only 13 months after the death of his father—Duncan devoted himself to transforming the family's private collection into a public memorial to his beloved father and brother. In the fall of 1921, eight years before the founding of the Museum of Modern Art in New York City, the Phillips Memorial Art Gallery, occupying two rooms of the family home, opened to an appreciative public.

That same year Phillips married Marjorie Acker, a talented painter in her own right, and the couple embarked on a period of active collecting. During the 1920s they acquired many of the collection's most famous paintings, including Renoir's *Luncheon of the Boating Party*, which was purchased for the record sum of $125,000 in 1923. By 1930 the collection had assumed its basic form, containing paintings by all the major French Impressionists, post-Impressionists and Cubists as well as outstanding works by several 17C and 18C masters, including Goya, El Greco and Chardin. In 1931 Phillips and his family moved out of their home in order to provide additional space for the expanding collection, which by that time comprised some 600 works. A new wing was added in 1960, and the following year the museum was renamed the Phillips Collection. From 1987 to 1989, the renovation and expansion of the wing (renamed the Goh Annex) was undertaken to improve exhibit conditions.

Luncheon of the Boating Party (1880-81) by Pierre Auguste Renoir

Collection Highlights

The Repentant Peter	**El Greco**	c.1600
A Bowl of Plums	**Chardin**	c.1728
Self-portrait	**Cézanne**	1880
Luncheon of the Boating Party	**Renoir**	1881
Miss Van Buren	**Eakins**	1890
The Blue Room	**Picasso**	1901
The Palm	**Bonnard**	1926
Ranchos Church	**O'Keeffe**	c.1930
Arab Song	**Klee**	1932
Painting No. 9	**Mondrian**	1942
Ochre and Red on Red	**Rothko**	1954

The Collection – Throughout his life Duncan Phillips eschewed the cold formality of the art establishment. He and his wife relied on their judgment and taste, rather than the advice of curators or art dealers. Phillips did not adhere to any one specific doctrine or school of art and largely avoided the avant-garde and cult movements of the day. While concentrating primarily on modern art, he frequently juxtaposed 19C and 20C works with Old Masters paintings to suggest sources from which modern artists might have sought inspiration. In fact, Phillips conceived his collection as "a museum of modern art and its sources."

The Phillips Collection is, in every respect, a reflection of its creator. Most of the museum's 2,500 works, primarily from the 19C and 20C, were selected by Phillips and his wife. Artists represented in the collection include Daumier, Degas, Cézanne, Monet, Bonnard, van Gogh, Matisse, Klee and Picasso, along with noted American painters such as Ryder, Marin, Dove, O'Keeffe and Tack.

Visit

1600 21st St. NW. Ⓜ Dupont Circle. Open year-round Tues–Sat 10am–5pm (Thu til 8:30pm), Sun noon–7pm (Sun til 5pm in summer). Closed Jan 1, July 4, Thanksgiving Day, Dec 25. $7.50. ✗ ♿ ☎ 202-387-2151. www.phillipscollection.org. "Artful Evenings" of music, gallery talks and videos on art are held year-round Thu 5pm–8:30pm. $5.

Paintings are hung in simple yet tastefully furnished rooms to create an informal domestic setting that Phillips considered conducive to the appreciation of art. The works, which are rotated frequently, are not arranged chronologically, but earlier pieces are generally found in the ground-floor rooms, including the foyer with its dark oak staircase and molding; and the house's largest room, the oak-paneled **Music Room**, which features a ceiling decorated with raised plaster medallions. Added to the house in 1907 as a library, this room is a congenial setting for Sunday concerts *(Sept–May 5pm)*.

The second floor contains additional gallery space for the permanent collection and a room devoted exclusively to the delightful works of the renowned Swiss painter **Paul Klee** (1879-1940). The Goh Annex is linked to the original building by two glass-enclosed walkways. Above the annex's street-level entrance hovers the bas-relief of a bird in flight, based on a work by Georges Braque, one of Phillips' favorite painters. Among the works displayed on a rotating basis in the annex are paintings from the popular **Bonnard Collection**, reputed to be the country's largest collection of the French artist's paintings.

A small gallery on the first floor displays four important works by Abstract Expressionist **Mark Rothko** (1903-70), known for his hauntingly simple canvases of large expanses of color. On exhibit in a second-floor gallery is the museum's most renowned treasure: *Luncheon of the Boating Party* (1881) by Renoir. The third-floor galleries are devoted to temporary exhibits.

NATIONAL GEOGRAPHIC SOCIETY EXPLORERS HALL

17th and M Sts. NW.
Ⓜ Farragut West or Farragut North.

The National Geographic Society's century-long support of explorers, archaeologists, oceanographers and other scientists is showcased in this museum. Housed in the society's three-building headquarters complex, the hall was opened in 1964. It occupies the ground floor of a 10-story marble and glass structure designed by Edward Durell Stone, architect of the Kennedy Center.

 Soul food
Map p 15. Just east of the National Geographic Society, the historic **Metropolitan AME Church** *(1518 M St. NW ☎ 202-331-1426)* serves great soul-food lunches on Thursdays and Fridays from September to June. The set-price, cafeteria-style meal features generous portions of old favorites: ribs or chicken, greens, black-eyed peas, corn bread and iced tea. In 1993, during Bill Clinton's initial swearing-in, this church became the first African-American church to host a presidential inaugural prayer service; the church held the service for Clinton's second inaugural as well.

VISIT

🧒 *Open year-round Mon–Sat 9am–5pm, Sun 10am–5pm. Closed Dec 25.* ♿ ☎ *202-857-7588.*

Explorers Hall features changing exhibits whose contents may be cultural, geographic or scientific.

B'NAI B'RITH KLUTZNICK NATIONAL JEWISH MUSEUM

1640 Rhode Island Ave. NW.
Ⓜ Farragut North or Farragut West.

Located on the ground floor of B'nai B'rith International, the world's oldest Jewish service organization, this museum houses an extensive collection of Judaic ceremonial, folk and fine art.

VISIT

Open year-round Sun–Fri 10am–5pm. Closed Jewish holidays and major holidays. ♿ ☎ *202-857-6583.* http://bnaibrith.org/museum.

Changing exhibits from the permanent collection feature antique and contemporary ritual objects, such as Torah implements, spice boxes, Esther scrolls, Hanukkah menorahs and kiddush cups. Photographic and other temporary exhibits are presented in the gallery to the left of the entrance hall.

9

Embassy Row

E mbassy Row is the popular name of the two-mile portion of Massachusetts Avenue between Scott Circle and Observatory Circle where some 50 diplomatic missions are concentrated. The buildings housing the chanceries (the embassies proper) and the ambassadors' residences (which may be separate from the chanceries) are recognizable by the colorful flags or plaques that generally adorn their facades. The area from 22nd Street to Observatory Circle is considered the most distinctive and elegant segment of Embassy Row.

Historical Notes – The portion of Massachusetts Avenue beyond 22nd Street developed in the first decade of the 20C as an extension of the exclusive Dupont Circle residential enclave. Situated on a wooded ridge overlooking a large expanse of Rock Creek Park, this pristine area offered spacious and relatively inexpensive lots well suited to the construction of the palatial residences fashionable in the early 20C before the advent of income tax. By 1915 the area around Sheridan Circle was home to some of the capital's wealthiest residents.

The 1929 stock-market crash and the ensuing Great Depression marked a turning point in the lifestyles of affluent Americans. Unable to maintain their sumptuous homes, the area's residents were forced to set up households in more modest quarters. In 1931 the governments of Great Britain and Japan led the way in the area's development as a diplomatic quarter by constructing new embassy compounds in the upper reaches of Massachusetts Avenue beyond Sheridan Circle. They were soon followed by several diplomatic missions and private firms, which purchased former private residences along the avenue. Before long the two-mile stretch between Scott Circle and Observatory Circle, dubbed Embassy Row, supplanted the Meridian Hill district around 16th Street NW as the capital's premier diplomatic quarter.

In the construction boom that followed World War II, some of Embassy Row's buildings were sacrificed to make way for intrusive modern structures, but the avenue's upper portion (north of Florida Avenue) has managed to conserve its elegant character.

In **Kalorama**, the pleasant residential neighborhood situated north of Florida Avenue between Massachusetts and Connecticut avenues, additional diplomatic missions have been established in reconverted upper-middle-class dwellings.

Beaux-Arts Architecture – Like the adjoining Dupont Circle area, the upper portion of Embassy Row preserves a concentration of outstanding private residences designed in the Beaux-Arts style. Derived from the preeminent art academy in Paris, the École des Beaux-Arts, this term, as applied to American architecture, generally refers to the wide gamut of classically inspired styles advocated by the École in the second half of the 19C. Among the scores of Americans who trained in Paris during this period were the Washington-based architects George Oakley Totten Jr. (1866-1939), Waddy B. Wood (1869-1944), Nathan C. Wyeth (1870-1963) and Jules Henri de Sibour (1872-1938). The returning expatriates imported the grandiose European styles that satisfied wealthy Americans' appetites for edifices reflecting their aspirations and opulent tastes. These styles included the Chateauesque and Georgian and Renaissance Revivals, but the most popular Beaux-Arts style was derived from tall apartment buildings that rose in Paris' elegant residential quarters at the turn of the century. The American edifices were characterized by symmetrical design, exuberant decorative details (swags, garlands, carved panels, ornamented keystones and brackets), a rusticated first floor generally with an entry canopy, and a mansard roof rising above a stone balustrade.

WALKING TOUR

M Dupont Circle.

Distance: about 1 mile (not including visits). Map below

The following walking tour describes the most noteworthy portion of Embassy Row—Massachusetts Avenue between 22nd Street and Observatory Circle. Part of Massachusetts Avenue below 22nd Street is included on the Dupont Circle walking tour *(p 196)*. Unless otherwise specified, all sights described or mentioned on the tour are located on Massachusetts Avenue NW.

Access to Embassies – *Consulates and ambassadors' residences are usually open for official business only. The general public can visit selected embassies on a special tour organized annually in early May to benefit Goodwill Industries. The self-guided tour (10am-5pm) includes free shuttle bus service to the participating embassies and refreshments. Tickets: $30. Reservations required. For details and reservations ☎ 202-636-4225. www.dcgoodwill.org.*

Begin the tour at the corner of Massachusetts Ave. and 22nd St.

2200 Block – This gently sloped portion of Massachusetts Avenue, flanked by attached town houses, provides a pleasant entry to Sheridan Circle, situated on a rise to the northwest. Occupying a choice corner lot, the limestone mansion at no. 2200, which today houses the **embassy of Luxembourg**, was designed by Jules Henri de Sibour for Alexander Stewart (1829-1912), a lumber magnate and congressman from Wisconsin. Completed in 1909 at a cost of approximately $92,000, the building incorporates characteristic Beaux-Arts features: symmetrical design, a rusticated first floor, arched windows and a mansard roof rising above a stone balustrade. The embassies of Togo and the Sudan are located at nos. 2208 and 2210 respectively. At **no. 2230** stands the smallest of the four Embassy Row residences built by the prolific Washington architect George Oakley Totten Jr. Completed in 1907, this brick-faced row house was designed in the so-called Chateauesque manner—an eclectic style briefly in vogue around the turn of the century. Derived from large-scale 16C European estates, Chateauesque buildings are characterized by gabled dormers, steeply pitched hipped roofs and balconies carved with reliefs or tracery. With elegant facades on both Massachusetts Avenue and Sheridan Circle, **no. 2234** was erected in 1909 as a private residence by William Cresson (1873-1932), an architect turned rancher, diplomat and eventually law professor. Cresson's training at the École des Beaux-Arts is reflected in the building's overall design and ornamental details. Since 1949 the building has housed the embassy of Ireland. The freestanding structure across the avenue at no. 2221 is the embassy of Greece.

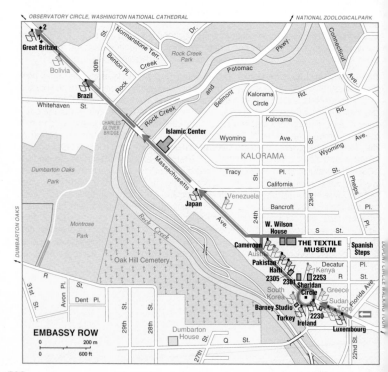

Sheridan Circle – Originally called Decatur Circle in honor of the early-19C naval hero Stephen Decatur, the park was renamed in 1890 after Gen. Philip H. Sheridan (1831-88), leader of the Union cavalry. Sheridan is known for his victory in the Shenandoah Valley on October 19, 1864, and for his role in bringing about General Lee's surrender at Appomattox in 1865. Dedicated in 1908, the vigorous bronze equestrian **statue** of Sheridan at the park's center was designed by Gutzon Borglum, renowned for the colossal presidential heads at Mount Rushmore.

A harmonious 19C addition to L'Enfant's plan for the capital, this circle, with its well-tended park rimmed with age-old ginkgo and linden trees, provides a graceful setting for the surrounding palatial mansions and town houses. At **no. 2301** the striking four-story mansion with a convex facade and monumental Palladian arch that dominates the circle's north side is the residence of the Egyptian ambassador. Other embassy buildings facing the circle are the residence of the ambassador of the Philippines at **2253 R St.** and the embassies of Kenya *(2249 R St.)* and South Korea *(2320 Massachusetts Ave.).*

Continue to the corner of 23rd St. and Sheridan Circle.

Embassy of Turkey (Everett House) – *1606 23rd St.* Reputedly Embassy Row's most sumptuous mansion, this grandiose structure (1915) was the home of Edward H. Everett, multimillionaire industrialist and inventor of the fluted soft-drink bottle cap. The costly residence (1915 tax assessment: $230,000) was designed by George Oakley Totten Jr.

The glass-covered carriage porch, the semicircular columned portico and the balustrade crowning the roof lend an air of opulence to the structure. Totten added an exotic touch by incorporating a colonnaded porch above the south wing. Instructed to spare no expense in the decoration of the house, the architect created a building befitting the grand lifestyle of the Everetts.

The interior, richly appointed with carved wood paneling and inlaid floors, featured an indoor swimming pool and a fabulous ballroom with walls hung with gold-thread damask. Mrs. Everett, an opera singer, hosted a concert series known as "Evenings with Music," a coveted social event featuring world-renowned divas and attended by Washington's cultural elite. The Turkish embassy was established in the mansion in 1936.

Continue clockwise along the circle.

Barney Studio House – *2306 Massachusetts Ave. Not open to the public.* Rather modest by Embassy Row standards, this charming town house tucked away on the southwestern rim of Sheridan Circle played a pivotal role in the cultural life of Washington at the beginning of the 20C.

Built about 1902 by Waddy B. Wood, the five-story structure, inspired by Spanish Colonial architecture (stucco facade, quatrefoil windows, curved parapet and red tile roof), was the home of Alice Pike Barney (1857-1931), one of the city's most enterprising and creative women. Painter, playwright and trendsetter, Barney established her studio-home to serve as one of the capital's earliest private artistic centers. During Barney's lifetime the studio provided the setting for much-needed cultural events, including art shows, small theater presentations, poetry readings, musical performances and informal parties. In 1960 the building was donated to the Smithsonian Institution by Barney's two daughters. Natalie Clifford Barney (1876-1972), Alice's eldest daughter, spent most of her life in Paris, where she hosted a celebrated salon frequented by renowned artists and literary figures, including many American expatriates.

Continue north on Massachusetts Ave. (right side).

2300 Block – Occupying adjacent lots just steps away from Sheridan Circle, the handsome Beaux-Arts mansions at **nos. 2305** and **2311** were designed between 1909 and 1910 by the Paris-trained architect Nathan Wyeth (who also drew up the plans for the Key Bridge linking Georgetown with Arlington). Sold to the Chilean government

> The annual **Dupont-Kalorama Museum Walk Weekend,** held on the first Saturday and Sunday in June, is a neighborhood festival featuring musical performances, special exhibits and activities, and tours of local museums and cultural institutions. Sights open to the public free of charge on that day include the Textile Museum and the Woodrow Wilson House. For information ☎ 202-667-0441.

in 1923, no. 2305, with its gracefully curved central section and roof balustrades, is the ambassador's residence. No. 2311, faced with colossal Corinthian pilasters and surmounted by a steeply pitched mansard roof, was owned by the Nationalist government of China (Taiwan) from the 1940s to the 1970s; it was subsequently purchased by the government of Haiti.

Located on a prominent triangular lot on the corner of Massachusetts Avenue and Decatur Place, the magnificent mansion now housing the **embassy of Pakistan** *(no. 2315)* boldly completes this distinguished block. The stucco Beaux-Arts pile, built in 1909 for the Moran family by George Oakley Totten Jr., is dominated by an imposing round tower adorned with limestone and terra-cotta detailing—oval cartouches, swags and bas-relief decorative panels.

Cross Decatur Pl. and continue past the Austrian embassy (no. 2343) to the intersection of Massachusetts Ave. and 24th St.

R. Corbel/MICHELIN

Pakistan Embassy

Embassy of Cameroon (**Hauge Mansion**) – *No. 2349*. This prominently situated limestone "chateau" was the first of the four Embassy Row residences designed by George Oakley Totten Jr. (the three other buildings—2230 Massachusetts Ave. and the Turkish and Pakistan embassies—are described above). Christian Hauge, Norway's first minister to the US, commissioned the building to serve as both his private residence and his government's legation offices. However, in 1908, less than a year after the mansion's completion, Hauge died accidentally in Norway. For 19 years thereafter it was the home of Hauge's American wife, Louise, a prominent East Coast socialite. Like the sumptuous Sheridan Circle mansion of the Everetts (now the embassy of Turkey), Mrs. Hauge's residence was, according to a local newspaper, "the scene of much of Washington's most brilliant entertaining." After almost 40 years as the Czechoslovakian foreign mission, the mansion was sold to the Cameroon government in 1972.

The Hauge mansion is architecturally significant as the city's finest example of the Chateauesque manner. Much bolder in scale and design than the row house at 2230 Massachusetts Avenue that Totten designed at about the same time, this freestanding structure is based on the 16C French chateau Azay-le-Rideau, in the Loire Valley. The mansion's outstanding architectural feature is the imposing rounded tower with its candlesnuffer roof. Like the nearby Pakistan embassy (no. 2315), this building displays Totten's skillful and dramatic handling of irregular corner lots.

Turn right on 24th St. and right again on S St.

Woodrow Wilson House – *2340 S St. Visit by guided tour (1hr 15min) only, year-round Tue-Sun 10am-4pm. Closed major holidays. $5.* & ☎ *202-387-4062. www.woodrowwilsonhouse.org.* The 28th president of the US chose this residence as his place of retirement upon completing his second term in the White House in 1921. The brick Georgian Revival town house, designed in 1915 by Waddy B. Wood, was described by Wilson's wife as "an unpretentious, comfortable, dignified house fitted to the needs of a gentleman's home."

The house has been converted into a **museum**, which preserves the lifestyle of an upper-middle-class family in the 1920s and serves as a window on the family life of the president who led the US through World War I and into a position of world leadership.

Continue on S St.

★The Textile Museum – *2320 S St. Open year-round Mon-Sat 10am-5pm, Sun 1pm-5pm. Closed major holidays & Dec 24. Contribution suggested ($5). Guided tours (1hr) available.* ☎ *202-667-0441. www.textilemuseum.org.* Founded in 1925 by George Hewitt Myers, this small private museum occupies a pair of elegant town houses built by two renowned Washington architects. The building serving as entrance to the museum was designed in 1913 by the prolific John Russell Pope as a private home for Myers. In 1908 the adjoining house was designed by Waddy B. Wood, who later constructed the adjacent Woodrow Wilson House.

The museum focuses on the collection, study and preservation of handmade textiles and carpets. Its holdings comprise more than 14,000 textiles and 1,400 rugs primarily from the Near and Far East and South America, including an outstanding **pre-Columbian collection** from Peru. Changing exhibits present textiles from the US and abroad.

Less than a block east, the **Spanish Steps**, which connect S Street with Decatur Place, offer a quiet spot to sit and enjoy the lion-head fountain and seasonal plantings.

Return to Massachusetts Ave.

Note the embassy of Venezuela (nos. 2443-2445), a low complex of white buildings on impeccably maintained grounds.

Cross the avenue.

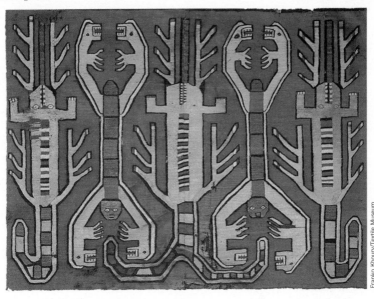

Peruvian Nasca Tunic Fragment (c.700 AD)

Embassy of Japan – *2520 Massachusetts Ave.* This handsome Georgian Revival structure dominating a tree-lined cobblestone courtyard was built in 1931 for the Japanese government. The design, conceived by the architectural team Delano and Aldrich and reputedly approved by Emperor Hirohito, contains a hint of Oriental aesthetics in the delicately curved roofline. Note the depiction of a chrysanthemum, the imperial symbol of the Japanese emperor, that emerges from the balcony recess over the front entrance. The starkly modern chancery building to the right was added in 1986.

Continue on the opposite side of the avenue.

Islamic Center – *2551 Massachusetts Ave. Open year-round Sat-Thur 10am-5pm. Proper attire is required while visiting the mosque: arms, legs (and women's heads) must be covered and shoes removed. ☎ 202-332-8343. www.theislamic center.com.* This long white edifice, surmounted by a slender minaret, serves as a place of worship and instruction for the metropolitan area's sizable Islamic population (estimated at 65,000). Completed in 1957 with funds and materials donated primarily by the governments of Islamic countries, the center houses one of the first mosques in the US.

Operation of the Center – A board of governors, composed of the heads of Islamic diplomatic missions in Washington, sets policies and provides guidance for the center's activities. In accordance with Muslim practice, prayer services are held five times daily: before sunrise, after noon, in the late afternoon, immediately after sunset, and before retiring for the night. The call to prayer, traditionally chanted from a raised place by the muezzin, can be heard *(10am-5pm only)* from the loudspeaker installed on the minaret. Every Friday, the Muslims' holy day, the faithful meet for congregational prayers. Marriages and funerals are also performed in the mosque. Through its publications and a program of lectures, seminars, language and religious classes, the Islamic Center strives to meet the needs of its congregation and to promote better understanding of Islam among Americans of all faiths.

Visit – The limestone construction incorporates characteristic features of Islamic architecture, including horseshoe arches, roof cresting and a minaret, which reaches a height of 160ft. The two-story buildings facing Massachusetts Avenue house the library and the administrative offices. The double row of arches linking the two buildings leads to a small courtyard enclosing a pink marble fountain that serves as a sort of atrium to the mosque. From this point the visitor should note the oblique alignment of the mosque's facade. This curious configuration is explained by the fact that, like all mosques, this building is oriented in the direction of Mecca. The **mosque** proper is an open square space flanked by colonnades richly ornamented in a profusion of calligraphy and geometric and floral patterns (the Koran forbids the representation of human or animal forms). The lower parts of the walls are faced with 7,000 blue tiles donated by the Turkish government. The gifts from Egypt include the 2-ton copper chandelier in the center of the mosque and the carved wood pulpit, or *minbar*. To the left is the *mihrab*, the niche that indicates the direction of the holy city of Mecca to which the faithful pray. The silk rugs were donated by the last Shah of Iran.

Cross the Charles Glover Bridge, a 420ft-long single-span construction (1940) that rises 75ft above a heavily wooded section of Rock Creek Park.

Continue to the corner of Whitehaven St.

Embassy of Brazil – *3000 Massachusetts Ave.* This handsome edifice, set back on a spacious lawn, was built in 1909 for an American diplomat by John Russell Pope. Inspired by Italian Renaissance palaces, the renowned architect designed four elegantly proportioned stories topped with a prominent cornice. The sober facade is punctuated by a recessed entry graced with two pairs of columns. The building, which was purchased by the Brazilian government in 1934, today serves as the ambassador's official residence.

The dark-glass rectangular structure resting on concrete legs at **no. 3006** houses the chancery. Erected in 1971 by the Brazilian architect Olavo Redig de Campos, it is noteworthy as one of the few buildings of contemporary design constructed on Embassy Row.

Continue beyond the embassy of Bolivia *(nos. 3012-3014)* to the **Winston Churchill statue (1)** on the left. One of the greatest public figures of the 20C, Prime Minister Churchill was given honorary American citizenship in 1963 by President John F. Kennedy. Three years later, this statue by William McVey was unveiled. The realistic work depicts Churchill with his familiar attributes—cane and cigar—and his hand raised in the "V for Victory" salute. The location of the statue was carefully chosen to symbolize Churchill's American and British attachments: the statue's right foot is placed on American soil (Churchill's mother was born in the US), while his left foot is resting on the property of the British embassy.

Monumental Sculpture in the Capital

The following is a selection of noteworthy works of modern sculpture adorning the public spaces of Washington, DC (*see also* **Memorials** and **National Gallery of Art Sculpture Garden**):

Mountains and Clouds by Alexander Calder. Atrium of the Hart Senate Office Building, Constitution Ave. and 2nd St. NE.

Mobile (untitled) by Alexander Calder. Atrium of the National Gallery's East Building.

The Gwenfritz by Alexander Calder. Constitution Ave. and 14th St. NW on the grounds of the National Museum of American History.

The Spiral by Alexander Calder. Courtyard of the Old Patent Office Building.

Infinity by José de Rivera. Outside the Mall entrance of the National Museum of American History.

The Awakening by J. Seward Johnson. A striking aluminum sculpture depicting a giant emerging from the ground. Hains Point in East Potomac Park SW.

Mountains and Clouds by Alexander Calder

Architect of the Capitol

The plaza and the sculpture garden of the Hirshhorn Museum provide an open-air showcase for works by prominent modern artists such as Rodin, Matisse, Calder, Moore, Maillol and Smith as well as pieces by contemporary sculptors.

British Embassy – *3100 Massachusetts Ave.* Completed in 1931, this embassy complex was the first to be erected in the area north of Sheridan Circle, thereby leading the way for the avenue's subsequent transformation into Embassy Row. Designed by the period's leading British architect, **Sir Edwin Lutyens** (1869-1944), this sprawling compound resembles an early-18C English country estate. The building facing the avenue is the main chancery—a U-shaped brick structure trimmed in white stone with steep roofs accented by tall chimneys. The ambassador's residence is linked to the rear of the chancery (the two chimneys rising above the chancery's roof are the only parts of the residence visible from the avenue). Traditional and elegant, the embassy is a stately presence among embassies in Washington. Its social functions, often charity benefits, are among the most popular in diplomatic circles.

The nondescript office building rising to the west of Lutyens' building is the chancery annex. In 1957 the cornerstone for this addition was laid by Queen Elizabeth during her visit to the US. The circular glass capsule near the entrance gate is a multifunctional space used primarily for conferences.

Opposite the embassy is the **Kahlil Gibran Memorial (2)**, a 2-acre landscaped site in Normanstone Park commemorating the author of *The Prophet (open daily year-round)*. At the entrance, a bronze head of the Lebanese-born American (1883-1931) rests on the curved wall above a small pool. Paved walkways rise to a circular, fountained terrace where his writings are inscribed on limestone benches.

10

Anacostia and the Eastern Riverfront

Decidedly off the beaten track, the banks of the Anacostia River host several historic military installations and the southeast neighborhood known as Anacostia, an area rich in black history.

The Beginnings – The Nacotchtank Indians inhabited the area along the east branch of the Potomac River when Capt. John Smith explored it in 1608. Later explorers misheard Nacotchtank as "Anacostia," the name now applied to the eastern branch of the Potomac and its southeast shore. Throughout much of the 17C, this area was in the hands of prominent landholders. By midcentury, lucrative tobacco plantations, worked predominantly by black slaves, dotted the riverfront. The incidence of escaped slaves here was high, as they were given refuge by local Indians.

When the federal district was formed in 1790, the area was incorporated into it as a part of Washington County. Thomas Jefferson had recommended that the land south and east of the eastern branch of the Potomac, now the Anacostia River, be included in the district, as it offered a strategic position from which to defend the city militarily. Both Jefferson and planner L'Enfant expected the shores of the Anacostia River to become a naval bastion for the capital and its commercial hub. Though the lower Southeast did not develop commercially, it did become the site of military installations, the first being the Navy Yard, established on the north bank of the river in 1799. The US Arsenal (on the present-day site of Fort McNair) was established in 1803 on the peninsula known as Greenleaf Point, at the confluence of the Anacostia River and the Washington Channel. By the late 18C tobacco had depleted the soil in this area and farmers turned to such crops as wheat, corn and maize. With the demise of the labor-intensive tobacco economy, slaves were increasingly given or allowed to buy their freedom, and the area had a large population of freed blacks by the early 19C. In addition, the liberal attitude of the federal circuit court of Washington County toward black landownership and the rights of blacks to claim their freedom encouraged many freemen to settle here.

The First Suburb – In the 1850s the area took on a suburban tenor with the establishment of a community called Uniontown, whose row houses still stand along U, V, and W streets east of Martin Luther King Jr. Avenue. Along with the nearby Navy Yard, the US Government Insane Asylum (now St. Elizabeth's Hospital), which opened in 1855, provided employment opportunities. Eventually people seeking relief from the congested city moved to what promoters called "the most beautiful and healthy neighborhood around Washington."

In 1862 Congress enacted a bill emancipating slaves in the District and compensating their owners. While the country was at war 11 forts were erected in Anacostia and along the eastern riverfront. Most were dismantled after the war, and their grounds now serve as public parks. After the war a Freedman's Bureau was established under Gen. O.O. Howard, for whom Washington's **Howard University** is named. The bureau quietly purchased the 375-acre Barry Farm in Anacostia in 1867 and resold plots to black families eager to own land. Within a year 500 families lived here. In 1877 **Frederick Douglass**, the nation's most prominent black spokesman, moved to Anacostia. The area remained sparsely populated until the 1920s and 30s when additional housing developments were constructed. Throughout the first half of the 20C, Anacostia's demographics reflected a mix of black and white working-class residents, who lived in single-family homes. Low-income housing projects were built here in the 1950s and 60s. By 1970 the population of the area was predominantly black (86 percent).

In recent decades the area has suffered the serious social and economic problems afflicting many city neighborhoods. In 1986, however, the district government designated Anacostia one of three development zones for the city, and a line of the Metro has been extended into the area.

FREDERICK DOUGLASS NATIONAL HISTORIC SITE⋆

1411 W St. SE.
Map p 259 BZ

Known as Cedar Hill, this quaint Victorian house was the last residence of black statesman, orator and abolitionist Frederick Douglass. The estate tops a grassy, shaded knoll overlooking the Anacostia River and the Mall area beyond, and serves as a perpetual monument to Douglass' ideals and spirit.

Historical Notes

Father of the Civil Rights Movement – Born into slavery in Talbot County, Maryland about 1818, Frederick Douglass, christened Frederick Augustus Washington Bailey, was the son of a black mother and an unidentified white father. As a boy he worked as a house servant in Baltimore, where he was taught the rudiments of reading and writing by the household's white mistress. However, as a young man he was sent to work in the fields and suffered physical deprivation and abuse at the hands of a notorious slave overseer. Later his owner allowed him to leave the fields and learn the trade of ship's caulker.

In 1838 Douglass escaped bondage and fled north, settling with his wife Anna Murray in New Bedford, Massachusetts. In 1841 he became involved with the Massachusetts Anti-Slavery Society and was soon a respected and well-known abolitionist and publicist. Soon after the publication of his first autobiographical work, *Narrative of the Life of Frederick Douglass, An American Slave*, in 1845, Douglass departed for Europe. While abroad Douglass became a free man thanks to English sympathizers and friends who purchased his freedom in 1846. During the Civil War Douglass exerted his efforts in re-

cruiting black troops and in persuading Lincoln to legally end slavery. After the war he was involved with Reconstruction and moved to Washington, first settling in a row house on Capitol Hill, then in 1877, on his Cedar Hill estate. During his years in Anacostia, Douglass received several presidential appointments to serve in district government. In 1882 his wife died, and in 1884 his remarriage to Helen Pitts, a white woman, caused controversy but did not ultimately detract from Douglass' influence as a powerful spokesman for civil rights. In 1895, after attending a women's rights meeting, Douglass died suddenly of a heart attack at his home.

Frederick Douglass

National Archives 200(s)FL-22

Cedar Hill – The neat white house with its broad columned front porch was originally built as a speculative property in the late 1850s by John Van Hook, one of the developers of the area's first planned residential community, Uniontown.

> *"It [Washington] is our national center. It belongs to us, and whether it is mean or majestic, whether arrayed in glory or covered with shame, we cannot but share its character and its destiny."*
>
> Frederick Douglass, 1877

When Douglass purchased the 9-acre estate from Van Hook, the house had never been lived in. Douglass expanded the property to 15 acres and added seven rooms to the rear of the house.

In 1900 Douglass' widow, Helen, founded the Frederick Douglass Memorial Assn., which, in conjunction with the National Assn. of Colored Women, opened the house for public tours. The house was donated to the National Park Service in 1962; the Park Service restored the estate and opened the historic site to the public.

Access – **By car**: *From downtown, cross the 11th St. Bridge to Martin Luther King Jr. Ave., turn left on W St.* **By Tourmobile**: *in summer (p 50).*

VISIT

Visitor center open mid-Apr-mid-Oct daily 9am-5pm. Rest of the year daily 9am-4pm. Closed Jan 1, Thanksgiving Day, Dec 25. House visit by guided tour (1hr 15min) only, year-round daily 9am-4pm. $3. ♿ 🗏 ✆ *202-426-5961. www.nps.gov/frdo.*

The house is decorated with Victorian furnishings and memorabilia, most of which belonged to the Douglass family. The ground floor consists of a formal parlor and a family parlor, a dining room, kitchen, Douglass' study and a pantry and washroom. Note the rare Douglass portrait by Sarah James Eddy in the formal parlor. Douglass sat for the artist during a visit to Massachusetts. The five bedrooms on the second floor include those of Douglass and his two successive wives and two guest rooms. Behind the house, a small reconstructed stone building served as a second study, which Douglass called "the Growlery."

ANACOSTIA MUSEUM

1901 Fort Place SE.
Map p 259 BZ

Located on the high ground of old Fort Stanton, a Civil War fortress now converted into a public park, this museum was conceived by the Smithsonian Institution as a neighborhood museum.

Since its inception in 1967, the museum has moved from its original Anacostia location to its present site and expanded its focus to encompass African-American heritage more broadly. The facility also contains the museum's education and research offices.

Access – **By car**: *From downtown, cross the 11th St. Bridge to Martin Luther King, Jr. Ave., and turn left on Morris Rd., which becomes Erie St. before ending at Fort Pl.*

VISIT

Open year-round daily 10am-5pm. Closed Dec 25. ♿ 🗏 ✆ *202-287-3369. www.si.edu.*

The museum features changing exhibits on black history, culture and achievements.

CONGRESSIONAL CEMETERY

1801 E St. SE.
Ⓜ Potomac Ave.

Established in 1807 by a group of private investors, this grassy site above the Anacostia River was intended to serve as the burial grounds for the new federal city. In 1812 the cemetery was deeded to nearby Christ Church, whose vestry in turn allocated 100 plots for the burial of members of Congress, adding a further 300 in 1823. Congress bought more sites, provided funds for walls, a gatekeeper's house, vaults and other improvements, and in the process named it the Congressional Cemetery.

VISIT

Open year-round daily dawn-dusk. Closed Jan 1 & Dec 25. 🗏 ✆ *202-543-0539. www.congressionalcemetery.org.*

Many prominent individuals involved with the history of the nation are buried on the 32-acre grounds. Notable among these are Civil War photographer Mathew Brady; "March King" composer John Philip Sousa (who was born in nearby Anacostia); Push-ma-ta-ha, a Choctaw chief who served with Andrew Jackson in the War of 1812; and three architects who played important roles in the development of the federal city: William Thornton, Robert Mills and George Hadfield. In addition, more than 70 former members of the House and 20 former senators lie here. The graves of congressmen who died in office are uniformly marked by distinctive sandstone monuments, clustered in two locations in the cemetery. From 1839 to 1875, these monuments were also erected as cenotaph ("empty grave") markers in memory of congressional members buried elsewhere.

WASHINGTON NAVY YARD

9th and M Sts. SE.

Ⓜ Navy Yard.

Historical Notes

In 1799 the first secretary of the Navy, Benjamin Stoddert, authorized this shipbuilding yard as the US Navy's first shore facility. The prominent architect Benjamin H. Latrobe was commissioned to design the complex. The Navy Yard expanded rapidly until the British occupation of Washington in 1814. At that time the yard's commandant, Capt. Thomas Tingey, ordered the facility burned down, to avoid its takeover by the enemy. The yard was rebuilt and continued ship production until the mid-1850s, when it increasingly turned to ordnance manufacture. By 1886 it had become known as the Naval Gun Factory. In both world wars its involvement in weaponry production necessitated expansion. The facility ceased operation in 1961 and now serves primarily as an administrative center and as a historic precinct used ceremonially as the "Quarterdeck of the Navy." Two military museums open to the public are located on the premises.

VISIT

The grounds are open daily year-round. A photo ID is required to enter the Navy Yard.

Navy Museum – *Entrance on Sicard St. Open April-Labor Day, Mon-Fri 9am-5pm, weekends & holidays 10am-5pm. Rest of the year Mon-Fri 9am-4pm, weekends & holidays 10am-5pm. Closed Jan 1, Thanksgiving Day, Dec 24-25. Guided tours (1hr) available (2-week advance reservations suggested).* ✗ ♿ 🅿 ☎ *202-433-4882. www.history.navy.mil.* Housed in a cavernous workshop of the former gun factory, this exhibit hall was opened in 1963. Its permanent displays of naval memorabilia, dioramas, ordnance and equipment interpret the history of the US Navy from the Revolutionary War through the space age. Among the highlights of the museum are an extensive collection of scale-model ships, including a 25ft-long, elaborately detailed model of a World War II landing craft (LSM); the fighting top from the USS *Constitution*; a World War II Corsair plane; and the bathyscaphe *Trieste*, which carried two men to a depth of 35,800ft underwater in 1960. A number of gun mounts on display may be manipulated by visitors. A gallery to the left of the museum entrance features changing exhibits.

Permanently docked near the annex at Pier 2 is the **USS Barry**, a destroyer maintained for public display. The below-deck living and working quarters are open to the public.

Marine Corps Museum – *Located in the Marine Corps Historical Center, Parsons Ave. near the 9th St. gate. Open year-round daily 10am-4:30pm. Closed Jan 1, Thanksgiving Day, Dec 25.* ♿ 🅿 ☎ *202-433-3840.* This museum displays weaponry, uniforms, medals, papers, musical artifacts and memorabilia related to the history of the Marine Corps. Interpretive exhibits on major battles are also featured.

At 8th and M streets, note the Greek Revival brick **entrance gate** with iron grillwork designed by Benjamin H. Latrobe in 1804 *(admittance through this gate is restricted to authorized personnel).*

FORT LESLEY J. McNAIR

4th and P Sts. SW.

Strategically positioned at the confluence of the Anacostia River and the Washington Channel, this complex, dating back to 1794, is one of the nation's oldest military installations in continuous operation. Known by various names over the years—Turkey Buzzards Point, Fort Humphreys, and the US Arsenal—the post was renamed Fort Lesley J. McNair in 1948 in honor of the commander of the army ground forces who was killed in Normandy in 1944.

It was on this site in 1865 that four of John Wilkes Booth's alleged fellow conspirators in the Lincoln assassination plot were imprisoned and hanged. One of them, Mary Surratt, was the first American woman executed by federal order. At the turn of the century, Maj. Walter Reed, who was instrumental in identifying the carrier of yellow fever, conducted research in the fort's military hospital.

Occupying a 98-acre site, Fort McNair today is the headquarters of the US Army Military District of Washington and the home of the prestigious National Defense University.

Access – **By Metro:** Ⓜ *Waterfront.* **By bus:** *Take bus nos. 60, 70 or M2 from central Washington.*

VISIT

Because the fort is an active military base, buildings are open only to military personnel. Visitors are allowed to drive or stroll around the grounds. ♿ 🅿.

Resembling a university campus more than a fort, the post is laid out in a long quadrangle with a central esplanade bordered by rows of neat brick houses that serve as residences for officers and enlisted personnel. At the southern tip of the grounds rises the **National War College** (1907), an imposing brick structure designed by McKim, Mead and White.

The waters of the Anacostia River and the Washington Channel provide an attractive backdrop to the impeccably maintained grounds and buildings. Various points along the quadrangle afford pleasant **views** of East Potomac Park across the channel. Among the other noteworthy institutions on the post are the Industrial College of the Armed Forces and the **Inter-American Defense College** (1962). The Defense College trains senior officers from 19 countries in the Western Hemisphere.

Additional Sights in DC

WASHINGTON NATIONAL CATHEDRAL★★

Massachusetts and Wisconsin Aves. NW.

Officially named the Cathedral Church of St. Peter and St. Paul, the imposing Gothic-style edifice overlooking the city from its 57-acre site on Mount St. Alban is popularly known as the Washington Cathedral or National Cathedral. This magnificent 20C anachronism—replete with flying buttresses, dizzying vaulting, gargoyles and stained-glass windows—was raised to celebrate Christian faith as well as the American nation and key figures and events in its history.

Historical Notes

A Long Time Coming – The inspiration for a national cathedral dates back to the beginning of the Republic. In his grand plan for the capital, planner Pierre Charles L'Enfant proposed "a great church for national purposes," but the idea won little initial support, the new nation being committed to the separation of church and state. Finally in 1893 Congress chartered the Protestant Episcopal Cathedral Foundation and authorized the building of the cathedral complex. Since no federal funds were allocated for the project, support had to be provided exclusively by private donors. Under the tireless leadership of the Right Rev. Dr. Yates Satterlee, first Episcopal bishop of Washington, the foundation was able to purchase the Mount St. Alban site at the turn of the century. Satterlee shaped both the philosophy and the design of the cathedral. He insisted that the cathedral welcome all, regardless of faith or nationality, and that it be built in what he considered the only truly Christian architectural style —Gothic. He envisioned "a genuine Gothic cathedral on this side of the Atlantic that will kindle the same religious, devotional feelings and historic associations that are awakened in the breasts of American travelers by the great Gothic cathedrals of Europe."

Construction – The foundation stone was laid by President Theodore Roosevelt on September 29, 1907, before a crowd of 10,000. In 1912 the first service was celebrated in Bethlehem Chapel, and services have continued in the cathedral every day since. Interrupted only by world wars and intermittent financial difficulties, construction was carried out primarily under the supervision of Philip Hubert Frohman, the project's chief architect from 1912 to 1971. The cathedral, built primarily of Indiana limestone, was erected by applying traditional techniques known to medieval European masons. However, work was accelerated by the use of pneumatic tools, and modern cranes were employed to lift the blocks and carved stonework into place. Thousands of people donated time and energy as well as money toward the construction, embellishment and furnishing of the cathedral, and the landscaping of its grounds.
In a ceremony held on September 29, 1990—exactly 83 years after the laying of the foundation—the final stone was set in place on the St. Paul Tower *(south side of main facade)* in the presence of President George Bush.

A National Cathedral – Although the cathedral is administered by the Episcopal Church, it strives to extend its reach across the nation, beyond religious and state boundaries. Constructed largely from funds provided by Americans nationwide, the cathedral continues to receive support from members of the National Cathedral Assn. throughout the US. Every US president since Theodore Roosevelt has visited the cathedral. In 2001 President George W. Bush's inaugural prayer service took place here. Holiday services are often broadcast to a national audience, and the cathedral has hosted several special memorial services such as those organized for the Vietnam War casualties, the Iran hostages, the Americans killed in the Persian Gulf War, and the victims of the September 2001 terrorist attacks. Great religious leaders from the US and abroad have preached their messages in this place of worship, and several prominent figures are among the more than 100 Americans interred in the cathedral.

Access – **By bus:** *Take any no. 30s bus to the intersection of Wisconsin and Massachusetts Aves.*

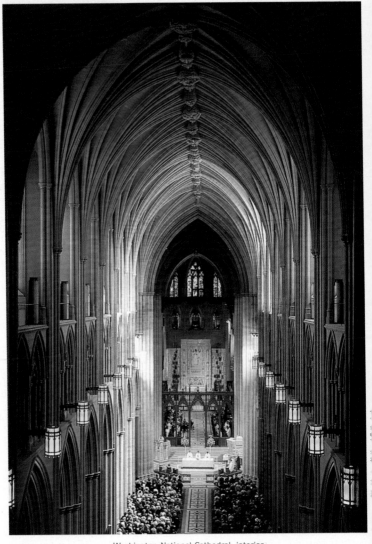

Washington National Cathedral, interior

VISIT

Open early May-Labor Day Mon-Fri 10am-9pm, weekends 10am-4:30pm. Rest of the year daily 10am-4:30pm. Guided tours (45min) available year-round Mon-Sat 10am-3:15pm, Sun 12:30pm-2:45pm (no tours during services). ☒ 🅿 ☎ 202-537-6200. www.cathedral.org/cathedral. Organ recitals Sun 5pm (in summer 4:45pm); carillon recitals Sat 12:30pm (in summer 5pm).

Exterior – Modeled after 14C English Gothic cathedrals, this massive structure is among the world's 10 largest churches in size and second in the US after St. John the Divine in Manhattan *(THE GREEN GUIDE New York City)*. From west facade to apse, the cathedral measures 514ft long. Crowning the crossing, the **Gloria in Excelsis Tower**, with its 53-bell carillon and 10-bell peal, rises 301ft and dominates the skyline of much of northwest Washington.

The **west facade**, designed by Frohman, is flanked by two identical towers dedicated to St. Peter *(left)* and St. Paul *(right)*. The carved tympanum above the central portal was designed by Frederick Hart, also known for his Vietnam Veterans Memorial sculpture group on the Mall. Hart's interpretation of Creation is a swirl of human figures emerging from nothingness. The bronze gates of the central portal are finely decorated with scenes from the lives of Abraham and Moses, and a statue of Adam adorns the portal's *trumeau*, or central pillar. The centerpiece of the facade is the 26ft rose window—an abstract composition of 10,500 pieces of glass by stained-glass artist Rowan LeCompte that celebrates the creation of light.

Designed to carry rainwater away from the walls, the gargoyles and grotesques around the flying buttresses that support the vaulting of the nave reflect the whimsies that carvers were occasionally allowed to indulge. With the help of binoculars, the visitor can spot these fanciful creatures. A sculpture of Darth Vader from the film *Star Wars* glowers from the St. Peter Tower.

Interior – The narthex, just inside the west entrance, is noteworthy for the inlaid seals of the 50 states and the District of Columbia that embellish its floor. The cathedral's vast proportions can be best appreciated upon entering the nave from the narthex. The nave extends approximately 565ft to the high altar. The nave's walls are divided into three levels: an arcade of pointed arches; the gallery, or triforium, which bears the state flags; and the upper section pierced with windows (the clerestory). The vaulted ceiling soars 102ft—about 10 stories. Side aisles flank the nave, and a series of bays opens onto the aisles.

The first pair of bays honors two famous presidents: Abraham Lincoln *(to the left of the entrance)* and George Washington *(to the right)*. Halfway down the right aisle *(over the 5th bay)*, the cathedral's most popular stained-glass window, the **Space Window**, commemorates the first manned lunar landing in 1969. A genuine moon rock is fitted in the center of the large red disc representing the moon. Just past the Space Window is the tomb of President Woodrow Wilson, adorned with symbols such as the crusader's sword representing his crusade to secure world peace after World War I.

Continue to the crossing and look back at the west facade to appreciate the blazing colors of the rose window *(best viewed in the late afternoon)*. The four colossal pillars in the crossing provide support for the Gloria in Excelsis Tower. Note the massive pulpit, built of stone from England's Canterbury Cathedral. From this pulpit, still used every Sunday, the Rev. Martin Luther King Jr. delivered his last Sunday sermon.

Above the high altar, the Jerusalem altar, is the **Ter Sanctus reredos**, an intricately carved stone wall dominated by a representation of Christ in Majesty surrounded by smaller sculptures of prophets and saints. To the left of the altar, note the Glastonbury Cathedra, a bishop's throne built of blocks from Glastonbury Abbey in England.

To the right of the choir, just past the crossing, the War Memorial Chapel commemorates those who lost their lives for the nation. A statue of a young Jesus welcomes visitors to the Children's Chapel, which contains furnishings scaled down for youngsters.

Crypt – *Access by the staircase on the north side of the choir.* Unlike crypts in medieval churches, which are generally limited to the area below the chancel, this vast underground labyrinth extends under the entire main floor. Of particular note is a group of chapels dedicated to the birth (Bethlehem Chapel), death (St. Joseph's Chapel) and resurrection of Jesus (Resurrection Chapel).

Among the notable Americans interred here are Helen Keller (1880-1968) and her teacher Anne Sullivan. A commemorative plaque honoring the two women can be seen in the Chapel of St. Joseph of Arimathea situated just beneath the crossing. The crypt also houses the cathedral's visitor center.

Observation Gallery – *7th floor. Open year-round daily 10am-4:30pm. Take either of the elevators in the narthex flanking the main entrance.* The enclosed gallery provides a **panorama** of Washington and its surroundings. The gallery's 70 windows also offer a bird's-eye view of the flying buttresses that support the nave. A slide show and a small exhibit illustrate the history of the cathedral.

Grounds – The lushly landscaped 57-acre site on which the cathedral stands, also known as the Close, comprises three schools, a college for clergy and the **Bishop's Garden** *(south side of the cathedral)*, which provides a fragrant haven of herbs, flowers and boxwood.

HILLWOOD★★

On a placid residential street above Rock Creek Park lies the 25-acre estate of **Marjorie Merriweather Post** (1887-1973), heiress to the Post cereals fortune. Her mansion, art collection and grounds are now open to the public and administered by a private foundation.

Historical Notes

A renowned businesswoman, hostess and philanthropist, Mrs. Post was also an avid collector. She transformed Hillwood, her final home, into a showcase for her extraordinary acquisitions. Though the columned brick mansion is somewhat unremarkable in both scale and appearance, its interior is lavishly decorated with 18C and 19C French furnishings. Displayed in its many vitrines and wall cabinets is the most extensive collection of **Russian decorative arts★★★** outside Russia.

Imperial Easter Egg (1895)
by Carl Fabergé

Marjorie Post accompanied her third husband, Joseph E. Davies, to Moscow, where he served as ambassador from 1937 to 1938. The timing was propitious. In the late 1930s the Soviet government began selling art confiscated from the imperial family, aristocracy and Russian Orthodox church during the Revolution of 1917. The Davies were among the last to be able to purchase some of these treasures in the commission shops of Moscow and Leningrad. Thus began Mrs. Post's abiding affection for Russian art.

The objects she collected during her sojourn in Moscow make up only about 20 percent of the collection she ultimately amassed. Hillwood's treasures illustrate more than 200 years of Russian decorative arts, from the reign of Peter the Great (1682-1725), who introduced a backward Russian court to the refined aesthetics of Western European art, to the days of the last Czar, Nicholas II (1868-1918), when jeweler Carl Fabergé created the fabulous Easter eggs and other precious bibelots that delighted an extravagant nobility.

Courtesy Hillwood Museum

Access – **By Metro:** Ⓜ *Van Ness (.5mi from Hillwood).* **By bus:** *Take an L1 or L2 bus along Connecticut Ave. to Tilden St. (.5mi from Hillwood).*

VISIT

Mansion and grounds open Jan & Mar-Dec Tue-Sat 9am-5pm. Visit by self-guided tour (audio tapes available); guided tours of the mansion offered 11am and 1pm. Docents available throughout the mansion 9am-11:15am & 2:30pm-4:45pm. Closed major holidays. $10. Garden tours (1hr) available in spring and fall. Reservations required. ✗ & ▣ ☏ 202-686-5807. www.hillwoodmuseum. org.

Begin your visit by stepping through Hillwood's new "front door" into the visitors center, built in 2000 on the site of the former head gardener's residence, directly across from the mansion. View an exhibit on decorative arts and an orientation video *(14min)*, obtain information and audio tapes, and browse an upscale museum shop. The second floor contains a resource center and an interactive computer kiosk.

Mansion – Reopened in fall 2000 after an extensive 3-year renovation, Hillwood boasts sumptuous interior furnishings that have been cleaned, restored, or replaced to reflect the elegance of the estate's heyday during Mrs. Post's occupancy, from 1955 to her death in 1973. The entry hall—with its Louis XV rock-crystal chandelier, Sèvres porcelain, and portraits of Russian royalty, and four 18C French commodes of wood marquetry, bronze and marble—provides ample preface to the regal exuberance of Hillwood.

The small, octagonal **Russian Porcelain Room** is lined with lighted wall cases containing dinner services commissioned by Catherine the Great (who reigned from 1762 to 1796) and produced in the Moscow factory established by the Englishman Francis Gardner. The oldest of the porcelains is a simple white pattern with pink rosettes, commissioned by Elizabeth I (daughter of Peter the Great) from the Imperial Porcelain Factory she established in 1744.

Off the hall, the small **Icon Room**★★ contains the finest Fabergé pieces in the collection, including elaborate boxes, clocks and two of the more than 50 **imperial Easter eggs** commissioned by the Romanovs as gifts for one another. The **diamond nuptial crown**, worn by Alexandra at her 1894 wedding to Nicholas II, is reputedly the only piece of Russian imperial regalia known to exist outside Russia. In addition to many superb icons, other ecclesiastical pieces, such as chalices and incense burners, are exhibited.

Three large reception rooms occupy much of the first floor: the **French drawing room** is elaborately appointed in Mrs. Post's favorite style, Louis XVI; the **dining room**, with its changing table settings, features an exquisite inlaid-marble Florentine table capable of seating 30 guests. The long pavilion at the northwest end of the house was used as a small movie theater and for square dancing, an activity Mrs. Post enjoyed. Note the large painting of *A Boyar Wedding Feast* (1883) by Konstantin Makovskii. The chalices and other decorative pieces depicted in the painting are similar to pieces on display throughout Hillwood. The **Russian Liturgical Gallery** off the kitchen contains Russian Orthodox robes brocaded with silver and gold threads and an exquisite 24-carat **gold chalice** commissioned by Catherine the Great.

The bedrooms on the second floor include an Adam-style guest room with blue and white Wedgwood jasperware and Mrs. Post's own Louis XVI room; arrayed in the dressing area adjacent to her bedroom are several of her elegant ball gowns, hats, evening bags, and personal jewelry made of diamonds and other precious stones.

Grounds – Several gardens surround the mansion, including an informal flower garden, a formal French parterre planted in boxwood, a rose garden encircling a pillar marking Mrs. Post's grave and a Japanese-style garden complete with a waterfall and arched bridge *(closed for renovation until spring 2002)*. A flowering pet cemetery endears itself to those who share Mrs. Post's fondness for four-legged family friends. Wooded paths connect the gardens and encircle the sweep of lawn on the mansion's south facade. Two dependencies also stand in the wooded area south of the mansion. The log **dacha**, a replica of a Russian cottage, was built by Mrs. Post to house part of her collection of Russian decorative art. The **Adirondack building**, a rustic wood cabin, displays the Native American basketry, rugs, pottery and silver objects that formerly decorated Mrs. Post's retreat in the Adirondack Mountains of New York.

NATIONAL ZOOLOGICAL PARK★★

3001 Connecticut Ave. NW.
Ⓜ Woodley Park-Zoo or Cleveland Park.

With plants and landscaped environments an integral part of its concept, this "biopark" exhibits more than 3,600 wild animals and serves as a research institution devoted to the study, preservation and breeding of threatened species. Nearly a third of the 475 species represented here are considered endangered.

Giant Pandas Tian Tian and Mei Xiang

© Brigitta L. House/MICHELIN

Historical Notes

Created in 1887 as the Department of Living Animals, the precursor of this zoo was originally located on the Mall and featured such indigenous American mammals as bison, mule deer and lynx. In 1889 Congress appropriated funds for the creation of a true zoological park, to be administered by the Smithsonian Institution. A 166-acre tract above Rock Creek Park was purchased, and renowned landscape architect Frederick Law Olmsted laid out plans for the new zoo. Because of disagreement among zoo administrators, however, Olmsted's project was only minimally realized.

Though it was an immediate popular success, the zoo was constantly plagued with financial problems. Not until 1964 when appropriations for it became part of the overall Smithsonian Institution budget was the zoo able to revamp and modernize its facilities.

VISIT

KB *Main entrance at Connecticut Ave.; other entrance at Beach Dr. (Rock Creek Pkwy.) and Harvard St. Grounds open May-mid-Sept daily 6am-8pm; rest of the year daily 8am-6pm. Buildings open May-mid-Sept daily 10am-6pm; rest of the year daily 10am-4pm. Closed Dec 25.* ✗ ♿ 🅿 ☎ *202-673-4717. www.si.edu/ natzoo.*

In recent years parts of Olmsted's original design have been implemented, and today the **Olmsted Walk** forms a continuous path through the zoo's numerous state-of-the-art exhibits. The highlight of this walk is the newly refurbished **Panda House**★★ and its popular inhabitants Tian Tian (b.1997) and Mei Xiang (b.1998), a breeding-age couple. The pair arrived in the US on December 6, 2000 and quickly made themselves at home in their new habitat, which includes air- and water-cooled grottoes, sand wallows and climbing structures in its 17,500sq ft outdoor area. The People's Republic of China receives $1 million per year for the loan of the pandas; these funds will assist research and conservation efforts to preserve the wild panda population.

The zoo's oldest building (1906), the original Small Mammal House, now contains the **Think Tank**★, a group of exhibits that focus on animal thought processes and communication skills. Here visitors may observe animal keepers working on symbolic language acquisition with resident orangutans, who commute between the Think Tank and the Great Ape House via the O line—vine-like cables suspended over the zoo's pathways some 20ft off the ground. Also on view along Olmsted Walk are large African ungulates (hippos, rhinos, giraffes and elephants) and a new exhibit on great cats, which focuses on the biology and conservation of lions and tigers. Adorned with fanciful bas-reliefs of animals, the Byzantine-style **Reptile Discovery Center** (1929) was voted "the outstanding brick building in the Eastern US" by the American Institute of Architects. It houses the world's largest lizard, the Komodo dragon, along with a variety of other reptiles and snakes.

The **Valley Trail** follows the wooded fringe of the zoo, where outdoor enclosures hold endangered Mexican wolves, birds, river otters, beavers, seals and sea lions. More than 40 species of waterfowl frequent the **Wetlands**, a natural setting of grasses and aquatic plants. The trail leads to the **Amazonia** exhibit, where a 15,000sq ft tropical forest habitat has been re-created. On the ground level visitors explore life within the Amazon River system and learn how villagers cope with frequent floods. An aquarium here contains Amazon River fish; nearby, an Amazon field station illustrates how biologists study the region's varied flora and fauna. Upstairs lies a humid rain forest that sustains more than 350 plant species. The adjoining Science Gallery gives visitors the opportunity to see Smithsonian scientists at work.

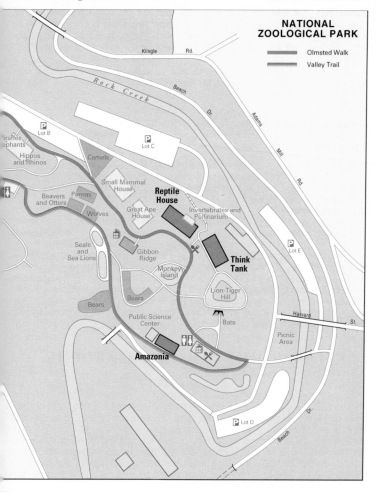

THE KREEGER MUSEUM★

2401 Foxhall Rd. NW.
Map p 258 AY

Ensconced behind a high wall in a well-to-do neighborhood, this unadorned post-Modern mansion (1967, Philip Johnson) contains the formidable art collection of former residents David and Carmen Kreeger. Rife with 19C and 20C European paintings by renowned artists, the 200-piece collection also includes African and 20C art.

Historical Notes

The Collector – A resident of Washington since the 1930s, Kreeger made his fortune in the insurance industry. An accomplished musician and patron of the arts, he became an avid collector, particularly of works by European Impressionists and post-Impressionists. To house the growing collection, Kreeger hired Philip Johnson, designer of Kennedy Center's Terrace Theater, to build a house that could function as a museum and performance venue. After her husband's death in 1990, Mrs. Kreeger vacated the house. In 1994 it was opened to the public as a museum.

The Building – Situated on 5.5 wooded acres, the 24,000sq ft travertine dwelling comprises three core modules of stacked cubes topped by barrel-vaulted ceilings. Most rooms have no doors, and the large entryways are more suggestive of an art gallery than a home. Designed as a concert hall and gallery, the Great Hall (22ft by 66ft) provides ample space for hanging art on its carpeted walls. Punctuated with floor-to-ceiling windows at each end, the hall opens onto a spacious, bench-lined terrace at the rear of the house. Also made of travertine, the terrace serves as a dramatic setting for the outdoor sculpture.

The Collection – European masters of the 19C and 20C are well represented in the collection, which includes paintings by Corot, Renoir, Degas and Bonnard, as well as multiple paintings by Monet, Picasso and Kandinsky. Works by Joseph Albers, Hans Hofmann, Clyfford Still and other 20C artists; sculpture by such renowned artists as Rodin, Brancusi and Maillol; and African art complete the collection.

Access – **By car:** *Drive north on Massachusetts Ave. to Nebraska Ave. At the circle, exit Nebraska Ave. to the west. Turn left onto Foxhall Rd.*

VISIT

Visit by guided tour only, year-round Tue-Sat 10:30am & 1:30pm. Closed Aug & major holidays. $5. Reservations required. 🅿 ☎ *202-338-3552. www.kreeger museum.org.*

Tours focus on one or two selected works in each room to illustrate historic trends, schools of art or specific techniques. Of particular interest are several early works by famous painters, such as Cézanne's *The Blue Vase* (c.1882) and van Gogh's *Bouquet of Zinnias* (1886), that do not resemble the styles for which the artists later became known.

First-floor galleries house 19C and 20C European art. Paintings and small sculptural works grace the Great Hall. Note Picasso's atypical *Café de la Rotonde* (1901). The dining room contains paintings by French Impressionists, including no less than nine by Monet. The works of Corot and Mondrian are highlights of the library, and the landing showcases paintings by Picasso, Miró, Man Ray and others. On the lower level, one gallery is devoted to large acrylic works representative of Abstract Expressionism and Color Field painting. An adjacent alcove contains African art, primarily large wooden masks.

Upstairs the terrace features larger sculptures by Henry Moore, Jacques Lipchitz, Isamu Noguchi and others.

KENILWORTH AQUATIC GARDENS

Anacostia Ave. and Douglas St. NE.
Map p 259 BY

Located on tidal marshland along the eastern bank of the Anacostia River, this peaceful haven in northeast Washington comprises some 40 diked ponds devoted to the cultivation of water lilies, lotus and other aquatic plants.

Walter B. Shaw, a Civil War veteran, began the gardens in 1880 for his private enjoyment. The lilies he grew multiplied so quickly that he soon began commercial cultivation. During the 1920s the Shaw family gardens were a popular destination for Washingtonians on Sunday outings and were visited by such luminaries as presidents Wilson, Harding and Coolidge.

In the 1930s a dredging project proposed by the Army Corps of Engineers threatened the survival of the ponds. To save them for public enjoyment, the Department of the Interior purchased them in 1938. The 12-acre tract is currently administered by the National Park Service.

Access – **By Metro:** Ⓜ *Deanwood.* **By car:** *Drive northeast on New York Ave. From New York Ave. take 295 South. Exit Eastern Ave. and turn right on Douglass St. (2nd right after exiting freeway). Continue on Douglass St.*

VISIT

Open year-round daily 7am-4pm. Closed Jan 1, Thanksgiving Day, Dec 25. ♿ 🅿 ☎ *202-426-6905. www.nps.gov/kepa. The blooms are most spectacular in the morning. Seasonal highlights: water lilies in Jun and Jul; tropical plants in Jul and Aug. Winter visits are not recommended. A brochure on the gardens, with a map of the ponds, is available at the visitor center.*

Among the park's exotic flora are the **Victoria amazonica**, a water lily whose platter-shaped leaves grow as large as 6ft across, and the **East Indian Lotus**, grown from seeds estimated to be hundreds of years old. In 1951 seeds for this rare plant were discovered in a dry lake bed in Manchuria and were subsequently germinated by the Park Service. They are believed to have been 350 to 575 years old, making them among the oldest viable seeds discovered to date. These ancient lotus plants can be viewed in the pond directly behind the visitor center. The Victoria lilies are located in a pond at the far western end of the gardens near the Anacostia River.

NATIONAL ARBORETUM

3501 New York Ave. NE.
Map below

One of the largest arboretums in the country, this federally owned 446-acre tract situated on the gentle slopes of Mount Hamilton provides a tranquil respite from the warehouses and thoroughfares of surrounding northeast Washington. Established by Congress in 1927, the arboretum did not become a reality until 1947,

National Arboretum in Spring

when the first azaleas were planted. It was opened to the public in the early 1950s. Today its hills and valleys are covered in evergreens, wildflowers and such flowering trees and shrubs as azaleas, rhododendrons and dogwoods, whose spectacular blossoms traditionally attract numerous visitors.

Access – **By car:** *From downtown, drive northeast on New York Ave. and enter the service road on the right after crossing Bladensburg Rd. Other entrance at 24th and R Sts. NE.*

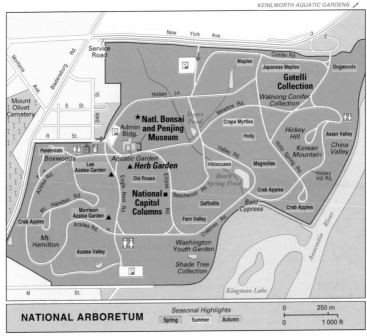

VISIT

Open year-round daily 8am-5pm. Closed Dec 25. ♿ ☎ *202-245-2726. www.usna.usda.gov. The arboretum is designed to be toured by car. Nine miles of paved roads lead past the various gardens, collections and designated parking areas along the route.*

Outstanding Collections – The walled Japanese garden complex, behind the modern administration building, comprises several small gardens and the **National Bonsai and Penjing Museum**★ *(open daily 10am-3:30pm)*, renowned for its outstanding collection of Japanese, Chinese and American bonsai.

The 2-acre **Herb Garden** comprises a formal 16C English knot garden; a rose garden with more than 80 varieties of "old" roses; and 10 specialty gardens, where herbs are grouped according to their uses throughout history. Atop a bluff stand the **National Capitol Columns**, which originally flanked the east entrance of the Capitol prior to its expansion in the late 1950s.

Pleasant stops along the drive include **Fern Valley**, the picturesque **Asian Valley** and the **Gotelli collection**, considered one of the finest groupings of dwarf conifers in the world.

NATIONAL SHRINE
OF THE IMMACULATE CONCEPTION

4th St. and Michigan Ave. NE.
Ⓜ Brookland CUA.
Map p 259 BY

A 20C blend of Byzantine and Romanesque styles, this massive Roman Catholic church is the official national tribute to Mary, the Mother of Christ and the patroness of the US. Official papal recognition of Mary as this country's patroness dates back to 1846, but it was not until 1914 that the plan for a national church for American Catholics was formulated, approved and designed. Construction of the crypt church began in 1920, and services have been held here since 1927. The shrine was dedicated in 1959.

VISIT

Open Apr-Oct daily 7am-7pm. Rest of the year daily 7am-6pm. Guided tours (1hr) available. ✗ ♿ 🅿 ☎ *202-526-8300. www.nationalshrine.com.*

Exterior – Constructed of brick, granite, tile and concrete, the shrine features the customary Latin cross design. Its dome is 108ft in diameter and 237ft in height to the summit of the cross. The dome's exterior is gold-leafed and adorned with blue, gold and red tiles depicting Marian symbols. The **Knights' Bell Tower**—a gift from the Knights of Columbus—is surmounted by a 20ft gilded cross and stands 329ft high. It houses a carillon comprising 56 bells cast in Annecy, France.

Interior – The church's nave rises 100ft and measures 58ft in width. The light from some 200 windows, including three rose windows accented in gold and amethyst, illuminates the sanctuary. The main altar is dominated by a monumental mosaic group depicting Christ in Majesty.

The mosaic in the chancel dome, the *Descent of the Holy Spirit*, was designed by Parisian artist Max Ingrand; it is the largest mosaic in the shrine. Seventeen chapels line the east and west sides of the upper church. Note especially the chapels dedicated to Our Lady of Czestochowa of Poland, Our Lady of Guadalupe of Mexico, and Our Lady's Miraculous Medal on the west side.

Among the richly adorned chapels in the **crypt**, note the Mary Altar *(below the main altar)* made of a block of golden Algerian onyx. The side chapels are dedicated to saints, martyrs, the Good Shepherd, Our Lady of Bistrica, and Our Lady of Lourdes.

POPE JOHN PAUL II CULTURAL CENTER

3900 Harewood Rd. NE
Ⓜ Brookland CUA.
Map p 259 BY

Opened in 2001, this modern, 100, 000sq ft facility designed by Leo A. Daly was built to provide a haven for exploring personal faith in the new millennium.

VISIT

Open year-round Tue–Sat 10am-5pm. Sun noon-5pm. $8. ✗ ♿ 🅿 ☎ *202-635-5400. www.jp2cc.org. Free shuttle service to and from Brookland/CUA Metro station on the half hour.*

The highlight of the main floor is the John Paul II Polish Heritage Room, which sheds light on Karol Joseph Wojtyla, the first non-Italian to be elected pope in 455 years. Among the keepsakes on view are a Tiffany clock, family photos, religious vestments, and downhill skis. Changing selections of art from the Vatican museums, accompanied by papal interpretation, occupy the second floor of the center. Bottom-floor exhibits demand a high level of participation: Interactive workstations, accessed by swiping a personal "smart card," cover everything from original sin to cloning. Visitors may also make virtual stained glass on a computer, collaborate on a song made from chimes or watch videotaped testimonials.

NATIONAL MUSEUM
OF HEALTH AND MEDICINE

Walter Reed Army Medical Center, 6825 16th St. NW.
Map p 258 AY

Housed in an undistinguished building on the grounds of the Walter Reed Army Medical Center, renowned for its presidential patients, this small museum depicts medical progress through displays of items ranging from Revolutionary War amputation implements to the medicinal leeches of modern microsurgery.

Begun during the Civil War by US Surgeon General William Hammond, the museum has advanced scientific knowledge through staff research conducted during wartime, epidemics, and national tragedies such as the Lincoln and Garfield assassinations. As curator, **Maj. Walter Reed** (US Army surgeon 1851-1902) and his team identified the carrier of yellow fever, paving the way for the disease's control. In 1909 Maj. Frederick Russell successfully tested a vaccine for typhoid at the museum. Today the institution fosters public education through permanent and changing exhibits on contemporary health concerns, such as AIDS and heart disease.

Access – By car: *Drive north on 16th St.; take the first right after Aspen St. into the compound. At the circle, take the second right (14th St.). Turn right at stop sign. Museum is the first building (no. 54) on the left.*

VISIT

Open year-round daily 10am-5:30pm. Closed Dec 25. ♿ 🅿 ☎ 202-782-2200. A floor plan is mounted on the wall near the gallery entrance. Some exhibits are not for the faint-hearted.

Highlights of the visit are photographs of injured Civil War soldiers taken before and after facial surgery, a large microscope collection dating from the late 16C to the 20C and such artifacts as the lead bullet that claimed Abraham Lincoln's life.

US NAVAL OBSERVATORY

3450 Massachusetts Ave. NW.

This naval facility is responsible for providing crucial astronomical and timing data to government agencies, the Navy and the country at large.

Originally established in 1830 in Foggy Bottom, the observatory was the first true scientific agency in the country. With its 26in telescope, Asaph Hall discovered the two moons of Mars in 1877. To avoid the detrimental noise, light and vibrations of the Foggy Bottom area, the observatory was moved in 1893 to a more secluded location on the upper portion of Massachusetts Avenue. Noted architect Richard Morris Hunt designed the main buildings.

Since 1974 a white brick Victorian structure initially built on the observatory grounds as the superintendent's house has served as the official residence of the vice president of the US *(not open to the public)*.

Access – By car: *Drive north on Massachusetts Ave. past Embassy Row to visitors' gate at Observatory Circle.*

VISIT

Kids *Entrance at South Gate. Visit by guided tour only, year-round Mon 8:30pm (limited to first 90 visitors). Closed major holidays. 🅿 ☎ 202-762-1467. www.usno.navy.mil .*

A video *(22min)* features the history of the observatory. Included on the tour is the **Master Clock** of the US, actually several rows of atomic clocks. Visitors are given an opportunity to view the sky through a 12in telescope.

Excursions

A s the focus of this guide is Washington, DC, we have limited our selection of excursions to those nearby sights whose histories are closely related to that of the capital. The five excursions described in the following pages are concentrated within a 36-mile radius south of Washington and are easily accessible by car

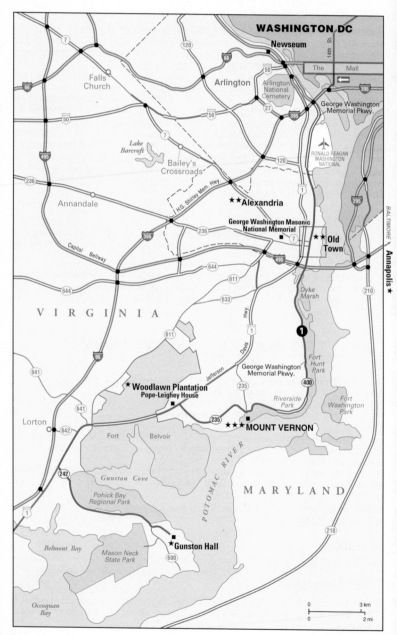

or public transportation. The well-organized visitor can take in two or more excursions in the same day *(expect long entry lines at Mount Vernon during the spring and summer)*. For those interested in longer excursions, the area offers a wealth of possibilities, including Annapolis *(36mi)*, Baltimore *(40mi from DC)*, and the vast Chesapeake Bay region in Maryland; and Manassas *(132mi)*, Fredericksburg *(53mi)* and Monticello *(near Charlottesville—115mi)* in Virginia.

ALEXANDRIA★★

Map p 228

Though it is situated just a few miles down the Potomac from the nation's capital, this enclave of historic homes and churches set along tree-shaded brick walks retains its colonial charm and an atmosphere of slow-paced Southern gentility. Alexandria's past is intimately bound with the founding of the country and with such preeminent Americans as George Washington, George Mason and Robert E. Lee.

Historical Notes

The Town Is Created – The area now called Old Town Alexandria traces its beginnings to the early 1700s, when a tobacco warehouse on the waterfront, near what is now Oronoco Street, spawned a small settlement. Prominent Scottish tobacco merchants and Virginia tobacco planters joined to petition the Virginia General Assembly to establish a town in the area, and in 1748 the assembly granted their request, stating that such a town "would be commodious for trade and navigation and tend greatly to the best advantage of frontier inhabitants." The 60-acre tract on which the town was to be sited belonged to members of the Alexander family, and thus the new town was named Alexandria.

The town was laid out in the grid pattern characteristic of 18C urban planning. Seven streets ran west from the river, bearing, as was typical of the day, the titles of royalty—Duke, Prince, King, Cameron (named for Virginia's Lord Fairfax, the Baron of Cameron), Queen, Princess and Oronoco (after the original tobacco wharf). The three north-south cross streets were named Water, Fairfax and Royal streets. Sale of the 84 half-acre lots was placed under the authority of 11 trustees, and on July 13, 1749, a public auction was held. Over a two-day period, 42 lots were purchased. The Spanish pistole, the most available hard currency at the time, was the predominant means of payment. Following stipulations laid down by the general assembly, no bidder was allowed more than two lots, and to ensure the growth of the town, a dwelling had to be erected within two years of land purchase.

A Prosperous Seaport – For the next quarter-century, Alexandria flourished as a rambunctious colonial seaport and trading center. It was a mixture of warehouses, shipyards, taverns, small clapboard dwellings and impressive Georgian mansions, like that of John Carlyle, one of the Scottish immigrants whose traditions still flavor aspects of Old Town. By 1763 the port had outgrown its original space and was beginning to expand westward, with the addition of more cross streets. It also grew eastward as land was filled on the marshy Potomac shoreline around present-day Union Street.

Growth abruptly ended with the coming of the Revolution in 1775. During the war Alexandria was a pivotal meeting point for such leaders as George Mason, whose plantation, Gunston Hall, was in the area, and George Washington, who maintained a small house in town and a large plantation, Mount Vernon, eight miles down the Potomac.

The townspeople themselves were divided during the Revolution: Some were ardent

Shops along Historic King Street

© Brigitta L. House/MICHELIN

Address Book

Dining in Alexandria

The venues listed below were selected for their ambience, location and/or value for money. Rates indicate the average cost of an appetizer, an entrée and dessert for one person (not including tax, gratuity or beverages). Most restaurants are open daily—except where noted—and accept major credit cards. Call for information regarding reservations and opening hours.

Additional restaurants are listed throughout this guide in the form of Digressions. See Index *for a complete listing of eateries described in the text.*

$$$$	over $50	$$	$15-$30
$$$	$30-$50	$	less than $15

Gadsby's Tavern – *138 N. Royal St.* ⅃ ☏ *703-548-1288. www.gadsbystavern.org* . **$$$ American**. Gadsby's Tavern bills itself as one of the few remaining 18C dining establishments in the US, aptly suited to the cobblestone streets of Old Town Alexandria. Costumed servers and entertainers gad about the historic hostelry, as patrons dine by candlelight on colonial favorites such as country-fried oysters and George Washington's duck. The attached museum *(see entry heading)* provides an intriguing glimpse into the history of the colonial port city.

La Bergerie – *218 N. Lee St.* ⅃ ☏ *703-683-1007. www.labergerie.com.* **$$$ French**. Housed in a historic brick warehouse, the elegant La Bergerie serves a tempting array of French dishes and Basque regional specialties. Crystal chandeliers sparkle above the comfortable dining room, where attentive servers patiently monitor casual lunches and intimate dinners. Order a raspberry or hazelnut soufflé for dessert before diving into the savory coq au vin or veal tenderloin mignonettes.

Majestic Café – *911 King St.* ⅃ ☏ *703-837-9117.* **$$ Southern**. The pink and blue neon signs that loom over colonial King Street join the 1700s and the 1930s in peculiar harmony. Now re-opened after a lengthy absence, the Majestic Café serves a tasty selection of stylish southern favorites. A cracker-crusted pork chop mixes nicely with a frosty glass of root beer, while the "cake of the day" perches in the window, begging to be sampled.

Stardust – *608 Montgomery St.* ⅃ ☏ *703-548-9864. www.stardustrestaurant.com.* **$$ Asian**. Guaranteeing "more atmosphere than the moon," Stardust is a whimsical departure from Alexandria's more traditional dining establishments. The menu successfully combines chef Pat Phatiphong's Thai expertise with far-reaching global influences. Oysters on the half shell are playfully doused with tropical fruit salsa, while a tasty stuffed rainbow trout overflows with leeks

patriots, while others resented the economic havoc war was playing with their lives. Battle threatened them only once, when a contingent of British ships sailed up the Potomac, fired a few shots, then left. At the height of the war, in 1779, Alexandria was incorporated as a town.

Part of the New Capital – With the coming of peace Alexandria's prosperity returned, and in 1789 the town's fortunes took a monumental turn when it was ceded by Virginia for the formation of the new federal city. Congress officially accepted it as part of the District in 1801.

Alexandria's prospects were curtailed, however, by a congressional amendment that prohibited the construction of any federal buildings on the Virginia side of the river. Historians believe that this amendment was enacted at the instigation of President Washington, who owned Alexandria lands and feared allegations of favoritism. Though no government buildings actually went up on Alexandria soil, the town had its heyday during the building of the new capital. Taverns, hostelries and businesses flourished, and the port became a major exporter of wheat, which had taken the place of tobacco as Virginia's cash crop.

In the early decades of the 1800s, Alexandria's fortunes declined as it lost trade to growing commercial centers in nearby Georgetown, Richmond and Baltimore. The town also incurred heavy debts in the building of the Alexandria Canal, which failed to stimulate the trade expected. Suffering economically from their association with the capital city and without representation in Congress, Alexandrians became disillusioned with their status as citizens of the nation's capital. In 1846 the County of Alexandria retroceded to Virginia, with whom it had always maintained strong social and political ties.

Civil War Years – From 1850 to 1860, with the coming of industrialization, a cotton gin and locomotive factory were built in town, and Alexandria once again thrived. Then federal troops moved in and occupied the town in 1861 for the duration of the Civil War, converting public buildings into Union hospitals and constructing a fort on Shooter's Hill, now topped by the granite tower of the George Washington Masonic National Memorial. During the Union occupation, Robert E. Lee, whose boyhood home still stands in Old Town, led the Confederate Army.

and crab in gorgonzola cream sauce. Vegetarians can feast on grilled vegetable brochettes with spicy peanut sauce or pan-fried linguini with Portobello mushrooms.

The Warehouse – *214 King St.* & ☎ *703-683-6868*. **$$ Cajun.** One of Old Town Alexandria's most well-loved casual eateries greets diners with hundreds of colorful, smiling caricatures of local personalities. Creole alligator stew and creamy she-crab soup usher in a Cajun-accented menu rich with meat and seafood dishes. A pleasingly old-fashioned caramel custard provides a rich finishing touch.

Staying in Alexandria

The properties listed below were selected for their ambience, location and/ or value for money. Prices reflect average cost for a standard double room (two people) in high season (not including any applicable city or state taxes). Room prices may be considerably lower in off-season, and many hotels offer discounted weekend rates. The presence of a swimming pool is indicated by the ⛴ *symbol.*

$$$$$	over $300	$$	$75-$125
$$$$	$200-$300	$	less than $75
$$$	$125-$200		

Alexandria & Arlington Bed and Breakfast Network – ☎ *703-549-3415 or 1-888-549-3415. www.aabbn.com.* The cozy cobblestone streets of Alexandria make staying at a bed and breakfast particularly inviting. If you're looking to ease into the tranquil pockets of Northern Virginia, the Alexandria and Arlington Bed and Breakfast Network maintains a listing of private homes and bed and breakfasts available for short- and long-term rentals.

Almost Heaven Bed and Breakfast – *6339 Brocketts Crossing*, Beulah St. ⊡ ⛴ ☎ *703-856-2355. 3 rooms.* **$$$** Lodged in a lovely four-story home outfitted with antique furnishings and comfy bedding, Almost Heaven lives up to its name with a terrific location, amiable hosts and welcoming amenities. Each bedroom has its own private bath, and the property also features a pool, Jacuzzi and sauna.

Morrison House – *116 S. Alfred St.* ⅹ & ⊡ ☎ *703-838-8000 or 1-800-367-0800. www.morrisonhouse.com. 45 rooms.* **$$$$** While built in the 1980s, Old Town Alexandria's finest hotel maintains the appearance of an ersatz Federalist-era townhouse and offers the remarkable service of an elite European inn. Elegantly furnished with period pieces and sparkling chandeliers, the Morrison House's early-American charm is neatly matched by the atmosphere of Old Town. Guests can collapse into cozy four poster beds against the backdrop of a decorative fireplace or enjoy some of Alexandria's finest cuisine at **Elysium**.

In 1870, soon after the war's end, Alexandria became an independent city, separate from the county of the same name (now called Arlington). Over the decades it spread west, annexing parts of the old county as it grew. Not until World War I did the town experience any real prosperity again, when the federal government constructed a torpedo factory on the waterfront.

Bird's-Eye View of Alexandria (1863)

Mariners' Museum, Newport News, VA

During World War II Alexandria benefited from the growth that infected the entire metropolitan area. Today the city encompasses nearly 16sq mi, with a population of 111,000.

Elegant Enclave – In recent decades the Old Town quarter of the city has paid increasing attention to its architectural heritage, fostering an image of genteel provincialism. The city government carefully monitors the appearance of buildings in the historic district, which in 1969 was placed on the National Register of Historic Places. Since the 1960s gentrification has overtaken what had been the working-class neighborhoods of the city. Professionals, lured by Alexandria's cachet, have bought and renovated the small colonials and elegant Georgians. Many now display the official metal plaques that designate buildings "of historic or architectural significance."

Today the city's waterfront is graced with parks, and restaurants and boutiques line King and Washington streets. At the foot of King Street, the **Torpedo Factory** *(map p 233)* has undergone a much-acclaimed urban renovation and now serves as an art center, housing the shops and studios of visual artists.

Access – *Alexandria is located on the west bank of the Potomac River, 6mi southeast of Washington.* **By car:** *Leave Washington by the 14th St. Bridge, take exit 11A (for National Airport), and continue south on the George Washington Memorial Parkway. One-day (24hr) visitor's parking permit is available at Ramsay House Visitors Center (King and Fairfax Sts.).* **By public transportation:** *Take Metro to King Street Station, then board an eastbound DASH bus no. AT 2 or AT 5.*

★★OLD TOWN *Walking tour*

Distance: 4mi. Map p 233.

Begin at the corner of King and N. Fairfax Sts.

Ramsay House Visitors Center – *221 King St. Open year-round daily 9am-5pm. Closed Jan 1, Thanksgiving Day, Dec 25.* ☎ *703-838-4200. www.funside.com.* The north portion of this colonial clapboard incorporates the remains of the oldest structure in Old Town. Built in 1724 by William Ramsay, a Scottish merchant, the small house was moved to Alexandria soon after the town's founding. It now functions as the official visitor and convention center.

Turn left on S. Fairfax St.

Stabler-Leadbeater Apothecary Museum – *105-107 S. Fairfax St. Open year-round Mon-Sat 10am-4pm, Sun 1pm-5pm. Closed Jan 1, Thanksgiving Day, Dec 25. $2.50.* ▣ ☎ *703-836-3713. www .apothecary.org.* An apothecary from 1792 to 1933, this shop has been restored to its mid-19C appearance. Shelving, cases, glass bottles and equipment used for preparing medicines and remedies are from the original store, which served as a major supplier of pharmaceuticals in the area.

Cross King St.

Market Square – Now modernized and dominated by a steepled city hall (1873), this square has served as the city's focal point since the mid-18C. It has been the setting for many historic gatherings, including Washington's drilling of his Revolutionary troops.

★**Carlyle House** – *121 N. Fairfax St. Visit by guided tour (45min) only, year-round Tue-Sat 10am-4:30pm, Sun noon-4:30pm, every 30min. Closed Jan 1, Thanksgiving Day, Dec 24-25. $4.* ♿ ☎ *703-549-2997. www.carlylehouse.org.*

Modeled after a Georgian manor house, this freestanding stone construction was built by John Carlyle, one of the Scottish entrepreneurs instrumental in founding Alexandria. Carlyle came to Virginia in 1741 as an agent for an English merchant, but he soon established his own trading concerns. His marriage in 1747 to Sarah Fairfax, daughter of one of the colony's most influential men, further

Carlyle House

R. Corbel/MICHELIN

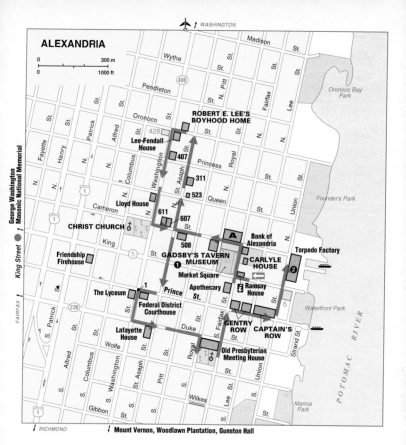

secured Carlyle's fortunes and position. He became a friend of George Washington, a founding trustee of the town and a respected merchant and builder. His impressive mansion, completed in 1753 and surrounded by stables, sheds, dependencies and a warehouse, dominated the Alexandria waterfront for several decades before the swampland along the Potomac was reclaimed in the late 18C.

The mansion's hour of glory came in April 1755, when the British general Edward Braddock, en route to his ill-fated campaign against the French and Indians, headquartered himself here. During his stay he commissioned George Washington to serve with him in the campaign, and he held the historic **Governors' Council**. At this unprecedented meeting, five colonial governors met with Braddock in Carlyle House. He petitioned them not only for advice on military strategy but for financial support from their local assemblies. The governors' contention that the colonists would refuse to provide funds to the British was an early sign of tension between England and the colonies.

When Carlyle died in 1780, his property passed to his daughter Sarah and her husband, William Herbert. After the Herberts' tenure, the house was sold out of the family. In 1970 the Northern Virginia Regional Park Authority purchased Carlyle House and began a six-year renovation to restore it to its colonial appearance.

Visit – The two-story building, with a projecting central section and prominent quoins (or cornerstones), is topped by a graceful hipped roof punctuated by a pair of chimneys. Inside, the mansion is authentically decorated in the style fashionable to its period. The popular tones of the day (verdigris, blue verditer and Prussian blue) predominate throughout the house. Note the fine woodwork cornices, pediments and paneling in the first-floor study and main parlor, the only two rooms that have retained their original architecture.

The second floor has bedrooms and an architectural exhibit room, where the restoration process is explained in captioned photographs and a section of the original rubble and mortar walls of the house is exposed. On the basement level is a servant's workroom containing various utensils of the day.

A formal garden behind the house is laid out in parterres with brick walkways.

Bank of Alexandria – *133 N. Fairfax St.* This restored brick Federal structure is the oldest building (1807) in Virginia that has been continually used as a bank. Carlyle's son-in-law, William Herbert, served as the bank's second president and a director.

Alexandria Calendar of Events

Listed below is a selection of Alexandria's popular annual events; some dates may vary each year. For more information contact the Alexandria Convention and Visitors Assn. ☏ 703-838-4200 or www.funside.com. The area code for all telephone numbers is 703.

Date	Event/Location	☏
Jan-Feb		
late Jan	**Robert E. Lee Birthday Celebrations** Lee-Fendall House, Old Town	548-1789
mid-Feb	**George Washington Birthday Celebrations**	
	Birthnight Banquet and Ball *Gadsby's Tavern Museum*	838-9350
	Revolutionary War Encampment & Skirmish *Fort Ward Park*	838-9350
	Parade *Old Town*	838-9350
Mar-Apr		
mid-Mar	**St. Patrick's Day Parade** *King Street*	237-2199
late Apr	**Historic Garden Week Tour** *Old Town*	838-4200

Turn left on Cameron St.

The row houses in the **300 block (A)** of Cameron Street, representative of the early- to mid-19C architecture of the area, now house the kinds of storefront boutiques for which Old Town is known. No. 309 has a picturesque side courtyard and loggia.

★**Gadsby's Tavern Museum** – *134 N. Royal St. Visit by guided tour (30min) only, Apr-Sept Tue-Sat 10am-5pm, Sun 1pm-5pm. Rest of the year Tue-Sat 11am-4pm, Sun 1pm-4pm. Closed major holidays. $4. ☏ 703-838-4242. www.gadsbystavern.org.*

This tavern is one of the most celebrated hostelries from the early days of the country. Functioning now as a museum and restaurant, it is actually two joined brick structures: the two-story Georgian-style tavern dates back to about 1770; the three-story Federal-style construction was built as a hotel in 1792 by John Wise, a local businessman. Englishman John Gadsby leased the larger building from Wise in 1796, and in 1802 Gadsby also took over the smaller one, which he operated as a coffeehouse. The Federal-style building became the renowned Gadsby's Tavern, considered the finest public house in the new capital. While the federal city was being built across the Potomac, Gadsby's Tavern frequently entertained its officialdom—the Jeffersons, the Adamses and George Washington himself, whose town house was just a block away at 508 Cameron Street. For years an annual gala celebrating Washington's birthday was held in Gadsby's ballroom.

The buildings functioned as a tavern until 1878. They were restored to their original appearance in 1975 and reopened in 1976. The ground floor of the Federal-style building is leased as a commercial restaurant, serving meals in the re-created ambience of a late-18C tavern. Much of the rest of the two buildings is devoted to a museum depicting the tavern as it appeared in Gadsby's day.

Visit – The first floor of the older building consists of an entrance hall and two public rooms. The larger room to the left is set as a dining room, with furnishings and food appropriate to the late 18C. The small dining room to the right contains a table set as it would have been for one of the private dinners that often took place here.

A large assembly hall dominates the second floor. Furnished with only a few chairs, this room was used by merchants to show their wares and by itinerant dentists to treat patients, as well as for social events.

Gadsby's famous **ballroom**, which occupies much of the second floor of the Federal building, was the scene of many elegant soirees. Its original paneling is now conserved in the Metropolitan Museum of Art in New York. A musicians' gallery is cantilevered out over the ballroom.

The canopied beds and pleasant decor of the two bedchambers on this floor contrast sharply with the spartan accommodations in the small third-floor bedrooms, where travelers sometimes slept two or three to a bed.

Alexandria Calendar of Events

May-Jun		☎
late May	**Memorial Day Jazz Festival** *Oronoco Bay Park*	838-4686
early Jun	**Red Cross Waterfront Festival** *Old Town*	549-8300
mid-Jun	**Civil War Camp Day** *Fort Ward Museum and Historic Site*	838-4848
all summer	**Ethnic festivals** *Market Square, Old Town*	838-4200
Jul-Aug		
all summer	**Ethnic festivals** *Market Square, Old Town*	838-4200
early Jul	**USA & Alexandria Birthday Celebration** *Jones Point Park*	838-4686
late Jul	**Virginia Scottish Games** *Episcopal High School*	912-1943
Sept-Oct		
late Sept	**Tour of Historic Homes** *Old Town*	931-9481
Nov-Dec		
mid-Nov	**Historic Alexandria Antiques Show** *Holiday Inn Hotel and Suites, Old Town*	549-5811
1st Sat, Dec	**Scottish Christmas Walk** *Old Town*	838-4200
mid-Dec	**Historic Alexandria Candlelight Tours** *Old Town*	838-4242

Return to Cameron St. and continue west.

The modest clapboard building at **508 Cameron Street** is a recent reconstruction of the town house George Washington built as a convenient town office and lodging.

Turn right on N. Saint Asaph St.

At the intersection with Queen Street, note **523 Queen Street** *(the second house from the corner)*, one of the smallest houses in Old Town. Among the quaint mid-19C clapboards in the 300 block of N. Saint Asaph Street is an example of a **flounder house** (no. 311). This vernacular architectural style, which dates from the first half of the 19C, derives its name from the flat, windowless side of the house, resembling the eyeless side of a flounder fish. There are about 20 such structures still standing in Old Town.

At the next intersection note Princess Street *(on the left)*, which has its original cobblestone paving. The cobbles often came across the Atlantic Ocean as ballast for ships.

Continue to the corner of Oronoco St. and turn left.

★**Robert E. Lee's Boyhood Home** – *607 Oronoco St. Not open to the public.* Constructed in 1795 by John Potts, a business acquaintance of George Washington, this gracious Federal town house soon became the residence of William Fitzhugh, a close friend of Washington.

Here in 1804 Fitzhugh's daughter Mary married Washington's ward and the squire of Arlington House, George Washington Parke Custis *(table p 191)*.

In 1812 Henry "Light-Horse Harry" Lee, a Revolutionary War hero, friend of Washington and father of Robert E. Lee, rented the house from the Fitzhughs, relatives of Henry Lee's second wife, Ann Hill Carter.

Soon after, Lee was wounded in a Baltimore riot. Crippled by his wounds and virtually bankrupt save for his wife's income, he sailed to Barbados in the Caribbean, reputedly to recover his health. Six-year-old Robert never again saw his father, who died away from home five years later.

Widowed and invalided by arthritis, Ann Carter Lee relied heavily on her fourth child and youngest son, Robert. The family lived here until 1825, with the exception of a four-year hiatus, during which William Henry Fitzhugh was in residence and the Lees occupied another Lee family property at 407 N. Washington Street. Robert left his boyhood home in 1825 to become a cadet at West Point Military Academy. Unable to maintain a household without his help, Mrs. Lee moved to Georgetown.

The intersection of Oronoco and Washington streets is known as "Lee Corners" due to the cluster of Lee family residences. The stately Georgian building at 428 N. Washington Street was the home of Light-Horse Harry's brother Edmund Jennings Lee, mayor of Alexandria from 1815 to 1818.

■ A dog friendly town

If your best friend has been trying to lure you into the car and pointing you in the direction of Northern Virginia, chances are your canine companion has heard the news about what's happening in Old Town Alexandria. After classes at the Olde Towne School for Dogs, most pups sniff their way to Fetch bakery for peanut-butter cookies or to pick up some after-dinner mints. On Thursday nights (a non-school night) during the summer, pets and their companions congregate for happy hour at the Holiday Inn Select for treats and drinks. The Animal Welfare League even sponsors a Halloween costume contest where dogs can dress up as their favorite human, and photo sessions at Christmas where they can have their picture taken with Santa Claus. Typically non-dog oriented businesses such as banks, coffee shops and florists get into the act by handing out treats (baked by Fetch of course) to their four-legged customers. Most dog walking routes pass by the Enchanted Florist for a snack from the bone box that is always stocked with treats and free to power-walking pups.

© Brigitta L. House/MICHELIN

Fetch Bakery – *101 S. St. Asaph St.* ☎ *703-518-5188.*

Olde Towne School for Dogs – *529 Oronoco St.* ☎ *703-836-7643.*

Enchanted Florist – *139 S. Fairfax St.* ☎ *703-549-0012.*

Lee-Fendall House – *614 Oronoco St. (Enter on Washington St.) Visit by guided tour (45min) only, year-round Tue-Sat 10am-4pm, Sun 1pm-4pm. Closed Thanksgiving Day & mid-Dec-Jan 1. $4.* 🅿 ☎ *703-548-1789. www.leefendall house.org.* This large clapboard house was built in 1785 by Philip Richard Fendall, a distant Lee relative who bought the half-acre lot from Light-Horse Harry Lee. Fendall successively married three different Lee women, and members of the Lee family continually lived in the house until 1904. From 1937 to 1969 it was the residence of the famous labor leader John L. Lewis. Today the house is decorated in early-19C style, with many authentic Lee pieces.

Continue down N. Washington St.

On N. Washington Street note the house at **no. 407**. Built by Charles Lee, another brother of Light-Horse Harry, this was the home in which young Robert E. Lee lived with his mother from 1817 to 1820.

Lloyd House – *220 N. Washington St.* John Wise, who established Gadsby's Tavern, built this attractive late-Georgian brick edifice as his residence in 1797. In the early 19C a succession of prominent Alexandrians lived in the house, including Benjamin Hallowell, a Quaker schoolmaster who briefly tutored Robert E. Lee. In 1832 the house was purchased by John Lloyd, whose wife, Ann Lee Lloyd, was a first cousin of Robert E. Lee. The house remained in the Lloyd family until 1918. In 1976 it became part of the Alexandria library system.

★**Christ Church** – *Corner of N. Washington and Cameron Sts. (Enter walled graveyard from Washington St.) Open year-round Mon-Sat 9am-4pm, Sun 2pm-4:30pm. Closed major holidays. Guided tours (20min) available. As the church may be closed for private use, it is advisable to phone before visiting. $5 contribution requested.* ᴛ ☎ *703-549-1450.* Encircled by a high wall, the church grounds provide a peaceful haven where trees shade 18C grave markers.

Both George Washington and Robert E. Lee worshiped in the simple brick and stone structure, with its pepperpot steeple. By tradition, 20C presidents have come here to worship in Washington's pew on the Sunday nearest February 22, his birthday.

Construction of the church began in 1767, but for unknown reasons the original builder did not complete the job. It was John Carlyle who finished the church in 1773, and in 1774 a member of the Alexander family, after whom the town was named, gave the parish vestry the acre of land on which the church is situated. In the church's unadorned and luminous interior, a raised wineglass pulpit and a large Palladian window provide the focal point. Silver plaques mark the **pews** of Washington *(no. 60)* and Lee *(no. 46)*.

Return to Washington St., cross and walk down the 600 block of Cameron St.

In 1811 the Georgian brick dwelling at **611 Cameron Street** was home to Light-Horse Harry Lee and his family, including his three-year-old son Robert E. Lee. Thomas, the ninth and final Lord Fairfax of Virginia, lived in the imposing Federal-style structure at **no. 607** in the 1830s.

Turn right on S. Saint Asaph St. and walk two blocks, past the intersection with King St., the main shopping street in Old Town. Turn right on Prince St.

The large brick structure with Palladian windows, at the corner of Prince and Washington streets, is the **Federal District Courthouse** for Virginia's Eastern District. A number of nationally publicized trials, particularly involving Pentagon espionage, have been heard here.

The statue (1889) **(1)** dominating the intersection of Washington and Prince streets commemorates Alexandria's Confederate dead.

Cross Washington St.

The Lyceum – *201 S. Washington St. Open year-round Mon-Sat 10am-5pm, Sun 1pm-5pm. Closed Jan 1, Thanksgiving Day, Dec 24-25.* ⚐ ☎ *703-838-4994. www.alexandriahistory.org.* In 1834 Benjamin Hallowell *(see Lloyd House above)* interested his fellow citizens in founding a lyceum, or cultural center, in Alexandria, and five years later this Greek Revival structure was built to house a library, lecture rooms and natural history exhibits. Many prominent 19C figures spoke here, including the renowned orator Daniel Webster. After serving as a Civil War hospital, private home and office building, the building was restored in 1974. Today it houses a museum featuring changing exhibits on state and local history.

Continue one block south on Washington St., then turn left on Duke St. and continue one block to S. Saint Asaph St.

① Alexandria specialties
Map p 233. A plethora of restaurants, proffering virtually every cuisine in the world, lines King Street. Half a block off King, sample the hardy roadhouse portions of soups, sandwiches, salads and superbly sinful side dishes, such as buttermilk-battered onion rings, at **King Street Blues** *(112 N. Saint Asaph St.* ☎ *703-836-8800).* The upscale **Geranio Ristorante** *(722 King St.* ☎ *703-548-0088)* excels in subtly prepared Northern Italian cuisine, and **Santa Fe East** *(110 S. Pitt St.* ☎ *703-548-6900)* has a strong following among Tex-Mex fans. It's worth strolling toward the upper end of the street for the bisques, pâtés, quiches and other French provincial classics at **Le Gaulois** *(1106 King St.* ☎ *703-739-9494).*

Torpedo Factory
Map p 233. (105 N. Union St. ☎ *703-838-4565).* In addition to its restaurants, Alexandria boasts this extensive arts-and-crafts center. The cavernous building was indeed used to manufacture torpedoes during the world wars, but now it houses the studios and shops of more than 150 professional artists and craftspeople.

Lafayette House – *301 S. Saint Asaph St. Not open to the public.* Built about 1815 by a prosperous shipping agent, this three-story brick building, with an elegant double doorway topped by a fanlight and flanked by lunettes, is a fine example of a Federal-style town house. In 1824 the Marquis de Lafayette stayed here during a state visit.

Continue down Duke St. two blocks to S. Royal St. Turn right and enter the brick gate marked no. 316.

Old Presbyterian Meeting House – *Between 300 block of S. Royal and S. Fairfax Sts. Open year-round Mon-Fri 9am-4pm, Sun for services only.* ⚐ ☎ *703-549-6670. www.opmh.org.* Alexandria's many Scottish immigrants established this church in 1772, contracting John Carlyle to oversee its building. Completed in the mid-1770s, it was the site of celebrations for Alexandria's Masons.

In 1799, at Washington's death, the church bell tolled continuously for four days, and his public funeral service was preached here, "the walking being bad to the Episcopal Church." In 1835 lightning struck the steeple, and the ensuing fire virtually destroyed the church. Within two years it was rebuilt essentially to its present state.

Visit – The old flounder house manse inside this walled churchyard on the left was built in 1787. The graveyard beyond contains markers for John Carlyle; Dr. James Craik, the surgeon general of the Continental Army; and other prominent Alexandrians. The sarcophagus enclosed by a wrought-iron rail on the north commemorates an unknown soldier of the Revolution. *(The box beside the sarcophagus plays a videotape on the church's history.)*

From the church walk through the cemetery. Turn left (north) on S. Fairfax St., then turn right onto Prince St.

Prince Street – The brick-paved 200 block of Prince Street is known as **Gentry Row★**, due to its dignified 18C structures. Considered one of the finest examples of this architectural period in Virginia, **no. 207** is believed to contain elements of a town house built by the George William Fairfaxes, Washington's close friends. At nos. 211 and 209 lived two of Washington's physicians, Dr. Elisha Cullen Dick and Dr. James Craik. The stuccoed, salmon Greek Revival **Athenaeum** (1852) on the corner was built as the Old Dominion Bank and now functions as a gallery for the Northern Virginia Fine Arts Assn. *(open April-late Oct Wed-Fri 11am-3pm, Sat 1pm-3pm, Sun 1pm-4pm; closed major holidays; ☎ 703-548-0035).*

George Washington Birthday Parade

The architecture changes abruptly along the roughly cobbled 100 block of Prince Street. Known locally as **Captain's Row★**, the street may derive its name from the 18C sea captain John Harper, who owned much of the land along the north side of the street. A preponderance of small residences were built here in the late 18C and early 19C, when the street bordered the Potomac River. Many of the original houses were destroyed in an 1827 fire, but the block retains a seafaring flavor.

Turn left on S. Union St.

The building on the corner *(6 King St.)* is an early-19C warehouse made of brick and stone. End the tour at the **Torpedo Factory**.

ADDITIONAL SIGHTS *Map p 233*

George Washington Masonic National Memorial – *101 Callahan Dr. King Street. Open year-round daily 9am-5pm. Closed Jan 1, Thanksgiving Day, Dec 25. Guided tours (1hr) available.* ♿ 🅿 ☎ *703-683-2007. www.gwmemorial.org.* Crowning historic Shooter's Hill, this memorial to George Washington, the first master of Alexandria's Masonic Lodge, is a city landmark, anchoring the western end of Old Town. The large granite building, topped by a tiered tower, is modeled after one of the Seven Wonders of the World—the lighthouse on the island of Pharos near Alexandria, Egypt. Begun in 1923, the memorial was built in increments over the course of 40 years.

Visit – Passing through the imposing columned portico, visitors enter **Memorial Hall**, dominated by a 17ft-high bronze **statue** of Washington. On either side of the hall are two 46ft-long murals by artist Allyn Cox, who executed other murals in the memorial, as well as in the Capitol. The mural on the left depicts Washington at the Masonic ceremony for the laying of the Capitol cornerstone; the mural on the right shows Washington with his fellow Masons at a religious service in Philadelphia's Christ Church.

The **Replica Room** (down the hall to the left of Cox's cornerstone mural) contains Windsor chairs and other furnishings originally in the late-18C Alexandria-Washington Lodge in Old Town. It also displays various Masonic articles associated with George Washington, including the silver trowel and the Masonic apron he used while laying the Capitol cornerstone. The **Assembly Room** (one floor below Memorial Hall) has eight polished green granite columns that act as structural supports for the entire memorial. The 350-year-old Persian royal meshed rug here measures 30ft by 50ft, supposedly the world's largest rug made on a single loom.

The seven-story tower houses a **museum** of Washington memorabilia, a library (open by appointment only) and five small rooms, each devoted to a different order or type of Masonry, such as the Knights Templar, Royal Arch and Grotto Masons. These chambers are decorated in the Persian, Egyptian, Hebraic and medieval motifs symbolic of the specific orders.

The top level opens onto an observation deck, with a **view** of Old Town and the Potomac River.

■ Freemasonry

Reputedly the world's largest and oldest global fraternal order, Freemasonry had its origins in the stonemason guilds of the late Middle Ages. Its official founding, however, was in England in 1717. Established in the American colonies in the late 1720s, it was embraced by prominent leaders of the Revolutionary period. Fourteen US presidents have also been Masons.

Though Freemasonry is not a secret society, as is often believed, it does maintain secrecy concerning its ritual practices, which include the symbolic use of architectural concepts and implements to recall stonemasonry. The George Washington Masonic National Memorial embodies many of these symbolic elements, such as the use of the five orders of architecture: Doric, Ionic, Corinthian, Composite and Tuscan.

Friendship Firehouse – 107 S. Alfred St. Ⓜ King Street. Open year-round Fri & Sat 10am-4pm, Sun 1pm-4pm. Closed major holidays. ㊤ ☎ 703-838-3891. Organized in 1774, the Friendship Fire Company lists among its honorary volunteers statesmen, governors and presidents, including George Washington himself. The current brick firehouse, with its quaint cupola, was completed in 1857. Though the company ceased active fire fighting in the early 1870s, the Friendship Veterans Fire Engine Assn. has continued to maintain a ceremonial and supporting function. Now the property of the city, the restored building features a first-floor exhibit room devoted to 18C and 19C fire-fighting equipment, including leather buckets, speaking trumpets and wheeled vehicles. The meeting room on the second floor displays memorabilia relating to the company's social role in the community.

MOUNT VERNON★★★

Map p 228

America's most visited historic estate, Mount Vernon sits on a grassy, shaded slope overlooking the Potomac River. Here, George Washington escaped the rigors of public office and enjoyed the life of a successful Virginia planter.

Historical Notes

Family Heritage – The Mount Vernon property came into the Washington family in 1674 through a land grant from Lord Culpeper to John Washington, George's great-grandfather. The land passed through the hands of several descendants before Augustine Washington bought it from his sister in 1726.

In 1735 Augustine moved his family, which included three-year-old George, from Westmoreland County to the newly purchased Potomac property, then called Little Hunting Creek Plantation. The family spent four years here before again moving to a farm on the Rappahanock River. Records of the period, though sketchy, indicate that Augustine probably built a small cottage near the current location of the Mount Vernon mansion.

Mount Vernon

In 1740 Augustine deeded the Potomac property to his son Lawrence, George's elder half-brother. Lawrence renamed his 2,500-acre estate Mount Vernon, after a British admiral he had come to respect while serving in the Royal Navy. In 1743, when George was 11, his father died, and he came increasingly under the influence of his brother Lawrence. Married to Anne Fairfax, the daughter of William Fairfax, one of Virginia's wealthiest landowners, Lawrence moved in prestigious circles. George, whose upbringing until that time had been more practical than formal, was exposed to genteel colonial society at Mount Vernon.

As a young man Washington spent several years surveying uncharted areas of western Virginia. When Lawrence died in 1752, the 20-year-old George took over the management of Mount Vernon, leasing it from Lawrence's widow. Though he eventually became the nation's greatest hero and its first president, Washington considered farming the "most delectable" occupation. "It is honorable," he wrote, "it is amusing, and, with judicious management, it is profitable."

The Gentleman Farmer – In 1759, after having distinguished himself in the French and Indian War, Washington married Martha Dandridge Custis, a widow with two children, John (Jacky) and Martha (Patsy). With his marriage to Martha, who owned some 15,000 acres in the Tidewater area near Williamsburg, Washington became one of Virginia's largest landowners. To accommodate his new family, Washington redecorated the simple 1.5-story farmhouse at Mount Vernon and added a full story to it. In 1761 his brother Lawrence's widow died, making Washington the legal owner of the estate. Over the years he increased Mount Vernon's holdings to more than 8,000 acres, which were divided into five independent but adjoining farms and worked by some 300 slaves. Washington believed that farms should be self-sufficient, and to that end he constructed outbuildings for such activities as blacksmithing, shoemaking, weaving and fish salting.

Washington enjoyed entertaining at Mount Vernon and was active in the social life of nearby Alexandria, where he owned a small town house. In 1773 he began an ambitious enlargement of Mount Vernon, adding two-story additions to the north and south sides of the house, the piazza on the east, the cupola and the curving colonnades. The project took almost 15 years to complete.

The Public Years – In 1774 Washington was elected one of Virginia's delegates to the First Continental Congress meeting in Philadelphia to protest British injustices. A year later the Second Continental Congress unanimously voted him head of its military forces, a position that would keep him engaged in war and, for the most part, away from Mount Vernon until 1783.

Returning home from the Revolution, Washington set about rejuvenating his farms and finances, which had suffered during the war. His fortunes were further drained by an endless stream of house guests, many of them uninvited strangers, who came to Mount Vernon to visit the famous general. For the next six years Washington devoted himself to farming, experimenting with crop rotation and introducing new plant varieties. He took great pleasure in his wife's two grandchildren, Eleanor (Nelly) and George (Little Wash). The Washingtons brought the two children to live at Mount Vernon after their father, Martha's son John, was killed in the American Revolution. From 1789 to 1797 Washington served as the country's first president. During his two terms, he managed to return to Mount Vernon on 15 occasions, sometimes for only a brief visit and at other times for several months. Refusing public demands that he serve a third term, Washington retired for a final time to Mount Vernon in March 1797.

The Final Years – The last two years of his life were spent once more as a planter. On December 14, 1799, having spent a snowy day overseeing work on the grounds, Washington contracted quinsy, an acute inflammation of the throat. Doctors administered gargles and bled him four times with leeches but to no avail. "I die hard," Washington said, "but I am not afraid to go." A day later he passed away in his bed at the age of 67. His body was interred in the old family burial vault overlooking the river. Two years later, Martha Washington was buried beside her husband.

After Washington – After Martha's death the mansion passed to Bushrod Washington, a nephew and Supreme Court justice. He bequeathed it in turn to his nephew John Augustine Washington. When the latter's son, John Augustine Jr., came into possession of Mount Vernon in 1850, the estate was no longer agriculturally productive. Realizing the need to preserve the home and without the means to do so himself, John Washington sought to sell it either to the federal government or to the State of Virginia, but neither was in a position to buy it.

Instead, a woman in South Carolina, Ann Pamela Cunningham, began a grassroots effort to save the historic house. In 1853 she founded the Mount Vernon Ladies Association, the first historic preservation society operating on a national level in the US. Through a public campaign, the association raised the $200,000 necessary to buy the estate. The association has owned and operated Mount Vernon since 1858.

Access – *Mount Vernon is located 16mi south of Washington. By car: Leave Washington by the 14th St. Bridge, take exit 11A (for National Airport) and continue south on the George Washington Memorial Parkway. Average round-trip driving time from downtown: 1hr. By public transportation: Take Metro to Huntington station, then board bus no. 101 (Fairfax Connector) for Mount Vernon. By Tourmobile: Sightseeing buses run several times daily. By boat: Potomac Spirit departs Tue-Sun from Pier 4 at 6th and Water Sts. SE mid-Mar-Oct; schedule varies in winter months.* ☎ *202-554-8000.*

 George Washington Memorial Parkway
Map p 228. This carefully planned highway, modeled on New York's Bronx River Parkway, is paralleled by a popular paved biking and walking path, the **Mount Vernon Trail**, that leads through the wetlands along the Potomac River. Areas such as Dyke Marsh offer great opportunities to spot shorebirds, occasional raccoons, deer and even foxes. Parking pull-offs, particularly south of Old Town Alexandria, allow you to park and walk—or bike—as far as you like. *Bike rentals are available in Old Town; see Yellow Pages of the phone directory. Bike trail maps may be obtained from Alexandria's visitor center.*

THE MANSION

Open Apr-Aug daily 8am-5pm. Nov-Feb daily 9am-5pm. Rest of the year daily 9am-4pm. $9. ✗ 🅿 ▥ ☎ 703-780-2000. www.mountvernon.org. A map of the estate is distributed at the ticket booth.

The estate's main building is entered from the carriage side, opposite the river side, which boasts the well-known broad, columned piazza that is Mount Vernon's hallmark. The Georgian farmhouse is set off by a rust-red roof and curved colonnades connecting two flanking wings. A weathervane bearing the dove of peace tops its distinctive cupola. A facade of "rusticated board," a wood siding beveled and plastered with sand to resemble white stone, testifies to Washington's frugality as using real stone was much more expensive.

First Floor – The large **dining room**, or "new room," was the last addition to the house and is the most lavishly appointed. Here, as in the rest of the mansion, the decor is authentic to Washington's final years, and many of the furnishings belonged to him. Verdigris, a color favored by Washington, dominates the room and provides contrast to the ornate white woodwork around the Palladian windows and in the ceiling trim. The 21 side chairs are part of an original set made for this room by John Aitken of Philadelphia, who also crafted one of the mahogany sideboards. Washington characterized the ornate marble mantel, which was the gift of an Englishman, as "too elegant and costly...for my republican style of living."

The east-facing door in this room opens onto the piazza, which affords a pleasant **view★** of the Potomac and the far Maryland shore. The center door in the piazza leads into the mansion's large central hall, whose pine paneling Washington had "grained" to resemble mahogany. Cross-ventilated from both the carriage and river sides, this hall was used for informal entertaining in the summer. On the south wall hangs a framed key to the Bastille prison in France, given to Washington by his French ally and friend, the Marquis de Lafayette.

Four rooms open off the hall. The small parlor used for informal family gatherings contains the harpsichord Washington ordered from England for his granddaughter, Nelly, who became an accomplished musician. Formal entertaining was done in the west parlor, which is painted in Prussian blue, a fashionable color at the time. A fine example of colonial Virginia architecture, the room retains its original ceiling molding, door and mantel pediments, and wall paneling. A number of portraits of family members hang here. The small dining room is appointed with richly glazed verdigris walls and mahogany furnishings. Over the mantel is an original **engraving** of the Washington family by Edward Savage. A bedroom opens off this room.

Second Floor – A heavy "grained" staircase leads to five bedrooms off a central hall. More lavishly decorated than Washington's simple bedroom, these guest chambers reflect Martha's tastes, with their worn, broad-planked floors and four-poster beds. So many guests visited the estate that Washington once called his home "a well resorted tavern, as scarcely any strangers who are going from north to south, or from south to north, do not spend a day or two at it."

The **master bedchamber** occupies a more private space in the south section. Simply furnished, this room contains the mahogany four-poster bed in which Washington died. The bedchamber also functioned as Martha Washington's office and contains the late-18C French desk at which she fulfilled her duties as an "old-fashioned Virginia house-keeper," as she called herself.

A narrow back staircase in this wing leads to Washington's own first-floor study. This large room contains many pieces intimately associated with him, including his desk and his presidential desk chair, which he brought back to Mount Vernon with him, and a terrestrial globe commissioned from a London manufacturer.

The two wings attached to the mansion by curving colonnades house a kitchen *(south)* and quarters for white servants *(north)*.

THE ESTATE

To locate the various outbuildings and points of interest throughout the estate, consult the map distributed at the ticket booth.

Outbuildings – Twelve small dependencies are scattered along the lanes leading from both sides of the house. These structures re-create the operations of a self-sufficient estate, from the curing, spinning and laundry houses to the living quarters for overseers and slaves.

The stable at the south edge of the lower garden houses a fine example of an 18C coach. At the eastern edge of the upper garden, a small **museum**, built in 1928 and fully renovated in 1999, houses Washington memorabilia such as jewelry, china, swords and other personal items. It also displays a **bust of General Washington** executed at Mount Vernon by the French sculptor Jean Antoine Houdon.

In the museum annex *(located in the greenhouse)*, a **model** of the mansion depicts the various stages of its evolution. Other exhibits explain the archaeological digs ongoing at the estate.

Grounds – As an admiring 18C European visitor observed, Mount Vernon's grounds conform "to the best samples of the grand old homesteads of England." Today the estate comprises 40 acres of landscaped gardens and forests. The carriage entrance to the house is fronted by a sweeping bowling green bordered by stately trees. Several of the larger tulip poplars here were planted during Washington's lifetime. On the river side of the house, a deer park slopes to the Potomac.

The upper garden on the north side of the bowling green is an ornamental flower garden, dominated by large boxwood hedges that date from Washington's day. The formal parterres are planted with annuals and perennials commonly found in 18C gardens. An imposing brick greenhouse, a reconstruction, forms the garden's north side. Opposite the upper garden, south of the bowling green, is the lower, or kitchen garden where a variety of fruits, berries and vegetables are grown.

Two different burial sites lie beyond the stables. George and Martha Washington were originally buried in the old family vault, a brick-fronted underground crypt. In the years following Washington's death, Congress proposed enshrining his remains in a crypt on the ground level of the Capitol. However, after years of complications and delays, his descendants decided against moving his remains. In 1831 they erected the present **tomb** for George and Martha Washington, building it of "Brick and upon a larger Scale," according to the wishes expressed in Washington's will. Beyond an iron grille, the couple's marble sarcophagi are visible within an open vault. Interred in the walls of the vault are 27 other family members. In front of the tomb are two marble obelisks in memory of Bushrod and John Augustine Washington, the 19C proprietors of Mount Vernon.

A path leads from the tomb to a shaded grove, where a small monument memorializes the slaves buried in unmarked graves at Mount Vernon.

Located near the wharf is the estate's most recent exhibit, a **pioneer farm** that features, among other activities, demonstrations of 18C animal husbandry, crop cultivation, brick making and timber transformation. Visitors are invited to join costumed staff in such activities as planting and harvesting crops.

WOODLAWN PLANTATION★

Map p 228

This gracious Georgian estate reflects the refinement of its original owners, Lawrence Lewis and Nelly Custis Lewis. Favored relatives of George Washington, whose own Mount Vernon lies only three miles away, the Lewises brought to their home many of the furnishings and memorabilia of the original Washington estate.

Historical Notes

A Wedding Gift – In 1797 Lawrence Lewis, Washington's nephew, came to Mount Vernon to serve as his uncle's personal secretary. There he met **Eleanor** (Nelly) **Parke Custis** *(table p 191)*, the granddaughter George and Martha Washington had raised from early childhood. Well-educated, talented and beautiful, Nelly had grown up in the influential society surrounding the Washingtons. Benjamin H. Latrobe, the prominent architect, said of her that she embodied more perfection "than I have ever seen before or conceived consistent with mortality." In 1799, after a quiet courtship, Nelly married Lawrence Lewis at Mount Vernon on February 22, Washington's birthday.

Washington ceded a 2,000-acre tract west of Mount Vernon to the Lewises and urged them to begin building a home. He also deeded them a nearby mill and distillery, because, as he advised Lawrence, "a young man should have objects of employment. Idleness is disreputable." Washington died less than a year after the wedding, but the young couple, following his advice, began building. In 1802 Martha Washington died, and the Lewises moved into the completed north wing of the house.

Woodlawn Plantation was praised by visitors as a "lovely place," with "much to delight all who have a taste for the comforts and elegancies of life." Though the Lewises pursued a lifestyle they felt befitted their Washington heritage, they did so with some difficulty. The estate lands were never very productive, and the couple grappled with financial problems throughout their lives. In 1839 Lawrence, then in his early seventies, died, and Nelly went to live with her son Lorenzo at Audley Plantation in Clark County.

An Era Ends – In 1846 the family offered Woodlawn at public sale. The land was purchased by a group of Quaker businessmen, who divided it into separate farms for a Quaker community. Four years later the house itself was bought by John and Rachel Mason. It passed through a succession of private owners, including a playwright and a senator, all of whom modified and embellished the original structure. In 1949 a locally formed group, the Woodlawn Public Foundation, purchased the house, and in 1957 the estate became the property of the National Trust for Historic Preservation.

Access – *Woodlawn is located 19mi south of Washington.* **By car:** *Leave Washington by the 14th St. Bridge, take exit 11A (for National Airport) and continue south on the George Washington Memorial Parkway to Mount Vernon. Continue 3mi west on Rte. 235 and follow the signs to Woodlawn. Average round-trip driving time from downtown: 1hr 30min.* **By public transportation:** *take the Metro to Huntington station and transfer to a 9A (Fort Belvoir) bus to Woodlawn.*

THE MANSION

Visit by guided tour (45min) only, Mar-Dec daily 10am-4pm, every 30min. Closed Thanksgiving Day, Dec 25. $7.50 (discounted combination ticket for Woodlawn and Pope-Leighey House $13). 🔲 ☎ *703-780-4000.*

The late-Georgian style of Woodlawn may have been more the choice of Lawrence Lewis than that of prominent architect Dr. William Thornton, who was involved in the construction of the house. Woodlawn bears a striking resemblance to Kenmore, Lewis' boyhood home located farther south in Fredericksburg, Virginia. Pleasingly proportioned, the structure has a two-story central core with symmetrical one-story wings that are connected to the main house by hyphens. From the simple portico over the entrance on the river side, the tops of several trees situated on the bowling green at Mount Vernon can be seen.

Decorated as it might have been during the Lewises' lifetime, this house contains many of the furnishings that belonged to the family, including several that were brought from Mount Vernon. Opening off the center hall are a formal drawing room and family sitting room. Adept musicians, Nelly and her daughters often gave informal performances on the harp and piano that still dominate the drawing room. The fire screen, which Nelly worked on, is embroidered in a floral pattern popular in the first half of the 19C.

In the family sitting room, a lithograph depicts the French Marquis de Lafayette on a visit to Woodlawn in 1824. Off the sitting room the master bedroom holds personal items of the Lewises. On a needlework frame by the fireplace is the unfinished piece Nelly was working on at the time of her death.

The one-story hyphens connected to the center house were kitchen and work areas in the Lewises' day. They now hold a reception room *(south side)* and a dining room *(north side)*, which were added at the turn of the century. The two wings connected to the hyphens are used as administrative offices.

The second floor contains four bedrooms and a sewing room, all of which open off a central hall.

The **grounds** are graced with large trees and boxwoods. The parterred garden is noted for its roses.

Woodlawn Plantation, West Front

POPE-LEIGHEY HOUSE

On the grounds of Woodlawn, below the parking lot. Visit by guided tour (45min) only, Mar-Dec daily 10am-4pm, every 30min. Closed Thanksgiving Day, Dec 25. $7.50 (discounted combination ticket for this house and Woodlawn available at Woodlawn mansion, $13). 🅿 ☎ *703-780-4000.*

This small, L-shaped house in a wooded setting is one of the few publicly accessible examples of what the 20C's most eminent American-born architect, **Frank Lloyd Wright** (1867-1959), called his "Usonian" architecture—functional, simply designed homes affordable to middle-class Americans.

Built in 1941 for Loren Pope, a journalist in nearby Falls Church, Virginia, the 1,200sq ft, five-room house cost roughly $7,000. The Leigheys bought the house from the Popes five years later. When it was threatened with demolition because of highway construction in 1964, Mrs. Leighey donated it to the National Trust for Historic Preservation, which moved it to its current site.

The house contains the furniture that Wright designed for it and is built only of cypress, brick, glass and concrete, following the Wright tenet to use as few materials as possible. Other Wright hallmarks—flowing space, strong horizontal lines and organic unity—are evident in the design of the house.

GUNSTON HALL★

Map p 228

This fine colonial Georgian estate reflects the style and substance of plantation life favored by wealthy 18C Virginia planters. The gracious manor house and grounds were the home of **George Mason** (1725-92), a respected thinker whose writings influenced the course of the Revolution and the development of the young Republic.

Historical Notes

The Forgotten Sage – Now a rather obscure patriot, George Mason drafted many documents critical to the birth of the US. During the Revolutionary period, he wrote a number of pivotal statements delineating the colonists' rights, including the Fairfax Resolves (1774) and the Virginia **Declaration of Rights** (May 1776). The latter contained the statement "That all men are by nature equally free and independent and have certain inherent rights...namely, the enjoyment of life and liberty, with the means of acquiring and possessing property, and pursuing and obtaining happiness...." This wording was echoed by Jefferson, Mason's friend and protégé, in his writing of the Declaration of Independence (July 1776). It was also employed by other colonies in their own declarations, and in 1789, by the French in their Declaration of the Rights of Man.

Mason strenuously opposed the original Constitution, because it had no Bill of Rights and did not call for the immediate abolition of the slave trade. His opposition was influential in the subsequent adoption in 1791 of the first 10 amendments to the Constitution, commonly known as the Bill of Rights.

The Squire of Gunston Hall – Born in 1725 and descended from British gentry, George Mason was a fourth-generation Virginian whose family possessed considerable landholdings along the Potomac. When Mason was 10, his father died, and as eldest son, George inherited the family property. He received his education from tutors and the extensive law library of his uncle and guardian, John Mercer. In 1755 he began constructing his own home, Gunston Hall, naming it after other family estates in America and England. He situated it on the Virginia shoreline about a mile above the Potomac and not far from the Washington family estate of Mount Vernon. As young men, Mason and George Washington developed a friendship and mutual respect. Over the years they frequently exchanged views on horticulture, politics and the direction the new nation should take. Mason was a prominent local figure, serving as a justice of Fairfax County, a member of the Alexandria Board of Trustees and a founder of the Fairfax militia company. Though he also served as a member of the Virginia House of Burgesses and a delegate to the Constitutional Convention of 1787, he disliked politics and preferred to exercise his influence quietly, through writing and private conversations. He also felt a great obligation to his nine children, who had been left motherless when Ann Mason died in 1773. Consequently, he did not often venture far from Gunston Hall.

Mason died at his home in 1792, just as the young Republic was being formed. Gunston Hall remained in the family until 1866. After passing through a succession of owners, it was purchased in 1912 by Mr. and Mrs. Louis Hertle, who restored it and ultimately deeded it to the Commonwealth of Virginia to be administered by the National Society of the Colonial Dames of America.

Access – *Gunston Hall is located 22mi south of Washington.* **By car:** *Leave Washington by the 14th St. Bridge and continue south on Rte. 395 (I-95). Take exit 163, then follow the signs for roughly 8mi to Gunston Hall. From Mount Vernon or Woodlawn, continue south on US-1 and follow the signs. Average round-trip driving time from downtown: 1hr 30min.*

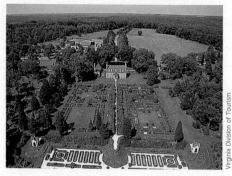

Bird's-Eye View of Gunston Hall

Virginia Division of Tourism

VISIT

Mansion visit by guided tour (30min) only, year-round daily 9:30am-5pm. Closed Jan 1, Thanksgiving Day, Dec 25. $7. 🅿 ☎ 703-550-9220. www.gunston hall .org. Brochures with map of the estate are available at the visitor center in the brick building.

The brick building where tickets are purchased houses a small **museum** and **orientation center** with dioramas, exhibits and a film *(20min)* explaining Mason's contributions and illustrating his life at Gunston Hall. Family and period memorabilia are also on display.

Mansion – Mason is presumed to have designed the exterior of his Georgian manor house, with its large symmetrical chimneys and dormer windows. The unembellished brick facade is offset with quoins, or cornerstones, of local buff-colored Aquia sandstone. The carriage entrance features a pedimented portico with a fanlight above the door. The river entrance portico is a semioctagonal porch with graceful ogee arches.

The interior of the house contains some noteworthy mid-18C carved **woodwork**. When George Mason was planning his dwelling, he asked his brother Thomson, then studying law in England, to procure the services of an English craftsman for him. **William Buckland**, a carpenter-joiner, was engaged under an indenture and arrived in Virginia in 1755. Since Gunston Hall was Buckland's first commission, he took great pains to embellish it with a variety of woodworking styles. The present house contains a combination of original and re-created woodwork and is decorated with period furnishings, a few of which, such as the portraits, belonged to the Mason family.

In the central hall connecting the carriage and river entrances, Buckland used pilasters, chair railing and a double arch offset with a pinecone finial. The Masons' bedroom opens off the left of the hall, and directly across from it is the **Chinese Formal Parlor**, the only surviving room in America featuring the scalloped Chinoiserie woodworking of the colonial period. Beyond the formal parlor, the dining room is embellished with intricate English Palladian-style woodworking. Across the hall from this room is an informal room that was used as Mason's study and as a family dining room and sitting room. A wide wooden staircase in the center hall leads to seven bedrooms on the upper floor.

Grounds – The fenced-in courtyard adjacent to the north side of the house encloses several reconstructed dependencies. Beyond the house on the south side is a small frame schoolhouse, a reconstruction of the one in which the Mason children were tutored. A gravel path connects the schoolhouse to an avenue of cedars that leads to the brick-walled family **graveyard**, where 16 family members are buried. The two raised sarcophagi contain the remains of George Mason and his wife, Ann.

A double row of magnolias and cedars lines Magnolia Avenue, the carriage approach to the house. On the river side, an impressive boxwood allée leads through **formal gardens** to an overlook above a garden terrace. In Mason's day the now-forested fields sloping to the river were cleared for planting and the Potomac was visible from here. A mile-long walk through a wooded area leads to the river.

ANNAPOLIS★

Set on the south bank of the Severn River, Annapolis, Maryland is known for its history and its harbor. The former dates back to 1649, when Virginia Puritans established Arundel Towne along the Severn. The latter shelters hundreds of yachts and sailboats tied up at City Dock, once home port for the Chesapeake Bay's oyster fleet.

Historical Notes

Annapolis became the seat of colonial government in 1695, named in honor of England's Queen Anne. Founding fathers laid out the new capital with the 1779 Georgian-style **State House★** *(center of State Circle ☎ 410-974-3400)*—which served as the US capitol between 1783 and 1784—occupying the highest point, while **St. Anne's Church** *(Church Circle ☎ 410-267-9333)* was given the second-highest site. The rest of the town spread out on narrow streets from these structures, symbolizing the key positions of church and state. In the 18C, Annapolis reigned as Maryland's premier port, as well as the colony's cultural capital.

Today, the city's economy revolves around tourism, state government and the US Navy. Visitors come year-round to sample the shops and bistros of Main Street and to wander the tree-lined side streets, where historic homes attest to the prosperity of the city's early years.

Access – *Annapolis is located 36mi east of Washington via US-50 East. Parking available at Gotts Garage on Northwest Street next to the Visitors Center. To access Visitors Center and parking, continue on US-50 to exit 24 (Rowe Blvd.). Proceed down Rowe Blvd., crossing College Creek Bridge. Stay in the right lane. Rowe will split into Northwest St. Look for signs to Visitor Center. To see the city from a different perspective, take one of the popular boat cruises that regularly ply the harbor (for cruise information, contact the Annapolis & Anne Arundel County Conference & Visitors Bureau, 26 West St., Annapolis MD 21401. www.visit-annapolis.org ☎ 410-280-0445).*

■ Blue Crabs

When summer settles into the Mid-Atlantic, there are few things more dear to a Marylander's heart than eating blue crabs. The small crustacean is the state's single most valuable fishery resource. Watermen harvested more than 26 million pounds of crabs in 1999, netting the state more than $30 million. Although found as far north as Cape Cod, the blue crab *(Callinectes sapidus)* thrives in greatest abundance in the Chesapeake Bay. In season, from May to October, this regional delicacy can be sampled in several forms. Some of the best ways to eat blue crabs are: by **picking crabs**, a messy but fun process of cracking the shell open and extracting the meat; as **soft shells**, a blue crab that has molted and not yet formed its new shell *(available May-Sept)*; or made into Maryland's justifiably famous **crabcakes**.

© Michael Ventura/FOLIO, Inc.

Blue Crabs

Sights

★★Hammond Harwood House – *19 Maryland Ave. Visit by guided tour only, year-round Mon-Sat 10am-4pm, Sun noon-4pm. $5. ☎ 410-263-4683.* This outstanding example of the Georgian style (1775), with its unusual bowed wings, is the work of William Buckland. One of the country's first and foremost architects, Buckland emigrated from England in 1755. A joiner by trade, Buckland had a keen eye for detail, and the elaborately carved rose garlands above the entryway fanlight and the ornate woodwork and plaster ornamentation within are glorious proof of his skill. Inside, the tall arched window above the staircase is modeled on one found in London's Church of St. Martin's in the Field.

★Chase-Lloyd House – *22 Maryland Ave. Visit by guided tour only, Mon-Sat 2pm-4pm. $2. ☎ 410-263-2723.* Built for Samuel Chase, a signer of the Declaration of Independence, this imposing three-story brick Georgian (1774, William Buckland) is best known for its breathtaking **entrance hall** featuring a split, cantilevered staircase and a tall Palladian window. Only the first floor and the public garden are open to the public as the rest of the house has served as a home for elderly women since 1890.

William Paca House – *186 Prince George St. Visit by guided tour only, Mar-Dec Mon-Sat 10am-5pm, Sun noon-5pm. Rest of the year Thur-Sat 10am-5pm, Sun noon-4pm. $8. ☎ 410-263-5553. www.annapolis.org.* Patriot and signer of the Declaration of Independence, lawyer William Paca based his design of this brick town house (1765) on the Georgian principal of attaching wings to the main structure with short corridors called "hyphens." The interior is sparsely furnished with period pieces; the lovely formal **gardens** behind the house have been restored to their 18C appearance.

★★US Naval Academy – *Armel-Leftwich Visitor Center, 52 King George St. Visitors Center open Mar-Dec daily 9am-5pm. Rest of the year 9am-4pm. Visit of campus by guided tour only, Jun-Labor Day Mon-Sat 9:30am-3pm, Sun 12:30pm-3pm. Rest of the year Mon-Sat 10am-2:30pm, Sun 12:30pm-2:30pm. Closed Jan 1, Thanksgiving Day & Dec 25. $6. ☎ 410-263-6933. www.navyonline.com.* Midshipmen study to be officers in the US Navy and Marine Corps on a peaceful, 338-acre campus along the Severn River and College Creek. In 1850 the five year-old Naval School became the official undergraduate college for the US Navy. More than a century later, competition is fierce to be one of the 4,000 midshipmen that gets a rigorous and free education at the academy.

US Naval Academy Cadets

Middleton Evans/Courtesy Maryland Tourism

The guided tour around "the Yard," as the academy grounds are called, includes massive **Bancroft Hall**, the 1906 Beaux-Arts structure in the center of campus that covers 33 acres and boasts 5mi of corridors. Few buildings in Annapolis rival the glorious gold-domed US Naval Academy **chapel★★** (1908, Ernest Flagg), modeled after the Hotel des Invalides in Paris. In the chapel's eerily lit crypt, the remains of the nation's first naval hero, John Paul Jones, are interred in a black marble sarcophagus. After the tour, be sure to visit the Preble Hall **museum**, where you'll find a superb collection of **ship models★★** made in England during the 17C and 18C, as well as other artifacts detailing the academy's history.

■ Maryland's Eastern Shore

Just across the Chesapeake Bay Bridge from Annapolis *(50mi east of Washington, DC)* is Maryland's Eastern Shore, a peninsula that lies between the bay and the Atlantic Ocean. Characterized by sleepy fishing villages and small farms, the low-lying coastline here is a conglomeration of quiet coves and lonely marshes. You can easily while away a couple of pleasant days exploring historic waterside villages such as **St. Michaels**★ and **Chestertown**, staying in some of the fine bed-and-breakfast inns, poking through antique shops, bird-watching, and sampling the region's bountiful seafood—especially the famous **blue crabs** and oysters.

One of the shore's most unique events takes place each summer on the southern end of **Assateague Island National Seashore**★ *(29mi east of Salisbury, MD, via US-50 & Rte. 611;* △ ♿ 🅿 ☎ *410-641-1441)*. This part of the 37mi-long barrier island harbors several hundred **wild ponies** that roam **Chincoteague National Wildlife Refuge**. The offspring of horses brought here by 17C settlers to avoid penning and taxation laws, the ponies are rounded up annually on Assateague Island and herded across the narrow channel (at slack tide) to the town of **Chincoteague, VA** *(across Chincoteague Bay on Rte. 175)*. Here the annual **Pony Penning**★, the public round up and sale of foals, is held on the last Wednesday and Thursday of July *(for information, call ☎ 757-336-6161)*.

Favorite viewpoints around Washington

Washington Monument

Lincoln Memorial (east side)

Old Post Office Tower

Capitol (west terrace)

Arlington House

Marine Corps Memorial

Market Square and City Hall, Old Town Alexandria

Practical Information

Calendar of Events

Listed below is a selection of Washington, DC's popular annual events; some dates may vary from year to year. For more information, consult the periodicals listed on p 267 or the quarterly Calendar of Events available from the Washington, DC Convention and Visitors Assn. (☎ 202-789-7000). Events for Alexandria are listed on p 234. Unless otherwise specified, the area code for all telephone numbers is 202.

Date	Event/Location	☎/Contact Information
Spring		
mid-Mar	**St. Patrick's Day Parade** *Constitution Ave. NW*	637-2474 www.dcstpatsparade.com
	Washington Flower & Garden Show *Washington Convention Center*	703-823-7960 www.flowergarden show.com
late Mar-Apr	**National Cherry Blossom Festival** *Tidal Basin*	547-1500 www.nationalcherry blossomfestival.org
Easter Sun	**Easter Sunrise Service** *Arlington National Cemetery*	703-697-2131 www.arlington cemetery.com
Easter Mon	**Easter Egg Roll and Egg Hunt** *White House*	456-7041 www.whitehouse.gov
early Apr	**Spring Garden Tours** *White House*	456-7041 www.whitehouse.gov
Apr 13	**Thomas Jefferson's Birthday** *Jefferson Memorial*	619-7222 www.nps.gov
late Apr	**Shakespeare's Birthday** *Folger Shakespeare Library*	544-4600 www.folger.edu
	Georgetown House Tour *Georgetown*	338-1796 www.georgetown housetour.com
early May	**Flower Mart** *Washington National Cathedral*	537-6200 www.cathedral.org
mid-May	**Goodwill Embassy Tour** *Embassy Row*	636-4225 www.dcgoodwill.org
	Memorial Day Weekend Concert *Capitol (west lawn)*	619-7222 www.nps.gov

---

US Military Band Summer Concerts are usually held at 8pm from **Memorial Day to Labor Day**. For information contact: US Army Band (☎ 703-696-3718; www.army .mil/armyband); US Marine Band (☎ 202-433-4011; www .marine band .usmc.mil); US Navy Band (☎ 202-433-2525; www.navyband.navy.mil); US Air Force Band (☎ 202-767-5658; www.af.mil/band).

Mon	Navy Band	Capitol (west front)
Tue	Army Band	Sylvan Theatre, Mall
	Air Force Band	Capitol (west front)
7pm	Marine Corps Sunset Parade	Iwo Jima Memorial
Wed	Marine Band	Capitol (west front)
Thu	Navy Band	Sylvan Theatre, Mall
Fri	Air Force Band	Sylvan Theatre, Mall
	Army Band	Capitol (west front)
Sun	Marine Band	Sylvan Theatre, Mall

US Army's **Twilight Tattoo Sunset Parade** is held at The Ellipse May-Aug Wed at 7pm.

Marine Corps Evening Parade *(1hr)* takes place at the Marine Barracks *(8th & Eye Sts. SE, Washington DC; May-AugFri 8:45pm; for reservations:* ☎ *202-433-6060; www.marineband.usmc.mil).*

Summer

Early Jun	Dupont-Kalorama Museum Walk *(p 207)*	667-0441
	Dance Africa Festival	269-1600
	Dance Place, 3225 8th St. NE	www.danceplace.org
Jun-Aug	Twilight Tattoo (military parade/show)	475-0685
	The Ellipse	www.army.mil/armyband
late Jun- early Jul	Festival of American Folklife	275-1150
	Mall	www.folklife.si.edu
late Jun-Jul	Jazz Arts Festival	783-0360
	various locations	
Jul 4	National Independence Day Celebrations *Mall*	619-7222
		www.nps.gov
mid-Aug	US Army Band's 1812 Overture Concert	703-696-3718
	Sylvan Theatre, Mall	www.army.mil/armyband

Fall

Early Sept	Labor Day Weekend Concert	619-7222
	Capitol (west lawn)	www.nps.gov
	Adams Morgan Day Festival	232-6113
	Columbia Rd. & 18th St. NW	www.adamsmorganday.org
mid-Sept	International Children's Festival	703-642-0862
	Wolf Trap Farm Park, VA	www.wolf-trap.org
Sept 17	Constitution Day Commemoration	501-5215
	Downtown DC	www.nara.gov
Late Sept	Rock Creek Park Day	426-6828
	Rock Creek Park	www.nps.gov/rocr
	Annual Open House	537-6200
	Washington National Cathedral	www.cathedral.org
	Arts on Foot Festival	www.artsonfoot.org
	Downtown DC & various locations	
Oct-Dec	US Army Band Fall Concert Series	703-696-3718
	Brucker Hall, Fort Myer, Arlington	www.army.mil/armyband
mid-Oct	Fall Garden Tours	456-7041
	White House	www.whitehouse.gov
	Columbus Day Ceremonies	244-6302
	Columbus Memorial Plaza	www.nps.gov
late Oct	Marine Corps Marathon	703-784-2225
	Marine Corps War Memorial,	www.marinemarathon.com
	Downtown DC and northern VA	
	Washington International Horse Show	301-840-0281
	MCI Center, Downtown DC	www.wihs.org

November

mid-Nov	Veterans Day Ceremonies	
	Arlington National Cemetery,	685-2892
	Vietnam Veterans Memorial,	619-7222
	US Navy Memorial	737-2300

Winter

Dec- Jan 1	National Christmas Tree Lighting & The Christmas Pageant of Peace	208-1631 www.nps.gov/
	The Ellipse (early Dec)	whho/pageant
Early Dec	Carol Singing	703-255-1900
	Wolf Trap Farm Park, VA	www.wolf-trap.org
	US Army Band Holiday Festival	685-2851
	DAR Constitution Hall	www.army.mil/armyband
mid-Dec	Holiday Candlelight Tours	703-780-4000
	Woodlawn Plantation, VA	www.nthp.org
	People's Christmas Tree Lighting	224-3069
	Capitol (west lawn)	
Dec 24, 25	Christmas Celebration	537-6200
	Washington National Cathedral	www.cathedral.org
late Dec	Christmas Candlelight Tours	456-7041
	White House	www.whitehouse.gov
1st week Jan	Congress convenes	www.senate.gov
	Capitol	www.house.gov

Taste of DC

mid-Jan	**Martin Luther King Jr. Birthday Observance**	619-7222
	National Mall	www.nps.gov
Late Jan	**Lee Birthday Celebration**	703-548-1789
	Lee Fendall House, VA	
late Jan-Mar	**US Army Band Winter/Spring Concert Series**	703-696-3718
	Brucker Hall, Fort Myer, Arlington	www.army.mil/armyband
Throughout Feb	**Black History Month**	357-2700
	various locations	
early Feb	**Chinese New Year Celebration**	357-2700
Feb 12	**Abraham Lincoln Birthday Celebration**	619-7222
	Lincoln Memorial	www.nps.gov
mid-Feb	**Washington Boat Show**	703-823-7960
	Washington Convention Center	www.washington boatshow.com
late Feb	**Imagination Celebration**	467-4600
	Kennedy Center	www.kennedycenter.com

Planning Your Trip

Visitors can contact the following agencies to obtain maps and information on points of interest, accommodations and seasonal events:

Washington, DC Convention and Visitors Association ....☏ 202-789-7000
1212 New York Ave. NW   www.washington.org
Suite 600
Washington DC 20005

Washington, DC Visitors Information Center ....☏ 202-328-4748
Ronald Reagan International Trade Center Building   www.dcvisit.com
1300 Pennsylvania Avenue, NW
Washington, DC 20004

Alexandria Convention and Visitors Association ....☏ 703-838-4200
421 King St.   www.funside.com
Suite 300
Alexandria VA 22314

Arlington Visitors Center ....☏ 800-677-6267
735 S. 18th St.   www.stayarlington.com
Arlington VA 22202

Advance Arrangements

Reservations for Sights – It is wise to make reservations in advance for any of the special **annual tours** of selected embassies *(p 206)* and Georgetown houses and gardens as well as guided tours of certain Washington sights (Diplomatic Reception Rooms, Hillwood). Consult the admission information that accompanies the sight descriptions in this guide for details on the attractions you intend to visit.

Tickets for **congressional visits** (special tours of some of the more popular sights, such as the White House, Capitol, FBI and the Bureau of Engraving and Printing) may be obtained by writing to your senators or representative *(below)*. As each member of Congress is allotted a limited number of tickets, requests should be made several months in advance. These visits, which are generally scheduled early in the morning, are sometimes more extensive than the standard tours and, best of all, you avoid the long lines.

Congressional Visits

Members of Congress can arrange special tours for the following sites:

White House	Capitol Building Gallery Pass
Supreme Court	FBI
Bureau of Engraving and Printing	National Archives
National Cathedral	Kennedy Center
Library of Congress	State Department
Treasury Department	

When writing your Congress member to request tours, be sure to include the following information:

Name, address & daytime phone number
Sites you would like to tour
Number of individuals in your group
Dates you will be visiting DC

Visiting Your Senators or Representatives – If you would like to meet the elected officials who represent you in Congress, you should write two to three months in advance to request an appointment. Call the Capitol (☎ *202-224-3121*) or write:

US Senate
Washington DC 20510

US House
Washington DC 20515

Capitol Flag

One of the many services offered by the members of the House and Senate is to honor Capitol Flag Orders. At the request of a constituent, a US Flag will be flown over The Capitol in honor of an individual on a certain date *(be sure to give at least 6 weeks notice)*. A dated certificate is then sent along with the flag. *For more information, visit www.house.gov or www.senate.gov.*

Washington DC's Seasons

Spring is Washington's peak tourist season. The mild temperatures and the blossoming of the famous cherry trees *(late Mar-early Apr)* attract the greater part of the capital's 19-20 million annual visitors. Hotel reservations should be made well in advance and long lines are to be expected at the main sights. The hot and humid **summer** weather can make touring uncomfortable and tiring, but the season's long days, extended operating hours for some sights and numerous outdoor events are a major draw. It is advisable to carry a lightweight jacket, since most buildings are chilly due to air-conditioning. **Fall** is a very pleasant season to visit Washington. Temperatures are moderate, the summer crowds have thinned out and the display of autumn foliage is often spectacular. **Winter** months are unpredictable, with temperatures ranging from the high 40s to well below freezing. Severe snowstorms are infrequent in Washington.

Washington DC Temperature Chart *(recorded at National Airport)*

	average high	average low	precipitation
January	43°F (6°C)	28°F (-2°C)	2.8in (7.1cm)
April	67°F (19°C)	46°F (8°C)	2.9in (7.4cm)
July	88°F (31°C)	70°F (21°C)	3.9in (9.9cm)
October	69°F (21°C)	50°F (10°C)	2.9in (7.4cm)

Getting to DC

By Air

Washington is served by three major airports *(map p 258)*.

Ronald Reagan Washington National Airport (DCA) – ☎ *703-417-8000. www.met-washairports.com. 4.5mi south of downtown DC, across the Potomac in Virginia.* Domestic and commuter flights arrive at and depart from National. **Traveler's Aid Booths** *(open Mon-Fri 9am-9pm, weekends 9am-6pm)* are located near the baggage-claim of each terminal. **Smoking** is prohibited in the airport except in designated restaurants. Restaurants with sit-down service are located in all terminals. Free airport shuttle buses provide transportation *(daily 6am-1am)* to and from all terminals, the satellite parking lots and garages, and the Metro station. Most **public transportation** departs from the curbside in front of each terminal.

Taxis – Taxis are available at the exits of Terminal A and the baggage-claim levels of Terminals B and C. Passengers are obligated to wait in line and take the dispatched cab. Taxi service to downtown DC takes approximately 10min and costs on average $8-$17, plus an airport fee of $1.25.

Shuttles – **Washington Flyer** express buses offer nonstop service between National and Dulles. Buses run daily 6:15am-9:15pm every hour *(45-55min; $16 one way/$26 round-trip; ☎ 703-685-1400 or 888-WASHFLY; www.washfly.com).* For transport to residences, businesses and hotels throughout the greater DC area, **SuperShuttle** provides shared-ride, door-to-door service year-round 24hrs daily *(☎ 800-258-3826).* Telephones for hotel/motel courtesy shuttles are located on the baggage-claim levels of the terminals.

Rental Cars – *p 264.* Rental-car company service counters are located on the lower level of Parking Garage A opposite Terminal A *(free airport shuttle buses stop at the garage).* At the airport, a sales tax of 10% plus an airport fee of $2.50 per day are added to the rental rate.

Public Transportation – The airport is served by the Blue and Yellow **Metrorail** lines. The Metro station is adjacent to Terminals B & C. Public bus service is available to areas not served by Metrorail. The **Metrobus** stop is located at the base of the Metrorail station *(☎ 202-637-7000).*

Washington Flyer express buses between National and Dulles Airports operate daily 5am-11pm every hour on the hour *(weekends every 2hrs; 45min; $16 one way/$26 round-trip; ☎ 703-685-1400).*

Dulles International Airport (IAD) – ☎ *703-572-2700. www.metwashairports.com. 26mi west of downtown DC, in Loudoun County, VA.* International flights and domestic flights arrive at and depart from Dulles. A **Traveler's Aid Booth** *(open Mon-Fri 10am-9pm, weekends 10am-6pm)* is located on the lower level of the Main Terminal. Smoking is prohibited in the airport except in **smoking rooms** located in the each of the concourses *(open 24hrs daily).* Restaurants with sit-down service are located on the upper level of the Main Terminal and in the concourses. Public transportation departs from the lower level of the Main Terminal.

Departure Hall, Ronald Reagan Washington National Airport

Taxis – Taxis are available at the exits of the baggage-claim level of the Main Terminal. Passengers are obligated to wait in line and take the dispatched cab. Taxi service to downtown DC takes about 30min and costs on average between $44-$50 *(Washington Flyer Taxicabs; ☎ 703-661-6655).*

Shuttles – Washington Flyer express buses offer nonstop service between Dulles and National. Buses run daily 5:20am-10:20pm every hour *(44-55min; $16 one way/$26 round-trip; ☎ 703-685-1400 or 888-WASHFLY; www.washfly.com).* For transport to residences, businesses and hotels throughout the greater DC area, **SuperShuttle** provides shared-ride, door-to-door service year-round, 24hrs daily *(☎ 800-258-3826).* Telephones for hotel/motel courtesy shuttles are located on the lower level of the Main Terminal in the ground-transportation centers.

Rental Cars – *p 264.* Rental-car company courtesy telephones are located on the lower level of the Main Terminal. An 9% sales tax is added to the rental rate; some car companies add a 10% airport access fee or a daily surcharge.

Public Transportation – An airport-Metro shuttle operates between Dulles and West Falls Church **Metro** station (Orange line). Shuttles run daily 6am-10:45pm *(weekends 7:45am-10:45pm; every half hour; 25min; $8 one way/$14 round-trip; ☎ 703-685-1400).* Public bus service is available to areas not served by Metrorail. The **Metrobus** stop is located at the base of the Metro station.

Baltimore-Washington International Airport (BWI) – *☎ 800-I FLY BWI. www. bwiairport.com. 28mi north of Washington and 8mi south of Baltimore.* Domestic, commuter and international flights arrive at and depart from BWI. **Airport Information Booth** *(open daily 9am-9pm)* is located at the entrance to Pier C on the upper level of the terminal building. Smoking is prohibited in the airport except in **smoking areas** located in designated restaurants. Restaurants with sit-down service can be found on the upper level of the terminal. Free airport shuttle buses operate 24hrs daily to and from the satellite and short-term parking lots and the BWI rail station. **Public transportation** departs from the lower level of the terminal.

Taxis – Taxis are available at the exits of the lower level of the terminal. Taxi service to downtown DC takes approximately 50min and costs on average $55. BWI Airport Taxi Management participates in the shared-ride discount program, wherein individual riders willing to share a cab pay a discounted rate. Inform the dispatcher if you wish to participate *(BWI Airport Taxi Management; ☎ 410-859-1100).*

Shuttles – SuperShuttle *(☎ 800-258-3826)* service is available from BWI to the downtown DC area. From 9am-2am, go to the Guest Services Desk in the Ground Transportation area in order to request shuttle service, or call ☎ 888-826-2700.

Rental Cars – *p 264.* Rental-car company service counters are located in the baggage-claim area on the lower level of the terminal. Some counters are open 24hrs a day. Rental cars are located behind the parking garage and can be reached by BWI airport car-rental shuttle buses. A sales tax of 11.5% is added to the rental rate. Some agencies may add a 10% concession fee as well as a $3 daily facility charge.

Trains – *below.* Maryland Rail Commuter Service, known as **MARC**, provides commuter service between the airport and Union Station in DC Monday-Friday 5:26am-10:05pm *(1hr; $5 one way/$8.75 round-trip; ☎ 800-325-7245).* **Amtrak** offers daily service between Baltimore and DC *(45min).* For fares and schedules: ☎ 800-USA-RAIL; www.amtrak.com.

By Train

Union Station is Washington's only railroad station and offers **Amtrak** and other rail service. Located near Capitol Hill at Massachusetts and Delaware Aves. NE, the station is accessible by Metrorail (Red line). Amtrak's Metroliner and Acela Express provide direct daily service between the nation's capital and major destinations throughout the Northeast (from DC to Boston via Philadelphia and New York), the Midwest and the South. Advance reservations are recommended to ensure the best fares and desired accommodations. Major short-distance routes to DC are from Philadelphia *(1hr 30min),* New York *(3hrs)* and Boston *(8hrs).* Amtrak also offers daily service between Baltimore and DC. Maryland Rail Commuter Service (**MARC**) operates trains between the two cities weekdays. Amtrak's longer routes include those from Atlanta *(13hrs 30min),* Chicago *(20hrs)* and Miami *(22hrs).* Travelers from Canada should ask their local travel agents about Amtrak/VIARail connections. The **North America Rail Pass** allows up to 30 days of travel throughout the US and Canada. The **USA RailPass** *(not available to US or Canadian citizens or legal residents)* offers unlimited travel within Amtrak-designated regions at discounted rates: 15- and 30-day passes are available. For schedules and routes, call ☎ 800-872-7245 *(toll-free in North American only; outside North America, contact your local travel agent)* or visit www.amtrak.com.

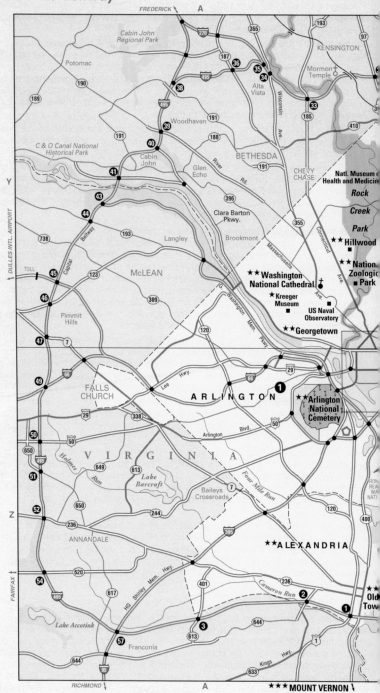

By Bus

Greyhound provides access to Washington, DC at fares that are generally lower than air or rail rates. However, some travelers may find long-distance bus travel uncomfortable due to the lack of sleeping accommodations. The **Discovery Pass** allows unlimited travel for anywhere from 4 to 60 days. Advance reservations are suggested. For fares, schedules and routes, call ☎ 800-231-2222 or visit www.greyhound.com. The capital's main bus terminal (☎ 202-289-5154) is located at 1005 1st St. NE, a short walk from Union Station.

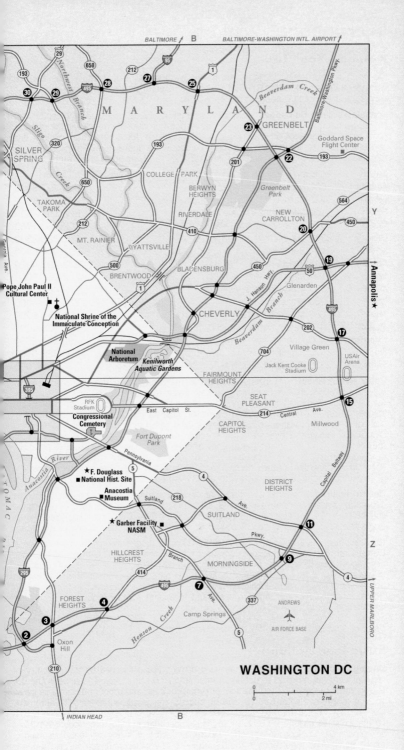

By Car

Map above. Washington is situated at the crossroads of several major interstate routes: I-95 (north-south), I-66 (east), Rte. 50 (west) and I-270 (north-west). These and other roads leading to the capital connect with the Capital Beltway (I-495), which encircles the city at a distance of about 12mi from the center.

International Visitors

Planning Your Trip

For tourist information, visitors from outside the US can contact the **Meridian International Center** (☎ 202-667-6800; www.meridian.org), the US embassy in their country and the organizations listed on p 254.

Consulates and Embassies – Since Washington, DC is the nation's capital, all embassies and many consulates are located here. International visitors can contact the consulate or embassy of their country of residence for information. Below are addresses and phone numbers of several. To obtain the phone numbers of others, call the Washington, DC Information line (☎ 202-555-1212) or go to www.embassy.org.

Country	Address	☎
Australia	1601 Massachusetts Ave. NW	202-797-3000
Belgium	3330 Garfield St. NW	202-333-6900
Britain	3100 Massachusetts Ave. NW	202-588-6500
Canada	501 Pennsylvania Ave. NW	202-682-1740
China	2300 Connecticut Ave. NW	202-328-2500
France	4101 Reservoir Rd. NW	202-944-6000
Germany	4645 Reservoir Rd. NW	202-298-4000
India	2107 Massachusetts Ave. NW	202-939-7000
Ireland	2234 Massachusetts Ave. NW	202-462-3939
Italy	3000 Whitehaven St. NW	202-612-4400
Japan	2520 Massachusetts Ave. NW	202-238-6700
Mexico	1911 Pennsylvania Ave. NW	202-728-1600
Netherlands	4200 Linnean Ave. NW	202-244-5300
Spain	2375 Pennsylvania Ave. NW	202-452-0100
Switzerland	2900 Cathedral Ave. NW	202-745-7900

Entry Requirements – Citizens of countries participating in the Visa Waiver Pilot Program (VWPP) are not required to obtain a visa to enter the US for visits of fewer than 90 days. For more information contact the US consulate in your country of residence. Citizens of nonparticipating countries must have a visitor's visa. Upon entry, nonresident foreign visitors must present a valid passport and round-trip transportation ticket. Canadian citizens are not required to present a passport or visa to enter the US, although identification and proof of citizenship may be requested (a passport or Canadian birth certificate and photo identification are usually acceptable). Naturalized Canadian citizens should carry their citizenship papers. Inoculations are generally not required, but check with the US embassy or consulate before departing.

Health Insurance – The US does not have a national health program. Before departing, visitors from abroad should check their health care insurance to determine if doctors' visits, medication and hospitalization in the US are covered. Prescription drugs should be properly identified, and accompanied by a copy of the prescription.

US Customs – All articles brought into the US must be declared at the time of entry. **Exempt** from customs regulations: personal effects; one liter (33.8 fl oz) of alcoholic beverages (providing visitor is at least 21 years old); 200 cigarettes or 100 cigars or 2 kilograms (4.4 lbs.) of smoking tobacco; and gifts (to persons in the US) that do not exceed $100 in value. **Prohibited items** are plant material, firearms and ammunition (if not intended for sporting purposes) and meat and poultry products. For further information, contact the US embassy or consulate before departing, or the US Customs Service, 1300 Pennsylvania Ave. NW, Washington DC 20229 *(open Mon-Fri 8:30am-5pm; ☎ 202-927-6724; www.customs.ustreas.gov)*.

Basic Information

Driving in the US – Visitors bearing valid driver's licenses issued by their country of residence are not required to obtain an International Driver's License to drive in the US. Drivers must carry vehicle registration, or rental contract, and proof of automobile insurance at all times. Rental cars *(p 264)* in the US are usually equipped with automatic transmission, and rental rates tend to be less expensive than overseas. Gasoline is sold by the gallon (1 gallon = 3.8 liters) and is cheaper than in many other countries. Most self-service gas stations do not offer car repair, although many sell standard maintenance items. Road regulations in the US require that vehicles be driven on the right side of the road. Distances are posted in miles (1 mile = 1.6 kilometers).

Electricity – The voltage in the US is 110 volts AC, 60 Hz. Foreign-made appliances may need voltage transformers and North American flat-blade adapter plugs (available at specialty travel and electronics stores).

Emergencies – In all major US cities you can call the police, ambulance or fire service by dialing 911. Another way to report an emergency is to dial **0** for the operator. See p 267 for emergency phone numbers. A **language hot line** (☎ 202-939-5538) provides assistance in 42 languages *(Mon-Fri 9am-5pm)*.

Telephone/Telegram – *See also p 267.* Instructions for using **public telephones** are listed on or near the telephone. Some public telephones accept credit cards, and all will accept long-distance calling cards. Post offices, convenience stores and supermarkets sell pre-paid phone cards for long distance and international calls. For **long-distance** calls in the US and Canada, dial 1+area code+number. To place an **international call**, dial 011+country code+number. A list of country codes can be found in the Yellow Pages. To place a **collect call** (person receiving call pays charges) dial 0+area code+number and tell the operator you are calling collect. If it is an international call, ask for the overseas operator.

The cost for a local call from a pay phone is generally 35¢ (any combination of nickels, dimes or quarters is accepted). Most phone numbers in this guide that start with **800** or **888** are toll-free (no charge) in the US only and may not be accessible outside of North America. Dial **1** before dialing an 800 or 888 number in the US. The charge for numbers preceded by **900** can range from 50¢ to $15 per minute. Most hotels add a surcharge for local and long-distance calls. For further information dial **0** for operator assistance.

You can send a **telegram** or money, or have money telegraphed to you, via the Western Union system ☎ 800-325-6000.

Temperature and Measurement – In the US temperatures are measured in degrees Fahrenheit and measurements are expressed according to the US Customary System of weights and measures.

Equivalents

Degrees Fahrenheit	95°	86°	77°	68°	59°	50°	41°	32°	23°	14°
Degrees Celsius	35°	30°	25°	20°	15°	10°	5°	0°	-5°	-10°

1 inch = 2.54 centimeters 1 pound = 0.454 kilograms

1 foot = 30.48 centimeters 1 quart = 0.946 liters

1 mile = 1.609 kilometers 1 gallon = 3.785 liters

Money

Credit Cards and Traveler's Checks – *Money p 266.* Rental-car agencies and many hotels require credit cards. Most banks will cash brand-name travelers checks and give cash advances on major credit cards (American Express, Visa, MasterCard/ Eurocard) with proper identification.

Currency Exchange – Foreign currency exchange, travelers checks and wire transfers are available through many banks in central DC, including **Riggs National Bank**, 1919 Pennsylvania Ave. NW (and other branch locations); ☎ 301-887-6000. Private companies offering exchange services include **Thomas Cook Currency Services**, 1800 K St. NW and at Union Station *(opposite Gate G;* ☎ 202-872-1233); and **American Express Travel Service**, 1150 Connecticut Ave. NW; ☎†202-457-1300. Visitors can also exchange currency at National Airport (Main Terminal, upper level, near Travelers Aid booth); Dulles International Airport (Main Terminal, upper level east end and west end; and Midfield Concourses, upper levels of C & D concourses); and BWI (in the business center, upper level of the Terminal).

Taxes and Tipping – *p 267.* Prices displayed or quoted in the US do not generally include the **sales tax** (5.75% to 14.5% in Washington, DC). Sales tax is added at the time of purchase and is not reimbursable as in other countries (it can sometimes be avoided if purchased items are shipped to another country by the seller). In the US it is customary to give a **tip** (a small gift of money) for services received from waiters/ waitresses, porters, hotel maids and taxi drivers.

Getting Around DC

Lay of the Land

DC Street System – *Map below.* Based on L'Enfant's design, the layout of DC's streets is logical. The focal point of Washington's street system is the US Capitol building. From this prominent landmark, the two cardinal axes—North Capitol and South Capitol Streets, and East Capitol Street and the Mall—divide the city into four quadrants: Northwest, Northeast, Southeast and Southwest.

Numbered streets running north-south are laid out in ascending order on either side of North and South Capitol Streets, while **lettered streets** running east-west begin on either side of the Mall/East Capitol axis. This arrangement gives rise to two sets of numbered streets and two sets of lettered streets. For example, the street one block east of the Capitol and the street one block west of the Capitol are both named 1st Street; similarly there is a C Street three blocks north and three blocks south of the Capitol. Since the same address may be found in each of the four quadrants, it is imperative that the appropriate designation (NE, SE, SW, NW) be attached to the address to avoid confusion. **Avenues** bearing the names of the states of the Union run diagonally across the grid pattern and generally radiate from **circles** named after prominent Americans such as Washington, Sheridan and Dupont.

Note the following particularities: in the NW and SW quadrants there is no A Street owing to the location of the Mall; B Street is replaced by Constitution Avenue (NE and NW) and Independence Avenue (SE and SW); there is no J Street; and I Street is commonly spelled Eye Street. The lettered streets end at W Street, beyond which a new alphabetical series begins with two-syllable names (Adams, Bryant, Channing, etc.).

How to Find an Address – Once you understand the city's rational street layout, you should be able to locate an address in central DC with ease. Bear in mind that the quadrant designation (NW, NE, SE, SW) indicates the location in relation to the Capitol and that building numbers run in series of 100 per block. The odd-even numbering of buildings in each of the four quadrants follows a distinct pattern according to the street's orientation in relation to the Capitol. As a general rule, in the **Northwest quadrant**, the north and east sides of streets and avenues are odd-numbered, while the south and west sides are even-numbered. Some examples:

❶ The intersection of 2nd and C Streets SE is two streets east of the Capitol and (C being the 3rd letter of the alphabet) three streets south of East Capitol Street.

❷ The Hart Senate Office Building, located at the intersection of 2nd and C Streets NE, is two streets east of the Capitol and three streets north of East Capitol Street.

❸ Ford's Theatre at 511 10th Street NW is ten numbered streets west of the Capitol and five lettered streets north of the Mall between E (the 5th letter of the alphabet) and F Streets. The number 511 indicates that the theater is located on the east side of 10th Street.

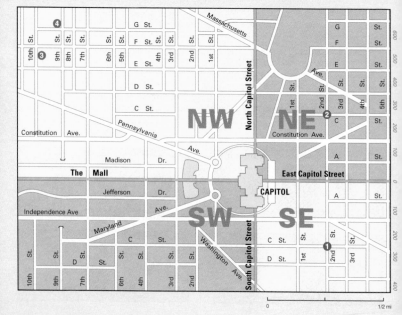

4 The Martin Luther King Library at 901 G Street NW is located on G Street in the northwest quadrant between 9th and 10th Streets. The odd-numbered street address (901) indicates that the library stands on the north side of G Street.

A City for Walkers – The principal sights, government buildings, and entertainment and business centers are concentrated in the northwest quadrant and on Capitol Hill. The logical street layout, the well-manicured appearance and the abundant greenery of this quadrant make orientation easy and walking a pleasure. The city's most heavily visited areas, such as the Mall, Capitol Hill and Georgetown, where parking is limited, are best visited on foot. However, most visitors will find walking uncomfortable and tiring during the summer months, when temperatures and humidity are high. *It is advisable to remain in the northwest quadrant of the city after nightfall.*

During **rush hours**—the peak transit times for business commuters *(7am-9:30am and 4pm-6:30pm)*—when no street parking is permitted, visitors should be aware of fast-moving vehicles in traffic lanes close to the sidewalks. Compliance with pedestrian walking signs is expected. Violators may be fined for crossing in the middle of the block rather than at corners.

Public Transportation

The **Washington Metropolitan Area Transit Authority** *(☎ 202-637-7000; www.wmata.com)* operates a public rapid transit (Metrorail) and bus system (Metrobus) that links Washington, DC and areas of Maryland and northern Virginia. Other bus service is provided by Alexandria's **DASH** buses *(☎ 703-370-3274; www.dashbus.com)* and Fairfax County's **Fairfax Connector** buses *(☎ 703-339-7200; www.fairfaxconnector. com)*, both of which join with Metrobuses and Metrorail *(service to Mount Vernon, p 58)*. Montgomery County's **Ride On** buses also connect to Metrorail and Metrobuses *(☎ 301-217-7433; www.rideonbus.com)*.

Rapid Transit System – The Metrorail subway system, known locally as the **Metro**, provides an efficient, dependable means of transportation. The Metro carries commuters to and from the suburbs during peak commuting hours *(5:30am-9:30am and 3pm-7pm)* and is convenient and inexpensive for sightseeing in the city. Stations are open 5:30am-midnight Mon-Thur, 8am-2am Fri-Satand most holidays, 8am-midnight Sun. *For easy reference, you'll find a Metro system map and information about fares, ticket purchase and transit lines inside the back cover of this guide.*

City Buses – Metrobuses operate daily, hours of operation differs by route, please contact the information line *(☎ 202-637-7000)* or the Web site *(www.wmata.com)* for more detailed information. Bus stops are indicated by red, white and blue signs. The buses display the route number and final destination above the windshield. **Fares** are determined by the time of day and length of trip; fares are higher during peak commuting hours *(5:30am-9:30am and 3pm-7pm)*. The base fare for most rides is $1.10. Exact fare is required. Some surcharges and transfer fees may apply. Bus-to-bus transfer is free with in a two-hour period. If a bus trip follows a ride on the Metro, transfers for the bus are free providing you collect the transfer at the originating station (machines distributing transfers are located at the escalators descending to rail level). There is no free transfer from buses to the Metro. Many routes are accessible to riders with disabilities *(p 60)*. To request a *Metro Visitor's Kit*, call ☎ 202-962-2733 or consult the Web site www.metroopensdoors.com.

Taxis

Within the District of Columbia, you can hail a taxi on the street or at taxi stands at hotels and transportation terminals. Numerous taxi companies operate under the supervision of the DC Taxicab Commission *(☎ 202-645-6005)*. When the "TAXI" sign on the roof of the cab is lit, the vehicle is available for hire.

DC taxis do not have meters; instead, the fare is calculated according to a **zone system**. The District is divided by a zone system that approximates concentric circles radiating from the Capitol. A ride within one zone is $4. The fare increases to $5.50 if crossing into a second zone, $6.90 if crossing into a third zone, etc. as described in the chart below:

Charge for Number of Zones/Subzones Traveled

1 = $4.00	3 = $6.90	5 = 9.25	7 = $11.75
2 = $5.50	4 = $8.25	6 = $10.25	8 = $12.50

A **zone map** with charges is displayed in the taxi, along with a list of passenger rights. It is not unusual for the driver to request payment before setting out or to pick up another passenger en route. However, each passenger pays the full fare. If riding as a group, one passenger pays full fare; all others pay $1.50 each.

If a rider enters the taxi during rush hours *(below)*, there is an additional $1 sur-charge. A rider can expect **additional charges** for radio-dispatched telephone requests, multiple stops, waiting time, more than one piece of luggage, special assistance, or service during official snow emergencies.

If traveling to the suburbs from the District, fares are based on mileage.

Driving in DC

Given the efficiency of the public transportation system, the availability of taxis and the ease with which many sights can be reached on foot, a car is not necessary to visit central Washington. Keep in mind that street parking is limited and rush-hour traffic jams are frequent. If you are staying outside the District, consider leaving your car at the parking facilities of one of the fringe Metro stations *(see Metro map on the inside back cover)* and riding the Metro into the city (it is advisable to arrive early on weekdays, as these lots are often filled with commuters' vehicles).

For excursions outside the city, a vehicle is recommended. Visitors are encouraged to avoid driving during **rush hours**: 7am-9:30am and 4pm-6:30pm.

Road Regulations – The maximum **speed limit** on major expressways is 55mph in rural areas and 55mph in and around cities. The speed limit within the city is 25mph unless otherwise posted. The use of **seat belts** is mandatory for driver and passengers. Child safety seats are required for children under four years or weighing less than 40 pounds (seats available from most rental-car agencies). Drivers must always yield the **right of way** to pedestrians. DC school bus law requires motorists to bring vehicles to a full stop when warning signals on a school bus are flashing. Unless otherwise posted, drivers may turn right at a red traffic light after coming to a com-plete stop.

Parking – In the city, parking space on the street is limited and parking regulations are strictly enforced. Some metered parking is available. Arterial streets in the District have posted **rush-hour restrictions** that generally prohibit parking from 7am-9:30am and 4pm-6:30pm. Parking in some residential areas is by permit only (restricted to area residents). Nonresidents are allowed to park in these areas for a maximum of two hours between 7am and 8:30pm. Parking signs are color-coded: **green and white** signs indicate hours when parking is allowed; **red and white** signs indi-cate hours when parking is not allowed. Parking spaces reserved for specific use by permit only (e.g., diplomatic or government vehicles) are reserved 24hrs daily unless otherwise specified. Parking spaces identified with &. arereserved for people with disabilities; anyone parking in these spaces without proper identification is subject to a heavy fine. Private parking garages are easy to find throughout the central sec-tions of the city.

Car Rentals – Major rental-car agencies have offices downtown and at the airports *(p 256)* serving the metropolitan area. Most agencies will rent only to persons at least 25 years old, although some will rent to younger drivers for a daily surcharge. A major credit card and a valid driver's license are required for rental (some agencies also require proof of insurance). The daily rate for a compact car when renting for 5-7 days ranges from $35 to $44. Note that a 10% sales tax and a 10% concession recoup fee are added to the daily in DC. Also, be aware when renting from airports that in addition to the 10% sales tax and a 11.11% recoup fee, there is also a $2.50/day contract fee.

Rental Company	☎ Reservations
Alamo	800-327-9633 www.alamo.com
Avis	800-331-1212 www.avis.com
Budget	800-527-0700 www.budget.com
Dollar	800-800-4000 www.dollar.com
Enterprise	800-325-8007 www.enterprise.com
Hertz	800-654-3131 www.hertz.com
National	800-227-7368 www.nationalcar.com
Thrifty	800-331-4200 www.thrifty.com

(Toll-free numbers may not be accessible outside North America.)

Accommodations

The Washington area offers a wide range of accommodations, from elegant down-town hotels *($149-$425/night)* to moderately priced motels *($65/night and up)* found mostly outside the city core and in the suburbs. Rates tend to be lower on weekends. Amenities include television, restaurant, and smoking/nonsmoking rooms. The more expensive hotels also offer workout facilities, room service and valet service. Downtown hotels may charge a fee for parking. A free listing of DC and area accom-modations (including campgrounds) is available from the Washington, DC Convention and Visitors Assn. *(p 254).*

Hotels/Motels – For information about specific hotels in the city, see the Address Book section in the front of this guide. Major hotel chains with locations in the DC area include:

	☎		☎
Best Western	800-528-1234 www.bestwestern.com	**Hyatt**	800-233-1234 www.hyatt.com
Comfort Inn	800-228-5150 www.comfortinn.com	**ITT Sheraton**	800-325-3535 www.sheraton.com
Crowne Plaza	800-227-6963 www.crowneplaza.com	**Marriott**	800-228-9290 www.marriott.com
Days Inn	800-325-2525 www.daysinn.com	**Omni**	800-843-6664 www.omnihotels.com
Four Seasons	800-819-5053 www.fourseasons.com	**Radisson**	800-333-3333 www.radisson.com
Hilton	800-445-8667 www.hilton.com	**Ramada**	800-228-2828 www.ramada.com
Holiday Inn	800-465-4329 www.holiday-inn.com	**Ritz-Carlton**	800-241-3333 www.ritzcarlton.com
Howard Johnson	800-446-4656 www.hojo.com	**Westin**	800-848-0016 www.westin.com

Reservation Services   ☎

Accommodations Express 800-906-4685
www.accommodationsexpress.com

Alexandria Hotel Accommodations 800-296-1000

Capitol Reservations 800-847-4832
www.hotelsdc.com

Clever Traveler 800-962-8958
www.clevertraveler.com

Hotel Reservations Network..800-964-6835
www.hoteldiscounts.com

Quikbook 800-789-9887
www.quikbook.com

RMC Travel Centre 800-782-2674

Washington DC Accommodations 800-554-2220
www.wdcahotels.com

(Toll-free numbers may not be accessible outside North America.)

Bed and Breakfasts – Many privately owned homes located in residential areas of the city are operated as B&Bs *($45 to $115/night)*. Continental breakfast is custom-arily included. Private baths are not always available and smoking indoors is usually not allowed. The following reservation services represent different properties throughout the DC area: Bed & Breakfast Accommodations Ltd., PO Box 12011, Washington DC 20005 ☎ 202-328-3510, www.bnbaccom.com; Bed & Breakfast League/Sweet Dreams and Toast, PO Box 9490, Washington DC 20016 ☎ 202-363-7767 *(booking fee)*.

Other Accommodations – A no-frills, economical option, **Washington International Youth Hostel** *(1009 11th St. NW;* ☎ 202-737-2333; www.hostels.com) charges between $19 and $22/night and is open year-round (250 beds). Various **campgrounds** in the surrounding area have access to Metrorail and trains. For information: **Capitol KOA Campground**, 768 Cecil Ave., Millersville MD 21108; ☎ 410-923-2771 or 800-KOA-0248; www.koakampgrounds.com. AAA also has approved campground listings. Furnished **apartment** rentals are available through B&B reservation services *(above)*.

Basic Information

Business Hours – Most businesses operate Monday to Friday 9am-5pm. Banks are generally open Monday to Thursday 9am-3pm with longer hours on Friday; some banks offer limited Saturday service. Department stores and shopping centers operate Monday to Saturday 10am-9pm, and many are open Sunday noon-5pm or 6pm; some extend their hours on Saturday.

Fax Services – Many hotels, as well as businesses that offer copying or mailing services, will send or receive faxes for a per-page fee.

Liquor Law – The legal minimum age for purchase and consumption of alcoholic beverages is 21. Proof of age is normally required. Establishments can serve alcoholic beverages Monday to Thursday 8am-2am, Friday to Saturday 8am-3am and Sunday 10am-2am. Beer and wine can be purchased in some convenience stores seven days a week. Liquor stores are closed on Sunday.

Mail – National Capitol Station Post Office, at Capitol St. and Massachusetts Ave. NE (next to Union Station) is open Monday to Friday 7am-midnight and weekends 7am-8pm. For location and hours of local post offices and other information, contact the Postal Service Customer Call Center *(Mon-Fri8am-6pm, Sat 7:30am-4pm)* ☎ 202-635-5300, www.usps.com. First-class rates within the US: letter 34¢ (1oz), postcard 21¢. Overseas: letter 80¢ (1/2oz), postcard 70¢. Letters can be mailed from most hotels. Stamps and packing material may be purchased at post offices, grocery stores and businesses offering postal and express shipping services located throughout the city *(see Yellow Pages of the phone directory under "Mailing Services" or "Post Offices")*.

Major Holidays – Most banks and government offices in the District are closed on the following legal holidays *(many retail stores and restaurants remain open on days indicated with *)*:

New Year's Day	January 1
Martin Luther King Jr.'s Birthday*	3rd Monday in January
Presidents' Day*	3rd Monday in February
Memorial Day*	Last Monday in May
Independence Day*	July 4
Labor Day*	1st Monday in September
Columbus Day*	2nd Monday in October
Veterans Day*	November 11
Thanksgiving	4th Thursday in November
Christmas	December 25

Money – Most banks are members of the network of Automatic Teller Machines (ATMs), which allows visitors from around the world to withdraw cash using bank cards and major credit cards 24hrs a day. ATMs can usually be found in banks, airports, grocery stores and shopping malls. Networks (Cirrus, Honor, Plus) serviced by the ATM are indicated on the machine. To inquire about ATM service, locations and transaction fees, contact your local bank, Cirrus ☎ 800-424-7787 or Plus ☎ 800-843-7587. **Travelers checks** are accepted in banks, most stores, restaurants and hotels. To report a lost or stolen **credit card**: American Express ☎ 800-528-4800; Diners' Club ☎ 800-234-6377; MasterCard ☎ 800-307-7309 or the issuing bank; Visa ☎ 800-336-8472. **American Express Travel Service** offices are located at 1150 Connecticut Ave. NW ☎ 202-457-1300.

Newspapers and Magazines – The city's leading daily paper, the *Washington Post* (established 1877), known for its investigative reporting, is one of the country's most influential newspapers, providing national and international coverage. The weekend section in the Friday edition lists entertainment, special events, and attractions for children. The Sunday edition contains a section highlighting the performing arts. The *Post* also publishes the day's congressional and Supreme Court schedules. The *Washington Post* is also accessible online: www.washingtonpost.com. Another daily, the *Washington Times*, was established in 1982 *(www.washingtontimes.com)*. The *Washingtonian*, a monthly magazine, features listings of restaurants, upcoming events and stories about the city *(www.washingtonian.com)*. Free alternative papers include *City Paper*, a weekly publication *(distributed Thursday)* covering the local entertainment scene *(www.citypaper.com)*. Several free publications found at hotels (such as *This Week in the Nation's Capital*, *The InTowner* and *Where Washington*) feature practical information and listings of cultural events, restaurants, nightspots and shops. *Sports Focus* and *Recreation News*, sports and recreation monthlies for the DC area, are available free at workout facilities, some stores and newspaper stands.

Safety Tips

In Washington, DC you are relatively safe throughout the day in the major tourist areas, but visitors should heed the following commonsense tips to ensure a safe and enjoyable visit:

- Avoid carrying large sums of money, and don't let strangers see how much money you are carrying.

- Keep a firm hold on purses and knapsacks, carry your wallet in your front pocket and avoid wearing expensive jewelry.

- Stay awake when riding on public transportation, and keep packages close by. Buses and trains are equipped with devices that enable riders to notify personnel of emergencies.

- Always park your car in a well-lit area. Close windows, lock doors and place valuables in the trunk.

- Exercise extra caution when visiting or traveling outside the Northwest quadrant of DC.

Taxes and Tipping – In Washington, DC the general sales tax is 5.75%. The hotel tax is 14.5%. Rental-car tax is 10% in DC. The food and beverage tax (restaurants) is 10%. Sales taxes in neighboring areas outside DC vary depending on the state and city.
In restaurants it is customary to tip the server 15-20% of the bill. Taxi drivers usually receive 15% of the fare. Skycaps and porters are generally tipped $1 per bag and hotel maids $1 per night.

Telephone – *p 261*. A local call generally costs 35¢ from a pay phone. Most calls within a distance of 12mi from the Capital Beltway *(Interstate 495, map p 258)* are charged as local calls but require dialing 1 and the area code.

Area Codes

Washington DC	202
Suburban Virginia	703
Eastern Maryland	410
Suburban Maryland	301

Important Numbers

Emergency Police/Ambulance/Fire Department *(24hrs)*	**911**
Police (nonemergency)	202-727-1010
Hotel Docs *(24hrs)*	800-468-3537
Dental Referral *(Mon-Fri8am-4pm)*	202-547-7615
Pharmacies *(24hrs)*:	
CVS, 6 Dupont Cir. NW	202-785-1466
CVS, 1199 Vermont Ave. NW (Thomas Cir.)	202-628-0720
Poison Control Center *(24hrs)*	202-625-3333
Time	202-844-2525
Weather	202-936-1212

Television and Radio

Major TV Networks

ABC	Channel 7	CBS	Channel 9	PBS	Channel 32
NBC	Channel 4	FOX	Channel 5	CNN	*cable channel varies*
WB	Channel 50				

Major FM Radio Stations				**Major AMRadio Stations**	
NPR	88.5	Soft Rock	97.1	News/ talk	630
Country	98.7	C-span	90.1	News/sports	1500
Rock	107.3	Contemporary	93.9	Oldies	1600

Time Zone – Washington, DC is located in the Eastern Standard Time (EST) zone, which is five hours behind Greenwich Mean Time. Daylight Saving Time is observed from the first Sunday in April (clocks are advanced 1hr) to the last Sunday in October.

Memorials

The following list is a selection of the principal memorials and commemorative public sculpture in central Washington and nearby Arlington:

Thomas Jefferson Memorial

Korean War Veterans Memorial

Other memorials

Arlington *Main memorials and graves on the grounds of Arlington National Cemetery are shown on the site map p 189.*

Washington DC

7	José Gervasio Artigas	18th St. & Constitution Ave. NW
8	Commodore John Barry	Franklin Park, 14th & K Sts. NW
9	Mary McLeod Bethune	Lincoln Park, E. Capitol & 11th Sts. NE
10	Sir William Blackstone	Constitution Ave. & 3rd St. NW
11	Simón Bolívar	18th St. at C St. & Virginia Aves. NW
12	Boy Scouts of America	Ellipse, west of 15th St. NW
13	President James Buchanan	Meridian Hill Park NW
14	Butt-Millet Memorial Fountain	Ellipse
15	Columbus Memorial	Columbus Plaza (Union Station) NE
16	Dante	Meridan Hill Park NW
17	DAR Founders	C St. between 17th & 18th Sts. NW
18	Jane A. Delano	American Red Cross, 17th & D Sts. NW
19	DC World War Memorial	Mall SE, West Potomac Park
20	Andrew Jackson Downing Urn	Mall SE, east of the Castle
21	Albert Einstein	22nd St. & Constitution Ave. NW
22	Emancipation Monument	Lincoln Park, E. Capitol & 11 Sts. NE
23	Robert Emmet	24th St. & Massachusetts Ave. NW
24	John Ericsson	Ohio Dr. & Independence Ave. SE
25	Admiral David G. Farragut	Farragut Square, 17th & K Sts. NW
26	First Division Memorial	Between E St. & Executive Ave. NW
27	Benjamin Franklin	Old Post Office, 12th St. & Pennsylvania Ave. NW
28	Freedom Bell	Columbus Plaza (Union Station) NW
29	Albert Gallatin	North side of Treasury Bldg. NW
30	Bernardo de Gálvez	Virginia Ave. & E St. NW
31	Grand Army of theRepublic Memorial	Indiana Ave. & 7th St. NW
32	President James A. Garfield	Capitol Reflecting Pool, Mall SE
33	Edward Gallaudet	Gallaudet University, Florida Ave. NE
34	Thomas Gallaudet	Gallaudet University, Florida Ave. NE
35	Samuel Gompers	Mass. Ave. & 10th St. NW
36	President Ulysses S. Grant	Capitol Reflecting Pool, Mall SE
37	General Nathanael Greene	Stanton Park, 5th & C Sts. NE
38	Alexander Hamilton	South side of Treasury Bldg. NW
39	General Winfield Scott Hancock	Pennsylvania Ave. & 7th St. NW
40	Joseph Henry	Mall SE, north of the Castle

41	President Andrew Jackson	Lafayette Park NW
42	Japanese Lantern	Tidal Basin
43	Japanese Pagoda	Tidal Basin
44	Joan of Arc	Meridian Hill Park NW
45	Commodore John Paul Jones	Mall SE at 17th St.
46	Benito Juárez	Virginia & New Hampshire Aves. NW
47	General Thaddeus Kosciuszko	Lafayette Park NW
48	General Lafayette	Lafayette Park NW
49	President Abraham Lincoln	Judiciary Square, Indiana Ave. NW
50	General John A. Logan	Logan Circle, Vermont Ave. at 13th & P Sts. NW
51	Martin Luther	Vermont Ave. & 14th St. NW
52	Chief Justice John Marshall	John Marshall Park, C & 4th Sts. NW
53	General George M. McClellan	Connecticut & California Aves. NW
54	Maj. Gen. James B. McPherson	McPherson Square NW
55	Maj. Gen. George C. Meade	Penn. Ave. & 3rd St. NW
56	Andrew W. Mellon Memorial	Constitution Ave. at 6th St. NW
57	National Grange Marker	Mall at Madison Dr. & 4th St. NW
58	Nuns of the Battlefield	Rhode Island Ave. & M St. NW
59	Original Patentees of DC	Ellipse, west of 15th St. NW
60	Peace or Naval Monument	Penn. Ave. & 1st St. NW
61	General Albert Pike	3rd & D Sts. NW
62	General Casimir Pulaski	Freedom Plaza, Pennsylvania Ave.at E & 13th Sts. NW
63	General John J. Pershing	Pershing Square at Pennsylvania Ave. &14th St. NW
64	General John A. Rawlings	Rawlings Park at 18th & E Sts. NW
65	Red Cross Memorial	American Red Cross, 17th St. between D & E Sts.
66	Sarah Rittenhouse	Montrose Park, R St. NW, Georgetown
67	Count Jean-Baptiste Rochambeau	Lafayette Park NW
68	President Franklin D. Roosevelt	Pennsylvania Ave. & 9th St. NW
69	President Theodore Roosevelt	Roosevelt Island NW
70	General José de San Martin	Virginia Ave. & 20th St. NW
71	Lt. General Winfield Scott	Scott Circle, 16th St. & Massachusetts Ave. NW
72	Second Division Memorial	Ellipse, southwest corner
73	Serenity (William Henry Scheulze Memorial)	Meridian Hill Park NW
74	General William Tecumseh Sherman	Sherman Square, 15th & E Sts. NW
75	Taras Shevchenko	22nd, 23rd & P Sts. NW
76	Signers of the Declaration of Independence	Constitution Gardens, Mall NW
77	General Friedrich von Steuben	Lafayette Park NW
78	Taft Memorial	Constitution & Louisiana Aves. between 1st & 2nd Sts. NW
79	Maj. Gen. George H. Thomas	Thomas Circle, 14th St. & Vermont Ave.NW
80	*Titanic* Memorial	Waterfront at P St. SW
81	US Navy Memorial	Market Square, 8th St. & Pennsylvania Ave. NW
82	George Washington (statue)	Washington Circle NW
83	Daniel Webster	Massachusetts Ave., west of Scott Circle NW
84	John Witherspoon	Connecticut Ave. & N St. NW
85	National Law Enforcement Officers Memorial	Judiciary Square, E St. between 4th & 5th Sts NW
86	Francis Scott Key Memorial	Francis Scott Key Memorial Bridge, Georgetown
87	Japanese American Memorial	Louisiania and New Jersey avenues and D St., NW.

Index

White House .... Building, street or other point of interest
Washington, George .... Person, historic event or term
Accommodations .... Practical information

Embassies, Memorials, Museums, Professional Sports, and Recreation are listed respectively under those headings. Sights of special interest to children are grouped under 🧒. Hotels and Restaurants are listed separately under those headings. Accommodations and restaurants for Alexandria are listed separately.

271

Notes

Please write to us !
Your input will help us to improve our guides.

Please send this questionnaire to the following address:
Michelin Travel Publications.
Post Office Box 19001, Greenville, SC 29602-9001

---

1. Is this the first time you have purchased THE GREEN GUIDE? yes   no

---

2. Which title did you buy? :

---

3. What influenced your decision to purchase this guide?

	Not important at all	Somewhat important	Important	Very important
Cover				
Clear, attractive layout				
Structure				
Cultural information				
Practical information				
Maps and plans				
Michelin quality				
Loyalty to THE GREEN GUIDE collection				

Your comments :

---

4. How would you rate the following aspects of THE GREEN GUIDE?

	Poor	Average	Good	Excellent
Maps at the beginning of the guide				
Maps and plans throughout the guide				
Description of the sights (style, detail...)				
Depth of cultural information				
Amount of practical information				
Format				

Please comment if you have responded poor or average on any of the above:

5. What do you think about the establishments provided in the guide?

HOTELS :	Not Enough	Sufficient	Too many
All categories			
"Budget"			
"Moderate"			
"Expensive"			
RESTAURANTS :	Not Enough	Sufficient	Too many
All categories			
"Budget"			
"Moderate"			
"Expensive"			

Your comments:

6. On a scale of 1-20, please rate THE GREEN GUIDE (1 being the lowest, 20 being the highest):

How would you suggest we improve these guides?

1. Maps and Plans:

2. Sights:

3. Establishments:

4. Practical Information:

5. Other:

Demographic information: (optional)

	Male	Female	Age

Name:

Address: